THE MIND OF THE OLD SOUTH

The
MIND
OF THE OLD
SOUTH

Clement Eaton

REVISED EDITION

LOUISIANA STATE UNIVERSITY PRESS

Revised edition, 1967

Copyright 1964 and 1967 by
Louisiana State University Press
Library of Congress Catalog Card Number: 67—11684

Manufactured in the United States of America by
Edwards Brothers, Inc., Ann Arbor, Michigan
Designed by E. S. Diman

To Ben,
lover of adventure and strange lands

PREFACE

THE most important change in the revised edition of *The Mind of the Old South* is the addition of two chapters. The first of these, entitled "The Young Reformers of 1832," centers about the life of the brilliant young liberal Jesse Burton Harrison and makes a fitting introduction to the study of the development of the Southern mind after 1830. The new chapter on the mind of the slave and the free Negro, entitled "The Mind of the Southern Negro: The Remarkable Individuals," is a recognition of the rising importance of the Negro in American life and of the incompleteness of any study of the Southern mind that leaves him out. If one wishes to study American patricians he should not neglect the highly conservative South Carolina aristocrat; accordingly I have added to Chapter II the portrait of one of the most attractive of this special breed, Robert W. Barnwell. I have often pondered the inconsistency of liberal-minded Southerners who believed slavery to be wrong yet refused to seek to emancipate their own slaves. In the remarkably frank diary of John Hartwell Cocke of Bremo Plantation in Virginia I have recently found an answer to this question that seems the most reasonable explanation I have encountered in the primary sources.

To define the term "Southern mind" in a few words is not easy. I have interpreted it to mean the thinking of the Southern people—

often inconsistent, ill-informed, prejudiced, and confused by cross-currents—on the great problems of their region and of human destiny. The term also comprises the sense of values, the nuances of regionalism, that Southerners developed. I have limited the time period of this study to the years 1820–60, the period in its history when Southern civilization was most unique and more different in its characteristics from the culture of other sections of the United States. Here in the antebellum period were laid the foundations of long-enduring regional attitudes, especially in regard to the Negro and the federal government.

I have adopted the method of studying the Southern mind through a study of representative individuals. By focusing on the lives of these typical men of the Old South we can glimpse the process of historical change in this unique region and understand better why the Southern people made some of the decisions they did. Professor William R. Taylor of the University of Wisconsin, who read the original manuscript, has pointed out the advantage of using such case histories—the inductive method—to grasp the picture of the larger unit, the sectional society. Thus, he observes, "We watch one man (or woman) draw conclusions, conceive of ideas, change his (or her) mind, develop inconsistencies, struggle to resolve them, lose hope, etc. We see the process of history from the *inside out* and our understanding of group behavior is increased in accordance. We see the range of difference between individuals who hold the same [general] views, and come to appreciate the complexity of human motivation." The validity of this method depends, however, on using not a single biography but several biographies of representative men, who usually are not great men.

I wish to express my appreciation to Professor Robert W. Johannsen of the University of Illinois who generously sent me three reels of microfilm that gave me information on Stephen Douglas' plantation in Mississippi and its Negro slaves. Also, I owe a debt of gratitude to Professor Edward M. Steel, Jr. of West Virginia University for giving me the opportunity to read a rare diary of a Southern yeoman that has enabled me to add a new dimension to my chapter on the mind of the Southern yeoman.

Lexington, Kentucky   CLEMENT EATON

CONTENTS

ILLUSTRATIONS

Chapter I

THE YOUNG REFORMERS
OF 1832

THE young Virginia reformers of 1832 pose somewhat of a mystery. It is easy to understand why they arose although their motivation was complex. It is far more difficult to understand why they abandoned so quickly their effort to reform the society of their state by the gradual emancipation of the slaves and by the establishment of a more democratic form of government. Among the reformers was the brilliant young humanist Jesse Burton Harrison of Lynchburg. Although he was not a member of the legislature of 1832 that voted on a plan of gradual emancipation, he aided the liberal cause with his pen. His reply to the tremendously influential proslavery pamphlet of Thomas Roderick Dew is one of the noble documents of Southern liberalism.

Jesse Burton Harrison was a very appealing young man whose zest for culture reminds one of a Renaissance personality. Unlike the Renaissance humanists, however, who were usually conservative in political and social affairs, and whose striving for self-culture was thoroughly egoistic, the young Virginian had a strong social conscience and a desire to reform the society in which he was born. He became one of the most cultivated of the generation of South-

erners which succeeded the distinguished generation of the early
republic. Professor George Ticknor of Harvard College, who taught
the young Virginian, described him in 1823 as possessing an extensive knowledge of "elegant literature." Ticknor said that Harrison,
though diffident, had shown in the law school at Harvard "singular
talents for extemporaneous debate." (Jesse Burton Harrison
Papers, Library of Congress) Harrison did not belong directly to
the plantation aristocracy. His father was a merchant and tobacco
manufacturer of Lynchburg who had been reared in the Quaker
Church, but was too independent to remain in it.

Following his graduation from Hampden-Sydney College, Harrison entered Harvard College where he studied law and literature.
His early ambition was to become a professor; after leaving
Harvard he applied for a teaching position both at the University
of North Carolina and the University of Virginia. Despite the
support of Jefferson, Madison, and Professor Ticknor, he was not
appointed at either institution. Disappointed and humiliated, he
decided to go to the University of Göttingen for further study.

At this time the University of Göttingen was among the most
renowned universities in Europe. The researches of Daniel B.
Shumway in "The American Students of the University of Göttingen" and of John T. Krumpelmann in *Southern Scholars in
Goethe's Germany* reveal its pre-eminent attraction to American
students and especially to Southern students. Between 1830 and
1860 South Carolina sent more students to that ancient university
than any other American state, with the possible exception of
Massachusetts. Although Virginia did not contribute as many
students to German universities as did South Carolina, the Virginians were, with the exception of Hugh Swinton Legaré, more
distinguished—including Thomas Roderick Dew, Jesse Burton
Harrison, and the great professor of classics at the University of
Virginia, Basil Lanneau Gildersleeve.

In 1829 Harrison sailed for Europe, carrying letters of introduction from Henry Clay, Ticknor, and Legaré. The journal which
he kept while he was a student in Germany (the manuscript of
which is now in the library of the University of Virginia) contains
lively accounts of the German professors and students and of his
travels. It shows that he thought not only of himself but of the
welfare and progress of his country. Shortly after his arrival,

Harrison wrote to his cousin Henry Clay for suggestions on suitable topics to observe and study abroad that would be useful in evaluating American society. Clay replied (January 3, 1830, Clay Papers, Library of the University of Kentucky) that the young Virginian should seek information concerning serfdom, "in view of reasoning upon it in relation to that of our African slaves"; he should also examine the effect of tariffs upon German economy; and he should observe "the practical inconveniences resulting from division [of Germany] into so many states." Such handicaps of fragmentation, the great statesmen of union observed, should warn Americans against division of their own Union, "the greatest misfortune that could befall our Country." Accordingly, Harrison made notes on the Prussian tariff and talked at length with a Russian princess whom he met at the Court of Weimar about serfdom in Russia. He may also have had in mind a comparison of the condition of the Southern slave with that of the European peasant when he made the following observation in his journal: "Til in Germany I had never a just idea of the misery and filth with which a loutish peasantry (I speak now of the villages) can be content to live on, never advancing one step from generation to generation; the same from carroty-headed youth to blue-shirted old age."

When Harrison returned to Lynchburg in the summer of 1831 he wrote to a friend in Germany that he found "a prodigious revolution" in progress in his native state. "The whole Town," he lamented, "with scarce any exception is over-run with a fanatical religious spirit that employs all thoughts, interrupts all business, forbids all social parties, treats all dancing as the greatest of crimes (compassionate the necessities of my legs, so long used to the gallopade), and in fact is a Schwärmerey which leaves the English Evangelicals a thousand leagues behind." He compared this religious despotism to "an age of barbarism rushing in upon us, an inroad of Vandals."

To the liberal-minded young Virginian, fresh from the German universities, life in the tobacco manufacturing town of Lynchburg now appeared crude and raw—a society in which an intellectual was looked upon as odd. Even before he left America he had become the advocate of an intellectual reform in Virginia, a movement to encourage the advancement of education and culture. In an address at his alma mater entitled *The Prospects of Letters*

and Taste in Virginia, which was later published as a pamphlet
(1827), he lamented the decline of culture in his native state.
The state of education among the upper class in Virginia he declared, had deteriorated since the Revolution, especially "in the
very vital point of learning, namely classical knowledge." He
observed that while the masses in the period before the Revolution
were scarcely at all instructed "the richer classes were vastly better
educated in proportion to the light and spirit of the age, than the
present generation are." The principal cause for the decline of
culture in Virginia, he maintained, was the premature desire of
ambitious young men to rush into politics, using the profession of
law as a stepping-stone. He noted also that his fellow citizens
seemed to be content to rest upon the laurels of the great generation of Virginians of the early republic; instead of themselves
achieving, they had become eulogists of the deeds and glory of
the past. He issued a call for the people of the state to arise from
their lethargy and reform their old system of education. Especially,
he advocated, should they encourage the young men of the state to
develope a genuine taste for culture, "a hot eagerness for knowledge," such as he himself possessed. "We want," he said, "men of
refined minds in our country residences."

In the increasingly materialistic atmosphere of Virginia—of the
South—society gave little encouragement to the development of
the scholar and gentlemen, or to the Renaissance type of personality
characteristic of the later colonial period. Among the relatively few
Virginians of this type was Francis Walker Gilmer of Albemarle
County, whom Jefferson had described in 1824 as "the best educated subject we have raised since the Revolution," and whom he
had sent as agent to Europe to select professors for the first faculty
of the University of Virginia. But before Gilmer could realize the
promise of his brilliant literary gifts he died in 1826 at the age of
thirty-six. William Short, Jefferson's secretary in France, was
another highly cultivated young Virginian, who preferred, however, when he returned to America to settle in Philadelphia.
Edward Coles, Madison's secretary, because of his idealistic opposition to slavery, also emigrated from his native state to Illinois,
where he became governor and led a notable fight to save the state
from adopting a form of slave labor. Another brilliant and cultivated Virginian of this generation was Thomas Mann Randolph

(d. 1829), who married a daughter of Jefferson and was a man of broad intellectual interests. The most widely known exponent of culture in the state was a Richmond lawyer, William Wirt, author of the *Letters of a British Spy* (1803) and a life of Patrick Henry (1817), but he devoted most of his energies to the law and politics. These literary individuals, as well as some brilliant conversationalists, such as John Randolph of Roanoke, seasoned Virginia society somewhat, but they could do little to affect its general tone.

After his return from Germany Harrison sought to arouse a broader enthusiasm for culture and letters in Virginia. One of the most important steps toward this goal, he believed, was to eliminate the provincialism of his own state and of America in general. In an article entitled "English Civilization," published in the Charleston *Southern Review* in 1832, he criticized Americans for their extravagant fondness for British society and literature to the virtual exclusion of interest in other literatures and ways of thought. The great fault of English literature and culture, he observed, was that they were permeated with class prejudice, which was alien to American ideals. The Bristish exhibited, he thought, an exclusive, aristocratic spirit and a lack of "a love of the ideal" which made them a poor model for his countrymen to follow. Instead, Americans should look abroad to the civilization of the European continent, read German, French, and Dutch newspapers and literature, and abandon their intellectual isolation. His efforts to encourage the growth of intellectual culture seem to have been directed toward the education of the upper class of society rather than to lifting the level of popular education.

Though the young Virginia advocate of a catholic culture thought that the South had too many lawyers and politicians, he himself was so strongly affected by the sense of values of his native section that he abandoned his youthful desire to become a professor and entered the ranks of both of these professions. Before he returned to America he wrote to his brother-in-law in Lynchburg that he had lost the desire to become a professor. Even in Europe, he observed, only moderate honor was accorded to the most learned professors. He perceived "the vanity of striving for a name for myself in a branch where there are already so many giants, unrewarded by fame—in which branch, too, reputation is perhaps least of all to be hoped for in America." Accordingly, not wishing to sacrifice himself as "an unaspiring Pedagogue," he settled briefly in Richmond in the honorable profession of a lawyer.

In August, 1831, two months after Harrison's return from Germany, the Nat Turner insurrection occurred in Southampton County, Virginia, resulting in the death of sixty whites and many Negroes. This dramatic event so frightened the people of the state that when the legislature met in December, numerous petitions were presented to that body requesting the adoption of a plan for removing the slaves and free Negroes from the state. A group of ladies from Augusta County in their petition even offered the supreme sacrifice of giving up their domestic servants who relieved them from the drudgery of household work in a hot climate. The governor, John Floyd, was strongly affected by this agitation so that, even though he was the owner of twelve slaves, he recorded in his diary on November 21, 1831: "Before I leave this Government I will have contrived to have a law passed gradually abolishing slavery in this State, or at all events to begin the work by prohibiting slavery on the West side of the Blue Ridge Mts."

A great struggle now took place between the liberals and the conservatives in the legislature over the issue of the gradual emancipation of the state's slaves. It was initiated on January 11, 1832, by a resolution of William O. Goode of the Tidewater County of Mecklenburg. His resolution proposed to discharge the select committee to which antislavery petitions had been referred from considering them and declared it inexpedient to legislate upon the subject of emancipation. Thereupon, Thomas Jefferson's grandson, Thomas Jefferson Randolph of Albemarle County, introduced a counter resolution. Randolph's resolution embodied his grandfather's plan for ridding the South of the evil of slavery by a *post nati* system. He proposed that all slaves born after July 4, 1840, should become the property of the state, the males at the age of twenty-one and the females at eighteen, to be hired out until they earned a sum sufficient to deport them from the United States.

The debate that followed lasted two weeks and brought forward an impressive group of young liberals, including two nephews of the governor, Charles James Faulkner and James McDowell, twenty-five and thirty-five years old respectively. The oldest of the active liberal group was Randolph, thirty-nine, and none of the others was over thirty-five years of age. The movement of the young liberals represented essentially a revolt of the younger generation against the leadership of the older generation that had triumphed in the constitutional convention of 1829–30.

There was a liberal tradition in Virginia upon which they drew for support and for arguments for their cause. Most of the leaders of the great generation of the Revolution and early republic had condemned slavery as an evil and had supported the emancipation cause either by example or precept. One of the most influential of the older generation's liberals was George Wythe, signer of the Declaration of Independence and law professor at William and Mary College, who had influenced both Thomas Jefferson and Henry Clay toward their antislavery sentiments. Wythe was so advanced in his libertarian thought that he would appeal to the civil rights activists of today. Virtually all of the Southern liberals of the antebellum period believed that after the emancipation of the slaves, the freedmen could not live successfully in a free black and white society and accordingly must be deported. Wythe, on the other hand, was almost unique in his views on the irrelevance of the color line (even more advanced in thought on this subject than was Abraham Lincoln). "Mr. Wythe," according to one of his students cited by Joseph Robert in his excellent study *The Road From Monticello,* "to the day of his death was for simple abolition, considering the objection to color as founded in prejudice—." He illustrated his liberal principles in regard to race by becoming the father of an illegitimate mulatto son, of whom he was exceedingly fond. It is ironic that this great liberal was poisoned by his nephew, who in a fit of jealousy intended to murder the favorite slave boy but instead accidently poisoned his uncle.

Prior to the great debate of 1832 a liberal sentiment in regard to slavery seems to have been widespread among the people of Virginia, especially west of the Blue Ridge. This state of mind can be explained partly by tradition—by the survival of ideals of liberty from the Revolutionary period, and by the influence of Jefferson and Madison, which predisposed many Virginians to adopt a liberal view in regard to slavery. Furthermore, economic conditions, especially a long period of declining prosperity in which slavery seemed to be a powerful cause, bolstered altruistic sentiments. A number of travelers such as the Englishman Isaac

Candler, Levasseur, the secretary of Lafayette during his visit to America in 1825, and the Northern traveler Henry Knight observed that the planters generally lamented the existence of slavery as an evil, which they believed would some day pass away, though they were appalled by the practical difficulties of eradicating the long-entrenched institution.

In contrast with Virginia sentiment, public opinion in South Carolina, where slavery was a thriving institution, was decidedly more conservative. Captain Basil Hall of the British Navy found in 1827–28 much support for the continuance of the peculiar institution; one man with whom he talked defended the institution as no evil at all, but a positive good, while another admitted that it was an evil but one that was attenuated by long habits of thinking both on the part of the master and the slave. Captain Hall himself was convinced that the people of South Carolina would maintain slavery inviolate "in spite of their admission that it is a grievous evil and certainly in spite of all efforts to compel them to change it."

The Virginians, though believing slavery to be a social evil, were content to leave the emancipation of the slaves to Providence and the slow action of time until the Nat Turner insurrection shocked them out of their lethargy. This revolutionary episode coincided with a renewed discontent on the part of the Virginians west of the Blue Ridge over the failure of the constitutional convention of 1829–30 to redress fully their grievances. Accordingly, the motives of the young reformers of 1832, most of whom were from the West, in attacking slavery were mixed, including a feeling of sectionalism as well as genuinely liberal ideas on the emancipation of the slaves. In the western part of the state there were relatively few slaves as compared with the eastern part where slaves constituted the majority of the population. The westerners felt that in the past their interests had continually been sacrificed to the interests of the eastern slaveholders, who constituted a minority of the white population. The young reformers from the West even went so far as to threaten the dismemberment of the state if their demand that some action be taken to eradicate slavery from the state were not adopted. On the other hand, extreme conservative eastern members spoke of the same dread eventuality if their slave property should be sacrificed. The governor, who had at first favored the emancipation movement, became alarmed over the violent course the debate in the legislature took with regard to sectionalism and reversed his position.

The arguments of the young reformers for the gradual abolition of slavery attributed most of the evils of Virginia society to the institution of slavery, neglecting other important factors. They arraigned slavery as the cause of the declining prosperity of the state, the exhaustion of the soil, and the emigration of many families. They said slavery prevented the growth of industry, degraded manual labor and thereby encouraged idleness of many productive workers, promoted sensuality, caused an accumulation of debt to furnishing merchants, and prevented the adoption of a free public school system and of needed internal improvements to give the West a larger market for its crops. In addition to these materialistic arguments, some of the young reformers appealed to the inalienable rights of man as the basis for giving the slaves their freedom. One of the finest men among the reformers, Samuel McDowell Moore, emphasized the bad moral effects of slavery in its debasement of the character and personality of the Negro. Some of the most radical proponents of the abolition of slavery, notably Charles James Faulkner, maintained that property in slavery existed not by any law of nature, but by the acquiescence and consent of society; when such property became an evil to society, or a public nuisance, he felt that the government had a right to abolish it and he favored the adoption of such a drastic policy. The reformers agreed with the conservatives, however, that the slaves in Virginia were kindly treated—or as Thomas Marshall, the son of the great Chief Justice put it, "The ordinary condition of the slave is not such as to make humanity weep for his lot."

The speeches of some of the members contained remarkable anticipations of future developments in the South. Randolph, in defending his proposal of gradual emancipation, said, "There is one circumstance to which we are to look as inevitable in the fulness of time; a dissolution of this Union"—and when it should occur, "border war follows it—." William H. Roane, grandson of Patrick Henry, in his defense of slavery anticipated the rejection of Jeffersonian principles of natural rights by extremists of the Southern region, as well as the growth of the proslavery philosophy, when he declared, "I am not one of those who have ever revolted at the idea of the practice of slavery, as many do. It has existed, and ever will exist, in all ages, in some form and to some degree. I think slavery as much a correlative of liberty as cold is of heat: —Nor do I believe in that Fan-faronade about the natural equality of man."

The speeches of the prominent antislavery advocates in the legislature as well as those of the conservatives were published in the Richmond *Constitutional Whig* and the Richmond *Enquirer*. The latter began printing the speeches of the reformers (Philip A. Bolling, Samuel McDowell Moore, and Thomas Jefferson Randolph) on January 19. In an editorial on that day, the editor, Thomas Ritchie, declared: "The seals are broken which have been put for fifty years upon the most delicate and difficult subject of state concernment. We publish speeches in the House of Delegates today, which at no other period would have been delivered but behind closed doors. In the same spirit the press fearlessly speaks its own sentiments—unawed by the tocsin of denunciation or the menaces of proscription."

But all this fine fervor and high talk for the freedom of the slaves came to naught. The reformers could not agree on a practical plan of emancipation, and some men of liberal sentiment did not support the antislavery cause because they had not been elected to the legislature on this issue and they felt their constituents should be consulted before taking any action. The conservatives rallied; and finally on January 25, a vote was taken on the strongest antislavery measure to be voted on in the House of Delegates— the amendment of William Ballard Preston from the trans-Alleghany section of the state to the effect that the legislature should take some action for the abolition of slavery. The reform movement was defeated by a majority of 73 to 58 votes.

The delegates from west of the Blue Ridge voted overwhelmingly for Preston's amendment; those from the Tidewater and Piedmont, where most of the slaves were held, voted just as decisively against it. Shining exceptions of liberalism among the latter were Thomas Jefferson Randolph and Philip A. Bolling, who owned 36 and 16 taxable slaves, respectively, and whose counties had a slave population of well over 50 per cent. Instead of adopting some provision for the gradual abolition of slavery, the legislature tightened the bonds of the slave and restricted the liberty of the free Negro by

harshly revising the black code. Furthermore, the Senate defeated
a colonization bill that might have contributed toward the gradual
emancipation movement.

The debate in the Virginia legislature on the emancipation of
the slaves has been regarded as a turning point in the development
of the Southern mind. In other Southern states responsible leaders
watched its progress with great concern, for the decision of the
Virginia legislature might greatly influence public opinion in their
own states toward emancipation. One of these leaders, Judge
Alexander Porter of Louisiana, wrote to Senator Josiah Stoddard
Johnston of that state on February 1, 1831: "I am looking with
intense interest to the proceedings in the Virginia Legislature.
They are debating a more important question for the happiness of
the human race than any set of men ever did except the old Continental Congress. If gradual emancipation should be adopted
there the whole of the Southern states will before the lapse of one
century follow their example." Yet the judge, a native of Ireland,
a large slaveholder, and a prominent Whig politician, was, unlike
young Harrison, a realist. "I do not think the people of this state,
or Mississippi," he wrote "are yet in a state to bear the discussion
of emancipation, no matter how remote the time is fixed, and I am
confident it could destroy the usefulness of any public man who
would propose it. The object (and no more desirable one exists)
can only be obtained by approaching the subject by slow and
almost imperceptible degrees." Again, he warned the Louisiana
Senator: "You cannot act with too much caution in this matter. A
single false or precipitate step which would alarm the public mind
in the South would throw us back in the great work a quarter of
a century."

The conservative reaction in Virginia was far-reaching in its
effects, for it not only set an example of conservatism, but gave
a powerful rationale to the incipient proslavery defense throughout
the South. Before this event, in the 1820's, prominent South
Carolinians had begun to develop a proslavery philosophy that
maintained that Southern slavery was not an evil but a positive
good. Now, two able Virginians joined their ranks by publishing
pamphlets justifying the retention of slavery in the South. The
first of these, Benjamin Watkins Leigh, was a brilliant Richmond
lawyer, a great admirer of the philosophy of Edmund Burke, and

the former leader of the eastern conservatives in the constitutional convention of 1829–30. In two letters to the Richmond *Enquirer*, February 4, and 28, 1832, entitled "The Letter of Appomattox to the People of Virginia," soon republished as a pamphlet, he argued against the practicability of any scheme of emancipation, minimized the danger of insurrection, strongly advocated leaving the solution of the slavery question to the action of Providence, and concluded by urging Virginians to withdraw their subscriptions from newspapers, such as the *Enquirer* and the *Whig*, that printed liberal emancipation speeches and articles. The other proslavery apologist was Thomas Roderick Dew, a young professor at William and Mary College, whose career will be considered later. In an article in the *American Quarterly Review* of Philadelphia, September, 1832, entitled "Abolition of Negro Slavery," Dew gave a classic statement of the proslavery argument. This article was enlarged and published subsequently as a pamphlet, *Review of the Debate in the Virginia Legislature of 1831 and 1832*. His ideas were to have a profound effect upon the development of the Southern mind.

It was at this point that Jesse Burton Harrison joined the fray on the liberal side. In his youth and early manhood, he had associated with some of the great men of Virginia of an older generation. Jefferson had introduced him to George Ticknor, his Harvard mentor, when the Northern professor had visited Monticello. Madison also influenced him; on a visit to Montpelier he took notes on the former President's opinions on various subjects, including slavery, which are among the Jesse Burton Harrison Papers in the Library of Congress. From these two great liberals he seems to have derived his views of the evils of slavery. He seems also to have adopted their plan of gradualism in getting rid of slavery and of deporting the emancipated Negroes. He was, moreover, active in the American Colonization Society, contributing an article in 1827 to the organ of the society, the *African Repository*.

In December, 1832, he published in the *American Quarterly Review* a reply to Dew's proslavery article. The story behind the publication of this notable article is to be found in the Harrison Papers in the Library of Congress. There are a number of letters from R. R. Gurley, the executive secretary of the American Colonization Society, urging Harrison to take a more active part in the great cause, and there is a commission to serve as an agent to speak to the legislatures of New York and Pennsylvania. When the letter of "Appomattox" appeared in the Richmond *Enquirer* Gurley wrote to him expressing the wish that "you would enter the lists against this Champion of Slavery & denouncer of all plans for its removal." As soon as Dew's article appeared in the *American Quarterly Review* Gurley again urged Harrison to reply to the proslavery argument, advising him to go deeply into the whole subject of the Scriptural argument. On September 21 he wrote a second letter to the hoped-for young champion, saying that he had heard from Robert Walsh, editor of the *American Quarterly Review*, "who desires a good reply to the article on slavery." Gurley urged Harrison to undertake the task, observing that Dew had "left unnoticed all the moral elements which are at work for us."

The result of these urgings by Gurley was the appearance in the *American Quarterly Review* in December, 1832, of the article "The Slavery Question in Virginia." Both the articles of Harrison and Dew were anonymous, but when they were published early in 1833 in pamphlet form their authorship was acknowledged. Harrison began his essay with the statement that, "Every thing tells of a spirit that is busy inspecting the very foundations of society in Virginia—a spirit new, suddenly created, and vaster in its grasp than any hitherto called forth in her history. There is a serious disposition to look the evil of slavery (nothing less!) in the face, and to cast about for some method of diminishing or extirpating it." He observed that the people of the state had not only permitted but encouraged the open discussion of a subject in the legislature that never before had been thought "fit to be mentioned but in a whisper."

In dealing with the great problem that confronted the people of Virginia, Harrison showed his discipleship to Jefferson and Madison. Rather than employ legislative action and compulsion, he advocated the exercise of reason and persuasion to effect the reform he sought. Convince the great majority of the people of the state, he advised, of the wisdom of adopting "a plan of heroic justice." In support of his idealistic proposal he quoted the encomium of Milton of the man of moral courage who against the crowd would be willing to be "the sole advocate of a discountenanced truth." The confidence of the young Virginian in the power of reason to prevail over the minds of men caused his Charleston friend Hugh Legaré to write on March 12, 1832: "Perhaps in ten years, or even *five*, you will qualify your confidence in reason."

In the state-wide debate on the emancipation of the slaves, Harrison took his stand, not with the extremists such as Faulkner and Preston, but with the more moderate reformers, particularly Thomas Marshall. His article in the *American Quarterly Review* commented on the mildness of slavery in Virginia and expressed the view that there was no moral turpitude chargeable to Virginians in holding slaves "under the present circumstances." Nevertheless, he regarded slavery as a great social and economic evil, and he repeated the various arguments for the gradual abolition of slavery advanced by the young reformers in the legislature. His plan for the removal of the evil of slavery was for the state to encourage voluntary emancipation and to buy up the young slaves annually and eventually deport them to Africa. To finance this enormous undertaking he advocated appealing to the federal government for a grant of public lands.

Harrison's literary antidote to Dew's proslavery article brought him some local fame. A review of Dew's publication in the Richmond *Enquirer* on March 12, 1833, referred to Harrison as one who had been "bellowsed and puffed by the abolitionists in Virginia as if the whole weight of their sinking cause rested upon him." The reviewer, on the other hand, wrote sarcastically of Harrison's arguments and announced that the young champion of the liberal side had not overturned the able arguments by Professor Dew supporting the continuance of slavery. Harrison's brother-in-law, William W. Norvell, wrote to him that Dew's pamphlet was on sale at all the bookstores of Richmond "and cracked-up as something great."

But by this time Jesse Burton Harrison had emigrated to New Orleans, on the advice of Henry Clay, to seek money, honors, and political office in the Creole metropolis. Here, in addition to establishing a law practice, he edited in 1836 the *Louisiana Advertiser* in support of the cause and candidates of the Whig party. The clippings of his editorials, preserved in the Harrison Papers at the University of Virginia, show that he placed patriotism above the interests of partisanship. His brief career in Louisiana can be followed to some degree by the letters to him from William Norvell, who continually admonished him as to the steps he must take to advance his career—mix with society, advertise yourself to the public in your newspaper, and "cultivate influential men for politics and black legs and scoundrels for your law practice." Norvell praised him for his good article on the U.S. Bank, his excellent parody of Van Buren in the style of Terence, and for addressing a public rally in New Orleans on behalf of Clay.

In the pleasure-loving and commercial city where he had made his home, the cultivated young lawyer sought, as he had in Virginia, to promote the growth of culture. He was one of the founders of the Louisiana Historical Society, and he spent many hours of laborious work editing four volumes of Louisiana Law Reports. But his great ambition was to be elected to high political office. In this quest he was handicapped by being a reserved Virginian, unsuited temperamentally to the rough and tumble politics of Louisiana at that time. Christian Roselius, an eminent lawyer of the city, in a letter on September 10, 1839, tried to dissuade him from running for office against Preston, arguing that his candidacy would split the American vote and inevitably result in the defeat of both candidates. "My experience," he admonished, "has taught me that the Creoles and French have very strong prejudices against the *Americans* as they call them *par excellence,* they look upon them as intruders." Nevertheless, Harrison was planning to become a candidate for the Senate of the United States when yellow fever caused his untimely death at the age of thirty-six on January 8, 1841.

In Louisiana there is no indication that he tried to continue the mild crusade against slavery that he had begun in his native state. Success in politics which he so ardently desired would have precluded such quixotic endeavor. And the same fate befell the other young reformers that he had left behind in Virginia. Once the issue was decided, the young liberals virtually ceased, as far as I have been able to ascertain, their efforts to abolish slavery from the state. If they were animated by a truly humanitarian spirit, it is surprising that, even though they could not accomplish the gradual emancipation of the slaves, they apparently made no effort through the remainder of their lives to change the slave code in order to ameliorate some of its harsh features. They could have, for example, pressed for a law such as Louisiana had, forbidding the sale of a child under ten years of age from its mother; they could have advocated giving to the Negro the right of testimony against whites in the courts; they could have demanded laws recognizing the sanctity of slave marriages; they could have urged the adoption of laws giving greater protection against sadistic masters and mistresses, and they could have supported efforts to enlighten the slaves, to liberalize the laws in regard to free Negroes, and to enact legislation facilitating the self-emancipation of slaves by purchase of their freedom on an installment plan.

The reform movement of 1832 died almost as quickly as it had arisen. Originally it was inspired by the panic that seized the people of the state after the Nat Turner insurrection. But the fear of servile insurrection receded into the dark corners of the Virginia mind, not to be exorcised again until the John Brown raid of 1859. In 1831–32 the Virginians were alarmed by the dangers to be apprehended from the steady increase of the ratio of the Negro population over the white; but the rapid development of the internal slave trade soon solved that problem, carrying thousands of surplus slaves to the expanding cotton plantations of the Southwest. The violent debate also raised the bogey of the division of the state along the line of the Blue Ridge, which alarmed many conservatives to seek to suppress the reform movement. Then just at the height of the movement, the nullification controversy intervened to divert attention from social reform. Furthermore, the unprofitable condition of slavery in Virginia in 1832, resulting from the worn-out soils, began to change. In the very year of the celebrated debate Edmund Ruffin published his epoch-making *Essay on Calcareous Manures*, which pointed the way to the renaissance of Virginia agriculture. Also there were formidable mental handicaps interfering with Virginians considering the proposals of the young reformers with open minds; the most insurmountable one perhaps was the almost universal opinion in the Old South that any emancipation of the slaves must be followed by their deportation. Southerners of this period could not conceive of the two races living peaceably together in freedom and equality. Also, the supreme difficulty of working out a plan of emancipation that appeared practicable to that generation of Virginia induced a conservative attitude of mind. Finally, the rise of "abolition fanaticism" in the Northern states and religious fundamentalism strengthened the conservative mood.

The subsequent course of the young 1832 reformers in politics affords a melancholy rubric on the changeability of human opinions. Most of them came from the western part of the state where their antislavery stand did not injure them in local and congressional elections. Philip Bolling, on the other hand, the delegate from a strong slaveholding county, was defeated for reelection in 1832; and James McDowell, Jr., was also defeated in the same year in his bid for election to the U.S. Senate, although a division among the Jackson Democrats in the legislature seems to have been the main cause for his downfall. Thomas Jefferson Randolph, who was more interested in farming than in politics, retired from active politics a few years after the debate but reappeared when a crisis arose; he was elected to the constitutional convention of 1850 and served in the secession convention. Although opposed to secession he became a loyal Confederate. The same was true of William Ballard Preston who, after a distinguished career as a Whig congressman and Secretary of the Navy under Tyler, served in the Confederate senate.

Four of the young reformers publicly recanted their former opinions on slavery and were thus able to stay in politics. The ardent young radical Charles James Faulkner retired temporarily from public life in 1833, but returned to the legislature in 1838; from 1851 to 1859, he was a member of Congress. In a speech in the constitutional convention of 1850, he repudiated the antislavery views which he had voiced so eloquently and boldly in the legislature of 1832. Another apostate was George W. Summers from the Kanawha Valley, who became a Whig member of Congress and in 1851 was a candidate for governor. During the campaign his antislavery utterances in the legislature of 1832 were brought up to discredit him and he was charged with being friendly with abolitionist Methodist ministers. He tried to defend himself by adducing extenuating circumstances, explaining his aberration as a young legislator, and by condemning the Northern abolitionists, but he was nevertheless defeated.

The most striking recantation of antislavery views was made by James McDowell, Jr., a Princeton graduate and perhaps the best educated of the group of young reformers. He was elected governor in 1842 and served in Congress from 1846 until his death in 1851. In the House of Representatives he delivered on February

24, 1848, a eulogy of John Quincy Adams—a typical flowery Southern oration. When he spoke in Congress against the Wilmot Proviso on September 3, 1850, he attempted to reconcile his support of slavery expansion with his 1832 antislavery sentiments. He declared that the Virginia legislature had the legal right to adopt the plan of emancipation that he had then advocated, but the Wilmot Proviso on the other hand, was unconstitutional, denying equality of rights to the Southern states. "Whatever opinions I have expressed or entertained upon the institution of slavery in the abstract," he explained, "I have never doubted for a moment, that as the white and black races now live together in the southern states, it is an indispensable institution for them both." It was needed, he said, to prevent physical amalgamation (he did not explain why). Emancipation of the slaves—with the rights of remaining in the South and holding property but exclusion from social, civil, and political equality—he predicted, would lead to a bloody war of colors, ending in the extermination of the Negroes. In contrast to his view of 1832, advocating state action for the eradication of slavery, he proclaimed that the correct policy of the federal government was to let slavery alone, not to try to prevent its expansion into the federal territories.

There was one prominent advocate of emancipation in the legislature of 1832 whose changing attitude on human liberty was particularly sad. He was Samuel McDowell Moore of Rockbridge County, in the Shenandoah Valley. When Moore spoke so ardently in behalf of the cause of emancipation in 1832 he was the owner of three slaves, but at the same time he was devoted to the natural rights philosophy of the Virginia Bill of Rights and the Declaration of Independence. He then maintained that the slaves were entitled to freedom as an inherent and inalienable right of man. In 1845 he published "An Address to the People of West Virginia" in the Lexington papers, bitterly assailing the eastern slaveowners for placing the protection of their slave property above the welfare of the state and thus sacrificing the needs of the west. He declared that the west, containing a majority of the white population, would not accept vassalage to the conservative east, and that unless a constitutional convention were called and justice done to western Virginia, the westerners would as a last resort form a new state.

Two years later he revealed that he still held to the liberal views he had expressed as a young man in the legislature of 1832. A debate was held in Lexington in the Franklin Literary Society; Dr. Henry Ruffner, president of Washington College, presented his antislavery views and his advocacy of the separation of western from eastern Virginia. Moore was one of the twelve signers of a formal letter requesting Ruffner to publish his views. Ruffner responded by publishing an *Address to the People of Virginia Shewing that Slavery is Injurious to the Public Welfare* (Lexington, 1847). The publication of this mild antislavery document caused so much criticism and ill-feeling that Dr. Ruffner the next year resigned the presidency of the college and moved away.

Moore and John Letcher, at that time editor of the *Valley Star* of Lexington, were among the signers of the call for Dr. Ruffner to publish his views. Twelve years later when Letcher was the Democratic candidate for governor he was attacked because he had been an endorser of the Ruffner pamphlet. In repudiating his former support of Ruffner's views, he drew a fine distinction by saying that in 1847 he had regarded slavery to be a social and political evil but not a moral one. Later he had reexamined the question and had become convinced of the error of his earlier opinions on slavery and had publicly acknowledged his mistake as early as 1850. He was elected governor.

In the following year (1860) Moore was also attacked for endorsing the Ruffner pamphlet. In the Whig state convention of February, his connection with the Ruffner pamphlet was brought forward as an objection to his name being placed on the ballot as a Whig candidate for presidential elector. He arose and declared that he offered no apology for signing in 1847 a call for Ruffner to publish his pamphlet. He preferred, he said, to keep "the esteem of that able, patriotic, and good old man, Henry Ruffner, which was worth more than the inconvenience of incurring the ill-will of those who condemned him" (Norfolk *Southern Argus*, March 20, 1860). In order not to injure the Whig cause, however, he withdrew his name as a candidate for presidential elector. This part of Moore's conduct was truly admirable, but then came a sad admission of change of views. He declared that he was not in favor of educating the Negroes and that previously he had advocated ridding the state of the slaves, not by freeing them, but by selling them (both sentiments drawing applause from the Whig convention). He proclaimed also that the Southern slaves, well fed and well cared for, were the happiest class of laborers in the

world. At another Whig meeting a month later he confessed that
he had modified his views since 1832 and 1847; the conditions of
1832 favorable to the emancipation of the slaves no longer existed,
and now it had become impossible to devise a practicable plan of
emancipation and deportation. He took virtually the same position
that McDowell had expressed in Congress ten years earlier—that
the two races could not live together in equality. Slavery was,
therefore, a necessary evil; it had become a stern necessity.

Whether Jesse Burton Harrison would also have changed his
views on the emancipation of the slaves is of course a question
that cannot be answered. It is highly probable that he would have
succumbed, as did the other young reformers of 1832 who were
politically ambitious, to the great shift of Southern thought on the
subject. The story of the defeat of the young reformers and their
later apostasy, if that is the correct word, is one of the tragic pages
in the intellectual and social history of the South. In their young
manhood the reformers had aspired to change their society on a
heroic plan; they were social critics and idealists. But after their
defeat in the legislature, they found the world as constituted too
strong for their puny efforts; in their maturity and old age they
accepted the social order and became realists. The opportunity for
radical reform, if it had ever really existed in the South of their
time, was lost—partly because they gave up the fight too quickly,
partly because they had no organization and little means of propaganda, but mainly because economic interest and inertia prevailed
over idealism. They asked of the men of their slave-based society,
the owners of slave property, the hard sacrifice that Christ asked of
the rich young man who came to inquire the way of salvation.
Furthermore, the people of the Old South were the victims of
powerful denigratory stereotypes of the Negro and of a fixed conception that whites and blacks could not live together in freedom
and equality without conflict and without racial amalgamation,
the latter so abhorrent in idea to them yet actually practiced to a
far greater degree then than after the slaves were freed. Following
the death of the young liberal Jesse Burton Harrison, the outstanding social reformer of Virginia in the antebellum period was the
great planter and gentleman John Hartwell Cocke of Bremo, whom
I shall discuss in the next chapter as the representative of the liberal facet of the Southern mind.

Chapter II

THE LIBERAL MIND
IN A SOUTHERN CONTEXT

GREAT ideas rule and form the minds of men fully as much as do the mores and economic conditions of the society in which they live. *Noblesse oblige* was one of these imperial ideas that permeated the upper class of Southern society in the antebellum period of history. Inherited from the colonial gentry, it survived, though in an attentuated form, into a later less aristocratic age. *Noblesse oblige* as practiced in the Old South had a quixotic side, exhibited in a high sense of honor, and a very practical side, shown in a sense of responsibility for public service. It animated the lives of numerous country gentlemen scattered over the South—of the planter Thomas Spalding of Sapelo Island in Georgia, of Joel R. Poinsett in South Carolina, and of *émigré* planters from Virginia in Alabama and Mississippi such as Colonel Thomas Dabney; but especially was the spirit of *noblesse oblige* perpetuated in the Old Dominion, where united with the Christian tradition it produced such symmetrical personalities as Robert E. Lee and John Hartwell Cocke of Bremo.

These men would be exceptional individuals in any society, yet they bore a certain family likeness—the imprint of their re-

23

gion. Such homogeneity was not incompatible with the development of well-marked varieties of Southerners in the subregions,
constituting to a degree a federalism of cultures. The Virginia
type, for example, differed from the Gulf Coast type, for it was
a unique blend of aristocracy and democracy and it had a mel-
lowness that was largely absent from the society of the cotton
kingdom. Consequently, during the heated controversy over the
expansion of slavery that led to the Civil War, Virginia acted as
a moderating influence, somewhat like a wise old patriarch, and
wherever the Virginia gentleman emigrated, he carried with him
something of the refinement and moderation that characterized
the society he had left. This society had many conservatives,
very few radicals, and a small minority of quiet liberals. Among
the latter John Hartwell Cocke of Bremo was outstanding, and I
have accordingly selected him as an exemplar of the liberal
facet of the Southern mind of the antebellum period.

Approximately midway between Richmond and Charlottesville on the James River stands Bremo, a stately brick residence,
designed in part by Jefferson, one of the beautiful houses of
America. Here from 1820 until his death in 1866 General Cocke
lived with simple dignity, unambitious of political honors. Everything about Bremo reveals his strong and distinguished personality. Even the barn, built of stone, has style about it, resembling
a Roman temple with columns and a white frieze. His Negro
cabins are well made and comfortable, showing his concern for
the welfare of his slaves, and the brick schoolhouse demonstrates
his interest in education. And on the estate is the famous "Temperance Well," housed in a Greek Revival structure, a monument
to his zeal for temperance. Not as cultivated as Thomas Jefferson
or possessing his versatile personality, Cocke equaled the great
Virginian in his respect for the dignity of the individual and in
his desire to reform his native state and the South.

Cocke belonged to the great tradition of Virginia gentlemen.
He developed a remarkably independent attitude toward the
mores of his society, partly at least because he had no political
aspirations and was a gentleman of assured social position and
wealth. General Cocke, as he was called, was one of the few
social reformers that the Old South produced. The group in
Southern society from which one might have expected leader-

ship in urging social reforms—the ministry—produced scarcely any critic of the social order after 1835. Yet Cocke derived his reform impulses primarily from his deep religiousness; he was truly a Puritan cavalier. There is something very touching in the zeal for religious improvement that permeates Cocke's papers and the diary of his wife Louisa. On December 1, 1834, she records that they began a course of reading the Bible early in the morning by candlelight. It is no wonder, therefore, that on Sundays they often became drowsy during the sermon. Ashamed of such weakness of the flesh, Louisa wrote in her diary, "Lord, be merciful to a poor weak sinner." These good people, whose thoughts were probably as pure as snow, at intervals reviewed their "sins" and sought to correct them. Louisa strengthened her soul by reading *The Imitation of Christ* by Thomas à Kempis, with its melancholy renunciation of worldly life. General Cocke's puritanism expressed itself in refusing to travel by train on the Sabbath day and in rebuking his married son Cary for not observing his own custom of a family altar, at which prayer and the reading of the Scriptures took place at the beginning and end of each day.

Born in 1780 into a family of French Huguenot origin, Cocke acquired the fine sense of responsibility and of *noblesse oblige* that characterized the older Virginia gentry. After attending William and Mary College, he rendered his first notable public service in the War of 1812, when he rose from the ranks of captain of artillery to brigadier general, commanding troops in Virginia. One of his aides, William Fitzhugh Gordon, observed that he was "universally respected and looked up to by the officers under his command." As a result of his military career, a movement arose to elect him governor of the state, but he refused to allow his name to be presented to the legislature as a candidate.

Like John Taylor of Caroline, Cocke regarded the life of the Southern planter as the ideal occupation, and he refused to be lured into entering politics as a profession. He was a progressive planter who read books on scientific agriculture, including a German work and a book on Chinese millet, which he sent to one of his sons to interest him in experimenting with this crop. Not only did he closely supervise the cultivation of his Virginia estates, but he had two cotton plantations in Alabama, which he visited regularly in the winters. In his early career as a farmer he followed the custom of his region in planting tobacco at Bremo, but he disliked the speculation that developed in marketing the crop. To his Richmond factor he wrote in 1827 that he wished a fixed price could be established for tobacco, "to get rid of the ruinous spirit of speculation which is invading the ranks even of our Country Gentlemen." His ideal of the country gentleman, however, was entirely too high for the competitive society which had arisen since the spread of cotton culture.

This aristocratic gentleman sought to promote the improvement of Virginia agriculture both by example and by precept. In the early days of the founding of the University of Virginia he advocated establishing a professorship of agriculture. His son Philip St. George Cocke of Belmead offered the legislature $20,000 to endow a professorship of agriculture at the university, but nothing came of it. Cocke was active in promoting agricultural societies, in experimenting with horizontal terracing to prevent erosion, in applying marl to exhausted land, and in breeding superior livestock. He imported Merino rams to improve the quality of his sheep, and though he had a puritanical attitude toward pleasure, he raised race horses, notably the stallion Roebuck, whose picture by Edward Troye hangs today on the walls of Bremo.

He extended his efforts for agricultural reform to his Alabama plantations. In 1854 he wrote to his son Cary Charles: "Nevertheless, I am much encouraged in the prospect of being able to work out my problem for Alabama agriculture—viz. that it is far better to improve the worn out lands of this originally gifted region than to abandon them and remove to virgin forests of the West & South & run the same course of destruction there—my marling, manuring & Rotation of crops is beginning to attract attention—and will soon be imitated by all who are not looking forward to removing to fresh lands."

There was a Jeffersonian side to Cocke's nature that caused him to seek to improve the lot of mankind by useful inventions. As a result of his yearly trips to Alabama on the railroad cars he realized the need for a more comfortable seat than those in use, especially one that could be adjusted to allow the passenger to sleep during the journey. Accordingly, in 1854 he invented an improved sleeping seat for railroads and spent $120 for lawyer's fees in obtaining a patent. He journeyed north to Philadelphia, New York, and Albany to interest the railroad companies in his invention but had no success.

Cocke's notable services in the founding of the University of Virginia and in cherishing its interests throughout the rest of his life constitute one of his most liberal achievements. Cocke ranks next in importance to Jefferson and Joseph C. Cabell in the founding of the university. He and Jefferson had charge of the construction of the buildings. Prudent businessman that he was, he believed that Jefferson was spending too much money on the beauty of the buildings, or on a "raree show of architecture." He, on the other hand, wished to keep expenses as low as possible so that the cost of a higher education would be within the means of the sons of independent farmers. He also upheld the strict enforcement of the "Uniform Law" of 1828 requiring the students to wear a plain gray uniform and no boots, for he regarded it as a wholesome measure against extravagant clothing.

Nor did Cocke sympathize with Jefferson's desire to import foreign professors. He wrote to Joseph C. Cabell on April 10, 1824, "Do save us from this inundation of foreigners, if it is possible." Indeed, his greatest disagreement with Jefferson's ideas arose over the appointment of Dr. Thomas Cooper, an immigrant Englishman, as professor of science and law, the first faculty member selected for the university. Cooper's unorthodox ideas on religion and a rumor that he was intemperate in strong drink resulted in a crusade against his appointment, especially among the Presbyterians of the state who were led by John Holt Rice, editor of the *Evangelical Magazine* at Richmond. Cocke supported this movement to reject Cooper, although it cost him great agony of mind. To Joseph C. Cabell he wrote on March 1, 1819: "The thought of opposing my individual opinion upon a subject of this nature against the high authority of Mr. Jefferson and Mr. Madison has cost me a conflict which has shaken the very foundations of my health, for I feel now as if I should have a spell of sickness. But I could not act otherwise, for if I had expired under the trial I should have held out to the last."

Jefferson vigorously defended the appointment, declaring that

Cooper was "the greatest man of America in the powers of his mind." But the board of visitors overrode his wishes and repudiated their contract with the free-thinking professor. In this episode the limits of Cocke's liberalism were revealed, while Jefferson stands forth pre-eminently as the greatest of the Virginia liberals.

The "sage of Monticello" had tried to keep the university a liberal intellectual institution, unhampered by sectarian religious influences. But Cocke, who served on the board of visitors for many years after the death of Jefferson, strongly supported the movement to establish a chapel on the grounds of the university and to encourage an orthodox religious atmosphere among the students. The appointment of Professor William H. McGuffey in 1845 as professor of moral philosophy was a notable step in this direction. Also when Professor Albert T. Bledsoe's book *On the Freedom of Will* was published in 1854, Cocke expressed the hope that it would be "an instrument of Providence to convert the university from a school of infidelity." He rejoiced when in 1855 he succeeded in having a "Temperance Hall" erected among the classic buildings on the campus.

Cocke's interest in education was exhibited not only in the founding of the University of Virginia but in the seminary that he established on Bremo plantation. Probably the initial impulse in founding this school was the desire to give his children a good education. In 1820 he advertised for students in the Richmond *Enquirer,* limiting the number to twenty between the ages of ten and fifteen. Two male teachers were employed to give instruction in Latin, Greek, French, Italian, surveying, Euclid, and algebra. A list of schoolbooks found in a bill in the Cocke papers includes McGuffey's *Eclectic Readers,* Greek New Testaments, Hebrew grammars, and arithmetic and geography texts. Aristocratic planters from various parts of Virginia wrote to Bremo seeking admission of their children into the school there. After Jefferson's death Cocke advocated the founding at Monticello of a gymnasium on the German model to prepare boys to enter the University of Virginia. The Bremo school was still in operation in 1857 with sixteen "scholars"; the teacher wrote to Cocke, who was away from Bremo, that he was having trouble with discipline and had been forced to use the rod; therefore he wished him to return, for the respect that the boys had for the firm old gentleman aided in the maintenance of discipline.

Why Cocke became a zealous reformer in the matters of temperance and the use of tobacco can only be surmised. There is a tradition in the family that during his early years at Bremo he served wine and liquor, and he also raised tobacco as his primary cash crop until he was past middle age. In his later years, however, he became an extremist in condemning both the drinking of wines and liquors and the use of tobacco. In 1834, when he was fifty-four years old, his attitude toward what he called "the great moral revolution" of temperance was reasonable and free from extremism. Writing to a Northern friend, he described the progress of the temperance movement in Virginia, which he said had begun in the middle division of the state in 1828 or 1829. The lower part of the state, he observed, had been the seat of many apple orchards and of the production of brandy, but a pest of caterpillars, particularly in Southampton County, had recently caused the farmers to turn to the cultivation of cotton. Upper Virginia was engaged in distilling whiskey from grain because of the difficulty of transporting crops to market. As soon as good transportation facilities were provided, he anticipated that the inhabitants would abandon whiskey distilling and turn to other occupations. Moreover, "the old grog & toddy drinking Christians in whom the power of habit is stronger than the spirit of Christ," he predicted, must soon die out. He himself advanced the cause of better transportation facilities in the state by promoting the construction of the James River and Kanawha Canal, being an active member of the board of directors of the canal company.

The master of Bremo rose to such national prominence in the temperance movement that in 1836 he was elected president of the American Temperance Union. Years later he wrote to various prominent Virginians and to Neal Dow, the author of the Maine prohibition law, to obtain their opinions as to whether the Bible prohibited the drinking of wine. Dabney Carr Harrison, named after Jefferson's intimate college friend, sent an equivocal reply. He agreed with Cocke that the spirit of the Scriptures was clearly against the use of intoxicating liquors as a beverage, yet he observed that Christ had not specifically condemned wine drinking and had even miraculously manufactured wine. Thus Cocke and his temperance friends were led to the same expedient that the abolitionists adopted, of appealing from the letter to the spirit of the Bible.

One of the persons with whom he corresponded on the temperance question was the tutor on the old James River plantation of Westover, then owned by John A. Selden. In April, 1857, the tutor, William G. Strange, wrote to Cocke agreeing with him that every school should be both a Bible school and a temperance society. But he pointed out the handicaps in inculcating the principles of temperance in tidewater Virginia: "Now as for the temperance society—this part of Va. preserves too decidedly still her old grog-drinking habits to make such a movement as the temperance reformation a very pleasing one—even among the young. Mr. Selden himself makes no regular business of drinking every day, but I don't think he speaks of the temperance cause in a way to make his children think it very deserving of their attention." He observed that he himself was regarded as a perfect prodigy because he did not drink. During the Christmas holidays he had been invited to a party where he was an object of curiosity because he was "a live specimen of a *cold water* man."

In his reforming zeal Cocke went to the greatest extremes in attacking the use of tobacco for pleasure. He raised his last crop of tobacco at Bremo in 1839, and a close student of his agricultural activities has observed: "The original motivation for his restriction of tobacco acreage was economic, but was swiftly transformed into a moral crusade." He corresponded in the 1850's with Northern crusaders against tobacco, who urged him to write letters to save the beautiful Connecticut Valley from being polluted by the spread of tobacco culture. One of his Virginia friends, Cornelius Carrington, undoubtedly reflected Cocke's own views in writing to him on November 10, 1857: "The use of tobacco should certainly be discontinued by all refined society; its appearance when chewed is filthy, as the claims of *decency* plead against its use; the tobacco quid & and segar are the ornaments for the mouth of the *drunkard, gambler* & rowdy, as well as other low & dissipated characters—therefore a desire of some distinction between the refined and low classes

JOHN HARTWELL COCKE, liberal reformer of Virginia.
Portrait by Edward Troye

should lead to its abandonment by the higher, refined, & decent circles."

The great blast which Cocke delivered against the tobacco evil was the publication in 1860 of a pamphlet entitled *Tobacco, the Bane of Virginia Husbandry*. In this work he argued that the raising of tobacco in Virginia ought to be completely abandoned, for it quickly exhausted the soil and required more continuous labor than any other crop. The tobacco farmer, he maintained, spent so much time on the numerous tasks of tending the tobacco crop that he neglected other crops, resulting in his buying a large portion of his meat from western drovers and raising a short crop of corn. Furthermore he imported northern hay and was usually deprived of milk for his coffee after Christmas because his cows had gone dry for lack of hay.

Cocke's principal argument against raising tobacco, however, was the moral objection. The use of the noxious weed by "tobacco idolaters," he maintained, produced delirium tremens, nervousness, dispepsia, insanity, indolence, the loss of teeth, discoloration of the skin, and dwarfishness. Such extreme and fantastic attitudes toward the use of tobacco and alcoholic liquors might seem to deprive John Hartwell Cocke of the valid title of being a liberal of the Old South, but these were only the foibles of a noble and generous nature.

"General Cocke" was essentially a gentleman of the old school whose views on the emerging feminist movement were those of his age and section. In September, 1853, he attended a "World Temperance Convention" in New York, where feminists struggled for recognition. His letter to his friend Professor McGuffey at the University of Virginia describing the occasion reveals that this fine old Virginia liberal was extremely conservative when the rights of women were involved: "You have doubtless seen in the newspapers the struggle we had with the strong-minded women as they call themselves in the World Temperance Convention. If you have seen the true account of the matter, you will see that we gained a perfect triumph, and I believe have given a rebuke to this most impudent clique of unsexed females and rampant abolitionists which must put down the petty-coats —at least as far as their claim to take the platforms of public debate and enter into all the rough and tumble of the war of words. The ladies of New York and New England will be greatly indebted to us for the line of demarkation [*sic*] we have drawn between the bloomers and the old school."

The professor of moral philosophy replied: "I most heartily rejoice with you in the defeat of those shameless Amazons who gave so much trouble at the World Convention—I trust and believe that it will be *final*."

Cocke's ideal of womanhood was distinctly Victorian. He described the wife of a kinsman in New Orleans as "a woman after my heart, accomplished both by education & travel, plane [*sic*] in her tastes & domestic in her habits—she soars above the whole class of affectations of the fashionable world and maintains herself in all the high-toned dignity of Christian character." In contrast, he drew the portrait of another New Orleans woman, the widow of a relative, who was a Catholic Creole. This lady, he wrote: " . . . has not an aspiration above a certain style of dress & jewelry and money enough to go to the opera or some other like exhibition every night—Sunday night not excepted. These Creoles are too lazy to comb their own heads & make their own dresses but employ professional hair dressers, and having no resource in Books, they never read, and talk only of the Opera, the Theatre & the Dancing parties, & thus passes the life of the greater part of the creole female population of New Orleans. The children of such Mothers are regarded as incumbrances, of which they are willing to get rid upon any reasonable terms. . . . "

Cocke's greatest claim to being a Southern liberal rested upon his antislavery views. A month after Nat Turner's insurrection, on September 23, 1831, he expressed his cautious but liberal views on the eradication of slavery in a long letter to a Northern correspondent. He pointed out the tremendous difficulties in freeing the slaves of the South, especially because of the great ignorance of the mass of field hands, most of whom could not count up to twenty and were totally unprepared for the responsibilities of freedom. Although he regarded slavery as a great curse, he believed that emancipation would have to be accomplished very slowly; it could be done only "by a process so slow as to preclude the men of any one generation from the honor of its accomplishment."

The members of Virginia society most disposed toward this great liberal reform, he observed, were the large slaveholders who had inherited their slaves, for only one-third to one-half of their slaves were productive, and they had to support the unproductive ones. The classes most strongly opposed were the middle class of slave-owners and the yeoman slaveholders; these two latter groups had as a rule purchased their slaves and therefore owned a large proportion of productive workers. Nevertheless, he believed that the great majority of Virginians would acquiesce in an enlightened plan of gradually removing the slaves from the state if they were paid a fair evaluation for the loss of their property. Anyone, however, who should venture to advocate the freeing of the bondsmen without their deportation, he declared, would bring upon himself "deep & universal execration."

Cocke looked to economic rather than to political or moral forces to bring an end to slavery. The "peculiar institution" in Virginia appeared to be in a moribund condition, unprofitable to many slaveholders, especially to those who on account of humanitarian reasons were reluctant to sell any of their slaves. Besides the economic problem of slavery (he apparently did not foresee the rejuvenation of slavery as a result of the cotton kingdom's rapid expansion), he suspected that another force was working toward the eventual abolition of slavery, namely, the relaxed discipline and government of slaves which he observed had developed within less than a generation. This lessening of firm control over the bondsmen, he believed, accelerated the growing unprofitableness of slavery and encouraged the spirit of insurrection among them.

The Southampton insurrection resulted in what Cocke called an "astonishing vibration of the public mind" on the question of liberating the slaves. Up to this time, he observed in a letter to his daughter Sally, "no man or set of men in our public councils have had the moral courage to encounter the popular current & declare publicly the magnitude of the evil & advocate the necessity of removing it." The famous debate on emancipation in the legislature of 1831–32 resulted in the adoption of nothing significant toward the abolition of slavery except the mild support of a plan to colonize free Negroes in Africa, but Cocke did not condemn the members for failing to face the problem: he commented that no plan had been suggested that had the general approbation of the legislature. So formidable were the difficulties involved in freeing the slaves that it is not surprising that Cocke expressed no deep disappointment at the meager result of the reform movement. He placed his hopes for the gradual abolition of slavery in the colonization of the slaves in Africa, in the providence of God, and in the operation of economic forces.

In 1835 Cocke wrote to the Virginia Senator William C. Rives that he was disturbed over the agitation of Southern politicians against the abolitionists. Some of these ambitious men, he declared, would rather be first in Hell than second in Heaven and accordingly would agitate the slavery question to advance their political careers. "They know full well," he wrote, "that the few enthusiastic and well advised abolitionists would soon fall into oblivion if let alone—but they also know that slavery is our sorest sin, and to touch it excites feelings allied to madness. I can't but fear there is dark trouble for us growing out of this cause—and I am inclined to think so the more readily because we deserve it. There is nothing clearer to my mind than our ability as a nation to free ourselves from the disgrace & curse of slavery if we were really as willing as we profess to be to get rid of it."

A method of gradually eradicating slavery which Cocke thought held great promise was the colonization plan. He was vice-president of the American Colonization Society for many years. In the University of Virginia library are a group of letters marked "Bremo Slave Letters," from slaves whom he had colonized in Liberia. They are full of affection and respect for him, grateful that he had taught them trades and given them religious instruction. Mrs. Cocke recorded in her diary October 3, 1834, that she had taught the colored children during the preceding week every day but one. And Cocke, while he was away from Bremo visiting his Alabama plantation in 1857, wrote to his son Dr. Cary Charles Cocke that he was glad to learn that he had secured a preacher for the chapel, which had been built for the slaves. "This is but a part of the religious instruction we owe to our Slaves," he observed, " . . . if we were faithful in this respect, we might with more propriety use for defense the Scriptural arguments which so distinctly recognize the Institution."

The letters of Lucy Skipwith, a slave on his Alabama plantation, reveal more poignantly than any other documents Cocke's efforts to elevate the Southern slaves. Lucy, according to her master, was the vilest sinner on his plantation before she was converted to Christianity and was born again to a new life. After this dramatic change she performed the function of chaplain on the plantation and was installed by Cocke as teacher of the children on the Alabama plantation both in the day and the Sabbath schools. On May 19, 1855, she wrote to her master at Bremo that she was teaching the children to write and that some of them could make letters very well. She also taught a night school for the older children who labored in the fields, but they improved very slowly. The children loved to work on the blackboard, she wrote, and little Mariah was so apt that she could add, multiply, and subtract. Lucy herself delighted in arithmetic and wished to go further in this study, but she lamented that she had no one to instruct her. The slaves at Bremo were also taught to read and write. In both Alabama and Virginia it was against the law to instruct slaves in reading and writing; Cocke seems to have paid no attention to this law but was not prosecuted.

The education of his slaves was an essential part of Cocke's program to prepare them for the responsibilities of freedom in Liberia. He used his Alabama plantation Hopewell especially as a training ground for those he intended to send to Liberia because its climate approximated that of the African colony. But when the master was not present, the Negroes would not work and made the life of the overseer miserable. In 1856 Cocke wrote to his son Cary that he had been greatly disappointed in his hopes for the moral and intellectual improvement of the slaves at Hopewell. There had been some progress in certain individuals, but the majority had no motivation "to bring their minds up to the conception of the dignity of Liberty." If they could not accomplish this, he observed, it would be better for them to remain in America in the charge of a humane master. In his will of 1859 he left the Alabama slaves to his grandsons with the request that they treat them with a Christian sense of responsibility for their physical and moral welfare. Only Lucy Skipwith, her husband, and children, were to be granted freedom and their expenses paid to Liberia if the faithful Lucy desired to go.

Toward the close of the antebellum period Cocke seems to have lost some of his early feeling that slavery was a great evil. N. F. Cabell of Liberty Hall wrote to him in April, 1857, that he was glad Cocke had approved of what he had written on the "peculiar institution," for he had anticipated Cocke's dissent. In the same year Cary wrote to his father a long justification of slavery and cited the failure of his father's methods of relying on moral incentives in managing the slaves on his Alabama plantation and of the excellent results obtained by a new overseer in using a strong hand over the Negroes. The son commented that he did not believe slavery was an unmixed blessing nor necessarily perpetual, but he regarded it as an institution of God's providence, necessary for the time being. He concluded by observing that a perusal of his father's recent letter induced him to believe "that our views herein are not so far apart as you have thought."

Nevertheless, Cocke retained a humane attitude toward slaves and recognized their dignity as human beings. He was attacked by the Richmond *Examiner* in 1854 because he wished to have the slaves educated. He permitted some of his slaves to obtain their emancipation by a plan of extra work. In regard to James, one of these freedmen, Cocke rebuked Cary for making a severe ruling concerning visits to his wife and children who remained slaves of Cary. Of this Negro, Cocke wrote that "he has shown himself man enough to work out his own emancipation in seven years—and I believe he will under God in seven years more be able to claim his wife & children for their value—I do not expect to live to that period but I trust you will and that you and Nannie Oliver [his wife] will find it in your hearts to reward such distinguished nobility in human nature."

The Virginia reformer was very much like Jefferson in placing a great trust in the idealism of human nature, whether residing under a white or black skin. In the Cocke Papers is a letter dated October 14, 1857, from R. S. Bissell of Greenwich, Connecticut, formerly the chaplain at Bremo, which illustrates this point. Bissell expressed regret that the old reformer was having so much trouble in emancipating and colonizing his slaves. He observed that Cocke expected more improvement in their character than experience and the depravity of human nature entitled him to expect. "When I was with you," he remarked, "I sometimes questioned whether a sanguine temperament & high toned sentiment did not dispose you to elevate your standard of Expectation (not to say requisition) higher than experience & practical acquaintance with men as they are warrants."

Cocke approached the problem of elevating the Negro from the point of view of paternalism, but there was a more viable attitude illustrated by John McDonogh, the great merchant and philanthropist of New Orleans. Except for a common devoutness, two men could hardly have been more different than the aristocratic Virginian and this self-made merchant. A poor boy from Baltimore, McDonogh had come to New Orleans in 1800 to make his fortune. By the time of his death in 1850 he had accumulated an immense fortune from merchandising and speculating in real estate. Though he was regarded penurious in his manner of living as a withdrawn bachelor, there was a nobler side to his nature shown in his efforts to liberate the slaves. He established a system of self-emancipation for slaves on his plantation which encouraged them to work extra hours and save the money that he paid them to be used in buying their freedom and paying their way to Liberia. He appointed a capable slave to be their overseer, called "the commander," and he established a jury system that worked admirably. He tried to induce other planters to follow his example by publishing letters in newspapers and a pamphlet describing his plan of self-liberation for the slaves. After he had established his system on his plantation, a striking change took place in the conduct of the slaves: they became industrious workers, cheerful, and devoted to their master. In the McDonogh Papers at Tulane University there are letters from a free Negro planter, A. Durnford, to McDonogh, signed "Yours Affectionately" which indicate that the colored planter and the white merchant–planter treated each other very much as equals.

A notable aspect of Cocke's liberalism was his relative freedom from sectional prejudice. In attending conventions of temperance, Bible, tract, Sunday school, and missionary societies in the Northern states, he tended to become less sectional in his feelings.

At these gatherings, he found, politics sank into utter insignificance. In 1854 he wrote: "Our Northern brethren are widening the gap between us sensibly, to my mind at every visit I make to the North, in all the arts of life—but this is not to be wondered at when we see how much they are doing for the education of the people & the propagation of the Gospel." He deplored the crimination and recrimination that went on between the two sections, threatening the preservation of the Union. Even when sectional feeling was reaching its height in the fall of 1860, he could write: "The more I have seen of our Yankee brethern, the more highly I appreciate them and rank them beyond comparison as the best part of our Nation." He praised former Senator William C. Rives, who later was to play a prominent role in Virginia in opposing secession, as a man who had contributed toward "breaking up the Mason and Dixon line."

The nearest Northern counterpart of John Hartwell Cocke that I can find is Edward Everett of Boston. I can imagine this polished Northern gentleman sitting in the parlor at Bremo chatting easily and with great geniality—though not with a mint julep in his hand—with John Hartwell Cocke. Both men were natural aristocrats in a republican society; both had a classical background; both were idealists interested in moral reforms. Everett had a broader and deeper culture than the Virginia planter, for he had received a Ph.D. degree from the University of Göttingen (1817) and had taught at Harvard College as professor of Greek literature. Unlike Cocke who had refused to become involved in politics, Everett was the scholar in politics, serving as Congressman, Whig governor of Massachusetts, minister to England, secretary of state in Millard Fillmore's cabinet, and finally in 1860 as vice-presidential candidate of the Constitutional Union party. Cocke was given to plain speech and avoided public speaking, but Everett was a famous orator who made the principal (though now forgotten) speech at Gettysburg when Lincoln gave his brief but immortal address.

Different as the two men were in many respects, their lives illustrated the likenesses and nuances of difference between the gentlemen of the South and of the North. Both men were deeply religious, but Everett's religion was more intellectual and flexible (he had been a Unitarian minister for a short while after his

graduation from Harvard) than that of the Southern planter;
both men were interested in promoting college education, Cocke
as a founder and long-time trustee of the University of Virginia,
Everett as professor and later president (1846–49) of Harvard
College; both were ardent patriots; both were advocates of
moderation in national affairs and of intersectional comity; and
both wished to eliminate slavery from the national life. Separating
them psychologically, notwithstanding, was an important dividing line, a different way of life of the Southern gentleman from
that of the Northern gentleman; the one had been molded by the
plantation environment and Jeffersonian traditions; the other, by
the urban and commercial society in which he had been reared.

John Hartwell Cocke may not seem much of a liberal in the
light of our twentieth-century preconceptions. But he was the
best that the Old South had to offer, save possibly James G. Birney or Professor Benjamin Sherwood Hedrick of the University
of North Carolina, whom I shall consider later. Far from being a
zealot such as the Boston patrician Wendell Phillips, he sought to
effect reforms in his society through the influence of a quiet
gentleman. Particularly disappointing to a modern liberal was his
failure to emancipate his slaves in his will. In 1799 Washington
had done so; but would he have emancipated his slaves if he had
lived fifty years later? Conditions had so changed by 1859 when
Cocke wrote his will that it would have been extremely difficult
to comply with the law and still liberate them. Furthermore,
Cocke's noble efforts to train slaves for freedom and colonize them
were a failure, a fact which may have tended to reconcile him to
the continuance of slavery; and finally there is reason to believe
that he was persuaded by the proslavery argument that the Bible
sanctioned slavery. He was caught in the wave of religious conservatism that inundated his section. We assume today that all
right-minded Southerners of the decades 1840–60 were struggling with their conscience over the rightfulness of slavery; there
is not much firm evidence to support this view.

In the period before 1840, on the other hand, there were many
men, especially in the upper South, who had a sense of guilt over
the existence of slavery in their region. Cocke declared in a letter
to Jesse Burton Harrison in 1827 that the colonization movement
might save the South from the horrors of a servile war and be "the

means of removing from our national escutcheon the only stain that defaces it"—slavery. He also praised Harrison for his 1827 article in the *African Repository* and for his opposition to the election of Andrew Jackson to the presidency. After the death of Louisa in 1843, Cocke rededicated himself to noble causes, especially "the ultimate extermination of the sorest and most afflictive evil of our day and generation in the Southern States."

Years later, in July, 1850, he ruminated in his diary over the change that had come over Southern opinion in respect to slavery and to democracy. The occasion for his reflections was an oration by William Garnett before the alumni of the University of Virginia, in which the speaker defended aristocracy and maintained that slavery was a blessing to the Southern states. In seeking to explain these "monstrous" doctrines, Cocke observed that "until the rise of Calhounism the vast majority of intellegent and reflecting men of my acquaintance uniformly regarded slavery as the curse of the land." The growth of Southern extremism and Northern abolitionism had been responsible, he maintained, for a great change of opinion in the South (he neglected to mention the growing profitableness of slavery); it had produced such "mad cap philosophy" and such "an impudent assault on political liberty" as he had just witnessed at Charlottesville.

On September 7, 1852, while he was at Hot Springs, he finished reading Wayland's letters upon slavery. This Northern antislavery book caused him to review his own thinking about the rightness of the peculiar institution. The reflections that he recorded in his diary constitute one of the best explanations that has survived of the apparent inconsistency of those Southerners who believed slavery to be wrong but nevertheless continued to hold on to their slaves:

While I protest against [the idea] of holding Slaves being a sin under all circumstances, I am equally fixed in the opinion that no sanction can be brought from the Bible for defending American slavery interminably. Where slavery is recognized by Law & they have been obtained by inheritance I cannot conceive it criminal to hold them in bondage until there is a fair prospect of bettering their condition or leaving them equally well off by giving them freedom, but I conscientiously believe that Virginia slaves in the hands of humane masters cannot be emancipated to their advantage in their present ignorant and debased state. I therefore feel no compunction at holding my slaves but I feel it is my

duty to do so for their good. I believe also that they have been reduced
to this state of unfitness for liberty by the debasing influence of their
bondage. I can't therefore get rid of the obligation of preparing them
for freedom and bestowing it upon them when so prepared.

The failure of General Cocke to carry out his enlightened program of reform illustrates the difficulties of being a liberal in the
Old South. The cards were stacked against the liberals then just
as they have been in most periods of history. The inertia opposed
to change was extraordinarily powerful in the Old South. The
overwhelmingly rural condition of society, the existence of slavery, the masses of illiterate and provincial voters, the strongly
orthodox religion of the people were allied forces to defeat liberalism. But stronger than these influences was the fact that Southerners of this period were living under abnormal emotional stress.
Their society was being violently attacked from outside; in fact,
a cold war existed.

Under such conditions, the liberal political leader, the liberal
editor, or the liberal minister was placed at a great disadvantage
in communicating his thoughts freely, for he was likely to be
suspected of disloyalty to his section. The advocate of the gradual
emancipation of the slaves, for example, was hounded, not merely
by the McCarthys of that period, but by the whole community.
Against the weight of this force, average human nature was too
weak to stand, for as Lord Acton has written, "from the
absolute will of the entire people, there is no appeal, no redemption, no refuge, but tyranny." Cocke did not meet this fate,
for he did not seek public office nor did he directly challenge the
passionate prejudices of the people by publishing his antislavery
views.

A transitional figure, John Hartwell Cocke carried over into a
new age some of the qualities and ideas that had distinguished
the Virginians of the eighteenth century—the generation whom
Dumas Malone has called "The Great Generation." That generation, which had won the independence of the country and
established the early republic, was led by a liberal aristocracy
who had a fine sense of public responsibility and *noblesse oblige*.
They had a larger more philosophic horizon than the succeeding
generation of Southerners who seceded from the Union. A
prominent leader of this later generation was James H. Ham-

mond, a man quite different from Cocke, an archconservative, whom I have chosen to represent the growing conservatism of the Southern mind.

Chapter III

THE HAMLET
OF THE OLD SOUTH

THE intellectual is rarely found in American politics—among
the Presidents, only Jefferson, the Adamses, Madison, and
Wilson. In the antebellum period South Carolina produced two
notable intellectuals among its public men—Calhoun, and at
some distance below him, James H. Hammond. Calhoun recognized Hammond's great potential ability, writing to him shortly
before he died in 1850: "Without flattery, I know no one better
informed, than you are, on the great subject that now agitates the
country, or more capable of deciding what should be done. . . ."
Hammond's friends, especially William Gilmore Simms, who
admired his unsurpassed intellectual equipment, expected him
to succeed Calhoun as the leader of the South, the man of the
hour in a dangerous world that confronted the South after 1850.

Why did he fail? In the first place, Hammond was a Hamlet-
like statesman with a brilliant encompassing intellect, very
practical but also fatally weakened for action by his capacity to
see the complexities of life and by an overweening pride and a
wavering will. Furthermore, could anyone from South Carolina
have united the South and led it to victory over the Northern

and Western congressmen before the Civil War? In a recent study of the American Presidents based on a poll of historians Professor Arthur M. Schlesinger has concluded that all the five men designated as "great" in the poll espoused the liberal side in American politics and the general welfare against the status quo. Hammond, on the other hand, chose the side of conservatism. He could not otherwise have been elected to office in South Carolina. Moreover, his early acquisition of great wealth undoubtedly influenced his political opinions and "principles."

The South Carolina mind in 1860 was the product of one of the most conservative societies in the civilized world, though this society did contribute some men of liberal views, notably Joel Poinsett, Benjamin F. Perry, and James L. Petigru. The basic reason for this conservatism was the feeling of its people that their safety and welfare depended upon preserving slavery against the attacks of the North. Slave labor seems to have been more imperatively required in the low country of South Carolina than in the upper South because the climate was hotter and the swampy rice fields were more unhealthy than most parts of the South. Here malaria was prevalent—malaria of a virulent kind—which was more enervating and fatal to whites than to blacks. Although the slaves, particularly the younger ones, did contract the disease at times, the majority of the Negroes apparently developed greater resistance to its ravages than did the white population. The slaves were more numerous in proportion to population and blacker in color in South Carolina than in any other Southern state. In 1860 they constituted 57.2 per cent of the population, whereas in Virginia the ratio was only 30.7 per cent. Moreover, the Carolina slaves, primarily because of their long isolation, seem to have been more primitive in culture than elsewhere in the South. The Gullah Negroes, particularly those on the sea islands, retained more of their African speech and culture than slaves in other states.

Accordingly, aside from powerful economic reasons for retaining slavery, South Carolina had perhaps greater justification for maintaining slavery as a police institution than any other state. Here also there were frightening memories of the slave uprising at Stono in 1740, of tales told by Santo Domingo planters who fled to Charleston after the massacre of the whites in 1793, and of the dangerous Denmark Vesey plot of 1822. South Carolina was the last state to reform its black code by making the willful murder of a slave a capital crime—in 1821.

The little "Palmetto State" was less affected by the phase of liberalism on the slavery question which arose after the Revolution than any other state. While in Virginia, Maryland, and North Carolina the tobacco crop which nourished slavery was declining, the rice and sea island plantations of South Carolina were prosperous, and slavery was profitable. Moreover, the soil of the rice country did not suffer from depletion and erosion to the extent that the land of her neighbors to the north did. When the indigo staple became unprofitable after 1800, upland cotton took its place. After this crop, based on slave labor, expanded into the Piedmont, the old sectionalism of the state became largely submerged. Accordingly, there was no strong economic reason to be dissatisfied with slavery in South Carolina. Indeed, there seemed to be abundant reason to justify the institution.

In the 1820's before the rise of the abolition movement, South Carolina leaders developed proslavery propaganda well ahead of the other states. By 1852 with the publication of *The Pro-Slavery Argument*, a series of essays written largely by South Carolinians, the elaborate rationalization of the South's position on slavery had been virtually completed. Only the writings of George Fitzhugh of Virginia—*Sociology for the South* (1854) and *Cannibals All* (1857)—were needed to complete the edifice of the great apology for slavery.

Into this highly conservative society James H. Hammond was born, not as a member of the ruling class, but as a commoner in the upcountry. His father, a native of Massachusetts and a graduate of Dartmouth College, had emigrated to South Carolina to teach school, had married a Southern woman, and had established an academy in the upcountry. In his father's academy young Hammond learned so rapidly that when he was barely sixteen years old he entered the junior class of South Carolina College and two years later was graduated near the top of his class. After a year of teaching school he studied law and was admitted to the bar. He settled in Columbia, where he not only practiced law but edited *The Southern Times* from January, 1830, to May, 1831. He later recalled with bitterness this period of his life of struggling to establish himself, for, as he wrote to his young brother, he had to work his way upward among people who "looked down" on him.

Then an event took place which greatly changed his life. He married a Charleston heiress, Catherine Fitzsimmons, daughter of a wealthy Irish immigrant merchant and distiller. Immediately after his marriage he quit the practice of law, abandoned his newspaper, and moved to his wife's plantation Silver Bluff on the Savannah River. From this time on he treated his wife's fortune and property completely as his own. In his reminiscences Professor Frederick A. Porcher of the College of Charleston wrote that Hammond was "the only intelligent man I ever knew in my life whom I considered to be 'a purse proud man'; he evidently and palpably valued himself more on account of his possessions than upon any of those intellectual powers for which the people admired him." His fortune made him indolent and gave him the leisure to indulge his immoral tendencies, his self-pity, and his morbid taste for being sick. William Gilmore Simms, his most intimate friend, believed that his marriage to a rich woman had a decidedly enervating effect upon him. To Beverley Tucker he wrote in 1851 concerning Hammond; "Upon this [his wealth] he recoils whenever the world goes wrong, instead of stripping to the buff and fighting through the thick of enemies. But for his fortune he would have been one of the most remarkable and most successful men in the country."

In his early manhood Hammond reminds one of the young Goethe, whom nature had showered with gifts. Like the German poet he was extremely handsome. Benjamin S. Perry, the South Carolina unionist, was impressed with the good looks of the tall young man. Years later, when Hammond had become a senator, Perry was amazed to see how greatly his appearance had changed; he was then "stout" and looked old at fifty, had become bald, and wore spectacles. In his youth he cultivated the social graces, and his quest for self-culture and desire to experience life deeply again remind one of Goethe. To his young brother John at the University of Virginia, he wrote, ". . . learn everything, not courses"; especially should he study French, which was more valuable than "Greek and Latin united." He should cultivate polished manners "as much as you do your mind." He should not neglect to learn dancing, ". . . without being able to dance & waltz tolerably, you can never get a wife."

Ever ambitious and self-seeking, Hammond accepted the values of the conservative and aristocratic society into which he had been born. In South Carolina a family tree was an asset, and accordingly, after he had arrived, he sent a genealogist to England to search for illustrious lineage among his ancestors. When the investigator reported that he was descended from honest yeomanry, the proud Carolinian tore up the documents sent to him and refused to pay the genealogist. In South Carolina, military rank was coveted, and Hammond zealously attended the encampments of the militia and in 1841 was elected general of the militia.

But above all he aspired to political honors. As a young editor in Columbia he had championed the popular cause of nullification and had won the certificate required in South Carolina of being regarded as a high-spirited gentleman: he had challenged one critic to a duel and horsewhipped another, the Northern editor of a Carolina paper. By his bold and uncompromising editorials in his newspaper he won the high regard of the leading nullifiers, including the master, Calhoun. After he retired from editing his paper, he continued to take an active part in the nullification movement. With the older heads, George McDuffie and James Hamilton, he conferred with Calhoun at Fort Hill in the summer and fall of 1832, planning the strategy of nullification. Governor Robert Y. Hayne appointed him one of his military aides in preparing the state for resistance. Hammond was energetic in recruiting volunteers and in making speeches to arouse the local patriotism of the people. He himself offered to the service of the state a hundred bales of cotton and the labor of his slaves to work on fortifications.

In 1835 the young nullifier was elected to Congress, the only election to office that he ever received by the vote of the people. Here he attracted national attention by a speech that he made on February 1, 1836, opposing the acceptance of petitions from abolitionists to emancipate the slaves in the District of Columbia. Displaying antislavery tracts with pictures of masters flogging their slaves, the young champion of the South, declared that the purpose of the abolitionist petitions was "to subvert the institutions of the South." Boldly he announced that the first step of Congress to emancipate Southern slaves would cause him to go home to preach secession even if it resulted in war. Shortly after his defiant speech, Hammond resigned his seat in Congress on account of ill-health and with his wife toured Europe for over a year.

When he returned to South Carolina, he held no public office for some years, devoting his energy to improving Silver Bluff. In 1841 he moved to Columbia to give his children better educational opportunities and to advance his political ambition. Here he built an expensive and imposing mansion and entertained lavishly. He collected a fine library and read much. From his travels in Italy he had brought back many pictures and statues. But his neighbors and associates appreciated neither literature nor art. On one occasion shortly after he had moved into his fine house in Columbia, he showed his pictures to a dinner party. As to their reaction he scornfully commented in his diary: "They gazed at them with the apathy of Indians."

In 1840 Hammond was a candidate for governor but was defeated by John P. Richardson, a former unionist during the nullification controversy. Two years later he was elected to the office that he coveted, but he won by the close vote in the legislature of eighty-three to seventy-six over the great rice planter R. F. W. Allston. As governor his main interests seem to have been the protection of states' rights and slavery. In 1844 when Robert Barnwell Rhett began "the Bluffton movement" for the calling of a state convention for "separate state action" on the protective tariff, he supported this extreme movement in his message to the legislature of November 26 of that year. He denounced the high protective tariff of the Whigs as violating the tariff treaty of 1833, and moreover he was embittered by Northern opposition to the annexation of Texas. He declared that when the compact of the Union was violated, South Carolina must look to the preservation of its interests and not be "overawed by the divine right of the Union." But Calhoun interposed to head off the Bluffton movement, and his lieutenants in South Carolina succeeded in getting the legislature to pass moderate resolutions that mortified the pride of the departing governor. Before he left office, Hammond had an opportunity triumphantly

JAMES H. HAMMOND, conservative intellectual of South Carolina.

to assert the sovereignty of the state. In accordance with a resolution of the legislature, he expelled from the state the Massachusetts emissary Samuel Hoar, who had been sent to Charleston to secure a judicial decision against the law requiring the imprisonment of free Negro sailors while their ships were in South Carolina ports.

Nevertheless, the intellectual but fire-eating governor accomplished very little of a constructive nature. He supported the movement to establish the Citadel, the state military college in Charleston, which was chartered in 1842 and opened the following year. He considered that the most important achievement of his administration was the passage of legislation regulating the powerful Bank of the State of South Carolina. Perhaps the most valuable service that he rendered as governor was his invitation to Edmund Ruffin to make an agricultural survey of the state in 1843 and his persuasion of the legislature to appropriate money for the survey. In the Southern Collection at the University of North Carolina is a series of letters from the governor to the Virginia agricultural reformer and also Ruffin's manuscript journal of his survey of the state, which present Hammond in a very favorable light. Ruffin discovered valuable marl beds in the state and preached the gospel of restoring worn-out lands by the application of marl. Hammond became an enthusiastic advocate of marl and of scientific agriculture in the South. He found, however, that he could not get his overseers to experiment with new methods, and the Southern farmers scoffed at a "Book-Planter." To Ruffin he wrote on February 8, 1844, "I cant get a soul to touch it [marling the land], have laid off some experimental acres along the public road with a sign board so as to *force* all who are not blind to see." Thus he showed one of the splendid sides of a nature that had much in it that was neurotic and unadmirable.

At the end of his term of office he returned to Silver Bluff, where for the next thirteen years he remained in political retirement. Here Solon Robinson, the Northern agricultural editor, visited him in 1850 and praised him for being a progressive planter. He described the master of Silver Bluff as "the most practical of men." At this time Hammond owned 10,000 acres of land, divided into several plantations, and 220 slaves. He gave close personal supervision to the work of the plantations, riding for hours over his lands, directing his overseers. He practiced the most modern methods of agriculture in his region, such as the enrichment of the soil with marl and guano, crop rotation, and the use of good tools. He carried on swamp drainage and the reclamation of arable land, according to Robinson, "to a greater extent than any person of my knowledge." In 1846 he wrote a pamphlet entitled *Marl* to aid in the improvement of the agriculture of the state. He also experimented extensively with new crops, such as Chinese millet and African imphee, hoping to develop a sugar-producing crop in South Carolina, and he established a vinery for the production of wine. In 1857 Edmund Ruffin visited Hammond at Redcliffe on Beech Island, near Augusta, to which he had recently removed, and talked with him until midnight on agricultural problems, concluding that his host unquestionably had the most powerful mind in the Southern states.

Hammond attained a reputation for being a severe slave master, partly because when he took over the management of Silver Bluff the slaves were unruly and lazy, and he had to extablish a severe regime to bring them into subordination. At the same time he performed acts of thoughtful kindness toward them: when he returned from his European trip he brought a large number of Italian briar pipes as gifts for them, and at various times he gave them barbecues, to which he invited the neighbors. In 1839 he shifted from the task to the gang system of labor because he believed that under the former system the slaves rushed through their work with no rest or food until three or four o'clock in the afternoon and used the leisure thus obtained to carouse and get into mischief. He always retained a low opinion of the Negro, and he also believed that the poor whites were no better than the slaves. He tried to encourage his slaves to work hard by offering prizes, and to his slave women he gave the reward of a calico dress for bearing children. Nevertheless, over a long period of time the number of deaths on his plantation exceeded the births. In 1854, however, he found a way to reduce the heavy mortality among the slaves by reducing the amount of medicine given to them and by changing the diet of the children from molasses and rice to skimmed milk and buttermilk.

Though he was an excellent farmer, Hammond was constantly complaining of the thin soil of Silver Bluff and its poor yields of cotton. In his diary (preserved in the Library of Congress) he wrote gloomily in 1841 that he had hung on to his South Carolina plantation rather than emigrate to the fertile lands of the Southwest because he did not wish to carry his family into "the semi-barbarous West." Also he confessed that he was detained in South Carolina by his political prospects and by his desire to give his children "a certain rank in society." One lucrative source of income, the selling of wood to steamboats on the Savannah River, had declined greatly after the introduction of railroads; in 1841 he estimated that he had thereby lost $2400 annually. Despite his complaints about the low returns of farming in South Carolina, his net income, varying from $6,000 to $15,000 annually, supported a life of considerable luxury.

During his long retirement from public office at Silver Bluff Hammond was restless and unhappy, not content to remain simply a country gentleman. His main resource against boredom was his friendship with the novelist William Gilmore Simms. In 1847 Simms said that Hammond had been his most confidential friend for nearly twenty-five years. This friendship was perpetuated despite Hammond's aloof and domineering nature because of his longing for conversation with intellectual men. Hammond made loans to the perpetually needy editor and novelist. He also gave Simms money to consult mediums when the novelist made trips to New York, for Hammond became a convert to spiritualism. Simms, in return, tried to cheer up his friend during his black moods and gave him sound advice concerning his domestic problems and his political ambitions. Both men were exceedingly frank in their criticism of each other, but their friendship remained unbroken.

Hammond's intellectuality was perhaps most clearly revealed in his correspondence with Simms. He gave the novelist excellent criticism of his literary work. He told him to curtail the long conversations of his characters. "Use the knife freely," he wrote, "& cut out everything that impedes the action. I used even when a boy to curse Scott for his long twaddling scenes & you must not blame me if I say that you have caught that failing from him." He upbraided Simms for his carelessness in violating the unities of time and place, and he insisted upon more realism. The two opinionated Carolinians discussed art, philosophy, literature, religion, politics, and farming. Hammond collected subscribers for Simms's magazines, *The Magnolia* and the *Southern Quarterly Review,* and wrote reviews and articles.

But Hammond's mind continually turned upon politics, which was honored in South Carolina as literature was not. Too proud openly to seek office, he constantly hoped that the legislature would elect him to the Senate. In 1846 when George McDuffie resigned from the United States Senate, an opening occurred for Hammond's election to the post. Just as he was about to seize the splendid prize, a mysterious scandal in his personal life came to light. It had happened three years before, when he was governor but had been kept a secret from the public. "The crisis in my fate which I have long apprehended would in some way come up," he wrote in his diary on December 4, 1846, "has at length arrived." It was then that Wade Hampton threatened to expose the hidden scandal if he did not withdraw from the contest for election to the office of senator. Accordingly, his managers in the legislature withdrew his candidacy, and Andrew P. Butler was elected.

This great scandal had a disastrous effect upon Hammond's political career, comparable to the disgrace that wrecked the career of the Irish nationalist leader Charles Parnell over the exposure of his adultery with Mrs. O'Shea. The element that made the scandal concerning Hammond's personal life so damaging was his silence about it, his refusal to gratify the prurient curiosity of the public. Rumors had begun to circulate as early as 1844 that he had seduced the teen-age daughters of Wade Hampton, who was his brother-in-law. In a letter to his brother Marcellus he declared that he would pay no attention to the gossip and cited the admirable course of the Charleston lawyer James L. Petigru toward a family scandal. Petigru, Hammond commented, never noticed the rumors about his daughter, who was accussed of having had an illegitimate child by a prominent Charlestonian, and events had proved the wisdom of his course.

Nevertheless, the proud man suffered the torments of the

damned, as he reveals in his letters to Simms and in his diary, which has all the frankness and fascination of Rousseau's *Confessions*. It was this scandal that forced him to give up his fine home in Columbia and not to return, except once, for a period of fourteen years because the Hampton plantation, Millwood, was nearby. In 1857 he wrote to Simms that "a little dalliance with the other sex" had kept him in political idleness for fourteen of the prime years of his life.

After his first defeat for election to the Senate, Hammond brooded at Silver Bluff over his personal tragedy. At times he thought that God had forsaken him because of his sins, but he was adept at rationalization and condoned his acts by citing examples from the Bible and from gossip about American politicians: Clay and Webster, he asserted, were notorious for immorality, and President Harrison had gotten his wife's niece with child. Although the distressed statesman admitted privately that he had done wrong in the affair of the Hampton girls, "the result of impulse, not design," he declared that if the truth were *fully* known it would not seriously injure him, but "fully known it never can be and I have been reduced to the humiliating course of endeavouring to smother everything."

In 1850 during the Southern movement Hammond again came momentarily into political prominence when he was elected by the legislature as one of the delegates at large to the Nashville convention. In February he wrote to Edmund Ruffin that he favored the South cutting loose from the Union as speedily as possible to avoid the fate of Jamaica. In April he wrote to W. B. Hodgson, a Georgia rice planter: "If I go to Nashville, I shall by no means enact Hotspur—but if I could, Washington." He declared that if he found the South prepared for secession, he would go into a secession movement head and soul in order to establish the "Republic of Washington." Nevertheless, when he departed for Nashville in May, he was deeply pessimistic that anything important would be accomplished by the convention, especially since Clay's Compromise had lowered the resistance spirit of the South. In the convention he made a speech which, according to his own account, "demolished" the unionist address of Judge Sharkey of Mississippi, but Robert Barnwell Rhett carried the ball for the South Carolina delegation. Hammond did not return to Nashville for the second meeting because he thought it would be dominated by a few ultras.

Back in South Carolina, he stood aloof from the movement for immediate secession led by Robert Barnwell Rhett and Langdon Cheves. In his diary he explained his attitude: "I should be [for secession] if I thought it judicious, as I have for near or quite twenty years been in favor of disunion & believed it inevitable. But no state save our own is ready to go to such lengths." Unlike Calhoun who loved the Union and tried to save it, at least on his own terms, Hammond was a Southern nationalist who had no love for the Union and believed that the South would be more secure in its institutions and more prosperous out of the Union than in it. But he was a practical man and a cautious one at the same time.

Calhoun's death in March, 1850, had left a vacancy in the Senate to which Hammond hoped to be appointed. But Governor Seabrook passed him over and appointed his rival, Franklin H. Elmore, president of the Bank of the State of South Carolina. Elmore died in May, and the legislature elected Robert Barnwell Rhett over Hammond to sit in Calhoun's seat. There were a number of reasons for his defeat, the most important of which were his failure to return for the second meeting of the Nashville convention, the opposition of the friends of the Bank of South Carolina whom he had antagonized, and the revival of the old scandal. Hammond wrote in his diary, "The public is still burning with curiosity to know all about the Hampton affair." He himself thought that it was extremely unjust for the legislature to let what he called a peccadillo in his private life influence their election of a successor to Calhoun. "Where," he exclaimed, "was a statesman ever put down before for his amorous & conjugal infidelity?" He cited the fact that Parliament ignored Lord Melbourne's affair with Mrs. Norton.

The Carolina leader was deeply hurt by the legislature's rejection of him for a man like Rhett. His gloomy and self-pitying thoughts over his defeat were heightened by his belief that he was the man for the crisis which the South then faced. Rhett and Governor Means, who were leading the state toward seceding alone from the Union, he regarded as rash and unwise leaders, belonging to "the violent bugle blast section" of politicians. He conceived of himself in a different role, or as he recorded in his diary on December 14, 1850, "I will further state my own firm belief, that with the help of God & tolerable health, I would guide the State and the South through all their present difficulties. And if there is another man who can do it, I do not know him—he is unknown now."

Crushed and embittered by his defeat, he sulked and refused to take any active part in the campaign for calling a state convention or a Southern convention to meet at Montgomery. If the state wished his services at this critical time, he declared, it must come *"cap in hand & beg them."* He did present a plan of resistance, which was published in the *Mercury,* namely, to cut all ties with the federal government, recall senators and representatives from Congress, and remain with one foot out of the Union. When the state convention met, it was apparent that the other Southern states would accept the Compromise of 1850, and accordingly it rejected Rhett's impracticable plan of secession by a single state. Thereupon, the Carolina fire-eater resigned his office in May, 1852. In the election of a successor Hammond was again passed over by the legislature in favor of a man of much inferior ability.

Hammond's conduct throughout the Southern movement of 1850–51 is puzzling and seems inconsistent. Although he was one of the outstanding Southern nationalists, in the crises of 1850 and later in 1860 he opposed actual secession. His attitude was ambivalent indeed, indicating a predilection to radical speech but conservative action. The explanation for this strange conduct seems to lie in his belief that the secession of South Carolina alone would be disastrous. But there was perhaps also an undeclared reason, a motive that he himself may not have fully realized—the conservatism of rich men, who fear to disturb the status quo and thereby endanger their vested interests. Moreover, his bad health tended to unnerve him for action. In his diary he wrote that he possessed "both moral & intellectual qualities that would enable me to lead an army or rule a nation," but that his health forbade such great efforts. Simms was constantly rebuking him for his overindulgence in food, drink, and the chewing of tobacco, and for lying on the sofa too much. He suffered from nervous dyspepsia, weakness of the eyes, and a severe case of piles. His ill health contributed to make him pessimistic and weakened his will for action.

In November, 1857, Hammond's fate turned dramatically. Senator Andrew P. Butler died and Hammond's friends once more brought his candidacy before the legislature. This time the proud Carolinian announced in the *Mercury* that he was not a candidate and would not serve if elected. The legislature, nevertheless, elected him over the prominent contenders, Robert Barnwell Rhett, James Chestnut, Jr., and Francis W. Pickens. Despite his previous disclaimer, he accepted the office, regarding his election as a signal defeat of his enemies.

The newly elected Senator revealed a curiously vacillating attitude toward the great problem of the future, the secession of the South. In a letter which he wrote to Simms shortly before leaving for Washington, he declared that he would not countenance any isolated movement of South Carolina or of any one state, "no matter what comes up." Reversing his former position, he wrote that he was not in favor of establishing a Southern confederacy if the South could remain in the Union and avoid submitting to "gross insult" or permanent "oppression."

When he arrived in Washington, he waited for more than two months before making a speech, and then he carefully prepared for his debut in Congress as the champion of the South. On March 4, 1858, he delivered the famous speech that contained the striking slogan, "Cotton is King." This argument contributed powerfully to the illusion of his section that if war should develop with the North, England and France were so dependent on cotton that they would have to come to the aid of the Southern states. Another important part of this speech was his argument for the continuance of slavery, namely, that every civilized society must have a menial class to do its hard physical drudgery and that the Southern slaves were peculiarly suited for this task, forming "the mud sill" of Southern society. Concerning the effect of this speech, Hammond commented in his diary that it "fixed me as the Peer of any of the Senators. That was glorious to me— but it finished me—prostrated me physically." Though he remained in the Senate until his resignation on December 11, 1860, he accomplished nothing constructive or notable. Like Calhoun, he tended to overvalue the effect of speeches in influencing the voters and actions of men.

When the session of Congress ended, Hammond returned to his home near Beech Island, where on July 22 at a public dinner honoring him he made a speech that dismayed the fire-eaters. He opposed a disunion movement by a single state—he would countenance such a movement only if four or five states acted in concert. Furthermore, he predicted that the first election of a Black Republican candidate would not lead to a dissolution of the Union, because fifteen or twenty Southern leaders in Congress had been mentioned as candidates for the Presidency. He also opposed the reopening of the African slave trade, which he had formerly favored.

The Beech Island speech was reported only in outline in the papers of the state, but it caused so much discussion and consternation that Hammond clarified his position in a speech three months later at Barnwell Court House. In this important pronouncement of his views he declared that the vast majority of Southerners preferred to stay in the Union if it were conducted in accordance with the true principles of the Constitution. He admitted that for many years he had been a disunionist but that now he cherished the hope that "we can fully sustain ourselves in the Union and control its action in all great affairs." He gave his reasons; the tariff of 1857 had reduced the average level from 40 per cent *ad valorem* where it was in 1828 to below 20 per cent; the Second National Bank had been destroyed; the federal government had retreated from a policy of internal improvements; but, most important of all, "the tide of abolition fanaticism is ebbing everywhere." He urged his fellow Southerners to give up as delusions any policies of adding new slave states by expansion of the United States into Cuba or Mexico and Central America. Instead, they should develop their own resources and trust and cooperate with their Northern allies.

Hammond did not himself participate in the fateful Democratic presidential nominating convention that met in Charleston in the spring of 1860. From Washington he telegraphed to the South Carolina delegation to secede from the convention if the Alabama delegation should walk out and should be followed by any other state. Brilliant though he was, he did not foresee the course of events that led to the breakup of the Union. He thought that Breckinridge, the candidate of the extremists, for whom he voted, would be elected. He utterly failed to realize the strength of Northern antislavery feeling, since he believed that the Northern people were guided principally by their economic interests. Lincoln's election in itself, he thought, was not a sufficient justification for the dissolution of the Union, because it was entirely constitutional. On November 15 he sent a letter to a committee in South Carolina advising the legislature to be calm and judicious in the crisis following the election of Lincoln, but the committee thought that this communication was so far "behind the times" that they suppressed it.

Despite Hammond's conservative views at this time, he contributed greatly to the swiftly growing Secession movement and to the emotionalism of the hour. When Federal Judge Andrew Magrath resigned after the election of Lincoln and the junior Senator from South Carolina, James Chesnut, Jr., on December 10, Hammond himself impulsively resigned the next day. He apologized to his brother Marcellus for this hasty act by confessing, "I thought Magrath and all those other fellows were great apes for resigning and have done it myself. It is an epidemic and very foolish. It reminds me of the Japanese who when insulted rip open their own bowels. . . . People are wild. The scenes of the French revolution are being enacted."

After his impulsive resignation, Hammond had very little part in the secession of his state and the formation of the Southern Confederacy. He himself recognized the peculiar irony of his position when he wrote to Simms on March 24, 1861: "A Southern Confederacy has been the cherishing dream and hope of my life. Yet it has been accomplished without apparent agency of mine. I did not see how the movement could succeed and fully believed that South Carolina would again have to eat dirt."

Though Hammond joined the Secession movement reluctantly and seemed to be out of step with the dominant trend of his state during this crisis, he was the ablest exponent after Calhoun's death of the ideology of the cotton kingdom. He was a strong believer in constitutionalism to protect Southern rights in the power struggle between North and South. In a letter to Calhoun in 1844 he lamented the decline of constitutionalism in the United States, observing that only South Carolina objected to any measure because it was unconstitutional. The people as a whole neither cared for the preservation of the Constitution (as it was in 1789), nor did they have any real knowledge of it. "We constitutionalists," he commented, "will soon be denominated the 'Ancien Regime,' and laid on the shelf." Although he had a low opinion of Calhoun as a practical politician, "a mere child in the ordinary affairs of life," he regarded him as the greatest political thinker in America. In a letter to Edmund Ruffin in 1857 he declared that Calhoun's *Disquisition on Government* was superior to any work that had appeared since Aristotle, and he predicted that it would be "the Text Book of the coming ages."

Hammond was foremost in the defense of slavery, even surpassing Calhoun in the reasoned defense of the institution. In his letters to the British abolitionist Thomas Clarkson and to the Free Church of Scotland in 1845, which were published and widely publicized, he gave a persuasive argument in favor of Southern slavery. He commented in his diary that the Old Testament should be expunged from the Bible because the Jewish God of that book did thousands of cruel actions, but he based his biblical defense of slavery largely on the Old Testament. He affirmed that the slaves were well treated and happy, noting that hardly a case of insanity existed among them. He concluded that the South owed a debt of gratitude to the Northern abolitionists because their attacks on slavery had caused the Southern people to examine the question of the rightness of the institution, which they had previously doubted. As a result of such examination, he declared, they had found that they had not violated any law of God and had thus obtained peace of conscience. Not only did he say this in public debate, but in a letter to Calhoun in 1849 he remarked that the discussion of the abolition question has "eased nearly every conscience in the South about holding slaves." He may have been correct in this opinion.

The defense of slavery led some proslavery advocates to reject Jeffersonian liberalism and the doctrine of majority rule. As Louis Hartz has observed in *The Liberal Tradition in America,* this sharp turn in Southern political theory marks the only important deviation from Lockian liberalism in American political thought.

Hammond was among the most important leaders in the South who severely criticized the philosophy of natural rights. In his Clarkson letter he proclaimed, "I indorse without reserve the much abused sentiment of Governor McDuffie that 'slavery is the cornerstone of our republican edifice;' while I repudiate, as ridiculously absurd, that much lauded but nowhere accredited dogma of Mr. Jefferson, that 'all men are born equal.'" He maintained that a government controlled by the numerical majority was necessarily a bad government, for in every part of the world more than half of the people were both poor and ignorant.

Hammond had not originally belonged to the South Carolina aristocracy, but by his marriage to a wealthy woman and by his great talents he elevated himself into it. The aristocracy of the state was not a closed corporation, as witnessed by the careers of George McDuffie, Langdon Cheves, and the great Calhoun himself. After Hammond joined the ranks of the large slaveholders, he became a strong conservative in the support of a stratified society. As one of the great planters, he himself held a privileged position in this society, which he said was equivalent to that of the nobility in European countries. Next to the planters in prestige he ranked the lawyers, "professed politicians," doctors, and merchants; he did not mention professors and writers in his classification of status.

His concern for the interests of his class and of the aristocracy of talents was expressed in his views on public education which he presented to the legislature in his governor's message of 1843. He announced that the free school system of the state had been a failure and should be replaced in each of the twenty-eight districts of the state by academies which would give a good classical preparation to those planning to go to college. Such schools should charge moderate tuition, enabling middle class families to educate their children as well as "such of the poor as really desire to educate theirs," for the latter should be permitted to send their children to these schools free of charge. Observing that this plan would save the tax-payers eight thousand dollars annually, he seemed to be completely oblivious of the need of educating the masses to read and write.

This advocacy of educating only the elite fitted in well with his aristocratic views of government and his repudiation of Jeffer-

sonianism. As early as 1836 he had written from Paris to
Francis W. Pickens that he was not a democrat; rather, he said,
"I go for a Republican government based on the institution of
slavery." He always entertained a dark and low opinion of
human nature. On October 10, 1845, he sent an abstract of South
Carolina's system of representation in the legislature to Edmund
Ruffin, noting that it worked admirably. The small slaveholding
parishes of the low country, he pointed out, were given the same
representation in the senate as the large populous upcountry
districts which contained relatively few slaves. "Thus the low
country [he remarked] rules the Senate—the upper country the
House. The result is that on the whole the wealth preponderates
in our Legislature & fully counterbalances the mere Democratic
tendency—Our Senate is in its constitution highly conservative
& aristocratic, nearly as much so as the English House of Lords—
We have the most perfect system of government in S. C.—yet
now and then the degrading dread of the Sovereign people sometimes invades the Senate. Aspiring men grow nervous when the
upper country gets on a high horse & make the Senate give way
sometimes when it should not."

Hammond believed that the South Carolina constitution was
so nearly perfect that it needed little change. He would have
liked to add a small property qualification for each voter. He
suggested to Ruffin that Virginia would do well to adopt the
South Carolina plan for the eastern and western parts of the state.
This balanced government would have a glorious result for the
South, he predicted. The election of the governor and presidential electors in South Carolina by the legislature rather than by
the people, he declared, had an immensely beneficial effect, for,
"We have no Federal parties *among the masses.*"

Five years later he reaffirmed in his diary (December 15, 1850)
his belief in an aristocratic form of government. He commented
approvingly on the evolution of an aristocratic type of government in his native state (which, however, he admitted was declining): "The government of S. Ca. is that of an aristocracy.
When a Colony many families arose in the Low Country who
became very rich & were highly educated. They were real noble-
men & ruled the colony & the state, the latter entirely until about
thirty years ago & to a very great extent to the present moment.

Our Legislature has all power. The Executive has none. The people have none beyond electing members of the Legislature—a power very negligently exercised from time immemorial. The Legislature governs, the old families ruled the Legislature. The abolition of primogeniture in 1790 was a severe blow to them. Extravagant, bad managers, & degenerating fast, they have been tottering with the death of every one who was in active life or at least had his character formed in the last century or the first fifteen years of this."

The old aristocracy, he asserted, had been temporarily rescued by the establishment of the Bank of the State of South Carolina. This powerful financial institution, which was closely connected with the state government, was run by a clique of politicians, headed by Franklin H. Elmore, who supported Calhoun: Simms wrote to Hammond in 1847 that Calhoun owed the bank $20,000. Hammond wished to replace this oligarchy by bringing to power another ambitious clique headed by himself, rather than by democratizing the government. Indeed, he was fearful of a revolt of the people who might seek to crush the low country by abolishing its "Rotten Boroughs" and changing the constitution so that the governor, presidential electors, and the judges would be elected by popular vote. These radical measures, he believed, would constitute "a Revolution." To head it off, he proposed a few minor reforms, such as making the governor eligible for re-election immediately after his first term, increasing his power, and making him and certain other public officers responsible for the conduct of the treasury rather than entrusting decisions to "a Secret Conclave of twelve men in a Bank Parlor."

Hammond wished to keep the status quo in South Carolina. He especially desired to put down "the influx of demagogism" and scorned the new vogue for electioneering, which, he wrote, even the old families were practicing by "their gross fawning on the vulgar." During the Secession movement he drafted a letter to the South Carolina legislature warning them against the danger of making any change in the constitution of 1808 with its compromises which protected slave property. "In this era of demagoguery," he declared, "the state must be protected against the little great men who will seek notoriety by proposing to elect Judges, Senators and Representatives annually and perhaps by universal suffrage; they must be kept from putting their hands upon this constitution or we shall soon have the guillotine at work upon good men." Thus, he echoed the sentiments of the great English philosopher of conservatism, Edmund Burke.

James H. Hammond was the Hamlet of the Old South, cast in the role of the defender of conservatism. In personality he was the very opposite of the national statesman of the twentieth century Franklin Delano Roosevelt, whom Justice Oliver Wendell Holmes described as "a second-class mind with a first-class temperament." Hammond's mind was both practical and contemplative, but his indecisive and mercurial temperament hampered him in resolute action and bold leadership. His wavering at crucial moments represented, indeed, the dilemma of the Old South.

Hammond was a self-made patrician, but the more typical Carolina gentleman was to the manor born. Such a person was Robert W. Barnwell of the Beaufort district in the Tidewater. Like many wealthy planters' sons, he was educated in the North, a member of the Harvard class of 1821. At Harvard he was first in scholarship in his class, was greatly admired by his classmate Ralph Waldo Emerson for his oratory, and was commander of the Harvard military company. With beautiful manners, a modest and unassuming personality, he possessed the poise and graces of an aristocrat of an old family. There must have been something very appealing, very Southern, in his personality, for when Emerson after the Civil War urged him to attend the class reunion, he referred to "the high, affectionate, exceptional regard in which I, in common I believe with all of your contemporaries of 1817–21, have firmly held you as our avowed chief, in days when boys, as we then were, give a tender and romantic value to that distinction which they cannot later give."

When Barnwell returned after graduation to his native state, he began a career as planter-politician. He was elected to the legislature and then to Congress without opposition. His culture was recognized by his appointment to the presidency of South Carolina College to succeed the skeptical Dr. Thomas Cooper; in this position he restored the confidence of the people of the state in their university. His complete accord with the political sentiments of the low country was demonstrated when he was chosen a delegate to the Nashville Convention and was appointed Senator to fill Calhoun's unexpired term. He presided over the Southern convention in Montgomery in 1861, declined the offer of secretary of state in the Confederate cabinet, but served as a loyal supporter of Davis in the Confederate senate. These offices should have been glory enough for an ordinary man, but the South Carolina aristocrat was a gifted individual who never fulfilled the brilliant promise of his youth.

Was it because of the enervating influence of his South Carolina environment? Inheriting many plantations and slaves and a secure social position, he was able to retire frequently from the strife of life to one of his plantations. At Harvard, Emerson noted, Barnwell was engaged in "a great struggle of ambition" for leadership; but in South Carolina everything came easy to him, and he seems to have lost his drive and ambition. Not only was he weakened by the great wealth for which he did not have to struggle, but even political office came to him without effort in the tight little oligarchy of his native state. Bound down by the mores of his society, he accepted conventional views of status, religion, and politics; he was not an independent thinker.

Nevertheless, he appeared to Benjamin F. Perry to be an almost perfect man—the Chevalier Bayard of the South. Mary Boykin Chesnut, on the other hand, noted some defects: he laughed uproariously at his own jokes, which she suspected he got from the same source that Lincoln did—"Joe Miller's Jokebook"; he looked through his spectacles with a benevolent, "a most Pickwickian expression," and though he was clever, she thought he was erratic. Moreover, some grave blemishes appear on his personality that even the sharp-sighted Mrs. Chesnut did not see. He viewed the Negro through a denigratory stereotype; he was a pious but a conventional Christian, little interested in social reforms; and especially, he was a "high-toned," conservative gentleman who placed loyalty to his state above loyalty to the nation.

His speech before the Senate on June 27, 1850 on the Compromise Bill was an accurate picture of the profound change of the Southern mind. He frankly admitted that there had been a time when the leading statesmen of the South regarded slavery as a social, moral, and political evil. But driven by the attacks of the abolitionists, Southerners had investigated the moral aspects of the subject; the result was that they had found nothing in the word of God condemning the institution, and they now felt that they could hold slaves in good conscience. They had changed their former view, too, that slave labor was unprofitable. They had concluded that all men are not capable of self-government and "experience has taught us that few nations are capable of self-government" — a far cry from the idealism of the Declaration of Independence (31st Cong., 1st Sess., 990–92).

America was changing rapidly, but Hammond and his class sought to preserve the old order. His brilliant highly critical mind did not detach him from his conservative environment. Instead, he became an exemplar of the ruling prepossessions of the South Carolina mind. Not only in major interests—the preservation of slavery, orthodox religion, and aristocratic government—was South Carolina highly conservative, looking backward to the eighteenth century, but also in lesser matters such as a fantastic opposition to divorce, a preference for the old writers of English literature, and a corresponding distaste for modern American writers, such as Emerson and Hawthorne, an archaic sense of honor, and an absurd emphasis on genealogy.

In 1860 the Southern people faced the prospect of a drastic change in their way of life imposed from without, as they do again a hundred years later. There is a great difference between reform that is forced on a society, and beneficial change that is brought about gradually by social evolution. Southerners believed then, with Sir Francis Bacon, that time is the great innovator. Indeed, the matter of timing is often the difference between liberals and enlightened conservatives. Conservatives may have a valid point in resisting outside pressure for a rapid reform of the old order of society, and they may rightly feel that outsiders do not have a realistic view of local conditions in trying to impose absolute norms upon them. At the same time it is their obligation to *begin* reforms now and to cooperate with the innovating force of time rather than to oppose it blindly. The unwillingness to do this was the mistake of the Southern mind on the eve of the Civil War. Insulating themselves from world criticism, Southerners did not realize the necessity of reforming their society, and they had no intention of initiating the reforms demanded of them by the North. It was a defiant stance, which undoubtedly hindered the emergence of a genuine reform spirit in the South. Nevertheless, conservatism in some matters is perfectly compatible with a vigorous championship of reform in other matters, as was illustrated in the career of the masterful business leader of New Orleans, Maunsel White.

Chapter IV

THE COMMERCIAL MIND

BEHIND the highest pile of oyster shells of any of the patrons of the old Gem Restaurant in New Orleans could frequently be found the great merchant Maunsel White. With a gourmet's taste for oysters, he concocted a peppery sauce which his Negro servant carried with him when they entered his favorite restaurant. Called "the Maunsel White sauce," it later received the name of tabasco sauce. This genial merchant was one of a remarkably able, wealthy, and public-spirited group of businessmen in New Orleans that included Glendy Burke, John McDonogh, Judah Touro, and John Burnside. Of these men White was the only one who kept a journal and a letter book that have survived to our time. From this source it is possible to get an insight into his mind and his way of life and therefore to understand better the commercial mind of the Old South.

New Orleans is the ideal city for the study of the business class of the Southern states. Although it had relatively few manufactures, it was the great commercial focus of the Mississippi Valley. In 1860 it exported over half of the enormous cotton crop of the Southern states, and approximately half of the sugar crop grown in Louisiana was sold by its factors. Thousands of flatboats and steamships transported to the Crescent City the agricultural surplus of the Ohio and Mississippi valleys—whiskey, flour, hams, dark tobacco, hemp, butter, and corn, as well as furs from St. Louis and the lead of Missouri and Galena. New Orleans was also a great slave-trading center, the antebellum Delos, where planters could buy prime young Negroes at the highest price in the Union.

New Orleans was destined to become the foremost commercial city of the southern United States, but when young Maunsel White arrived there in 1801, it was a small town controlled by Spain. He had left Ireland a penniless orphan when he was only thirteen years old. He never returned to his native land, but he retained a warm feeling for the Emerald Isle. Many years after his arrival in America when he heard that an Irish gentleman who had been kind to him in his youth was threatened with the foreclosure of a mortgage on his home, Jockey Hall, he sent thirty bales of his cotton to Liverpool to be sold to relieve the man's financial distress. Before the young adventurer came to New Orleans he spent several years in Louisville, Kentucky, where he formed a friendship with young Zachary Taylor. In New Orleans he clerked in a countinghouse for sixteen dollars a month, half of which he paid to a French teacher until he had acquired the ability to speak French. He described his early struggles in New Orleans in a letter of advice to his son off at school, "I had a proud spirit," he wrote. And he would let no obstacle discourage him.

The earliest record among his papers is a journal and memo book, dated April 22, 1802–July 14, 1804, which contains notations of personal expenditures. These indicate that he was a gay young blade, delighting in fine apparel, Florentine vests, silver buttons, and silk hose; that he gambled, attended the theater, went to dances, and drank wine. There are notations of the purchase of a fine German flute and of payment for tuition in French. Later he married the daughter of a prominent French Creole, Celestin de la Ronde, and when she died he married her sister Heloise.

In January, 1803, he embarked on the sailing ship *Mariner* for New York to purchase goods for a New Orleans firm. His journal indicates that he combined pleasure with business: it records expenditures at a play, a church coffee, and a sleigh ride. It also lists the purchase of oranges, almonds, apples, lottery tickets, books, brandy, beer, punch, oysters, and gambling. In New York he purchased various merchandise to be forwarded to New Orleans: silver spoons, gold earrings, gold breast pins, and gold finger rings—both "with Hair" and "Hoop Fashion." From New York he journeyed to Philadelphia, where he recorded paying 21/6½ to his landlady for one month's lodging, board, and washing. Here he visited Peale's Museum and Gray's Gardens. On this commercial trip he was away from New Orleans eight months and returned on September 23. Besides his expenses, he charged his firm, Wilson and Eastin, forty dollars per month salary. He purchased a total of $2,120 worth of merchandise, including cost of transportation and insurance. One curious item which he bought in Philadelphia was one dozen whip thongs.

The trip north was typical of the conduct of mercantile business by thousands of Southern merchants. They took pride in advertising that their stock had been purchased in New York. The textile industry in the South had to struggle against the prejudice of Southerners against homemade goods. In 1860 William Gregg, founder of one of the pioneer textile factories of the South at Graniteville, South Carolina, lamented, "Graniteville goods are more popular in New York and Philadelphia than at home."

White's early accounts show that he dealt in a variety of goods —lace caps, ribbons, skins, bonnets, cordage, lard, flour, pork, and beef. He lent small sums of money to his customers, and he acted as an agent in sending cotton to Northern ports. His son, commenting in his journal on the death of his father in 1863, explained his great success as a merchant: "he first made a *name* & his name made the money—none stood higher for integrity—his word was inviolate as an oath."

Gradually Maunsel White established himself as a reliable and successful factor in selling crops of the planters and forwarding plantation supplies to them. An important step in his progress was to secure the cotton business of Andrew Jackson. Jackson had become acquainted with the young merchant when White served as the captain of a volunteer company under him at the Battle of New Orleans. Some years later, disgusted with his New

Orleans factors, Jackson asked the former officer to be his agent in selling his cotton crop. This connection, begun in 1826, continued until Jackson's death in 1845.

In his dealings with the master of the Hermitage Maunsel White is revealed in an attractive light. He was frank in speaking even to so formidable a person as "Old Hickory." In a letter of January 28, 1845, the year Jackson died, he answered the latter's request to examine his last year's cotton crop, which had brought such a low price. White explained that it was the worst cotton that Jackson had ever shipped to him, containing much trash and broken leaf, and baled in a damp condition, which had materially injured its color. On another occasion when Jackson complained that White's firm had sold his cotton too quickly, thereby causing a loss, the New Orleans agent credited him with the difference between the price at which it was sold and the current price. Thereupon, Jackson sent to White a letter of gratitude beginning with "My dear Col," in which he first praised him for his brave and soldierlike conduct on the battlefield of Chalmette and then praised him for his action in regard to his cotton. White replied on May 1, 1845, thanking him for the letter of commendation, and saying that he would treasure it and leave it to his children and grandchildren, "to inculcate sentiments of Integrity, Honor, and Patriotism."

White's relations with some of his other clients were not as pleasant as those with Jackson. When Mary Coffee, widow of General John Coffee, an old comrade-in-arms of Jackson, insinuated that the firm of Maunsel White and Co. had cheated her by debiting her with nearly four thousand pounds less cotton than the amount she had weighed, he replied, "Common courtesy tells us to treat your communication . . . with respect, yet the writer of the same deserves no consideration from us, and we are somewhat surprised that after transacting the business of your husband & self, for so many years . . . the writer should insinuate that we had willingly wronged you out of a cent." He peremptorily rejected her demand for compensation. Indeed, he had a quick temper, or as he described himself, "his Irish would arise on occasions."

The factorage business in New Orleans was one of tremendous competition. In 1858 there were sixty-three sugar and molasses factors in the city, and the number of cotton factors must have been greater. It was important, therefore, for a factor to have the support and prestige of serving prominent planters. White wrote to Jackson in 1839 that he was grateful for the business of the former President. He observed that he had many rivals in the factorage business, "who are not delicate in endeavoring to get out of my hands, not only your Business, but [that of] many others."

Of all Southern businessmen the factors were most dependent on the vagaries of the weather. An overflow of the Mississippi and its tributaries could ruin planters and their agents. The devastating attacks of the army worm or a severe drought could so reduce fine crops that planters and factors had to go heavily in debt. The greatest financial hazard of the factor, however, was the granting of advances to the planters. This was usually effected through the agent's acceptance of drafts drawn upon him by the planter. Because of this practice many factors suffered heavy losses during the severe cotton crisis of 1839. White wrote to Jackson that despite the losses his firm had sustained as a result of planters being unable to repay advances made to them, they had not called upon any of "the monied institutions for relief but stand firm on our own means." Yet he was forced to decline an invitation of Jackson to visit the Hermitage because he had to remain in New Orleans to liquidate the debts of Maunsel White & Co.

Despite hard times Maunsel White & Co. increased rapidly. By 1840 they had given up their former policy of granting advances to planters except on cotton that was immediately shipped to them. White observed in a letter to Jackson that "it was those acceptances [of drafts drawn by planters on the factors] and the general custom of giving Credit facilities that brot [sic] on the ruin of the country and induced the planter to purchase more Land and negroes than he wanted and others who had no Capital, to buy large Estates on Credit, paying a part down, raised on merchants in this City at 12 mos."

White was a businessman with a sense of magnanimity. Zachary Taylor, who employed him as an agent to sell the cotton crop of his Mississippi plantation, praised him for this quality. In September, 1842, when both the officer and his factor were in

financial difficulties, he wrote to White, "I think you have acted
with great forbearance in not coercing those by legal process to
make payment who are largely indebted to you." White was
virtually forced, however, to acquire several Louisiana plantations to liquidate debts owed by planters to his factorage firm.

The year 1842 was a dark one in the history of Maunsel White
& Co. In April of that year White wrote to Jackson that prices of
produce were at their lowest ebb and the money market so un-
certain that he felt uncomfortable as never before. All the banks
except the Louisiana Bank suspended specie payment, and as a
result of the abuses of banking in the state, the legislature was
engaged in drafting legislation to put the Louisiana banks on a
sound basis. The crisis called forth Maunsel White's vigorous
fighting spirit and his great resourcefulness. He tried to borrow
funds and secure credits in New York. To a business acquaintance in that city he wrote that a host of people owed money to
his house but that it could not collect these debts, and the de-
rangement of the times prevented the firm from paying off its
own liabilities. He proposed to mortgage his home plantation
Deer Range with its slaves for a loan of £15,000 or even £10,000
payable in London at 6 or 7 per cent interest. He declared that
he did not owe a cent on his own account and that Deer Range
brought him a return of 10 per cent annually on a valuation of
$200,000. His Pointe Celeste and Deer Range plantations to-
gether, he wrote, had a prospect of making 1,100 hogsheads of
sugar.

He sought at this time to establish a business connection with
the New York merchant Joshua Clibborn that would enable him
to secure operating funds for his business. To Clibborn he wrote
that his firm was looking for a commercial house in New York
"to do for us what we do for the planters." His firm was in the
habit of authorizing reliable planters to draw upon them when
they were certain that they could deliver cotton to meet the
maturity of their drafts. Sometimes, he observed, the planters
were bad calculators and were disappointed in their expectations
by events beyond their control, but business was based on confidence in the people with whom they were dealing. White
proposed that a New York house should grant his company not
an outright loan but letters of credit authorizing it to draw upon

the New York agency for amounts of from one thousand to thirty thousand dollars, payable in ninety days to six months. In return, the New Orleans factorage house would throw all the fine cotton they received to the New York house for sale to Northern manufacturers and ship the ordinary and middling grades to Liverpool. This proposal, he commented, was a new mode of business, but his firm sought new channels. His company were agents, he pointed out, not only for cotton but for tobacco, pork, corn, molasses, and sugar.

During this crisis in his business career, White looked for aid in every direction. He wrote to an Irish relative in Liverpool to try to secure "a fat agency" there for his company. He looked to Congress for assistance, hoping that it would aid the sugar industry with a strong tariff. "If we get 3¢ on Sugar," he wrote on July 9, 1842, "I can soon bring the house out of the woods." His difficulties were increased by the loose way in which his partners managed business while he was away on his plantation Deer Range, forty miles below New Orleans. Indeed, he was so disgusted that he exclaimed, "If I had never formed the House of M. W. & Co. I might this day have called myself a man in the easiest circumstances in America. I have suffered torments, undescribable & my own aim is to wind up the whole concern."

Nevertheless, he weathered the storm, and retained both his business and his Deer Range plantation. By the summer of 1845 he had retired from active management of Maunsel White & Co. and devoted himself to superintending the operation of his plantation. Though his name remained in the mercantile house in New Orleans, he now proudly regarded himself as a planter. He returned often to the city, however, to supervise the affairs of the firm, for he found that his partners were frequently getting into what he called a "snarl," and he had to correct their mistakes.

To the task of superintending his four plantations White brought a keen sense of business and great energy. "I am up at from 3 to 4 o ck in the morning, and all day at the Sugar House or Field," he wrote during the grinding season of 1847 when he was sixty-four years old. He drove close bargains, both in buying plantation supplies and in trying to obtain the highest prices for his sugar by sending it to various markets besides New Orleans. His knowledge of human nature acquired in business made him aware of the necessity of guarding against trickery and dishonesty. In a letter to his factors in Richmond, Virginia, February 6, 1845, he wrote that he had recently taken a stroll among the sugar brokers on the levee at New Orleans. "The platform was crowded with them," he observed, "some selling, some buying, it was amusing to see the game of *over reaching* played in the drawing of sugar from the same hole, varying in its quality fully one cent a pound. The initiated laugh at the slight [*sic*] of hand, while the unpractised buyer or seller pays the Piper."

The operation of a large sugar plantation was almost as much a manufacturing enterprise as an agricultural occupation. Maunsel White was determined to produce a high grade of sugar on his Deer Range plantation. Accordingly, in 1845 he tore down the old sugar house and its machinery and bought the most modern machinery he could find—from New York manufacturers. In order to finance this purchase he borrowed heavily from his factors by means of drafts upon them. Besides his sugar machinery he purchased expensive pumps and machines to drain his fields.

Sugar cane had to be cut and windrowed before frost came; the grinding, or rolling, of the cane began about October 1. Consequently it was desirable to get the machinery in good order and the plantation force organized for the operation before that date. Delay in the arrival of machinery ordered from the North could be disastrous. White estimated that in 1844 he lost two hundred hogsheads of sugar—a third of his crop—from damage by frost because of the late arrival of clarifiers from New York. In the summer of 1845 while he was awaiting the shipment of new equipment from New York, he lived on "a bed of thorns," in dread that the machinery would not come in time. The machinery arrived late, and as a consequence he estimated that he lost $16,000.

One of his most trying problems was to find capable overseers for his several plantations and reliable white engineers for his sugar machinery. At Deer Range he employed both an overseer and an assistant overseer to supervise his labor force of more than two hundred slaves. On one occasion when he was negotiating for the hiring of an overseer, the prospect asked him what salary he would pay. White replied, "I never like to put a price on the service of any man—make up your mind like a man & say what will be the lowest price you will come here for or go to the Red River for." He finally employed him, but the overseer wrote such unintelligible letters that White ironically described him as "our learned friend Densen." On his Concord plantation he had a very independent overseer named James Bracewell, who received a salary of $500 and board as well as a bonus of $100 for good work at the end of a year. In making a contract with him for the year 1848 White wrote, "But I now tell you distinctly & to use your own beautiful phrase 'flat-footed' that while you stay with me I shall *examine, scrutinize* & enquire about your conduct & proceedings & if I find them unworthy of my confidence, you shall quit were it to cost me the crop. You have mistaken your man; I can never be driven into any measure." White rebuked his overseers for bad judgment, failure to communicate with him, and neglect of close supervision of the Negroes. To one overseer on a distant plantation, he remarked: "I can't bear to see things done in a careless slovenly way, in short, half-done." When an overseer asked for a raise in salary, he declared that the amount of salary would depend on the size of the crops.

The master of Deer Range strongly believed in maintaining a firm discipline over the slaves. When his overseer whipped one recalcitrant slave and put another in irons, he approved of this discipline, observing that "now that they know who is Captain," they worked well and were cheerful. He found it disagreeable to whip slaves personally, but he did not flinch from what he regarded as his duty. He also punished some slaves for bad conduct by putting them in the stocks, and those who feigned sickness were placed on a ration of dry bread and water.

Nevertheless, he was in many respects a patriarchal slave master. When one of his female slaves died from an accident at the sugar mill which crushed her hand and arm, he wrote to the Northern manufacturer of the mill, "this melancholy accident has caused myself and family the most sincere sorrow, as we view our Slaves almost in the same light as we do our children." Although he bought many slaves, he refused to sell any of his own servants, explaining, "I have made myself a solemn promise never to sell a negro—it is a traffic I have never done. I would rather give them their liberty than sell them." For good conduct he rewarded his slaves with wine, whiskey, extra clothes, holidays, and money. They seem to have respected him, and when a crevasse in the levee in 1858 threatened to ruin his crops, they worked heroically to fill it. On June 25 he wrote of this event in his diary that he was feeling "low-spirited and unhappy at the fatigue sustained by our good & excellent people to save our beautiful and fine crop. All the family exceedingly anxious, Blacks as well as Whites."

One of the questions which American historians have debated is whether plantation slavery was profitable. In Louisiana the employment of slave labor on sugar plantations under good management could be very profitable. Yet the hazards of the industry were great, and the expenses of the sugar planters were larger than those of any other type of planter. Maunsel White, for example, paid to his overseer toward the close of the antebellum period a salary of one thousand dollars, and to his engineer a similar sum. The cost of fuel to operate the sugar mills and to heat the vacuum pans was so great that on one occasion White bought an entire coal boat containing 6,889 barrels of coal at a cost of $3,100. Innumerable other expenses added to the cost of producing sugar, expenses that were typical of plantation operations in the lower South. There was need, for example, to purchase large supplies of pork, brogans, and clothing for the slaves, draft animals from Kentucky and Tennessee, and to replace slaves killed by cholera epidemics. There were also heavy medical charges: White paid a doctor $250 annually to visit the plantation twice a week.

Despite these large fixed expenses and the losses from failure of crops, the master of Deer Range made considerable profits from farming with slave labor. On July 23, 1843, he wrote to a businessman in New York that as bad as the sales of his sugar crop had been for the past four years, they had netted him, deducting all expenses and improvements, $20,000 a year. (In the good time of the 1850's planters made greater profits than ever before.) But White was an efficient manager who had rich land, plenty of capital, and excellent transportation facilities. Nor should it be forgotten that the sugar planters benefited from a protective tariff.

In 1850 Maunsel White had reached the height of his fortune.

MAUNSEL WHITE, New Orleans merchant.

Besides his interest in the factorage firm in New Orleans he had four lucrative plantations, one of them—Deer Range—worth at least $165,000. This spacious sugar plantation produced not only bountiful crops of sugar—from five hundred to a thousand hogsheads annually—but also large crops of corn as well as small quantities of rice and indigo. On Deer Range alone he had nearly a hundred mules and oxen and a herd of fine Southdown sheep. He bottled approximately twenty-four hundred gallons of orange wine, and in one year he sent nearly four thousand oranges to New Orleans to be sold. He dispensed informal but generous hospitality at Deer Range. In issuing an invitation to a guest, he wrote, "You cannot put us to any inconvenience, we are plain people, make no fuss; receive our friends 'sans ceremonie,' give them the best we have got & if they are not satisfied it is not our fault. Expect no great things—milk, Butter & corn Bread, perhaps some fresh fish & oysters should the season be good. had you come on Saturaday you could have had venison." In addition to his agricultural properties and slaves, White owned four hundred lots in New Orleans, stock in a Louisville, Kentucky, bank, railroad stock, and investments in a salt works in Florida and in a textile mill in Indiana.

While his fortune was intact, White made generous gifts to the recently founded University of Louisiana in New Orleans. He was elected a member of its first board of administrators. In September, 1847, he announced that he would donate to the infant university an endowment of lands to provide an income of one thousand dollars a year. He also circulated a subscription list to provide a general fund for the institution, seeking contributions even as low as a dollar a head. "No one ought to refuse," he wrote, "who is desirous of Education of his children at home." He thus became one of the early advocates of home education for Southern youths and the opponent of sending them to schools and colleges in the North, where they would be exposed to anti-slavery doctrine.

On February 8, 1848, he made a very modern proposal to the board of administrators. He offered to give fifty-six of his lots in the third municipality of New Orleans to the university for the purpose of endowing a chair of commerce and statistics to have equal rank with other professorships. If the returns from the endowment exceeded $1,200 annually, the surplus was to be used for establishing a commercial library to be attached to the chair and to be open to the merchants of the city. He proposed also that the city council should have the privilege annually of sending one student to the university free of cost from the high schools of the city. The university accepted this proposition and appointed his candidate, J. D. B. De Bow, editor of *De Bow's Review*, to the professorship. In 1849 De Bow began a series of lectures in his new post, boasting that the University of Louisiana was the first educational institution in the country to establish such a chair. Unfortunately, because of student indifference and the failure of the endowment to produce adequate funds, this enlightened project languished at the end of the first year and was abandoned.

White had an important role in sustaining the publication in New Orleans of *De Bow's Review*, the great commercial magazine of the Old South. During the early years of the founding of the review he lent money to the editor, and when De Bow worried over his inability to repay it, White assured him that "as regards a certain note, you need not feel any way uneasy about it, do all you can and only dream the rest." This imperious businessman tried at times to dictate to De Bow how he should run the review. On July 17, 1848, he wrote to the editor advising the publication of articles on yellow fever, the manufacture of sugar, and on the value of his drainage machine. He desired, he wrote, that practical and truthful articles be published.

In the autumn of 1850 White suffered disastrous financial reverses. A severe frost cut his sugar crop in half, and a fire that destroyed the planing mill which he had recently built resulted in a loss of $18,000. His partners in Maunsel White & Co. involved the firm in grave financial trouble, and he had to raise large sums to protect the good name of the house. One of the partners had misappropriated some of the firm's money, and both of them had endangered the credit of Maunsel White & Co. by their California speculations. He wrote to his son Maunsel, Jr., at the University of Virginia that out of the thousands of dollars owed to him, he could not collect enough money for his personal expenses. In this crisis he called his son from his studies to take charge of Deer Range while he himself returned to the city to rescue the firm.

Despite what he described as "the sleepless nights, loss of appetite and sickness of heart I suffer," he bestirred himself mightily to salvage the company and save his own fortune.

In the summer of 1852 he wrote to De Bow that he was working to pay all the debts of the late firm and to collect all debts due to it. A part of this letter was published in the January, 1853, issue of *De Bow's Review*, in which White wrote: "Full of confidence in my own integrity, and with the blessing of God, I made up my mind to bring everything I had under the hammer. The result is, that peace of mind which no mere worldly prosperity can give." De Bow requested that the newspapers which had heralded White's suspension should do justice to him by publishing the news of his resumption of payment. According to an account of Maunsel White's career published in the October, 1858, issue of *De Bow's Review*, White had accumulated an estate of nearly a million dollars when in 1850 he was brought to the verge of bankruptcy. During this crisis he had offered to the creditors of the firm over $800,000 worth of property to settle its obligations. Out of the wreck of his fortune he managed to save Deer Range plantation, where he spent the remainder of his life.

Just before financial disaster came upon him, White was having trouble with his only son, to whom he was devoted. Maunsel, Jr., off at school, had written to his father for permission to take piano lessons. White peremptorily refused, observing in a letter to him that "drumming" on the piano was a waste of precious time and ending the reply with "let me hear no more of pianos." While Maunsel was a student at the University of Louisiana, he importuned his father to get an appointment for him to West Point. White finally yielded and applied to his old friend Zachary Taylor, recently elected President. In the meantime he sent young Maunsel to Kingsley's military school in New York to prepare him for the entrance examination to West Point. Here the youth lost his enthusiasm for a military career and asked permission to return home. His father replied: "Your letter filled me with grief—that you become discouraged at the first obstacle. I call upon you to act like a man & exercise an iron will. If the cadets act improperly that is no reason that you should, nor are you bound to mix with them, or to enter into any of their vices.

No, my son, show yourself to be above such things." Finally young Maunsel did not enter West Point, but went instead to the University of Virginia.

White advised his son not to think of becoming a politician, because he questioned the happiness of politicians. He himself held only one political office during his long life: in 1846–50 he represented Plaquemines Parish in the state senate. He was drawn into politics by his zeal for the preservation of Southern rights and the institution of slavery. In the summer of 1847 he subscribed one hundred dollars to the project of establishing a newspaper in Washington to be independent of political parties and devoted to supporting "the great principle of Southern Equality." He shared the expansionist views of many Southerners, desiring even to annex Cuba. He was particularly incensed by the Wilmot Proviso, which he thought was calculated "to do more injury & make a wider breach between the North & the South than any other subject ever brought forth in our political strife."

Although he declared himself to be a Democrat, White also stated that he would never sell himself to any party. His friendship for Zachary Taylor led him as early as 1847 to advocate Taylor's election to the Presidency. He had known Taylor, he wrote, for over forty years, from the time that they were youths in Louisville, Kentucky. But his main reason for supporting the general was his assumption that as a Southern plantation owner "Old Rough and Ready" would uphold the rights of the South. Later he found that he was mistaken, for the Whig President did not put down the "Wilmot Proviso fanatics" or shut the mouths of the abolitionists as he had expected, and accordingly he regretted that he had ever voted for the apostate. Despite his disappointment in regard to Taylor, he shared the latter's devotion to the Union.

White's unionist views took a practical form. When he invested money in a cotton mill at Cannelton, Indiana, in 1849, he wrote that he wished to see the interests of the South and West united so that nothing on earth might separate them. In the same year he attended a railroad convention at Memphis out of a desire to promote the unity of the sections; for the same reason, as well as to tap the trade of China and India, he gave his support to the movement for a Pacific railroad, whether starting from St. Louis or Memphis. He pointed out in a letter to a Northern editor the strong economic advantages of the union between the South and the West through trade, citing his own extensive purchases of western produce as an example.

During the great controversy over the admission of California as a free state into the Union he declared that he would never yield to any compromise that went beyond "the land marks" pointed out by the Constitution. Though he affirmed his attachment to "the perpetuity of the glorious union," he said it must be "a Union of equals, jealous of their own & each others rights & submitting to no infractions of the constitutional compact as it was framed by our Republican Fathers." A supporter of Senator Pierre Soulé and the extreme Southern rights faction of the Democratic party, White applauded Soulé's action in opposing "the rascally compromise" of 1850. He declared in November of that year that the Great Compromise was no compromise at all and that, bad as it was, the North wanted to nullify an important provision of it—the Fugitive Slave Act.

White had a low opinion of politicians, a prejudice characteristic of many businessmen of this era. To Maunsel, Jr., he wrote in the summer of 1860: "look at our Senators Slidell and Benjamin & a hundred others. do they care a cent for the country. Look at Mason and Hunter from Virginia, sold the South! look at 'old Fogy Buck' and the rest of them, wanting to get in Kansas under the fraudulent Lecompton Constitution." Accordingly, in the presidential campaign of 1860 he supported Stephen A. Douglas, whom he described as "the most Honest & independent man of all those nominated for that office." He even "stumped" for him, a thing that he had never done before, and he served as an elector on the Douglas ticket. He condemned "the abstractionists" on the slavery question, who supported Breckinridge. When prices of commodities fell after the November election, he attributed the decline to the distracted state of the country which had been brought on by dishonest and infamous politicians. After Louisiana had seceded, he marched in a parade in New Orleans with the veterans of 1814–15 on Washington's Birthday, leading him to comment in his journal that "the machinations of corrupt & unprincipled Politicians" had rent the Union asunder by stirring up the most intense sectional hate. Fortunately for his peace of mind he did not live to see the devastation and defeat of the South and the decline of Deer Range with the introduction of free labor, for he died on his plantation on December 17, 1863.

White's long career illustrated, as he himself proudly pointed out, the opportunities that America offered to poor young men of energy and character. To Captain Graves in his native Ireland he wrote in 1847 that Andrew Jackson had been his most intimate friend and that his last letters to him were evidence "to shew that no one, no matter how humble, by good conduct & the aid of almighty providence may raise himself [in America] to consideration and respect from the highest." He returned to this theme in a letter introducing Judge John K. Elgee of Louisiana to the relatives he had left in Ireland. The judge's career, he wrote, was an example of America's generosity in rewarding merit and giving opportunities to hundreds of poor Irish immigrants in this country.

White's humble origin was characteristic of the business leaders of the Old South as well as of the rest of America of that period. In *De Bow's Review* of 1850–53 there appeared a series of twenty-eight sketches of prominent businessmen of the South, entitled "Gallery of Industry and Enterprise": nearly all of these commercial and industrial leaders had begun their careers as poor boys, with little opportunity for a formal education. The humble origin and the lack of an academic education of these early businessmen contrast with the social and educational background of American business leaders of the first half of the twentieth century, the majority of whom did not rise from the bottom and had the advantages of a college education. The most successful of the businessmen in the society of the Old South, such as Maunsel White or the South Carolina banker Franklin Elmore, who succeeded to Calhoun's seat in the Senate, mingled on terms of equality with the gentry.

The ideology of the businessmen of the Old South lay in a debatable ground between liberal and conservative attitudes. This position arose partly from the fact that Southern businessmen had not emancipated themselves from agrarian ways of thinking. Indeed, they were much closer to agriculture and agrarian ideals than were Northern businessmen; most of them wished to retire as planters and were probably like Maunsel White in wishing their sons to become either planters or professional men—not businessmen. Furthermore, their economic interests were less tied to the preservation of the old order than was the case of the planters.

In religion, however, they seem to have been just as conservative and orthodox as the planters. The society in which they lived did not question the literal interpretation of the Bible, the miracles, or the necessity to belong to a church organization to be "saved." Maunsel White was a vestryman and warden in the Episcopal Church. When Andrew Jackson wrote that he felt death was imminent, White replied that he hoped to meet the stern old soldier in "a Blissful Immortality." These men of business shared the belief of their rural neighbors that God constantly intervened in human affairs. In 1845 when gloom spread over the South as a result of the low prices of cotton and sugar, White wrote that they must submit to the will of God: "doubtless we deserve to be rebuked, for much is owing to our own folly." When his crops failed, he rationalized the misfortune to his overseer: they should be satisfied with "whatever the Almighty is willing to bestow—he gives us more than we deserve." When epidemics of yellow fever or cholera broke out, he regarded them as a visitation of God for the sins of the people. Like many of his contemporaries, White believed in the doctrine of the stewardship of the wealth which God permitted men to acquire. The wealthy man should spend the fortune which he had honorably acquired by hard work in "doing good to his fellow man." To a Philadelphia firm he wrote in 1850 that the capitalist should distribute his wealth as a good steward; he himself could not spend it in luxury or folly. Other notable examples of New Orleans merchants who carried out this idea of stewardship were John McDonogh, who left his great fortune for charity and education; Judah Touro, the outstanding Jewish merchant of the city, noted for his benevolence; and Glendy Burke, who was influential in founding the free school system of Louisiana.

White accepted unquestioningly the view of his section that slavery was a righteous institution approved by God. He maintained, moreover, that the Southern planters treated their slaves more humanely than Northern and European employers treated their factory and mining hands. He developed a strong prejudice against Yankees as a result of sectional strife, especially after the introduction in Congress of the Wilmot Proviso. On May 16, 1848, he wrote to his Richmond factor that he suspected that the Yankee captains of the ships which carried his molasses and sugar were dishonest, adding "Curse the Whole Race of Yankee Captains." He advised a factor in Philadelphia to whom he consigned his sugar crop to watch the captain of the ship carefully, for he was a shrewd Yankee. In a letter to his son at the University of Virginia he declared that he had bought three hundred shares of Tehauntepec Canal stock more to prevent "those grasping Yankees" from getting all the California trade rather than from any expectation of profit.

There were liberal aspects of the Southern commercial mind, however, that arose out of the very nature of business. Business expansion required enlarged transportation facilities—especially railroads—strong laws regulating banks and providing for a sound currency, liberal laws of incorporation, and good free schools. These were more important to businessmen than whether the South won the acceptance of the Lecompton Constitution or the right of slaveholders to take slaves into federal territory that was economically unsuited to "the peculiar institution." They thought such practical benefits were more useful than upholding Southern pride or an artificial sense of honor. Unlike the politicians who spent most of their energy fighting for party advantage and defending slavery, the businessmen sought state improvements. Indeed, they were too concerned with realities to indulge in Southern rhetoric or to fight duels over points of honor.

Southern business leaders as a whole valued the Union and were definitely opposed to the fire-eaters until after the election of Lincoln. Even in Charleston, the very citadel of Southernism, the businessmen in 1850, such as the prominent banker and capitalist Ker Boyce, were opposed to secession. In 1860 former governor William Aiken, "the Astor of Charleston," and Donald McKay, president of the principal bank, were also opposed to it. It is true that *De Bow's Review*, the great commercial magazine of the South, favored secession. Yet the New Orleans *Daily Picayune*, the organ of the commercial interests of the city, was pro-Union until December, 1860. The vote of New Orleans in the presidential election of 1860 strongly indicates that the commercial and business interests of the city were opposed to the fire-eaters. The vote for the moderate Union candidates, Bell and Douglas, constituted approximately 80 per cent of the popular vote, and the other Southern cities, with the exception of Savannah and Charleston, were of the same mind. In Mobile, the combined vote for Bell and Douglas was 71 per cent; Memphis, 89; Nashville, 66; Richmond and Norfolk, 75; Petersburg, 87; even in St. Louis, where the antislavery Germans were powerful, Bell and Douglas polled 57 per cent of the vote cast. In a study of urban and rural voting during this critical election, Ollinger Crenshaw argues persuasively that the city electorates, both in the South and in the North, supported the moderate candidates.

Yet after the secession of South Carolina and the failure of the Crittenden Compromise a striking change of opinion took place among the conservative class of the lower South. New Orleans, for example, apparently reversed its previous position and in the election of January 7 for delegates to the secession convention chose twenty-one immediate secessionists and four moderates. In the secession conventions, the business class was only slightly represented. In Mississippi there was not a single merchant or businessman among the one hundred delegates (unless a "saddler" could be so considered). The South Carolina convention of 169 delegates who voted unanimously for the secession ordinance contained sixteen businessmen, of whom only one was a manufacturer. In the Alabama convention of one hundred delegates there were only nine that represented the business class, four of them being secessionists and five, cooperationists. In Georgia, of the fifteen merchants in the convention of three hundred delegates, all but two were secessionists. There were fifteen merchants in the Florida convention of seventy-one delegates, eight of whom were cooperationists and seven, immediate secessionists. In the upper South the delegates from the business class in the conventions were almost evenly divided in their votes on the issue of secession. A recent study of the secession conventions by Ralph A. Wooster has concluded that in the lower South there was very little relationship between occupations and attitude toward secession.

This generalization, if it be true, applies only to a climactic moment in Southern history when the people were deeply swayed by emotion—the businessmen as well as other classes of Southern society. On the other hand, the previous course of the business leaders (with some important exceptions, such as Joseph R. Anderson, the West Pointer who was president of the Tredegar Iron Works in Richmond) had been to oppose the extremists and to apply the brakes to the Secession movement. Indeed, if the commercial mind had controlled politics in the Old South, there is strong reason to believe that the Civil War would not have occurred. Instead, the politicians and the editors guided their section into seceding from the Union. Of these, the governor of Virginia, Henry A. Wise, was foremost in his state (though not until the firing on Fort Sumter)—a strong personality, prone to rash action, who was alternately torn between his devotion to the Union and his violent sectional feelings.

Chapter V

A PROGRESSIVE
IN AN OLD STATE

G EORGE FITZHUGH, the author of *Cannibals All! or, Slaves Without Masters,* dedicated his outrageous advocacy of slaves for the white working class to Governor Wise of Virginia. Although this Virginia lawyer was a reactionary in his defense of slavery, he advocated some progressive ideas for the development of his native state. In his dedication to the governor he praised him for "endeavoring to Virginianise Virginia, by encouraging, through State legislation, her intellectual and physical growth and development"; no one but you, he wrote, "has seen so clearly the evils of centralization from without, and worked so earnestly to cure or avert those evils, by building up centralization within."

Henry Alexander Wise was the energetic governor of the Old Dominion on the eve of the Civil War—after the state had lost the leadership of the South and was looking backward to its former glory. He had entered public life in the 1830's at a time when the abolitionists were beginning to arouse the greatest intolerance toward antislavery men below the Mason-Dixon Line, and his excitable nature was strongly affected by the new militant attitude of his section. Although he ardently defended a system of labor that now seems the antithesis of progress, in many respects he represented the spirit of progress that was manifesting itself in various parts of the Old South.

In contrast to the tranquil and dignified philosopher-statesmen of the early republic, such as Jefferson, Madison, and Monroe, Henry A. Wise had a stormy and violent life, characterized by erratic changes of party allegiance. Following his graduation from Washington (now Washington and Jefferson) College in western Pennsylvania, he studied in the law school of Judge Henry St. George Tucker at Winchester. In 1828 he began the practice of law in Nashville, Tennessee, where he won the friendship of Andrew Jackson, who invited him and his bride to spend their honeymoon at the Hermitage. At this time he described himself as "a hot, whole hog Jackson man." His affection for Virginia drew him back to Accomac County, where in 1830 he settled on a farm and began the practice of law. Three years later, after a strenuous campaign in which he opposed nullification, he was elected to Congress at the age of twenty-six. An aftermath of the campaign was a duel between the two candidates, in which Wise seriously wounded his opponent.

During his early years in Congress the young Virginian displayed the conservative side of his nature. When the Jackson administration removed the government deposits from the Second National Bank, he joined the Whigs and became as violent in castigating Jackson as formerly he had been ardent in supporting him. For five years—from 1835 to 1840—he waged a a desperate war against corruption in the executive branch of the federal government, a struggle, he declared, "such as no man standing alone did in parliamentary life." His efforts resulted in the investigation of the executive departments and of the pet banks by two congressional committees—these, he claimed, broke down the Van Buren dynasty.

He especially distinguished himself in Congress as one of the foremost champions of the South in resisting the abolitionists. He refused to accept any compromise in the struggle over the reception of the abolitionist petitions in the House of Representatives. In the spring of 1836 when only ten senators voted against receiving abolitionist petitions, he exclaimed passionately in a

private letter, "The South lies low and bleeding. Oh God! for
energy for the occasion!" A year later when the Vermont Congressman William Slade attacked Southern slavery in a tirade
on the floor of the House of Representatives, the outraged Virginian led an exodus of the Southern members from the hall.

Throughout most of his Congressional career Wise kept up a
running debate with John Quincy Adams over the reception of
abolition petitions. After his retirement from the Presidency,
Adams served continuously in Congress from 1831 to his death
in 1848. Here he made it his mission to uphold the principle of
freedom of petition by presenting abolitionist petitions and
fighting against the gag rules of the House until they were abolished in 1844. Both Wise and Adams were pugnacious men:
Wise often took extreme positions out of defiance; and Adams,
his bald head crimson with anger, taunted the long-haired Virginian until, according to Adams's diary, Wise threatened to
murder him in his seat. Adams's venomous diary described one
encounter in 1841 as follows: "Wise began in a tone which I saw
would break him down—loud, vociferous, declamatory, furibund,
he raved about the hell-hound of abolition, and at me as leader
of the abolitionists throughout the Union for a full hour—till his
voice had broken into a childish treble two or three times." But
such tactics of Wise and other Southern members of Congress
injured rather than aided the cause of their section by denying
one of the cherished civil liberties of our government, the freedom of petition.

Adams's description of Wise's speeches indicates that the Congressman from Virginia was an emotional orator who had an un-
ceasing flow of language. Adams compared him to John Randolph of Roanoke "with his tartness, his bitterness, his malignity,
and his inconsistencies." The Southern champion was tall and
extremely thin, with a sallow complexion like the eccentric Randolph. He carried himself very erect and had something of the
appearance of an Indian, with long locks of auburn hair brushed
back of his ears, and aquiline nose, hazel eyes, and large mouth.
His angular frame was animated by a steel-spring energy. Although he was a teetotaler, he made up for his abstinence from
alcohol by intemperate chewing of the royal Virginia weed: he
spoke at times with a quid in his mouth. His combative nature

sought an outlet in profanity, fist fights, and verbal assaults on the floor of Congress, yet he fought only one duel. A reporter who observed him during his early career in Congress was impressed by his extreme carelessness in dress, his impetuosity, and his remarkable power of invective.

A Northern schoolteacher who heard him speak before a tavern in Puntoteaque on the Eastern Shore of Virginia described the contrast between his unprepossessing appearance and his unusual and violent oratory. "His mouth is very wide, his hair light, and grown very long. He is as plain a man as I ever saw," he wrote. "His forehead is rather low, but quite wide and prominent. He speaks very fluently and when he gets interested he is certainly eloquent. He then speaks exceedingly loud and twists his face into all kinds of shapes. The blood rushes into his face and he has the appearance of a man strangling."

His oratory was exactly suited to his constituents on the Eastern Shore, of whom one-fourth could not read. He knew how to inflame them with his rhetoric but he could also make them laugh with his humor and mimicry. The effect that his oratory had on a well-educated Southern audience has been described by the Virginia historian Hugh Blair Grigsby. After listening to him speak to the alumni and the Board of Visitors of William and Mary College on February 19, 1859, Grigsby wrote in his diary that Wise spoke in "a strain of eloquence extraordinary and overpowering. I never before saw such an extraordinary union of high tragic power blended in the same speech with the highest comic power. The speech was relieved with abounding and vociferous applause so that the rafters shook. The very black waiters could not be moved from their places but in the phrenzy of the moment applauded the speaker."

Although Wise became a Whig after 1834, he had little sympathy with the dominant faction in the party—the former National Republicans led by Henry Clay. He called them the "Exclusives" and "Latitudinarians," and he believed that the New England manufacturers dominated the group. Wise said that he himself belonged to the Democratic element of the party and believed in leveling society upwards instead of downwards. The great and controlling influence on his political life after he joined the Whig party was Judge Hugh Lawson White of Tennessee, prominent contender for election to the Presidency in 1836. In 1840 Wise was influential in getting White to support Clay for the Whig nomination for President in preference to Harrison, with the understanding that John Tyler, who represented the Democratic element in the Whig party, should be awarded the vice-presidential nomination.

When a rift developed in the Whig party after President Tyler vetoed the bank bills, Wise supported him and became his main spokesman in the House of Representatives. Wise was the leader of a forlorn group of Tyler adherents called "the Corporal's Guard." Wise's son, John Sergeant, in his reminiscences, *The End of an Era*, declared that his father's support of Tyler was the greatest political mistake of his career. So extraordinary was Wise's ascendancy over Tyler that when Abel P. Upshur, the secretary of state, was killed by the bursting of a cannon on a battleship, the Virginia Congressman without consulting Tyler offered the vacant cabinet position to Calhoun and then virtually forced the reluctant President to ratify his act.

Tyler rewarded his henchman by nominating him as minister to France, and when the Senate rejected this nomination, Tyler appointed him minister to Brazil. Here Wise exerted himself strenuously to stop the use of American ships (built or owned largely in New York, Baltimore, and New England) in the illegal slave trade from Africa. As a result of his zeal in this cause he became a *persona non grata* to the Brazilian government, which requested his recall, and in 1847 he returned to the United States, though at his own request.

Three years after his return, he was elected a delegate from Accomac County to the Virginia constitutional convention. The main purpose in calling the convention was to democratize the conservative constitution and reduce the sectional hostility of the western part of the state toward the Tidewater. The western counties had a serious grudge against the older slaveholding counties of eastern Virginia because of the mixed basis of apportioning representation in the legislature which had been adopted by the constitutional convention of 1830. This system, by which both population and the amount of taxes paid were counted, left control of the legislature to a minority of the white population residing in the eastern counties. This power had been used to prevent fair taxation of the slaves and the development of internal improvements in the West.

Wise was one of the four delegates from the East who had the courage to rise above sectional interests and vote for the democratic reforms demanded by the West, especially the adoption of the white basis of representation and the election of the governor by the people. Wise's economic interests (in 1860 he owned twenty-one slaves) as well as his associations and friends united him with the easterners who wished to preserve their privileged position. It is therefore difficult to explain his independence in rising above the viewpoint of his class other than because of a genuine devotion to democracy. "If there is anything in God Almighty's earth," he declared on the floor of the convention, "that stinks in the nostrils of my mind, as well as of my body, it is the monied aristocracy; and negroe [*sic*] aristocracy stinks worst of all."

Accordingly, Wise became the most prominent advocate in the convention of white democracy and was called by the Richmond *Whig* "the modern Jack Cade." The slaveholding aristocracy, he asserted, proposed that the 898,000 white people of the state should have no more representation than $495,000 worth of taxes, or in other words that a white person was equal to only 53 cents. Thus he proclaimed that the issue before the convention was money versus men: "It is the right of the people against the right of money—Mammon against liberty—and may God in his mercy, help the people in this fight." Moreover, he said that the old system of representation had held down the giant of the West for seventy years by preventing the adoption of a system of internal improvements. He maintained that Virginia needed to undertake a farsighted system of internal improvements, particularly by connecting the hinterland of the West with the ports of Norfolk and Portsmouth by railroad and canal lines running to the Ohio River.

Wise's powerful advocacy of the white basis earned for him the gratitude of the people of the West, which paid rich dividends to him five years later when he became a candidate for governor. The Virginia gubernatorial campaign of 1855 illustrates the value of tremendous personal effort in winning an election and reminds one of President Kennedy's strenuous

Henry Alexander Wise, progressive governor of Virginia.

campaign in 1960. The major issue of the campaign had virtually nothing to do with state concerns: it was a struggle to prevent the Know-Nothing party from capturing the state offices. Wise misrepresented the Know-Nothing, or American party in Virginia as the party of abolition since some of the prominent leaders of the party in New England were antislavery men— this was the big gun in his arsenal. But he also pointed out the absurdity of the major plank in the platform of the Know-Nothings, which inculcated fear of the Catholic and the foreign vote in a state which had less than eight thousand Catholic citizens and a ratio of one foreign-born to thirty-eight native-born inhabitants. Declaring that he feared Protestant popes more than Catholic popes, he protested against the use of the pulpit by ministers for political propaganda. He declared that the secrecy of the Know-Nothings was un-American and that the very essence of American democracy was freedom of opinion and liberty of conscience, which were opposed to the proscription of Catholics and the foreign-born.

The American candidate, Thomas Flournoy, failed to campaign, while Wise went all over the state speaking strenuously in behalf of his candidacy. In April he wrote to James Kemper, a Democratic political leader, "I am literally spent in the canvass. I must recruit when I am done at Leesburg—lungs & muscles are too sore to continue longer & the limestone water has scourged me to a shadow. . . ." The Richmond diarist Thomas Hicks Wynne, who had joined the Know-Nothing party, noted in his diary on May 6 that a friend in Staunton had described Wise's four-hour speech there: at its beginning he looked like a corpse, wrote his friend, worn-out with fatigue, and "his system debilitated by the scourging effects of the waters of the West," but after he began speaking he became animated, and his oratory changed the votes of many. He won the doubtful election by a smashing majority of ten thousand votes, a victory that gave a decisive check to the advance of the Know-Nothing party in the South.

The governor-elect belonged to a new type of politician who was arising not only in Virginia but all over the South. Unlike the dignified and philosophical statesmen of the early republic, these men sought office by demagogic appeals. They were prod-

ucts of the Jacksonian movement, of the spread of democracy
in a rural population. In his diary, October 30, 1857, Edmund
Ruffin delineated, though in an extreme form, the characteristics
of the new politician. The account is based on a description of
Wise: "He can speak 6 hours as easily as any less time, on any
subject. He is an actor in his oratory & a bad actor—though the
very faults of ranting and thundering seem to attract hearers &
admirers in proportion to his departure from correctness & good
taste. He is certainly a man of great powers of mind. But I believe that the greatest powers by which he has succeeded are,
not his superiority of intellect, but his unbounded ambition,
which impells him forward to seek his own personal advancement & his unbounded assurance & effrontery, which leave nothing untried that can push on his claims to popular favor. He is
not in the least held back from anything that can help him by
either sense of propriety, moderation or shame."

Wise might have made an admirable governor had not his
spectacular victory in 1855 encouraged him to seek the Presidency. During the gubernatorial campaign he had promised to
give Virginia a progressive administration, to complete the noble
plan of Jefferson for popular education, to finish Virginia's primary works of internal improvement, and to establish an Agricultural and Mechanical College. He had rebuked his fellow
Virginians for their obsession with federal politics to the neglect
of state concerns. He declared that "next to brandy, next to
card playing, next to horse-racing, the thing that has done Virginia more harm than any other in the course of her past history
has been her insatiable appetite for federal politics." Yet Wise
himself became obsessed with federal politics and failed to carry
out any of his promises.

He had a powerful rival for the leadership of the Democratic
party of Virginia in Senator R. M. T. Hunter, a descendant of
Pocahontas, who also wished to be President. In the contest
for supremacy, the governor had the disadvantage of having
changed party allegiance several times. He was therefore regarded by many as erratic and unreliable. After his return from
Brazil in 1847 he had rejoined the Democratic party, and in 1848
he voted for its candidate for President, Lewis Cass.

Wise's ambition to win the Presidency for himself was based

largely on his hope of forming a Virginia–Pennsylvania alliance. He had some strong connections with this great Northern state— his college education in Pennsylvania; his second marriage into a prominent Philadelphia family, the Sergeants; and his influential friends in the Democratic party of the state, notably James Buchanan and Robert Tyler, son of the former President and chairman of the Democratic executive committee of the state. In the Democratic convention of 1856 Wise planned that his friends in the Virginia delegation should go first for Buchanan, and then if the latter could not win, they should present his name. When Buchanan got the nomination, Wise proceeded to campaign vigorously for his election.

His principal campaign weapon was to warn the nation that the election of Frémont, the Black Republican candidate, would result in the secession of the Southern states from the Union. Wise called a conference of Democratic governors in the South to meet in Raleigh on October 13, ostensibly to consult on a course of action should Frémont be elected and to devise means of protecting the honor and interests of the slaveholding states. He probably hoped to influence the state elections of Pennsylvania and later those in other Northern states, but the conference was a fiasco, for only two other governors—Bragg of North Carolina and Adams of South Carolina—met with him.

Wise lost some of his popularity in Virginia by his political maneuvers of 1856, and still more by his repudiation of the Lecompton Constitution for Kansas during the next year. Thus he broke with Buchanan and stood with Stephen Douglas, although he detested Douglas's popular sovereignty principles. He refused to follow the Democratic leadership and the wishes of his section in regard to the Lecompton Constitution partly because he believed that the support of this disreputable measure would lose votes for the party in the North. Ardent pro-Southern men believed, however, that Wise was motivated in his opposition to the Lecompton Constitution by a desire to win votes in the Northern states for his candidacy for President. Robert Toombs wrote to a Baltimore editor on November 20, 1857, that Wise was "crazy for the Presidency and that disease unsettles the best of intellects." Though it is impossible to fathom his real motives in opposing the Lecompton Constitution, it seems probable that his feeling for democracy and justice was outraged by the Lecompton fraud.

Decidedly the most dramatic event in Wise's administration was the John Brown raid on Harpers Ferry, October 17, 1859. The governor arrived at the small Virginia town on the next day and found that John Brown and the raiders had been captured by some marines from Washington under the command of Colonel Robert E. Lee. Lee had offered the Virginia and Maryland militia the honor of attacking the engine house of the arsenal in which Brown and his men had stationed themselves, but they had refused this dangerous mission. Wise was deeply chagrined that United States troops had been used to suppress an invasion of the sovereign state of Virginia. In bitterness of soul, he declared in a speech at Richmond upon his return from the scene of the invasion that he would have given his arm to his shoulder if Virginia troops had captured John Brown. He wrote a letter to the superintendent of the insane asylum at Staunton to examine the fanatical leader but decided not to send it. Instead, he had an interview with the prisoner and concluded that Brown was not a madman, but "a man of clear head, of courage, fortitude, and simple ingenuousness." Undoubtedly it would have been wiser if the governor had carried out his original impulse to let an expert examine the desperate leader of this foolhardy attack on a federal arsenal. Brown himself rejected a proposal that he plead insanity even though nineteen of his relatives and friends sent affidavits showing a pronounced strain of insanity in his family. Wise made another serious mistake in handling the John Brown affair when he insisted that Brown be tried in the state courts rather than in the federal courts.

The Executive Papers in the State Library at Richmond contain many letters to the governor revealing the panic of the people over the fear both of a slave insurrection and of a large-scale attempt of abolitionists to rescue their hero from the jail at Charlestown where he was imprisoned. It may appear today that Wise deliberately magnified the dangers to be apprehended from such an invasion, as his political enemies maintained, but his correspondence shows that he was genuinely alarmed. When John Brown was finally executed, the governor assembled approximately thirteen hundred militia to form a hollow square around the gallows to prevent any attempt to rescue Brown. Among these troops was a company of V. M. I. cadets, in which marched the gray-haired Edmund Ruffin: the superintendent of the institute had allowed him to enroll temporarily as a student so that he might witness the hanging of the abolitionist leader. Wise used the panic of the occasion as an excuse to arm the state and reorganize the militia. He boasted in his recollections, *Seven Decades of the Union,* that when he left the executive office in 1860, Virginia was well armed with 85,000 stands of weapons, 130 fieldpieces, and $30,000 worth of Colt revolving arms.

Wise's dramatic and resolute handling of the John Brown raid retrieved some of his lost popularity. Edmund Ruffin, who was bitterly prejudiced against the Virginia governor, wrote in his diary, February 6, 1860: "Before the Harper's Ferry affair, he had but little support in Virginia (& none elsewhere) for the presidency which he was seeking so boldly and so shamelessly. But his conduct in and since that affair, though very blameable for indiscretion & [for a] foolish and useless & very expensive military parade, has given him more popularity than all he ever had acquired for real worth and ability. . . ." Nevertheless, the Virginia delegation in the Democratic convention at Charleston in April, 1860, supported Hunter instead of Wise as its candidate for the presidential nomination.

In the crisis of 1860–61 Wise's course appeared erratic and puzzling. He voted in the presidential election for John C. Breckinridge, the extreme proslavery candidate. When Virginia called a convention in February to determine whether the state should secede, he presented a peculiar plan of resisting Black Republican domination by fighting within the Union. He introduced a set of resolutions stating the conditions under which Virginia would remain in the Union—in effect, an ultimatum to the North. These conditions were so extreme that it was obvious the Northern people would not accept them. After Fort Sumter was fired upon and Lincoln called for troops from the various states, Wise became an outright secessionist. It was he who summoned the "Spontaneous People's Convention" in Richmond to put pressure upon the wavering group to pass a secession ordinance on April 17: he announced that an expedition had been sent to capture the United States arsenal at Harper's Ferry.

During the Civil War Wise did not serve in the civil government of the Confederacy where he probably would have been most effective but at the post of honor in the army. Unlike several of the political generals—John C. Breckinridge, Nathan Forrest, and John B. Gordon—Wise was a failure as an officer, ending his military service (at Appomattox) as he began—a brigadier general. He exhibited in the army the faults as well as the virtues of the romantic mind of the Old South. He wrote letters of high-flown rhetoric, such as the one to Mrs. Fleet of Green Mount, Virginia, thanking her for a Christmas present of homemade wine, molasses, and pickles; he praised Southern women for their superlative qualities of soul, which raised them far above the gross nature of ordinary men. Brave and gallant in war, though incompetent, he was intensely loyal to the cause of the Confederacy to the tragic end.

Wise can be regarded as an outstanding progressive leader of the Old South not because of his career in federal politics but because of his efforts to improve the state of Virginia. These included his powerful advocacy in 1850 of a democratic constitution for the state, his campaign against the illiberal Know-Nothing party, his attempts to unify the eastern and western sections of the state by works of internal improvement, and his efforts to persuade Virginians to establish an adequate free school system. The only important acts in his national career that might be designated as liberal in tendency were his struggle to suppress the African slave trade, his fight in Congress against corruption in the federal government, and his opposition to the disreputable attempt to force the proslavery Lecompton Constitution upon the people of Kansas.

Wise ranks with the plebeian governor Andrew Johnson of Tennessee as the most notable champion of free schools among the politicians of the Old South. Shortly before he left for Brazil in 1844 he issued a printed address to the constituents of his Congressional district urging them to tax themselves to establish an adequate system of free schools. He pointed out the appalling fact that one-fourth of the free white adults of his district, consisting of twelve counties, could not read—a larger number than those who voted. He condemned the Virginia school system in which the parents of a poor child had to make a declaration of poverty before the child's tuition could be paid by the state. "Common school education," he declared, "should not be a state charity, but it should be the chief element of the freedom of the State—There should be no distinction between the children of a republic. They are not in the school sense the children of their parents, but the State is *parens patriae*, and they should be regarded as the sons and daughters of Mother Commonwealth."

He proposed, therefore, that the board of education in each county should levy taxes sufficient to educate every child between seven and fifteen years of age and should also have power to fine parents, rich or poor, who did not send their children to school. He advocated, furthermore, that the state should give free tuition to those students at the university who would agree to teach in the common schools for a period as long as they had been maintained at the university. Recognizing that these were bold and drastic proposals, he tried to persuade all classes to realize that ignorance destroyed the equality of citizens. With consummate skill he appealed to those illiterates who had no use for "book learning": he compared education to a handspike, a tool which they all valued at a logrolling or house-raising. He urged them to hold meetings to stir up interest in free common schools, to petition the legislature, and "to shake the doors of the legislature down until you are heard."

On July 4, 1850, at the "Free School Celebration" in Northampton County in his Congressional district, Wise made a speech that displayed a remarkable feeling for democracy. He declared that the distinctions among men in the state, "those divisions into castes, however classified, shall, as far as our nature ordained by God will permit, be totally and absolutely abolished." How far men could become equal, he said, it was impossible to determine until education in its most comprehensive sense had been tried. Much of the inequality that people attributed to nature, he thought, was owing to want of education. He wished to mingle the children of the rich and of the poor in schools. "If you would 'down with aristocracy,'" he exclaimed, "you must 'up with the free schools!'" The free schools, he urged, should teach more than academic subjects; they should also inculcate manners and morals, develop the physical powers of the students, girls as well as boys, and teach them to honor labor.

When Wise became governor in 1856 he used his position to agitate for the establishment of an enlightened public school system in Virginia. Edmund Ruffin has described in his diary a speech that the governor made before a meeting of the state agricultural society in Richmond in October, 1857. He spoke for two and one-half hours "in his own remarkable & peculiar manner, in support of his grand scheme of general education for the state & in reply to strictures thereon by [Willoughby] Newton the night before." In spite of the fact that his audience began to slip away as the hour approached midnight, he continued to speak and "to make long pauses according to his artificial manner." In his campaign for the reform of the educational system of the state, Wise criticized the old system because it did not provide for the training of teachers and because it continued the feature of charity instruction. "The pride of our people," he observed, "withholds thousands of our poor children from the charity of our schools, even for the 53 days of time per annum & for the pittance of the cost of $2.57 per capita for the 53 days of time; whilst a sound republican *community* of instruction among the children of all classes would make all equally beneficiaries of public aid to instruction."

Though Wise received some works of the New England educational leader Henry Barnard (sent by his cousin Navy Lieutenant Henry Augustus Wise, who was stationed at Boston), his proposals show that he was primarily influenced by the educational ideas of Jefferson. He recommended that the state should be divided into 375 academy districts and into 13 male college districts, to which the state government should contribute funds. The state owed a duty, he declared, to provide opportunities for the children of the poor, not merely to acquire a knowledge of reading and writing, but "to taste of the more delicate food of the mind."

In order to advance the cause of free schools in Virginia, he selected President William A. Smith of Randolph-Macon College to investigate the condition of the schools and to act as a missionary by making speeches throughout the state. He hoped that this prominent educator and divine would arouse the people to put pressure on the legislature to do something constructive about popular education. Unfortunately, his choice was a poor one, for Dr. Smith was an ardent advocate of purging school texts of any sentiments hostile to slavery. In any case, he declined the appointment for petty reasons, including the failure of the governor to guarantee him a salary of $2,000 for six months' employment.

Even so dynamic a leader as Henry A. Wise could not effect a revolution in the attitude of the people toward public education. Before he became governor, other public-spirited men like Dr. Henry Ruffner, president of Washington College (now Washington and Lee), and Thomas Ritchie, editor of the Richmond *Enquirer*, had tried to arouse the state to adopt an effective public school system, but to no avail. The Virginia legislature did pass an act in 1846 permitting counties to tax property holders for free common schools, but only ten counties took advantage of the opportunity to do so. Samuel Janney, a Quaker and eminent Virginia liberal, charged the failure of other counties to tax their citizens for free schools to "the apathy and prejudices of the laboring classes whom it was intended to benefit and the jealousy of the slaveholders." In 1850 Moncure D. Conway, who had been educated at Harvard and later became a Unitarian minister, wrote a pamphlet entitled *Free Schools in Virginia,* which he published and circulated at his own expense. In his autobiography, he commented on this idealistic act of his youth: "But the social, physical, and financial condition of Virginia was little comprehended by me in my nineteenth year; there was little or no longing for education among the poor—probably more among the negroes. I was expecting echoes when there were no hills."

In addition to his efforts to provide an adequate free school system for Virginia, Wise strove mightily for the material development of the state. He devoted much attention to the improvement of the transportation system of Virginia. Fitzhugh praised him for urging forward to completion such works as the Covington and Ohio Railroad. He also sought to complete the James River and Kanawha Canal, whose construction had come to a standstill. In order to obtain revenue for internal improvements and education he advocated that the legislature tax oysters from Virginia shores at the rate of two cents a bushel—estimated at twenty-five million bushels annually. He made the revolutionary proposal that the state go into the insurance business and insure houses against arson, wheat against damage in the garner, and crops against destruction in the field. When some citizens protested to him against Eli Thayer's plan to establish a free labor colony of New England immigrants at Ceredo in western Virginia, he declared that the state needed settlers to improve her waste lands and that as long as they obeyed the law, he would encourage their settlement.

The letter books and executive papers of his administration, preserved in the Virginia State Library in over forty boxes, show that Wise was a vigorous and strong governor. Among his various reform projects he tried to improve the administration of the penitentiary, especially by insistence upon the maintenance of cleanliness and by urging the establishment of a workhouse apart from the penitentiary where youthful and less hardened offenders could be separated from the vicious criminals. He recommended to the legislature that the law providing for the sale and transportation of slave convicts out of the United States be repealed, for its observance had become a mockery, since most of the convicts were sold to traders who took them to the lower South: he proposed instead that such convicts should be used as laborers on public works. Although he pursued a firm policy in the exercise of the pardoning power, he granted leniency to young boys convicted of larceny, and he tried to see that slaves and free Negroes received fair trials.

Despite his great energy and ability, Wise accomplished very little in his enlightened plans for reviving the Old Dominion. His political ambitions, his desire for the Presidency, diverted him from vigorously prosecuting his plans for the development of the state. Accordingly, his request for the oyster tax was not enacted into law; the public schools were neglected; the insurance scheme was not adopted; an agricultural and mechanical college was not established. The reasons for this failure point to the overshadowing influence of slavery, which produced a conservative attitude of the legislature and the people. Far too much of Wise's splendid energy was devoted to defending the institution of slavery from Northern attacks—energy that might have been spent in improving the welfare of the state.

Yet he was not a proponent of the theory that slavery was a beneficent institution. In his reminiscences John S. Wise has described a conversation with his father on the night after he and his uncle from Philadelphia had attended a slave auction. Shocked by the cruelty of this event, they discussed their experience with the governor, who "agreed that a system in which things like that were possible was monstrous, and that the question was, not whether it should be abolished, and abolished quickly, but as to the manner of its abolition." Nevertheless, Wise intensely resented Northern interference with slavery in the Southern states, and both in Congress and in the governor's office he conceived of himself in the heroic role of "Defender of the South."

When Governor Wise is compared with the governor of the neighboring state of Pennsylvania, William Fisher Packer, there appears a remarkable similarity between the views of the Southern and the Northern governor. But when he is compared with the chief executive of Massachusetts, John A. Andrew, the differences between New England and the South are strongly contrasted. Packer struggled with many of the same problems that Wise did—internal improvements, education, and the financial stability of the state. Like his Southern counterpart, he was deeply involved in national politics, being an active supporter of Buchanan. Packer differed with Wise in his interpretation of the popular sovereignty doctrine, holding that it applied to the territorial stage of government, but he and the Virginia governor had almost precisely the same views in regard to the notorious Lecompton Constitution. Moreover, Wise himself could hardly have exceeded the expression of devotion to states' rights that Packer made in his message to the Pennsylvania legislature on January 5, 1859. "Every claim of federal power not granted by the Constitution," he declared, "should be sternly resisted. The tendency to centralization is so great, and the overshadowing influences of power and patronage so seductive, that liberty cannot long be preserved without the exercise of sleepless vigilance in enforcing a strict construction of the federal compact.

The doctrine of State rights is the doctrine of true liberty."

Especially at the time of the John Brown raid did the Pennsylvania governor show a friendly spirit toward the South. He promised the fullest cooperation with Governor Wise to prevent any attempt that might be made from Pennsylvania to rescue the leader of the insurrectionists. Packer revealed his sympathy with the South, moreover, when some Boston admirers of Brown asked him to address them on the subject of "How can American Slavery be abolished?" He declined, advising them that they "would better serve God and their country by attending to their own business. John Brown was rightly hanged and his fate should be a warning to others having similar proclivities."

The Pennsylvania governor was a Northern moderate who favored compromise on sectional issues. He therefore differed greatly from the extreme Republican leaders, such as John A. Andrew, who was elected governor of Massachusetts in the fall of 1860. This eloquent Boston lawyer was chosen governor by an overwhelming majority, almost solely because he had been prominent in the support of John Brown. Accordingly, he and the Virginia governor stood at opposite poles on sectional issues. Andrew had been affected deeply by the reform atmosphere of Boston and by his associations with Charles Sumner, Samuel Gridley Howe, and the Unitarian preachers. Henry A. Wise, on the other hand, had grown up in the conservative environment of the Southern plantation, from whose influence he could not escape.

Though dynamic and courageous, the Virginia governor was handicapped in carrying out progressive reforms by the conservative influence of slavery. Also he lived at a time when the *laissez-faire* conception of government prevailed in America, especially in the agricultural South. The people were not ready to adopt bold plans of state participation in the development of its resources. In most Southern states the governor had little real power; the legislature was supreme. Wise had unusual resources for influencing public opinion through his magnetic oratory and his control of the powerful Richmond *Enquirer*, which was edited by his son O. Jennings Wise. Nevertheless, he could not prevail against the inertia of legislatures that refused to tax the people to provide for the improvement of the state. Such progress as Virginia made in the last decade of the antebellum period, particularly in manufactures, came mainly from ineluctable economic forces—with little aid or direction from the government. Athwart the course of economic progress in the South lay the incubus of slavery; but few men in the region dared to attack this problem directly, as did the Kentucky crusader Cassius Marcellus Clay.

Chapter VI

THE EMERGENCE
OF THE RADICAL

IN THE 1830's when Cassius Marcellus Clay began his political
career, the North had become a prolific seedbed of radical
thought. The rural South, on the other hand, showed little tolerance for radicals. This hostility to the proponents of revolutionary
ideas seems at first view inconsistent with the individualism
which Southerners generally displayed. The Southern brand of
individualism, however, was of manners and character rather
than of the mind. The Southerner vigorously resisted the pressure of outside government; he was cavalier in the observance
of the laws; the planter on his semifeudal estate was a law to
himself. The yeomen, too, living largely on land that they owned
and regarding themselves as "the sovereign people," were among
the freest and most independent of Americans.

Nevertheless, this society after 1835 imposed a rigid conformity
of thought on its citizens in such vital matters as the preservation
of slavery, the status of women, and the upholding of orthodox
religion. Consequently, the few radicals that the Old South produced, such as the Grimké sisters of Charleston and Hinton
Rowan Helper of North Carolina, fled from their section. But one

prominent protoradical, an agitator who never became a fully fledged radical, Cassius Marcellus Clay of Kentucky, boldly stood his ground and attacked slavery in its stronghold.

Like Saint-Simon and Engels, born into a wealthy and aristocratic family, he had an unlikely background for the development of radical views. His father General Green Clay was a pioneer settler of Kentucky and a hero of the War of 1812. Cassius' boyhood was spent in roaming the fields and woods of his father's plantation in Madison County, where he developed the strong athletic body which was to serve him well in his fight for free speech. At any early age he was sent to the Jesuit school of St. Joseph at Bardstown, Kentucky, where he learned to speak French. Later, he attended Transylvania University for two years and then enrolled in the junior class of Yale College, from which he was graduated in 1832.

Clay's ambition was to attain distinction in a political career. To prepare himself for this profession upon his return to Kentucky he studied law at Transylvania University. He planned to combine a career in politics with the life of a planter. He had inherited the family estate in Madison County, Clermont, which he renamed White Hall. Here he engaged chiefly in raising livestock—buying young calves, fattening them, and driving the beef cattle to market in Cincinnati. He and his brother Brutus also operated a grist mill and a lumber mill on the nearby Kentucky River, but he neglected both his plantation and his mills for politics. In 1835 when he was twenty-five years old, he was elected to the legislature as representative of Madison County. In the next election he was defeated because of his vote in favor of internal improvements, but was re-elected in 1837. At this time he was a staunch Whig and had not yet become a crusader for the emancipation of slaves. He himself owned slaves inherited from his father, and he also seems to have managed his mother's slaves. One of them—"Luke"—broke into a house and stole twenty dollars. For this offense Cassius considered him "too outrageous to keep" and accordingly sold him to the lower South for $850.

Though he seemed at this time to conform to the type of a Kentucky country gentleman, the seeds had been sown that were to sprout into dissent. When he was a boy he had had the traumatic experience of seeing a slave cruelly mistreated. She was a mulatto girl owned by his father: he saw her covered with blood, after she had defended herself with a butcher knife from the attack of a drunken overseer. More affecting, however, was a fight that he had with a Negro boy named George, whom he had mistreated and who rebuked him by saying, "Mars' Cash, you would not treat me so, if you had not marster and mistress to back you." Clay replied by challenging him to a fight, in which he defeated the slave boy by superior strategy. "This fight with an African," wrote Clay in his autobiography, "was one of those instrumental influences by which Deity shapes the ends of life. George's courage won my respect, and his sad expression of defeat excited my sympathy; for he had one of those faces which in the blacks at times are so expressive of all the sentiments." Many other sensitive and compassionate Southern youths must also have suffered from witnessing some of the cruel aspects of slavery, but they grew accustomed to the institution, accepted it as the normal order of life, and did not become agitators against it as did Cassius Clay.

In New Haven Cassius had heard William Lloyd Garrison speak. This contact with the New England abolitionist aroused in him a desire to fight against slavery in his native state. He wrote to his brother Brutus on December 4, 1831: "The slave question is now assuming an importance in the opinions of the enlightened and humane, which prejudice and interest can not long withstand. The slaves of Virginia, Kentucky, and in fact all the slave holding States must soon be free! The voice of the civilized of Europe and the greater part of the United States is against slavery, not speculatively, but actively." He predicted, moreover, that there would be a dissolution of the Union before fifty years had passed.

Clay's public advocacy of the emancipation of the slaves developed after he had moved to Lexington in 1840 and was powerfully stimulated by a political quarrel. In August of that year he was elected to the legislature, defeating the Democratic candidate Robert Wickliffe, the son of the largest slaveholder in Kentucky. One of the issues of the campaign was the repeal of Kentucky's slave importation law of 1833, which prohibited the introduction of slaves into the state for sale. The Wickliffes, who formed a mighty clan of officeholders, supported the movement for repeal, while Clay defended the law. Robert Wickliffe, senior, "the Old Duke," delivered a bitter speech against Clay in Lexington, in which he criticized Clay for daring to speak on the merits of slavery. In reply, the young politician issued a pamphlet reviewing Wickliffe's charges, again stating his belief that slavery was an evil—morally, economically, religiously, and politically. He pointed out that slavery led to the emigration from the state of the non-slaveholder and that, "Every slave imported [into the State] drives out a free and independent Kentuckian." Slavery prevented the state from extensively using machinery and developing manufacturers. Yet, he declared that he was not an abolitionist, not even an emancipationist: "In part, I am like other slave holders, I know not what to do."

When the young liberal ran for re-election to the legislature during the following year, the proslavery forces rallied and used unfair methods to defeat him. According to a letter of Clay to the anti-slavery politician of Ohio Salmon P. Chase in March, 1842, the county officials refused to permit voters favorable to him to vote: they ruled that these prospective voters had no "fixed residence." But at the same time Clay's opponents imported into the county hundreds of illegal voters "to prostrate me and sustain their peculiar institution!!!" The son of "the Old Duke" was accordingly elected to the legislature. After this defeat Cassius never again held public office in Kentucky.

The letters of Clay to Salmon P. Chase in 1842 reveal the dilemma of a liberal in the Southern states. He wrote that he must proceed cautiously and with prudence in his community, for if he were openly to advocate emancipation of the slaves, he would be branded as an abolitionist and lose all power of doing good. The only course for him to pursue was "a gradual and quiet interchange of opinion [aided by] the general advance of liberal opinions in the world." Freedom of speech and of the press was essential, however, to this advance, and he strongly sympathized with John Quincy Adams' efforts to remove the gag rule in Congress. "Our light comes and must necessarily come from the house of Congress," he observed, "the press there is the only one that penetrates the homes of the great mass." He urged Chase to send him documents showing the comparative wealth, the state of the arts and sciences, and the numbers of the two sections, for these were more effective arguments against slavery than invective.

In his letters to Chase he strongly argued the economic case against slavery. Many noble Kentuckians, he wrote, had fled the state because of their antislavery views, but he was determined to stay. He lamented the economic effects of slavery upon his native state, citing the case of Bourbon County, the most extensive planting county of Kentucky, which was almost bankrupt "owing to the large emigration of its citizens to other states carrying off the proceeds of their lands & slaves." Moreover, he observed, slavery injured the mechanic class, for it was absurd to develop manufactures without a market, and the slave population were small consumers of manufactured goods. This was an important contribution to the economic argument against slavery, and he continued to use it in his later career. On June 10, 1845, in the newspaper that he founded—*The True American*—he used a striking and homely instance to demonstrate his point that slavery prevented the rise in the South of a home market for manufactures: "Lawyers, merchants, mechanics, laborers, who are your consumers; Robert Wickliffe's two hundred slaves? How many clients do you find, how many goods do you sell, how many hats, coats, saddles, bridles and trunks do you make for these two hundred slaves? Does Mr. Wickliffe lay out as much for himself and his two hundred slaves as two hundred freemen do?"

At the same time he continued to carry on his feud with the Wickliffes. When Robert ran for Congress, Cassius followed him from place to place in his campaign and caustically attacked the young aristocrat. Finally, according to Clay's unreliable memory, the Wickliffe family sent for a notorious fighter named Brown to kill him. Subsequently when Clay interrupted Wickliffe while he was speaking at Russell Cave near Lexington, the "hired assassin" attacked him, and a vicious fight with bowie knives and pistols took place. Though severely injured, Cassius came off the victor, horribly mutilating his opponent by slashing his skull to the brain, cutting an ear nearly off, slitting his nose, and putting out one eye.

This pugnacious side of Clay's personality was the most unattractive aspect of his character—a relic of the frontier stage of

Kentucky life. His fondness for the use of the bowie knife in self-defense was exhibited when he presented a specially designed dagger to another Kentucky antislavery man, the Reverend Robert Jefferson Breckinridge. Along with the gift he gave practical demonstrations in its most efficient use. Later, in 1869, he wrote a pamphlet entitled "The Technique of Bowie Knife Fighting."

By 1843 Cassius had developed his opposition to slavery more strongly and had written a letter to the New York *Tribune* expressing his antislavery ideas. The movement to annex Texas as a slaveholding state aroused him greatly, and in December, 1843, at a mass meeting at White Sulphur Springs, near Georgetown, Kentucky, he replied to a speech of Colonel Richard M. Johnson, who advocated the annexation of this territory. He declared that though he did not sanction insurrection or the confiscation of the property rights of slaveholders, he was an abolitionist in the sense that Washington and Jefferson were.

During the presidential campaign of 1844 he spoke in the Northern states in behalf of the candidacy of his distant cousin, Henry Clay. He later wrote in his autobiography that everywhere he spoke—from Ohio to Boston—he was received with "the wildest enthusiasm." So forthright was he in his attacks on slavery and on the annexation of Texas that Henry Clay wrote a letter to him urging him to be more cautious. The old statesman observed that his enemies were using the speeches of Cassius, whom they represented to be his son, to injure his prospects for election. In this speechmaking tour the Kentucky reformer established many contacts with the Northern abolitionists.

Shortly before he left for his campaign in the North, he emancipated his slaves. For this act he won the praise of the Northern abolitionists, particularly Gerrit Smith, the millionaire abolitionist of Peterboro, New York. In a public letter condemning Cassius for advocating the election of the slaveholder Henry Clay to the Presidency, Smith at the same time commended his unselfish action in sacrificing $40,000 worth of property by emancipating his slaves. The sacrifice was really greater than the loss of his own slaves, for in order to unite the families of those whom he emancipated he borrowed the money to buy and liberate thirteen of their relatives at a cost of $10,000. Moreover, the liberation of the working force on his plantation made it difficult for him to continue to operate it, and he appealed to his brother Brutus in Bourbon County to lend him some slaves to clean his pastures.

Clay found that he could not get a hearing for his antislavery views in the press of Kentucky. He wrote to Salmon P. Chase of Ohio on January 19, 1844, that his letter about the annexation of Texas to the New York *Tribune* had not been published in the slave states and that he had not been able to force editors in Kentucky to reprint it by any means. "The press is monopolized by the slaveholders," he observed, "and the people receive no light & are filled with prejudices carefully instilled into them."

Because the columns of the Kentucky newspapers were closed to his efforts "to throw light among the labouring people," he founded a weekly newspaper in Lexington, the *True American*, to agitate for the emancipation of the slaves. He tried to prepare the citizens of Kentucky for a favorable reception of his antislavery paper by a prospectus, very moderate in tone, which was published in the Lexington *Observer and Reporter* nearly three months before the appearance of the first issue. This document stated that the *True American* would work for the emancipation of the slaves through political action and that the reformer would not cut loose from the old political parties. The future editor promised that he would open the columns of his paper to various points of view, and he appealed to the people to preserve the freedom of the press and Jeffersonian principles.

In an "Address to the People of Kentucky" he gave the background of his antislavery sentiment. He had held such views, he declared, before he went to Yale College. Indeed, prior to his departure for New Haven he had authorized his older brother Sydney to enroll his name in an emancipation society founded in 1831 in Mercer County, and he and his idealistic brother resolved to emancipate their slaves. In an exaggerated form, his address described the adverse economic effects of slavery on Kentucky, and he closed with a stirring appeal: "Give us *free labor* and we shall, indeed, become *'the garden of the world.'*"

Clay's method of establishing his antislavery newspaper was ill-advised. Warned by the suppression of James G. Birney's emancipation paper *The Philanthropist* at Danville, Kentucky, nearly ten years before, he took precautions to defend his press if it should be attacked by a mob. He fortified his office as though he were in a hostile country. Two brass four-pounder cannon loaded with shot and nails were placed on a table commanding the entrance to his office. On the walls he hung Mexican lances and rifles. A trap door was cut in the roof and a keg of gun powder placed under the floor with a fuse attached so that if a mob drove the defenders out of the building, the invaders could be blown to pieces.

Before he started publication he sent an appeal to Gerrit Smith to secure subscribers for him in the Northern states. In a letter of February 14, 1845, he commented: "They threaten my life as usual and I fear it may go hard with me—but I was born a freeman and I intend to die one. I have about 240 subscribers in this county and I hope for more—will the North not send us 5 or 6000 names to the help of the great cause of the day—you may suppose that we dont go far enough—we go as far as we can. Let us judge for ourselves." When he issued the first copy of the *True American*, he had already obtained about three hundred subscribers in Kentucky and seventeen hundred in other states.

On June 3, 1845, the first issue of the *True American* appeared. The program which it presented to the people of Kentucky for the removal of slavery was mild and reasonable. The editor disassociated himself from the Northern abolitionists: instead of the Garrisonian program of the immediate abolition of slavery without compensation to the slave owners, he advocated a sensible plan of gradual emancipation. Clay conducted his paper with considerable restraint, and his editorials and arguments for the gradual removal of the great social evil certainly did not endanger the public safety. But the slaveholding leaders were waiting for the bold editor to make a misstep.

The issue of August 12 contained a lead article entitled, "What is to Become of the Slaves in the United States?" and an inflammatory editorial. The anonymous writer of the article advocated the gradual emancipation of the slaves in Kentucky, the provision of a system of educating them preparatory to their liberation, and the granting of full political rights to the freedmen, including the rights to vote, hold office, give testimony against the whites, and sit on juries. The editorial contained the ominous warning: "But remember, you who dwell in marble palaces—that there are strong arms and fiery hearts and iron pikes in the streets, and paines of glass only between them and the silver plate on the board and the smooth-skinned woman on the otto-man. When you have mocked at virtue and denied the agency of God in the affairs of men, and made rapine your honied faith; tremble for the day of retribution is at hand—and the masses will be avenged."

Two days later the storm came. A group of Clay's personal ene-mies held a meeting in the Lexington courthouse and sent him a letter demanding that he discontinue the publication of the *True American* and warning him that his safety would be involved in his reply. The intrepid crusader was very sick with typhoid fever at the time, but he summoned his strength to dictate a reply, treating their communication with "burning contempt" and clos-ing his note with defiant words: "Go tell your secret conclave of cowardly assassins that C. M. Clay knows his rights and how to defend them."

Thereupon a great public meeting was called to assemble in the Fayette County courthouse yard. Faced by this danger, Clay ap-pealed to the people in a series of broadsides. On August 15 he issued an extra to the *True American* explaining that his recent editorial applied only to the whites who were oppressed by the slaveholders and that it referred not to the present but to some future time. To the accusation that his paper was incendiary, he replied: "I regard the idea of an insurrection in Kentucky where there are about six whites to one black as ridiculous and only used by the Slaveholders as a Bug-a-boo, to maintain the ascendancy of their power in the State." He declared that he himself would shoulder his musket to suppress an insurrection of the slaves.

On the following day he published another broadside in which he sought to placate public opinion further. He wrote that al-though he believed slavery to be a violation of natural right, he was opposed to abolishing it by violence. Instead, he proposed the calling of a constitutional convention in Kentucky to adopt a plan of gradual emancipation. He advocated the freeing of fe-male slaves born after a certain date, when they had reached the age of twenty-one; and after the passage of thirty years, the state should buy and liberate all existing slaves. As to the freedmen, he said that he would not forcibly expel them from the state but would encourage them voluntarily to emigrate by financial inducements offered by the state. He declared further that he was opposed to amalgamation of the races and to giving the suffrage to the freedman, although he suggested that another generation might do so. Admitting that his paper might not have been conducted in "the most pacific manner," he concluded in a conciliatory but firm expression of intention: "I am willing to take warning from friends and enemies for the future conduct of my paper, and while I am ready to restrict myself in the latitude of discussion of the question, I never will abandon a right or yield a principle."

This statement of his principles and of his future course of action should have satisfied any reasonable group of men. But the feeling of the community had been deeply aroused against him: he was regarded as an outright abolitionist whose newspaper was sustained by the contributions of Northerners. For this reason the people seemed to be incapable of rational action in regard to his press. A huge public meeting, estimated to have been attended by twelve hundred people, met in the courthouse yard on August 18. Thomas F. Marshall, a bitter personal enemy of Clay who was smarting from a recent defeat in his bid for election to Congress, harangued the crowd, urging that the *True American* be suppressed. Marshall argued that an antislavery press in a Southern community constituted so great a danger to the public safety that the community was justified in suppressing it. Though the publication of the *True American* violated no law and therefore could not be legally stopped, he declared, the community had a right to abate the nuisance of an incendiary newspaper on the principle *salus populi suprema lex*.

The assembly accordingly resolved that they would not tolerate an antislavery publication in Lexington and chose a committee of sixty respectable citizens to carry out their will of suppressing the obnoxious paper. On the day that the meeting was held, the judge of the city court issued an injunction against the publication of the *True American*. The editor, thereupon, surrendered the keys of his establishment to the city marshal. When the committee arrived, they found the printing office undefended. They proceeded to dismantle the press, box it up with the type and appurtenances, and send them to Cincinnati. Shortly afterwards, feeling a need to publish a justification of their highhanded act, the committee issued a pamphlet in which they maintained that their arbitrary action was designed to prevent a violent attack of the mob.

Clay replied in a dramatic pamphlet entitled *Appeal of Cassius M. Clay to Kentucky and the World*. He declared that his enemies had insisted on branding him as an abolitionist—"a name full of unknown and strange terrors and crimes to the mass of the people." He emphatically denied that he was any more of an abolitionist than was George Washington. He appealed to the governor and people of Kentucky to preserve the liberty of the press, which should be the concern of the whole American people.

After the *True American* presses were sent to Cincinnati, Clay continued to publish his antislavery paper in that city but with the date line of Lexington, Kentucky. At the time of the forcible transference to Cincinnati, it had grown in circulation to three thousand subscribers. This number fell off after June, 1846, when Clay volunteered to fight in the Mexican War: Northern abolitionist subscribers felt that he had abandoned his principles. The idealistic Clay was determined that his paper should continue to be published, despite the fact that it involved a financial loss of $480 a month. His wife Martha Jane, however, could not bear to see the family funds continuously drained by the enterprise, and in October, 1846, ordered its publication suspended. John C. Vaughn, the assistant editor, took the subscription list to Louisville and on October 16, 1847, revived it under the name of *The Examiner*. Here the new editor—a native of South Carolina—was able to publish it unmolested and to advocate the emancipation of slaves and the election of antislavery delegates to the constitutional convention of 1849.

Cassius Clay's decision to volunteer for service in the war against Mexico was one of the inconsistent and ironic acts of his career. The Mexican War was regarded by the antislavery men of the North as a war for the expansion of slavery, and his fellow Whigs, including Henry Clay, also condemned it as unjust. In joining the conflict Cassius' motives were mixed: he confessed in a letter to Chase that he was tired of "the dray horse duties" of editing the *True American;* he was apparently influenced by the strong military tradition of the South; and, perhaps most impelling, his pugnacious nature made him feel restless at standing idle while his friends and neighbors were volunteering. He rationalized his decision to fight by saying that he wished to convince the people of Kentucky that he was not their enemy but only the enemy of slavery. Knowing that the Kentuckians were exceptionally fond of military glory, he hoped by volunteering to increase his influence in the state so that upon his return he could more effectively agitate for the abolition of slavery.

After many hardships he finally managed to arrive in Mexico, but in 1847 he was captured and spent much of the war period as a prisoner in Mexico City. Nevertheless, he won popularity among the Kentucky soldiers by bravery, by consideration for his men, and by sharing their hardships in campaigning and in prison. Upon his return to Kentucky he received an ovation from the mercurial citizens of Lexington and Fayette County, and his friends presented him with an elegant sword: Thomas F. Marshall made the presentation speech. Moreover, he won a suit in the courts for damages to the press of the *True American* against James B. Clay, the son of Henry Clay, who was the secretary of the "Committee of Sixty."

Temporarily restored to popular favor, Cassius resumed his agitation against slavery, but in a moderate fashion. He wrote Chase on December 27, 1847, that he planned to work for the cause by speaking, writing, and even publishing a book. He would not abandon the Whig Party, however, and he had resolved to be more moderate toward the Democrats, who in Kentucky were largely laborers. In the presidential election of 1848, having turned against his cousin Henry Clay, he supported Zachary Taylor. He wrote to William H. Seward in December of that year: "The cause of emancipation advances here—nearly all the papers are open to discussion—what a change in 3 years since the memorable 18th of August—!" He noted that his recently published book *The Writings of Cassius Marcellus Clay*, edited by Horace Greeley, was being sold in Lexington.

In the following year the political atmosphere changed, for the people were aroused by a campaign for the election of delegates to a state constitutional convention. The emancipationists agitated for the adoption of a clause in the constitution providing

CASSIUS MARCELLUS CLAY, radical agitator of Kentucky.

for the gradual emancipation of the slaves. Clay entered vigorously into the campaign and made a number of antislavery speeches in various parts of the state. When he arrived at Lawrenceburg, he was warned of the dangers of incendiary speech and was notified that if he spoke there, his life would be endangered. He paid no attention to threats but went to the courthouse with two revolvers in his carpetbag and a bowie knife concealed in his belt. The reputation of his kindness to Kentucky soldiers in the Mexican War came to his aid, and as a consequence he was allowed to speak without interruption. In 1849 when he spoke at Foxtown, a small village near his plantation, an attempt was made to silence him. Nevertheless, he spoke against the "peculiar institution," and when he was struck by one of his opponents, the son of Squire Turner, he killed the man with his bowie knife.

According to his autobiography, Clay was responsible for the meeting of the state emancipation convention at Frankfort in 1849. One hundred and fifty delegates attended from twenty-four counties, including Senator Joseph R. Underwood, Henry Clay, and the prominent Presbyterian minister Robert J. Breckinridge. Cassius made a speech urging the delegates to disregard party allegiance in working for the great cause of emancipation: since the non-slaveholders did not as a rule read the newspapers, the only way to reach them was by speaking on the stump. Despite the efforts of the emancipationists, they were not able to elect a single delegate. Indeed, a reaction against liberalism set in: the legislature repealed the law of 1833 prohibiting the introduction of slaves into the state, and the constitutional convention fastened the institution of slavery more firmly in fundamental state law by placing its protection in the bill of rights. The liberal Louisville *Examiner* gave up the fight for emancipation, and discontinued on December 8, 1849.

Clay's boldest political move for the emancipation cause was to become a candidate for governor in 1851. He campaigned in many counties for his candidacy and for the abolition of slavery in Kentucky—at times in defiance of threats. A story is told of Clay's method of meeting such threats that is highly characteristic of his personality. He would mount the rostrum carrying a Bible, a copy of the Constitution, and a pistol. "For those who support the laws of the country I have this argument," he would announce, placing the copy of the Constitution on the table before him: "for those who believe in the Bible I offer this argument," laying the Bible beside the Constitution, "and for those who regard neither the laws of God or man, I have this argument," and he would place the pistol in ready reach on the table. Although he received only 3,621 votes in the election, he believed that his candidacy had withdrawn so many votes from the Whigs that their long ascendancy in the state was broken: the Democratic candidate, Lazarus Powell, was elected governor.

The evolution of Clay from a liberal into a radical was a gradual process. After his press was mobbed, he received numerous invitations to speak in Northern cities, and early in 1846 he responded by giving a series of lectures to enthusiastic audiences, particularly in New York and Philadelphia. He also wrote to Chase in May of that year that he would give a hearing to the Liberty party in the *True American,* that he had nothing to say against Garrisonianism, and that he was now using the term "abolitionism" instead of "emancipation" in his newspaper. The sympathy of Northern antislavery men was impelling Clay to a more radical course. He corresponded sympathetically with such antislavery leaders as Salmon Chase, William H. Seward, Joshua Giddings, and Horace Greeley. He praised Seward's radical speech in the debates on the Compromise of 1850 and bitterly condemned Webster's moderate course in five letters that were published in the antislavery *National Era* of Washington. When Harriet Beecher Stowe's *Uncle Tom's Cabin* appeared, he praised it as an accurate picture of Southern life that did not exaggerate the horrors of slavery. In 1852 he joined the Free Soil party and campaigned in northern Kentucky with the party's vice-presidential candidate, George W. Julian of Indiana.

The pure idealism of Clay's early crusade against slavery now became alloyed with grosser elements of ambition and self-interest. Certainly by 1852 he was looking forward to the formation of a great national antislavery party with the hope that he would be the presidential or vice-presidential candidate. In thanking Seward for a letter of condolence on the death of his seventeen-year-old son ("who warmly sympathized with my views"), Clay urged the New York politician to leave the Whigs and join a new liberal party. The passage of the Kansas-Nebraska

Act gave him a splendid opportunity to agitate for the cause. He wrote Chase that he was continuing "to press the light into the mountains [of Kentucky] by papers and prints," and he organized anti-Nebraska meetings. When the Republican party was formed in 1854, he became an active member and spent the month of July canvassing Illinois "in the midst of cholera," giving nightly lectures on "The Despotism of Slavery." Accordingly, he was disappointed when the Republican convention of 1856 passed him by in nominating John C. Frémont and William L. Dayton. Feeling that he had been at the post of danger for many years and had worked hard for the cause, he complained to Chase that the Republican party had made a mistake in choosing both of its candidates from north of the Mason-Dixon Line.

Though he had become a staunch Republican and opposed the extension of slavery into federal territories, he repudiated the extremists of the party who advocated the higher law doctrine. In reply to an invitation to speak in Wheeling during the campaign, he wrote that he held strictly to states' rights; he believed that the federal government had no authority to interfere with slavery in the states. In 1857 Gerrit Smith offered him five hundred dollars for an outfit if he would go to Kansas; Clay declined to participate in the Kansas war, writing that he must stay in Kentucky to pay his debts. In the preceding year he had become bankrupt partly as a result of neglecting his private affairs while making antislavery speeches and campaigning in the Northern states for the election of John C. Frémont. Unsuccessful speculations in pork had also contributed to his financial ruin.

In 1860 his political ambitions were deeply aroused by the prospect of a Republican national victory. To Thurlow Weed he wrote in March that if Seward or Chase were not nominated at the national convention, he was willing to run for the Republician nomination for President. He listed his qualifications as follows: (1) he was a Southerner, and his nomination would therefore silence the cry of sectionalism; (2) he was a tariff man who would appeal to Pennsylvania; (3) he was popular with the Germans everywhere and not offensive to the Americans (the Know-Nothings); (4) he had served the party longer than any other man without reward; (5) he would form a Southern wing of the party and thus put down all hopes of disunion; and finally, (6)

"There are elements in my history that will arouse popular enthusiasm & insure success." Though he failed to get the nomination for either President or Vice-President, he was so much admired by the abolitionists that he received more than one hundred votes for the nomination for Vice-President.

Lincoln rewarded him for his services to the Republican cause by appointing him minister to Russia in 1861, although he seemed peculiarly unsuited for a diplomatic post. On his way to St. Petersburg he and his family stopped in London, and here Benjamin Moran, the secretary of the American legation, saw him stranded in the Westminster Hotel late at night without accommodations. In his journal Moran has left a vivid picture of this occasion: Clay "was walking up and down the magnificent hall like a chafed lion, and looked a man to be avoided, in the gas light, surrounded as he was by his suite of three tall, sharp-faced Kentuckians. I had never seen him before, was surprised to find him a man of some fifty years, 6 ft. high, [actually he was six feet three inches in height and weighed 215 pounds] well-proportioned, with a fine manly face and the form of a hero. Oddly enough he wore a blue dress coat with gilt buttons, and I could but smile to see an envoy of Russia in such a costume." Clay himself in his autobiography has added other details of his appearance at the time of the Mexican War: the color of his great mane of hair was jet black; his eyes were dark gray; and his skin was so fair that during his captivity some Mexican girls thinking that he used paint tried to wash it off.

After a year at the Russian court he was recalled to make a place for Simon Cameron, who had failed as secretary of war. Upon his return to the United States he was commissioned major general of volunteers, but he refused to fight unless the government abolished slavery in the seceded states. He desired to return to Russia as minister, and Lincoln placated him by reappointing him to that post. Proud of displaying his military dress uniform in the brilliant court of the Czar, he remained in Russia until he was recalled in 1869. While he was minister to Russia, the United States bought Alaska. In his old age he claimed credit for accomplishing this great object, but actually he had very little to do with it.

During the Reconstruction period he violently opposed the

policies of the Radical Republicans, especially their centralizing acts and their harsh vindictive treatment of the South. In 1872 he was active in the Liberal Republican movement, working for the nomination of Horace Greeley. So disgusted was he with corruption under Grant that in 1876 he became a Democrat and a Tilden supporter. But in 1884 he returned to the Republican fold and voted for James A. Garfield for President.

His later years were lonely and embittered; he quarreled with his wife, who divorced him; he was ostracized by Kentucky society, and when he went to the races he sat alone. He sent for his illegitimate son Launey in Russia to solace his cheerless life; when he was eighty-four years old he married a fifteen-year-old tenant girl, who later divorced him. He suffered under the delusion that his life was being threatened and one time killed a colored man who had come onto his estate against orders. He lived to be nearly ninety-three years old and died at White Hall in 1903.

Although Clay's life became absorbed in a cause, he had a considerable breadth of interests. One of his minor meritorious deeds was his patronage of Joel T. Hart, the Lexington sculptor. He encouraged this self-taught artist, who had begun as a stonemason in the Bluegrass. Clay commissioned Hart to execute a portrait bust of himself and paid him the large fee of five hundred dollars; he also helped the artist to go to Italy for study. Hart's marble bust of Clay, which now stands in the lobby of the University of Kentucky Library, is a striking work; the handsome face of the antislavery crusader is animated with a perverse and tantalizing smile.

As legislator and editor, Clay was a vigorous advocate of popular education in Kentucky. In 1835 during his first term in the legislature he introduced a bill for the establishment of free common schools, but it failed of passage. In his "Address to the People of Kentucky" of January, 1845, he observed that because of the existence of slavery it was impossible to establish free schools for all the children of the state. One of his notable contributions to education was a grant of land to the Kentucky antislavery agitator and preacher John G. Fee to found Berea Academy in 1858. But because Clay did not approve of the open racial policy of the college, he refused to serve as a trustee.

Like the radical Eastern abolitionists, Clay was in revolt against religious orthodoxy. He accused the orthodox ministers of "time serving" policies and boldly condemned the Southern churches for supporting slavery as a divine institution. The authenticity of the Jewish Bible, he maintained, should be judged by the same rules of evidence that were applied to the history of the Greeks and Romans. The Devil, he declared was simply "a figure of speech," and immortality could neither be proved nor disproved. Though he asserted his belief in the existence of God and in the validity of Christian morality, he rejected the current beliefs in miracles and the resurrection of the body, just as his deist father General Green Clay had done. Liberty of thought in religious matters he upheld as the right of every responsible human being.

Clay belonged to the aristocratic type of agitator. His counterparts in the North were men like Wendell Phillips and Charles Sumner, but unlike them he had a realistic view of slavery and of the difficulties in eradicating it. His relations with the Kentucky abolitionist John G. Fee illustrated disparate types of the antislavery radical. The background of the minister was quite different from that of the aristocratic Clay. The son of a small slaveholding farmer in northern Kentucky, Fee studied at Miami University of Ohio and Lane Theological Seminary in Cincinnati, where he was converted to a militant form of abolitionism. When he returned to his native state, he began preaching that slavery was a great sin and should be immediately abolished. As he carried on his crusade, this zealous little man with a bald head and a strange ascetic appearance seemed to be a reincarnation of Peter the Hermit. He courted martyrdom, and he was mobbed twenty-two times.

Clay at first befriended this zealot, not only by giving him a farm in the southern part of Madison County, but by protecting him from mobs so that he could preach his antislavery views. On June 4, 1855, Clay wrote to Chase that "the mobocratic spirit" had been invoked by the Louisville *Courier* against Fee in Lincoln County. A miniature Kansas fight was imminent when Clay marshaled his forces with guns to protect the abolitionist while the proslavery forces brought cannon from Frankfort to confront the bellicose antislavery leader. The Lincoln County people finally sent a committee to negotiate with Clay, and they agreed to disarm and allow Fee to speak.

But during the next year the cooperation between the two radicals abruptly ended, for Fee advocated the higher law doctrine—the ultimate in radicalism. He preached disobedience of the laws establishing slavery and the fugitive slave law because they were sinful. Cassius Clay, on the other hand, believed in obeying the laws; he proposed the accomplishment of reforms through a free press and the vote of the majority. In 1856 during a public meeting at Slate Lick Springs in Madison County where both reformers spoke, Clay declared, "Mr. Fee's position is revolutionary, insurrectionary and dangerous." After John Brown's raid, Fee spoke in Henry Ward Beecher's church in Brooklyn, praising the spirit of the fanatical leader. For such doctrine Clay had no sympathy and accordingly made no efforts to protect Fee and his followers at Berea when a mob expelled them from the state.

Cassius Marcellus Clay should be judged not by the follies of his old age but by the courageous and humanitarian deeds of his active career. His great work was to agitate for freeing the slaves and at the risk of his life to uphold the freedom of the press. Indeed, he had a quality of character that few Southern antislavery agitators possessed—a willingness to place his life in jeopardy for his opinions. Other prominent Southern antislavery men such as Professor Benjamin Sherwood Hedrick, Daniel R. Goodloe, and Hinton Rowan Helper—all from North Carolina—and James G. Birney of Kentucky did not defy the mob as Clay did but exiled themselves to the North. Often the radical is only interested in freedom of speech and the press for himself or his group, but Clay demonstrated his belief that the preservation of freedom of expression in a society was in itself a noble ideal, and he permitted persons whose views were obnoxious to him to have a hearing in his paper.

Chapter VII

THE SOUTHERN YEOMAN: THE HUMORISTS' VIEW AND THE REALITY

THE mass of Southern people did not share Clay's view of the wisdom of preserving freedom of speech and of the press. In any society the mass of the people are intolerant of ideas repugnant to them; nor are they creative thinkers but take their ideas mainly from the preachers, teachers, editors, and politicians. This does not mean, however, that in the Old South the great majority of slaveless farmers had no weight in determining the direction of the Southern mind. Indeed, after the 1820's the politicians usually moved in the direction of what they thought was the popular will. Often the weight of this pressure was exerted through partisan channels, particularly by legislative instruction of the federal senators.

The modern historian finds it difficult to fathom the mind of the Southern yeomen, who constituted the great majority of the people, because they were not vocal; they kept almost no diaries that have been preserved, and their personal papers, except for Confederate letters, are almost nonexistent. A few manuscript travel accounts written by yeomen (notably Micajah Clark's diary of a sentimental journey from Mississippi to his old home in

South Carolina in 1857) and some observations by travelers such as Frederick Law Olmsted, who had a special interest in the lower classes, cast a feeble light on their lives. Moreover, the election returns cannot be trusted as reliable indexes of the concensus of popular thought, partly because a large proportion of the lower classes did not vote. Some clues as to what the people thought and felt can be obtained from editorials, from the sermons of evangelical ministers, and from the appeals that politicians made to the electorate. In county courthouses and at state capitals are to be found legal documents such as wills, laws, and records of cases which throw light upon the activities of the common people, especially when they got into trouble. There are also various types of informal evidence—folklore, isolated newspaper items, occasional bits of memorabilia (such as the manuscript memoir of Newton Knight by his son), and the semirealistic writings of the Southern humorists with a rich vein of social history running through them.

This latter type of evidence—usually neglected in formal histories—is prejudiced, but valuable truth can be sifted from its distortions and bias. In studying the writings of the Southern humorists of the antebellum period the social historian has a different purpose from that of the folklorist, the student of American literature, or the investigator of the Southern vernacular. He is interested in the by-products of this type of literature —authentic details of manners, customs, amusements, and social institutions such as the militia muster, the religious revival, and the law courts. The historian must be able to distinguish between the bias of the humorists and the facts about their subjects, for these writers were not primarily reporters but creators of literature. Nevertheless, they present through their imagination and firsthand knowledge of the plain people a kind of truth that eludes the researcher in documents.

Some of the most important humorists sought faithfully to record the mores and manners of the common people by their descriptions of frontier life, courthouse scenes, militia musters, and the uninhibited amusements of the yeomen and poor whites. After Augustus Baldwin Longstreet, the author of *Georgia Scenes,* had become a preacher and a college president, he was disturbed at times by the frivolity and indelicacy of his humorous writing, but he justified his work on the ground that it was authentic social history which a later age would value. In his preface to *Major Jones's Chronicles of Pineville,* William Tappan Thompson also affirmed a historical purpose—to preserve a record of the "cracker" before education had changed him "by polishing away those peculiarities which now mark his manners and language, reduc[ing] him to the common level of commonplace people, and mak[ing] him a less curious 'specimen' for the study of the naturalist. As he now is, however, I have endeavored to catch his 'manners living as they rise.'" Likewise, Thomas Bangs Thorpe and Joseph M. Field seem to have purposely recorded characteristic features of frontier life and quaint customs in out-of-the-way places which were rapidly disappearing. In reporting Southern conditions the humorists had an advantage over most travelers, for they observed Southern life from within. The keen observations which they made were the fruit of a lifetime of association and understanding rather than the product of a hasty visit.

A recent student of Southwestern humor, Kenneth Lynn, has presented a thesis (which he rides hard), that these humorists were principally Whigs, who wrote with a strongly aristocratic bias. He maintains that they used their humorous writings as a weapon to combat and discredit the Jacksonian movement. Some evidence can be found, especially in the writings of Johnson J. Hooper and Joseph G. Baldwin, to support this tenuous thesis. But many of the writers wrote merely to entertain, to tell a good story, without political intent. Some of them—notably John Basil Lamar—had a genuine appreciation for the sterling virtues of the yeoman and the frontiersman—his independence, democracy, naturalness, courage, hospitality, and patriotism.

The attitude of Southern humorists toward the relatively small class of "poor whites" may have had something of aristocratic hauteur in it, but on the whole it represented the general attitude of Southern society to this debased class of people. To modern eyes the lowest class of whites of the Old South (often called "poor white trash" by the slaves) appear to be tragic figures, but to the planters and the residents of the towns they were a comic element. The upper plantation group as a class felt little sense of responsibility for the poverty, the illiteracy, the peculiar diseases of hookworm and malaria, and the drunkenness which beset the lower classes. What could be more laughable to these aristocrats than the quaint vernacular and the crude manners and dress of the "tackies" and "sand-hillers"? Even the slaves of the big house made fun of "poor white trash." In his *History of the Dividing Line* Colonel William Byrd set an example of snobbish aristocratic wit by his satire on the lubbers or backwoods people of North Carolina.

One of these aristocrats who was amused by the poor whites and collected their colloquialisms—"the piney-woods parlance" —was the Georgia doctor and poet Francis Orray Ticknor. Though Ticknor is known for his romanic poems, notably "Virginians of the Valley," his correspondence reveals that he had an earthy sense of humor. He lived on his planatation Torch Hill near Columbus, from which he made trips on his horse Kitty into the pine woods to minister to poor people. He described a learned reply that he gave to the question of a piney-woods mother: "What's the matter with my child's nose, he keeps a-picking of it?" His patients usually paid him with an X mark, but sometimes he got a cash case, "a temptation thrown in my way to reconcile me to my lot." He attended a sheriff's sale of the property of a poor white who had decamped owing him a bill. The property consisted of a cow and calf, a table, two chairs, a coffee mill without a handle, a tin pan with two holes in the bottom, and a pig of soft soap: all brought less than five dollars.

The customs and manners of the poor whites as well as of the yeomen of the South presented a rich tapestry of local material for the literary artist. This material, unsuited for use by the dominant romantic school of Southern writers, was exploited by the humorists who flourished in the period from 1830 to 1860. Unhampered by European traditions, except for the slight influence of Addison, these writers freshly observed the life about them and reported their findings without much effort at literary finish. They found around them the racy and individualized characters of the crackers and the yeomen, whose uncouth language and provinciality afforded substance for mirth. They could therefore create a native American humor based on realistic observation and illuminated by many sidelights of local color.

The Negro, on the other hand, was seldom or only incidentally used (as in Simms's novel *Woodcraft*), as a subject for comedy by antebellum Southern writers. Not until the time of Joel Chandler Harris did the "darky" assume a prominent place in Southern humor. Perhaps the detachment essential for seeing the ludicrous side of the poor white man was lacking in the case of the Negro, who was a form of property bitterly assailed by the abolitionists. Besides, the black slave was a congruous element in the plantation regime, whereas the cracker was not.

The origin of this semirealistic literature dealing with the common man can be explained partly by the democratic upsurge of the Jacksonian movement. The rise of the Nullification movement also stirred up an intense feeling of Southernism and an interest in Southern themes. In addition, economic and social conditions were ripe for the development of a school of broad humor below the Mason-Dixon Line. Georgia was the cradle of Southern humor. In this state a remarkable contrast developed between the yeomen of the red hills and the planters of the long-settled tidewater region. Indeed, the frontier had only recently been erased in the 1830's with the removal of the Cherokees. This juxtaposition of seasoned culture and the rude frontier produced incongruities and comic situations that evoked laughter.

The school of Southern humor was founded in Georgia by Augustus Baldwin Longstreet, a graduate of Yale and of Judge Tappan Reeve's law school at Litchfield, Connecticut, and editor of the Augusta *State Rights' Sentinel*. In his *Georgia Scenes,* published in book form at Augusta in 1835, Longstreet first set forth the ludicrous aspects of the life of Southern yeomen, crackers, and poor whites. He was soon followed by others, notably William Tappan Thompson, his protegé on the *State Rights' Sentinel;* Johnson J. Hooper, who had emigrated from North Carolina to Alabama where he became an editor and politician; John Basil Lamar, a Georgia planter; Henry Clay Lewis, the "Madison Tensas" of *Odd Leaves from the Life of a Louisiana Swamp Doctor;* Joseph M. Field, editor of the St. Louis *Reveille;* and Albert Pike and Colonel C. F. M. Noland of Arkansas.

Prominent among the humorous writers from the upper South were Joseph G. Baldwin, who emigrated from Virginia to the lower South during the flush times of the 1830's; George W.

Bagby, editor of the *Southern Literary Messenger* at Richmond; Hamilton C. Jones and Harden E. Taliaferro of North Carolina; and George Washington Harris, whose bold and earthy descriptions of the mountain whites of east Tennessee remind one of the pictures of Thomas Hart Benton such as "I got a Gal on Sourwood Mountain" and "In the Ozarks." The humor of the Old South found its most powerful expression in Harris's *Sut Lovingood's Yarns*. Unfortunately, the difficult dialect and the extreme realism of his work have hampered its popularity.

The creator of Sut Lovingood, after having long been neglected, has come in recent years to be regarded as the most original and imaginative of the Southern humorists. Born in Allegheny City, Pennsylvania, in 1814, he spent the formative years of his life in Knoxville and east Tennessee. Here he became a Jack-of-all-trades, never able to make much money from a succession of jobs; he was apprentice to a jeweler, farmer in the foothills of the Great Smokies, steamboat captain, railroad man, sawmill manager, and postmaster of Knoxville. Though many of the humorists were Whigs, he was a Democrat, an ardent secessionist, and a sympathizer with the common people. His writings are full of vivid pictures of the common folk—an old mountain lady with a pipe in her mouth standing by her ash hopper, a poor white riding on a bull with a saddle made with forks of dogwood, a hypocritical circuit rider who guzzled bald-face liquor, a Yankee razor-grinder cheating the gullible country folk, and mountain people dancing at a Tennessee frolic. His rich imagery is homely, almost Chaucerian in freshness, and redolent of the Southern countryside.

Some of these writers, by virtue of their background, held a position of detachment from the plantation culture. Dr. Henry Clay Lewis, who wrote *Odd Leaves from the Life of a Louisiana Swamp Doctor* under the name "Madison Tensas," was of part Jewish origin and though born in South Carolina, described himself as "a Southerner by adoption." He could make fun of the pretensions of the plantation aristocracy in such delineations as the "Man of Aristocratic Diseases." Writers such as Lewis, being outside of the aristocratic culture, could appreciate the antithesis between the folk culture and the culture of the colonnaded mansion.

A considerable number of writers who described the humorous aspects of Southern yeomen were Northerners who resided in the South. William Tappan Thompson, the creator of "Major Jones," was born in Ravenna, Ohio, and worked on Northern newspapers until he came to Georgia, where he was given a job by Longstreet on his *State Rights' Sentinel,* and later he founded the Savannah *Morning News.* Thomas Bangs Thorpe emigrated from Massachusetts in 1836 to Louisiana, where he worked as a portrait painter and journalist. John S. Robb, a journalist on the staff of the St. Louis *Reveille* who wrote *Streaks of Squatter Life,* was born in Philadelphia. Albert Pike was a native of Boston and attended Harvard College before he settled in Arkansas in 1832 to become an editor, lawyer, diplomat, and commander of an Indian brigade in the Confederate Army. William T. Porter of Vermont, who founded *The Spirit of the Times,* a sporting and humorous magazine of New York City, was the great encourager of the Southern humorists by publishing their stories in his periodical. In the 1850's the connection of the Southern humorists with Porter's magazine was one of the few friendly links between North and South.

The writers who exploited the vein of Southern humor were chiefly journalists seeking to enliven the pages of their newspapers by local anecdotes, or lawyers who entertained each other on the circuit by swapping stories. They collected tales and gave them literary form, and they described comic happenings of the yeomen and crackers. These anecdotes originated in village taverns, livery stables, barrooms, or at the campfires of wagoners and hunters; they represented a different standard of stories, as Shields McIlwaine has pointed out, from the type of polite and witty anecodotes told in the parlors and on the verandahs of the planters' homes. The former brand of humor bore the unmistakable stamp of the common man, having frequently evolved from the practical joking of the frontier. It had an earthy tang and was characterized by broad farce—a bull playing havoc with a quilting party, the antics of a preacher when some lizards were placed in his trousers, or the comedy arising from a horse swap in Georgia.

Despite the place of honor which romantic literature held in the estimation of Southerners, these amusing stories of low life were keenly relished. This Rabelaisian taste was indicated by the fact that ten editions of *Georgia Scenes* were printed before 1860, and *Major Jones's Courtship* appealed to such a wide circle of readers that it ran through eleven editions. Furthermore, some of the most droll personalities of the Old South—notably the plebeian Governor "Zeb" Vance of North Carolina, Judge Dooley of Georgia, and "Lean Jimmy" Jones, who defeated James K. Polk for governor in 1841—remained storytellers and wits who never committed their humor to the printed page.

From the pages of the Southern humorists we gain our most vivid descriptions of the appearance of the poor whites and of the crackers—a term often used to describe the upland farmers of Georgia as well as the poor whites. On court days they would come into the somnolent villages of the South, driving two-wheeled carts pulled by mules, bony horses, or oxen which they guided by a rope around their horns, and cracking their long whips. In the morning they seemed to be the most harmless individuals on earth; "their bilious-looking eyes, and tanney, shrivelled faces . . . wore a meek and pensive expression," according to *Major Jones's Chronicles of Pineville*. But towards noon, after they had imbibed heavily of bald-face corn liquor, a transformation occurred. "Then might be seen the cadaverous looking wiregrass boy in his glory, as he leaped out into the sand before the door, and tossing his linsey jacket into the air, proclaimed himself the best man in the country. Then, too, might be seen the torpid clay-eater, his bloated, watery countenance illuminated by the exhilarating qualities of Mr. Harley's rum, as he closed in with his antagonist," cursing, biting, and gouging.

The gregarious nature of the yeomen found an outlet in numerous social gatherings in which they combined work with pleasure. Their sports and amusements were an especially rich field for comic delineation. These diversions were mainly an outgrowth of frontier conditions. In the less developed sections of the South, as well as north of the Ohio River, wrestling matches and rude fights took place that were completely devoid of chivalry. The victor would jump up on a stump and crow like a cock, flapping his arms. Or he would boast: "I'm the yellow blossom of the forest; I'm kin to a rattlesnake on the mother's side; I'm the stepfather of the yearth; I'm a lion with a mangy

Augustus B Longstreet

Augustus Baldwin Longstreet, Georgia humorist.

tail, a bear with a sore head, a flying whale." A distinctive sport of the Southern backwoods was gander pulling, in which the contestant galloping on horseback, sought to pull off the head and neck of a well-greased gander hung high on a pole. The yeomen of Georgia indulged in a drinking game called "Bingo," in which gallons of liquor were consumed to the accompaniment of a song that began, "A farmer's dog sat on the barn-door and Bingo was his name, O!"

The tremendous vitality and optimism of Southern yeomen often found expression in tall stories with a Baron Munchausen flavor. Franklin J. Meine has collected some of these extravagant stories in his *Tall Tales of the Southwest*. This type of humor was especially prevalent on the frontier where the mysteries of an undiscovered country and the bigness of the mountains and the prairies excited the imagination. But the tall tale also flourished in the interior regions of the South. Harden E. Taliaferro has related some of these impossible stories which he heard in the back country of North Carolina in *Fisher's River Scenes and Characters*. There were stories of marvelous snakes that took their tails in their mouths and rolled along like a hoop, of people who ate impossible quantities of peaches or watermelons, of magical trees that grew so fast that a horse who was hitched to a branch was hoisted high into the sky, of incredible fights with catamounts, and of bears that displayed human sauciness and sagacity. Finally, there were ghost stories such as those which the superstitious old hatter told Joel Chandler Harris when he was a small boy on the Joseph Turner plantation near Eatonville, Georgia.

A peculiar quality of Southern yeomen humor was its emphasis on what Professor Alphonso Smith called "the humor of discomfiture." This laughter at the painful or embarrassing predicaments of others probably arose out of the practical joking of the frontier. Good examples of such roistering humor are to be found in the Sut Lovingood tales, such as "Bart Davis's Dance" and "Sicily Burns's Wedding," or the drover's tale related by Olmsted in his travel account *A Journey Through Texas*.

From the reports of travelers in the antebellum South we gain the impression that the poor whites, unlike the yeomen, were lacking in humor. The conditions of life were so hard for them, especially in the mountain regions, that they developed a fatalistic melancholy. James Lane Allen has described the unchanged mountaineers of Kentucky: "eyes with a slow long look of mild enquiry, or of general listlessness, or of unconcious and unaccountable melancholy; the key of life a low minor strain, losing itself in reverie, voices monotonous in intonation; movements uniformed by nervousness."

The ignorance and provincialism of these secluded people were a frequent theme of the humorist. "McAlpin's Trip to Charleston" by Hamilton C. Jones, for example contrasts the openmouthed naiveté of the country greenhorn with the sophisticated culture of the city. The countryman who had seen the wonders of "Augusty," Georgia, was looked upon as a man of the world, and a plausible Yankee with a common school education like the politician Franklin Plummer was regarded in the backwoods of Mississippi as a walking encyclopedia. The suspicion about city people entertained by the yeomen was portrayed in numerous stories, such as T. S. Lane's "The Thimble Game," and Thompson's *Major Jones's Sketches of Travel.*

One of the most valuable pictures of the rusticity of the natives is given by Johnson J. Hooper in "Taking the Census," a story based on his experience as a census enumerator in 1840. The old ladies in the rural districts of Alabama confronted the enumerators with grim countenances and with the threat of "setting the dogs on ye" for prying into such personal affairs as, "How many chickens have you?" and "How much cloth have you woven?" The government of Washington was regarded by the country people in these isolated sections of the South almost as an alien enemy.

Southern humorists presented the daughters and wives of the farmers and the poor whites in a realistic light, quite different from the romantic halo cast over the ladies of the gentry by the novelists. The humorists portrayed cracker women engaged in quite unladylike practices like fighting; they pulled out hair and scratched faces, dipped snuff, chewed tobacco, and smoked corncob pipes. The young doctor Henry Clay Lewis ("Madison Tensas") found on his first visit into the swamp country of Louisiana to attend a farmer's wife that the neighbors believed the hoot of an owl to be an omen of death. A favorite theme of the humorists was the embarassment of travelers who spent the night in a yeoman's crowded log cabin and had to go to bed in the presence of the female members of the family. The daughters of the farmers were usually modest girls, who became speechless before strangers and blushed deeply. The farmers' womenfolk were gullible patrons of Yankee peddlers, who sold them ribbons, pins, needles, nutmegs, clocks, and bustles. "Mike Hooter's" daughter in the backwoods of Mississippi did not have the money to buy a bustle—the latest in fashions—so she improvised one by tying a thick sausage under her dress. At a camp meeting when one end of the sausage came loose, she thought that the dangling object was a snake climbing up her leg; accordingly, she writhed with fear instead of with religious ecstasy.

The religion of the cracker was dramatized in the camp meeting, a method of soul-saving that gave spice to an otherwise monotonous rural life. Consequently the camp meeting holds a prominent place in Southern humor. A most realistic description of the emotional extravagance that often accompanied these religious gatherings is given in Hooper's *Some Adventures of Captain Simon Suggs, Late Captain of the Tallapoosa Volunteers.* The Captain stood on the outskirts of a great crowd of people at the Sandy Creek camp meeting in Alabama and coolly observed this mass of humanity in the throes of religious excitement. A half dozen preachers, serving in relays, were exhorting their audience, terrifying them with their somber theology and loud raucous voices. On the outer circle Negroes were singing, screaming, and praying with primitive African vehemence. Delicate women had become hysterical, so that their nerves played strange tricks known as "the jerks" or "the holy laugh"—a phenomenon that was terrifying because it resembled a maniac's chuckle. Some of the men wore a hideous grin; others were barking like dogs; while still others were shouting "Gl-o-ree!" In front of the mourner's bench the ground was covered with straw, upon which the converts were rolling in religious ecstasy or lay swooning upon each other in promiscuous heaps.

In sketching the political mores of the yeomen and crackers, the humorists emphasized their violent partisanship and their susceptibility to the arts of the demagogue. The autobiography of David Crockett tells how he won his elections by treating the

voters liberally to liquor and amusing them with his folksy
humor. On one occasion he defeated an opponent with a devastating smile by comparing him to a grinning coon. Crockett
then boasted of his own prowess in killing coons by outgrinning
them. Any sign of aristocracy exhibited by a candidate was a
distinct handicap in winning the votes of the "sovereigns." John
S. Robb's story of "The Standing Candidate" presents an old
Missouri squatter named "Sugar" who appeared at all elections
to the legislature as the standing candidate to represent Nianga
County. He always came equipped with a jug of homemade
whiskey and a bag of brown sugar. After one of the opposing
candidates had paid him generously for his liquor supply, he
would then make a speech yielding his claim to office to his
patron until the next election. When a fastidious candidate refused to drink his mixture of whiskey and brown sugar (a rustic
old-fashioned), he held up the unfortunate man to ridicule:
"He's got an *a*-ristocracy stomach, and can't go the *native-licker*."

The Southern yeomen and poor whites, indeed, were strong
advocates of democracy—a white democracy. They immediately resented any assumption of superiority of one class over
another. An amusing story illustrating this trait is told in Thomas
D. Clark's *The Rampaging Frontier*. John C. Breckinridge and
Robert Letcher were traveling together through eastern Kentucky in 1852, stump speaking as candidates for Congress. Letcher would make a short speech to "the sovereigns," and then
while his rival spoke would play his fiddle nearby. The lively
music invariably drained off the auditors of Breckinridge until
only a handful of followers resisted the lure. Finally the wily
Breckinridge concocted a scheme that ruined his musical opponent. At the next meeting, when Letcher began to play, a lank
fellow wearing a coonskin cap, yelled out, "Why don't you fiddle
with that t'other hand o'yourn?"

"T'other hand!" shouted the hillbillies.

Letcher, who was left-handed, became deeply embarrassed.
The man with the coonskin cap continued to roar: "T'other hand!
We've heard about you! You fiddle down thar in that d——n
Bluegrass country, 'mong rich folks, with your right hand and
think when you git up in the hills 'mong pore folks, left-hand

fiddlin's good enuf for us; you've cussedly missed it. Left-hand doin's won't run up hyar."

Indeed, the most notable trait that distinguished the Southern yeomen from European peasants was a conviction of the equality of all white men. This frontier attitude never disappeared from the great middle class of the South, a virtue that was perpetuated by the rise of Jacksonian democracy. John Basil Lamar's humorous story "Polly Peablossom's Wedding" caught the authentic spirit of this movement. At the wedding when the preacher failed to appear and a squire was asked to perform the ceremony, Mrs. Peablossom objected that "the quality" in her day in Duplin County, North Carolina, had a prejudice against being married by a magistrate. But old Mr. Peablossom remonstrated: "None of your Duplin County aristocracy about here, now. . . . Noth Ca'lina ain't the best state in the Union nohow. . . . *Quality*, eh! Who the devil's better than we are? An't we honest? An't we raised our children decent, and learned them how to read, write, and cipher? An't I *fout* under Newman and Floyd for the country? Why, darn it! We are the *very best* sort of people."

Southern yeomen had many virtues to balance against some of the ludicrous aspects of their rural lives. William Tappan Thompson paid a high tribute to their sterling qualities when he wrote in the preface to his *Chronicles of Pineville:* "As a class they are brave, generous, honest, and withal possessed by a sturdy patriotism. The vagabond and the dissolute among them are only the exceptions to the rule, and in a few generations more, education will have made the mass a great people." This prophecy was realized within two generations. During the building of the New South, the leadership in politics, in education, and in business was often taken over by the sons and the grandsons of yeomen.

The resemblances between the Southern yeomanry and the small farmers and villagers of the North were much greater than their differences. Major Jack Downing of Maine, whom Seba Smith created for his newspaper in 1830, has much in common with Major Jones of Pineville, Georgia. They belonged approximately to the same economic level, and they had that sturdy independence and fine disregard for class distinctions that were natively American. The Yankee farmer, however, was more likely to be thrifty and enterprising, with a down-East shrewdness that was caricatured in the stock figure of Sam Slick the clockmaker, whom Haliburton popularized. The Northern humorists of the antebellum period dealt more extensively with politics than did the Southern humorists, and they drew realistic pen pictures of female comic characters. There is no character in antebellum Southern humor to correspond to Mrs. Partington or to the Widow Bedott, those garrulous old New England ladies whom Shillaber and Whitcher portrayed so skillfully.

How far does the picture of poor whites and yeomen drawn by Southern humorists correspond to reality? With respect to the relative numbers of the poor whites, they did not exaggerate, as did the abolitionists. Contrary to the abolitionist stereotype, the poor whites formed only the shabby fringe of Southern society—not the mass of whites. When Governor Henry A. Wise of Virginia addressed the legislature in 1856, he estimated that 10 per cent of the children of the state belonged to families too poor to pay for elementary schooling. In South Carolina Governor Hammond estimated that the poor whites composed 20 per cent of the whole white population.

The humorists did not realize, however, that the degraded condition of the poor whites was largely owing to their environment and the enervating diseases which beset them. Living in the isolated and infertile areas of the South—the sand hills of Carolina and Georgia, the piney woods of the coastal plain, and the mountainous areas—the poor whites were primarily hunters and fishermen; many of them were squatters like Sam Bostwick in Simms's novel *Woodcraft*. Despite their poverty, the "crackers" and the "piney woods folk" had a striking personal pride. As the Northern traveler Frederick Law Olmsted observed in 1853, they would not deign to engage themselves to the planters to do menial work—wait on tables, carry water, bring wood, black boots, cut hair, drive a coach. Such was "nigger's work," as they phrased it.

The yeomen were often confused with the poor whites by contemporary travelers and even by native writers. They judged from appearances, for many of the independent farmers lived in log cabins that were no better than the dwellings of the poor whites. The yeomen dressed in homespun or blue jeans, and their cattle and hogs were frequently hidden in the woods where they grazed. Yet there was a real difference—not merely in material possessions, but in spirit—between the yeomen and the poor whites. The true poor white was a creature like Ransy Sniffle in Longstreet's story "The Fight" in *Georgia Scenes* or the clay eater in Hooper's *The Widow Rugby's Husband.* Such a type was comparable to the slum element in the Northern states. Besides these people, who were often scattered in the interstices of the plantations, there were the mountain whites. These secluded people preserved the ways of their ancestors, the pioneers, without the spirit and hope of the pioneers. As Rupert Vance has observed, they represented the ebb of the frontier.

In their writings the humorists described both the yeomen and the poor whites and occasionally the tradesmen in small villages. It is sometimes difficult to distinguish in their work between the yeomen, frontiersmen, and poor whites, for the classes shaded into each other. The small farmers and the villagers, in contradistinction to the poor whites, were respectable citizens forming the bulk of the population of the South. Thomas Bangs Thorpe has drawn an attractive portrait of a member of this class in "The Big Bear of Arkansas." This mighty teller of tall tales was a man in the prime of his life, enjoying perfect health and contentment: "his eyes were as sparkling as diamonds, and good-natured to simplicity. Then his perfect confidence in himself was irresistibly droll." Representative specimens of the yeomen class were sympathetically portrayed by Lamar in "Polly Peablossom's Wedding" and by Thompson in *Major Jones's Courtship.*

The humorists do not appear to have realized the importance of the middle class of small farmers. Daniel R. Hundley of Alabama, who studied at Harvard and the University of Virginia, was one of the first writers to recognize the significance of the yeoman class in the social structure of the Old South. In 1860 he published a pioneer study of Southern society entitled *Social Relations in Our Southern States,* in which he combated the abolitionist stereotype of Southern society as consisting of only three classes—planters, poor whites, and slaves. On the contrary, he maintained, its society was composed of five classes, of which the yeoman farmer constituted a large and important element.

Hundley noted some of the distinguishing characteristics of

this class—their independent and democratic spirit, their industriousness, and their warmhearted hospitality. He observed that yeomen who owned slaves worked side by side with them in the fields, treating them with great kindness, almost as equals; these slaves were often allowed to call their masters by their first or Christian names and both ate the same fare.

The yeomen of the South, Hundley maintained, were much like Northern middle-class farmers, fully as intelligent though not as sophisticated as the tradesmen and mechanics in the cities. They were superior to their counterparts in the North in handling the rifle, judging the quality of liquor and brandy (for they brewed or distilled their own), and in a grasp of politics, which they acquired not from newspapers but from public speakings, barbecues, and the talk of county courthouse gatherings. In confutation of Frederick Law Olmsted's criticism of Southern hospitality, Hundley cited the testimony of a Connecticut mechanic whom he had met. This man, thrown out of work by the panic of 1857, had traveled penniless through the South seeking employment and had found a warm welcome in the homes of the farmers along his route.

The yeomen who moved into the villages and became artisans or tradesmen retained the characteristics of their former rural life with its democratic spirit and sense of equality. The Scottish wool carder William Thomson who traveled in the Southern states in 1840–42 seeking employment reported that the mechanics and tradesmen in the South, unlike their class in Great Britain, considered themselves as "men of honour"; they resented any indignity that might be shown them "even at the expense of their life, or that of those who venture to insult them."

The humorists' view of the yeomen gives no indication of the most important economic fact about them—namely, that a very large proportion of them owned their farms. According to studies made by Professor Frank L. Owsley and his students at Vanderbilt in the 1940's, approximately 80 per cent of the farmers of the South in the decade 1850–60 owned the lands they tilled. This economic stake in society, as well as the wide participation of the people in their government after the emergence of the Jacksonian movement, made the Southern yeomen one of the freest and most independent groups in the world.

The independent spirit of the Southern yeoman and his outlook on life are reflected in a rare manuscript diary kept by a small farmer of Mississippi between 1838 and 1846. The diarist, Ferdinand L. Steel, was born in 1813 in Fayetteville, North Carolina. When he was fifteen years old his family moved to western Tennessee; Steel worked on his father's farm there, helped in his father's trade as hatter, and worked on river steamboats. At the time of his diary, he was farming near Grenada, Mississippi. His silence on the subject of slavery and his slight reference to politics suggest that to the yeoman farmer these subjects were much less important than were the practical concerns of earning a living.

Steel's diary portrays the rather primitive frontier life characteristic of small farmers of the lower Mississippi Valley throughout the antebellum period. The Steel family was largely self-sufficient; Ferdinand made shoes for himself, his brother, and his sister Julia; the mother and Julia made their dresses as well as the shirts and "pantiloons" for the men. They manufactured their own lye soap, fashioned gourds into dippers, and the farmers' wives and daughters spun and wove cotton into cloth. They often concocted their medicines from herbs and roots. When Ferdinand contracted malaria, for example, he treated himself with boneset tea, although he also used quinine and calomel bought from the store in Grenada. The principal commodities the family purchased from the village store were sugar, coffee, salt, calico and domestic cloth, powder and lead. The diary records a surprising and seemingly needless expense of buying bacon from the store, but this occurred in the summer when the supply of meat from the eight or ten hogs they had killed in the fall must have been exhausted. Their accumulated store account for the year 1839 was only $73.78, which was paid after the sale of their cotton crop. Together with the sale of watermelons, their cotton crop brought a cash income of approximately $200.

Cotton was the money crop of the small Mississippi farmers, and the Steels raised five or six bales. Like most of the other small farmers, they used the gin of the near-by planter to prepare their cotton for market, paying a toll of one-eleventh; and when they took their wheat and corn to the mill, they also paid a toll. Ferdinand and his brother spent most of the fall picking cotton, on their best days picking as much as 120 pounds, an amount that was below the average of good slave hands. On several occasions

Steel expressed the opinion that cotton was not a suitable crop for the yeoman farmer to raise. Cultivating cotton required such constant labor that other farm occupations had to be neglected. On June 5, 1838, in reference to his cotton crop, he wrote: "We are to [sic] weak handed. We had better raise small grain and corn and let cotton alone, raise corn and keep out of debt and we will have no necessity of raising cotton." But he was never able to abandon the crop, which indeed was his principal source of cash.

A typical day's activities in the life of Steel (and the yeomen in general) is recorded in the diary on March 22, 1839:

I arise regularly at 5 o clock in the morning. After the rest of the family have arisen we have Prayers. I then feed 2 horses and with the assistance of my Brother milk 3 cows, from then to Breakfast I jenerally do some little job about the house. After breakfast I go to my regular work which is cultivating the soil, and work until 12 o clock at which time I come to dinner. Rest jenerally 2 hours, during which time I dine, then Pray to God and endeavor to improve my mind by some useful study. At 2 o clock I again repair to work until sun down. I then come in, feed horses milk cows, and then the days work is done. I sup and then I have a few hours for study, at 9 o clock we have prayers and then we all retire to Rest. This is the manner in which my time is spent. My Life is one of toil, but blessed be God that it is as well with me as it is.

The monotony of a life of farm toil was broken by visits to Grenada on Saturday afternoons. There he met other farmers and made small purchases. He and his brother also hunted deer and wild ducks and searched for wild bees' hives to obtain honey. He attended a celebration of the Fourth of July in Grenada, at which there was a reading of the Declaration of Independence, an oration, a "sumtious" feast, cold water toasts, and the taking of temperance pledges. He belonged to a temperance society in Grenada that had 181 members. On December 25, 1845, he left a Christmas party early because the young people were engaged in "the silly play of marching Down to New-Orleans." He had no relish, he comments, for such nonsense: "I feel thankful to God that he has, by his holy Spirit, inclined my heart to abhor that which will not tend to his glory." He enjoyed going to a singing school and concerts in the Methodist church. The principal occasions for sociability and rude amusement among the frontier farmers were log rollings, corn shuckings, and communal work on the public roads, in which Steel participated.

Steel's diary gives a remarkable view of the religion of the common man of the Old South. Steel was a devout Methodist who frequently attended various religious services—Sunday School, preaching, and especially the exciting camp meetings which often lasted a week. These meetings were held in the summer after the cultivation of the crops was completed. After coming from such a meeting, he wrote in his diary, August 13, 1841, "My Faith increases, & I enjoy much of that peace which the world cannot give; Blessed be God for the blessed hope of being free from Sin while I lived on Earth, & for the blessed anticipation of living in heaven, O Lord!" At another time after attending the quarterly meeting of the Methodist Church at Coffeeville he reported: "We had a happy time in Love feast on Sunday morning. Brother Sullivan our Itinerant preacher professed Sanctification and truly he seem'd a happy man. The people of Coffeeville were truly kind. O! how is the Religion of the Lord Jesus Calculated to make mankind sociable." He often engaged in "secret prayer" and strove to live free from sin so as to be ready to die. Untimely deaths in the community and funerals admonished him to be "ready," for "surely in the midst of life we are in death." Yet these gloomy thoughts in the diary were relieved by a note of gratitude to God for his temporal life. He displayed a strong belief in the justness of mysterious Providence, even when disasters such as a long drought came. Mingled with his unworldly religion were some folk superstitions—when a calf died after being altered, he attributed this misfortune to performing the operation in the wrong time of the moon. The religion of Ferdinand Steel was that of the common people of the Old South—full of humility, deprecating the worldly life, and believing in the literal word of the Bible as revealed religion. Tinged with the romanticism of the period, this religion of the plain people was highly emotional—Steel, for example, speaks of the Lord melting his heart to tenderness.

The most striking aspect of the diary is its revelation of Steel's ardent desire for self-improvement and his ambition to rise in the world. Forced to quit school early, he resolved to make up this deficiency by self-education. Accordingly, he procured an English grammar and a Latin grammar at the village store and devised a method of attaching his Latin grammar to his plow so that he could study it as he worked. He borrowed books from the Sunday School

library and read the eight volumes of Rollins' history, the life of
Martin Luther, Blackstone's *Commentaries on the Law of England,*
Jones' chemistry, a Greek grammar that enabled him to translate
the book of St. John in the Greek Testament, and Abercrombie's
"The Intellectual Powers," which taught him rules of logic and
correct thinking. It was a heroic schedule of long hours of study
carried on despite adverse circumstances. Moreover, he helped his
sister Julia acquire some education by paying her tuition with hog
meat raised on the farm. Eventually, the serious young farmer
became an itinerant Methodist preacher. The record he left in his
diary contributes significantly to the opinion of the respectability
of the large class of yeoman farmers of the Old South held by the
modern revisionists.

The writings of the humorists, who made fun of the yeomen
and poor whites indiscriminately, do not mirror the relatively un-
stratified and fluid society of the South in the antebellum period.
This condition was partly owing to the constant emigration of the
slaveless farmers, especially to western lands. There were some
exceptions to the generally democratic organization of antebellum
Southern society, particularly in the low country of South Carolina,
among the "cotton snobs" of the black belt of Alabama and
Mississippi, in the delta country of the Mississippi Valley, and in
several enclaves of aristocracy in Virginia and Maryland.

Numerous examples could be cited of how easy it was for an
energetic and intelligent yeoman to rise high in Southern society,
but one of the most interesting was the career of David L. Swain
of North Carolina. This son of a hatter, small farmer, and postmaster of Asheville had a precocious and phenomenal success. He
was an unusually tall, ugly, and bumbling youth when he attended the academy in Asheville. Benjamin F. Perry, who was
his classmate, has left this description of him: "He was six feet
two inches in height, slender and ill-shaped, with a long pale
face, thick lips, sharp nose, and dull expression of the eyes. The
boys all loved him most affectionately. He was an accomplished
Latin and Greek scholar, and took great pleasure in reading for
the younger students any hard sentence which they came across
in their lessons. I remember with what pleasure I listened to his
reading of Homer, with a sort of musical drawl, that to me, was
sweet and charming."

Young Swain either did not have the money to attend the University of North Carolina longer than four months or he was too eager to enter a career in law and politics to stay for a degree. After being admitted to the bar in 1822 he represented Buncombe County in the legislature. Within a few years he was appointed a superior court judge and at the age of thirty-one was elected governor of the state. He proved to be a great liberal and constructive leader. A powerful figure in the constitutional convention of 1835, he advocated complete religious toleration in respect to the holding of state office, popular election of the governor, and a fair apportionment of representation in the legislature to heal the bitter sectional controversy between the western and eastern sections of the state. Also he opposed the disfranchisement of free Negroes.

In 1835 he was chosen by the trustees to become the second president of the University of North Carolina, a position that he held until his death in 1868. He taught law, history, and moral science in the university and did much to make that institution popular throughout the state. His manuscript diary in the Southern Collection at Chapel Hill reveals that he was a very religious man who constantly sought to educate himself by reading and observation. Particularly did he have a strong interest in the colonial history of North Carolina, which led him to do research in the manuscript papers of the colonial governors. Though he owned slaves, he seems to have emancipated himself from many of the illiberal prejudices of his society, and in 1860–61 he was one of the strong Union leaders of the state. David L. Swain was a living demonstration of the open society of the Old South. It was open to the movement of poor boys upward to wealth and leadership of the state, but it was closed to any criticism of its fundamental way of life, as the career of Hinton Rowan Helper demonstrates.

Chapter VIII

SPOKESMAN FOR THE NON-SLAVEHOLDERS

A S THE Civil War approached, the non-slaveholding men of the South began to show some signs of class consciousness. Such realization of class interest as existed in this group, however, was inarticulate and was intimately tied up with intrastate sectionalism. The antagonism of the Piedmont farmers and mountaineers toward the lowland planters was so identified with various sectional grievances that it is virtually impossible to separate class feeling in the Old South from sectional prejudice. On one issue, nevertheless—the taxation of slave property—class divisions were most clear-cut and articulate. In North Carolina a public-spirited slaveholder, Moses Bledsoe of Wake County, in 1856 led the non-slaveholders in a movement to tax all property, slaves as well as land, *ad valorem.* Four years later John Pool, the gubernatorial candidate of the Whigs, whose strength lay in the Piedmont and mountain counties, waged his campaign largely on the issue of the adoption of the *ad valorem* principle of taxation.

In western Virginia and other regions of the South where the hold of slavery was weak there were also rumblings of discontent on the eve of the Civil War against the favoritism shown by the state governments toward slave property. Bitter protests arose not only against the unfair distribution of the tax burden but also against the requirement of non-slaveholders to perform patrol duty; against the levying of taxes in Virginia to support the Public Guard at the capitol, which had been established to suppress slave insurrections; and against the taxation of non-slaveholders to recompense masters for the loss of criminal slaves who were executed.

Thus, there were latent grievances held by the non-slaveholders against the ruling planter class, wrongs which lay ready for some bold agitator to protest and dramatize. Lying deep beneath the surface of the consciousness of the poor whites and yeomen, north as well as south of the Mason-Dixon Line, was a negrophobia partly irrational and partly economic in origin. The principal agitator in the South who attempted to exploit this reservoir of ill-will as well as legitimate grievances was Hinton Rowan Helper of North Carolina, author of the revolutionary book *The Impending Crisis of the South and How to Meet It.* Helper's career as an agitator against Southern slavery was motivated not by the slightest humanitarian feeling toward the Negro but by his deep sympathy for the non-slaveholding class.

Born in Davie County in the Piedmont region of North Carolina in 1829, Helper came from German ancestors who had changed their name. Although his father owned a few slaves, the family belonged to the yeomanry of the South, not to the debased "poor whites." After graduating from an academy in Mocksville, he clerked in a store in nearby Salisbury. He was accused of embezzling three hundred dollars from his employer, a charge which he later admitted. In 1850 he went to New York, where he took passage on a ship bound for the gold fields of California. After three years of struggle he returned to the East disillusioned and penniless. In 1855 the disappointed gold seeker published a book about California entitled *The Land of Gold, or Romance Unveiled,* in which he displayed the same tendency toward broad generalization and extreme overstatement that characterized his later books.

Incidents connected with the publication of this book started him on his career as an antislavery crusader. It was published in Baltimore by the same firm that printed the ardently proslavery *Southern Quarterly Review*. The publisher objected to certain passages in the manuscript that made unfavorable comparisons between slavery and free labor, and forced the author to delete them before he would publish the manuscript. This censorship aroused the combative nature of Helper and led him to write *The Impending Crisis*. In a book that he published fourteen years later, *Noonday Exigencies in America*, Helper maintained that he had written his famous attack on slavery because the freedom of the press below the Mason-Dixon Line was suppressed, and he was determined to present his views on the evils of Southern slavery.

He composed *The Impending Crisis* in North Carolina and Baltimore and took it with him to New York to secure a publisher. When he applied to several established publishing houses, including Harpers, they refused to have anything to do with a book that might injure their Southern trade. Finally he persuaded a New York book agent, A. B. Burdick, to bring it out in June, 1857, on condition that the author would stand the financial responsibility for it.

The Impending Crisis was an attack on Southern slavery primarily from an economic point of view. It completely ignored any other factor but slavery as a cause of the backward condition of the South. To discredit the "peculiar institution" the author used a technique that other Southern antislavery men before him had employed, namely, the arrangement of census statistics to show that though formerly the Southern states were superior to the Northern states in many things, they had as a result of slavery declined to a relatively inferior status, except in politics. As early as 1841 Daniel R. Goodloe, a North Carolina printer, had published an attack on slavery entitled *Causes Which Have Retarded the Accumulation of Wealth and Increase of Population in the Southern States*, in which he used this technique of economic comparisons of slave and free states. Dr. Henry Ruffner, president of Washington College at Lexington, Virginia, in 1847 had published an *Address to the People of West Virginia Shewing that Slavery is Injurious to the Public Welfare*, which anticipated Helper in its similar manner of attack on the institution of Southern slavery. Both Goodloe and Ruffner were moderate and reasonable in their antislavery arguments.

It was Helper's peculiar contribution, on the other hand, to present the record of census statistics of the South in the most extreme and spectacular form, by a process of partisan selection and omission. He made the startling assertion, for example, that the hay crop of the Northern states was more valuable than the combined staple crops of the South—cotton, tobacco, sugar, rice, and hemp. Northern *dried grass*, not cotton, he announced, was king. He ignored the warm climate in the lower South which enabled livestock to graze throughout the year on green grass; moreover, the large corn crop raised in the South furnished abundant fodder so that it was used largely as a substitute for hay. Nevertheless, he sought by this striking illustration and other loaded statistics to prove that the South was far behind the North in that area of economic activity in which she boasted of superiority—agriculture.

Furthermore, he demonstrated from the census statistics the great inferiority of the South to the Northern states in numerous other categories—imports and exports, manufactures, railroad mileage, bank capital, and wealth. He failed to mention facts that were favorable to the Southern states—that they provided three-fourths of United States exports to Europe (thus largely furnishing the exchange needed to purchase European goods) and that the rate of growth of railroads in the South during the last decade of the antebellum period was greater than that of the Northern states. He correctly pointed out, however, that the South was economically dependent on the North for manufactured articles, which forced Southern merchants to buy their stock of goods in the great Northern cities. From the census of 1850 he also showed that the slave states were greatly inferior to the North in all cultural indexes—literacy, schools, colleges, libraries, newspapers, post office operations, and number of books published.

As to literature, Helper maintained that the South had produced virtually none. Indeed, Southerners read so few books and periodicals in 1857 that the head of Harper Brothers, the most prominent of Northern publishers, estimated that only 20 per cent of all their publications, including *Harper's Magazine* and

Harper's Weekly found a market in the slave states. From Duyc-kink's *Cyclopedia of American Literature* he arrived at the con-clusion that while 403 American authors had been born in the Northern states, only eighty-seven were natives of the slave states. Among the important causes of "the literary pauperism" of the South, he concluded, were the illiteracy of the people, the lack of educational opportunities (even Southern colleges as a whole, he asserted, were colleges in name only and would not rank with a third-rate Northern academy), and the evil effects of slavery, which inhibited freedom of mind and expression.

The most appealing and generous part of his book was the chapter entitled "Southern Testimony against Slavery." Here he quoted from letters and writings of the great Virginia statesmen who condemned Southern slavery—Washington, Jefferson, Pat-rick Henry, George Mason, Madison, and John Randolph of Roanoke. Especially effective were his quotations from the young Virginians of the following generation who spoke in the legisla-ture of 1831–32 in favor of the emancipation of the slaves in their state. He gave a long extract from the speech of Charles James Faulkner, in which the young legislator maintained that since slavery was a public nuisance, the state government had no ob-ligation to compensate the owners of slaves who were emanci-pated by the state. Helper observed that the liberal Southerners such as Jefferson, Washington, and Madison had supported the principles of the modern Republican party, a party to which he would give his vote.

The true policy of the South, he asserted in several places in *The Impending Crisis,* was to abolish slavery immediately. He thus seemed to accept the program of the radical abolitionists of the Garrison and Weld type. Yet the plan which he outlined for eradicating slavery did not call for the abolition of the entrenched institution at one stroke. By "the immediate abolition of slavery" he seems to have meant that steps should be taken promptly for the eventual abolition of the institution in the Southern states. His concrete proposals contained both sound and utterly imprac-ticable measures. He advocated first the thorough organization of the non-slaveholders into a political party and then the calling of a convention of non-slaveholders from all the slave states to de-liberate on a plan of speedy abolition of slavery. He proposed the elimination of slaveholders from politics by making them ineligible to hold office and by a stern boycott of slaveholding merchants, lawyers, hotel keepers, ministers, and editors. Emancipation should be accomplished by a tax on slaveholders of sixty dollars for each slave they held, the money to be used to colonize the freed blacks in Liberia or Central or South America; and after July 4, 1863, an annual tax of forty dollars per slave should be imposed on all masters who continued to hold slaves.

The masters were not to be compensated for the loss of their human chattels, because they were guilty of maintaining a nuisance. He contended that by fastening slavery on the South the planters had caused an enormous property loss to the non-slaveholders. His argument rested on his statistics that the average value of land per acre in the Northern states in 1850 was $28.07, while in the Southern states it was only $5.34. He declared, "emancipate your slaves on Wednesday morning, and on the Thursday following the value of your lands, and ours [the non-slaveholders] too, will have increased to an average of at least $28.07 per acre."

The invidious comparisons that Helper made in his book between the free and slave states were not what aroused the greatest intolerance in the South. Rather, the book contained some violent sentences that might fairly be interpreted as incendiary, tending to encourage the slaves to murder their masters. The author declared (on p. 149) that the Negroes "in nine cases out of ten would be delighted with an opportunity to cut their masters' throats," and join an army of the non-slaveholders against the slaveholders and their allies, the hirers of slaves, whom he dubbed "lickspittles." He modified this sanguinary statement, however, by saying that he hoped the issue would not come to a trial of arms but would be decided by the ballot box.

Also highly inflammatory were his attacks on the oligarchy of the slaveholders (whom he called "the lords of the lash") and his appeal to the non-slaveholders to arise, organize, and overthrow the control of the planters. He tried to convince the non-slaveholders that the institution of slavery was seriously injuring them and for that reason should be speedily abolished. The planters, he asserted, refused to support popular education because they wished to keep the non-slaveholding whites in "the grossest ignorance so that they might the more easily control them." Again and again he emphasized this point, declaring that the "unparalleled illiteracy and degradation" of the poor whites was "purposely and fiendishly" perpetuated by the planters. Thus they were able to control the government. They maintained their power as an oligarchy not only by keeping the common people in ignorance but by cajoling and flattering them by oratory and by bribery.

In his indictment of the slaveholding class he followed the abolitionist stereotype, which portrayed the planters as a haughty and immoral aristocracy and the masses of the Southern people as poor whites. He attributed far more of the Machiavellian spirit to the slaveholders than they possessed. Actually there was much democracy in the Old South—white democracy. Illiteracy among the poor whites was not the result of a deliberate plan but was owing primarily to the scattered population, the bad roads, and the apathy of the poor whites themselves to education. Moreover, Helper probably exaggerated the envy and ill feeling toward the planters which he maintained existed in the lower class. He seems never to have realized the importance of the great middle class of yeoman farmers, some of whom owned slaves or aspired to own them. By accepting the abolitionist image of the South, which his own observations must have belied, he exhibited a powerful tendency of mankind to think in terms of dominant stereotypes.

The Impending Crisis did not attract much attention until Horace Greeley published a compendium of it in 1859. The Republican politicians saw in the promotion of its circulation an opportunity to appeal to the factory workers and small farmers of the North. Accordingly, a committee was organized in New York to raise money to print and circulate 100,000 copies of the compendium in Pennsylvania, New York, New Jersey, Illinois, Ohio, and Indiana. The agent selected to raise this fund was John C. Underwood of Virginia, who was hailed in the North as "a martyr to his political opinions," but was notorious in the South as an antislavery agitator. A native of New York, Underwood had emigrated to Virginia as a teacher, but after marrying a Southern woman who owned a large farm in Clarke County, he became a planter. In 1856 he had attended the Republican convention that nominated John C. Frémont as the first Republican candidate for President. Describing himself as "a delegate from Virginia," he made an antislavery speech in the convention. For this "treason to the state," he was notified by a vigilance committee, headed by the famous Turner Ashby, that he would not be permitted to return to his community to live.

Republican sponsorship of the Helper book gave it a tremendous advertisement. Sixty-eight Republican congressmen, including John Sherman, candidate for speaker of the House of Representatives in 1859, endorsed it. During that autumn the whole country was deeply aroused over the John Brown invasion, and the South was in no mood to tolerate an endorser of *The Impending Crisis*. When Sherman's name was presented as candidate for the post of leader of the House, Representative John B. Clark of Missouri introduced a resolution that no man who had endorsed the Helper book was fit to preside over the House. Thereupon, a turbulent debate took place that lasted nearly two months, during which forty ballots were cast before Sherman withdrew his candidacy.

John Sherman's account of this celebrated affair, published in his autobiography in 1896, does no credit to the reputation either of himself or of Helper. In order to exculpate himself at the time of the election of the speaker, Sherman had read in Congress a letter to him from Frank Blair, Sr., dated December 6, 1859, in which Blair explained the Republican endorsement of *The Impending Crisis*. Helper, wrote Blair, had brought the book to him at Silver Spring, Maryland, to get him to recommend it to the leading Republicans. When the old Jacksonian editor objected to certain parts, Helper promised to omit or alter them in the proposed compendium, and upon this assurance the Republicans had agreed to endorse it. In his autobiography Sherman declared that he had never read either the original or the compendium and had no recollection of signing the endorsement. When the autobiography appeared in print, Helper wrote him a letter, stating that he alone had prepared the compendium of *The Impending Crisis*, that he had imbibed its general principles from the writings of Thomas Jefferson, and that he had refused to emasculate his work by eliminating from the compendium all the passages "that Tom and Dick and Harry and other wiseacres had objected to."

Actually, Helper, or the compiler of the compendium, omitted only a few statistics and several irrelevant paragraphs from the original work. To make up for these inconsequential omissions and to bring the book up to date, a chapter was added—"Testimony of Living Witnesses." Here the compiler included extracts from the speeches and writings of prominent Republican politicians, notably William H. Seward, John C. Frémont, Charles Sumner, and Henry Wilson; abolition leaders such as Garrison, Phillips, Weld, and Parker; journalists such as Greeley, Raymond, and Thurlow Weed; and antislavery men from the upper South, notably Cassius M. Clay, Daniel R. Goodloe, Frank Blair, Jr., Professor Benjamin S. Hedrick, and B. Gratz Brown, who was later prominent in founding the Liberal Republican party.

Thus, a freak of partisan politics catapulted an obscure young man, not yet thirty years old, into national prominence. The adoption of his book as a Republican campaign document was alone enough to arouse the deepest resentment against him in the South. Thereafter in some Southern states the circulation of *The Impending Crisis* became a criminal offense. In North Carolina the Reverend Daniel Worth, a Wesleyan preacher who was born in the state, was convicted in 1860 by the Guilford County Superior Court of the crime of circulating the obnoxious book and was sentenced to jail for a year. He appealed the case to the Supreme Court of the state, but it upheld the decision of the lower court. Justice Charles Manly in his written opinion held that "the expressed object of the book, as disclosed by the extracts, is to render the social condition of the South odious, and to put an end to that which is held up as the odious feature, by force and arms, if necessary."

In his preface Helper had expressed the hope that his "fellow-Southrons" would read his book and receive it in a "reasonable and friendly" spirit. He must have been extremely naive, for his attacks on the "slave oligarchy" and on Southern society were so violent that he defeated his purpose of attracting to his cause the non-slaveholders, many of whom could not read. As Jonathan Worth, the unionist leader and a first cousin of Daniel, observed,

"Nobody here will countenance the circulation of a book denouncing slave-holders as worse than thieves, murderers, etc."

There was one prominent Southerner who publicly recommended *The Impending Crisis*—Cassius Marcellus Clay. Speaking on the steps of the Capitol at Frankfort on January 10, 1860, Clay said that he had read it carefully and that there was not a single incendiary doctrine in it. He admitted, nevertheless, that it contained some foolish statements, particularly the proposal to abolish slavery by taxing the slaveholders exclusively on property to which they had a legitimate title.

John Hartwell Cocke also read the book and recommended it to his friends. One of them, Professor Lucian Minor of William and Mary College, replied on October 14, 1857: "Do not send me the Helper Book. I should not have time for more than a brief glance into it. What you say of its strange oscillations between sublimity and absurdity excites my curiosity to peep over some of its pages." Another correspondent, N. F. Cabell, wrote to Cocke: "From what you tell me of Mr. Helper's talk of Oligarchs & all that, I rather divine the school to which he belongs & hardly suppose that I shall agree with him either in premise or conclusion. I am not however afraid to read it."

Very different was the reaction of the Southern liberal Professor Benjamin Sherwood Hedrick, who had been dismissed from his position as professor of chemistry at the University of North Carolina because he had expressed his freesoil opinions during the presidential campaign of 1856. On December 14, 1858, he sent fifty dollars to William H. Anthon as a contribution toward publishing the compendium of *The Impending Crisis*. At the same time he wrote that Helper's book was a noble commentary on Judge William Gaston's antislavery address before the students of the University of North Carolina.

Though very few Southerners openly endorsed Helper's book, there was a small minority of leaders who sympathized with his desire to rid the South of slavery. In *The Impending Crisis* Helper listed the most prominent of these individuals, who were from the upper South only—Botts, Stuart, and Macfarland of Virginia; Rayner, Morehead, Stanley, Graves, and Graham of North Carolina; Davis and Hoffman of Maryland; Frank Blair, Jr. and Brown of Missouri; the Marshalls of Kentucky; and

Etheridge of Tennessee, all of whom were connected with politics. "All of these gentlemen, and many others of the same school," he wrote, "entertain, we believe, sentiments similar to those that were entertained by the immortal Fathers of the Republic— that slavery is a great moral, social, civil, and political evil to be got rid of at the earliest practicable period." He now urged them to show moral courage and come out frankly for the abolition of the pernicious institution.

After the fame of his first book had subsided, Helper's career became a long and sad anticlimax. Despite the enormous sale of *The Impending Crisis* and the compendium, he made little money from them. Unable to return with safety to the South, he remained in New York, where he attempted to earn money by lectures. A reporter of the New York *Herald* described his appearance on the lecture platform as that of a tall, slim, young man with short black hair and whiskers, a very bronzed complexion, and a countenance having "a fierce military expression." Surprisingly, his lecture tour was a complete failure. Sick and almost desperate for the need of money, he wrote to Hedrick from New York, April 20, 1861: "There is an immense number of cowards here and they are all afraid of me. Still, I incline to the opinion that late events are working somewhat in my favor and so I am managing to subsist on hope." He applied to President Lincoln in 1861 for an appointment as consul to one of the European countries, but Lincoln sent him to Buenos Aires. Here he served for five years, married an Argentine woman, and constantly importuned the State Department for a raise of salary.

When he returned to the United States, he resumed his occupation of writing extremist books, this time in a crusade to expel the Negroes from America. His curious works *Nojoque: a Question for a Continent* (1867) and *Negroes in Negroland* (1868) were dominated by a negrophobia fully as rabid as the hatred which the followers of Hitler displayed against the Jews. Indeed, he became so prejudiced against the Negro that he would not patronize any hotel, restaurant, or ice cream parlor in which Negro labor was employed. He also turned against the Radical Republicans because their reconstruction policy ignored the welfare of the white yeomanry and elevated the freedmen to political equality with white men.

Helper's latter years were consumed by a monomania over a project for an intercontinental railroad from Hudson Bay to the straits of Magellan. He spent the large sums which he had received for collecting American debts in South America in trying to realize this grandiose dream. In these tragic years he could be seen in the lobbies of Congress, in the hotels, and on the streets of Washington agitating for his pet project and expounding in dogmatic fashion his peculiar views, such as a belief that humanity was going to the dogs because of the vice of reading novels. A Kentucky newspaperman, Eugene W. Newman, saw Helper on one of these occasions talking to a group in a Washington hotel and has left a vivid description of him: "above six feet in height, straight as an arrow, and broad-shouldered as a giant, and long-armed as Rob Roy MacGreggor. His face wore the florid [look] of an Englishman, his eyes were sky-blue, and his hair [and beard were] white as cotton, but a vigorous white."

Another description of Helper in his old age has been given by Professor John Spencer Bassett of Smith College. Bassett expressed the opinion in a letter to the author that Helper was not a promising subject for a Ph.D. dissertation: "He was undoubtedly mentally unbalanced, at least when I knew him. He wrote a book which stated a very patent fact in a striking way, but aside from that, he was neither wise nor attractive." Penniless, lonely, despondent, declaring that there was no justice in the world, and that he was tired of living, Helper committed suicide in 1909 in a cheap rooming house on Pennsylvania Avenue in Washington.

The world was too much for the fighting spirit of Hinton Rowan Helper. He did not gather around him any devoted friends or disciples as did the great European radical of his period Karl Marx. One of the peculiarities of American liberalism (or radicalism) before the Civil War, as Cassius Marcellus Clay has observed, was its isolation, particularly the lack of cooperation between Northern and Southern liberals. It is true that there was some cooperation between temperance reformers of the two sections as well as a very limited cooperation between the advocates of free public schools. But a barrier existed between Northern and Southern antislavery men in attacking the great social evil of Southern slavery. Indeed, any open cooperation would have been dangerous for Southern reformers.

Helper's stirring call to arms in *The Impending Crisis* against the oligarchy of slaveholders has something of the ring of the *Communist Manifesto* of 1848: "Non-slaveholders of the South! farmers, mechanics, and workingmen, we take this occasion to assure you that the slaveholders, the arrogant demagogues whom you elected to offices of honor and profit, have hoodwinked you, trifled with you, and used you as mere tools for the consummation of their wicked designs. . . . By a system of the grossest subterfuge and misrepresentation, and in order to avert, for a season, the vengeance that will most assuredly overtake them ere long, they have taught you to hate the abolitionists, who are your best and only true friends." (p. 120)

Despite a certain similarity between the ideas of Karl Marx and Helper, there were vast differences between the two men and their doctrines. Marx was a writer of massive, if prejudiced, scholarship, who spent many years in the British Museum gathering material to support his ideas. Helper had a shallow education, and he went to little trouble to verify his evidence or ideas. Marx ignored Christian morality, indeed scorned conventional ethics; Helper, though radical in social matters, was thoroughly orthodox in religion and appealed to Christian doctrine to support his program. Perhaps the greatest difference between the two radical agitators lay in the methods which they proposed to use in effecting a drastic social change. Marx had no tolerance whatever for the gradualist approach to reform: he believed that gradualism— that is, compromise—was really a surrender to the class in power. The upper class, he held, could never be induced by moral suasion to give up their privileged position—in other words, to quit exploiting the proletariat. The ruling class must therefore be liquidated by violence, by a revolutionary movement. Helper, on the other hand, did not advocate the sudden abolition of slavery but proposed that it should be eradicated by taxation over a period of thirty years.

The remarkable aspect of Helper's agitation to arouse the non-slaveholders to class consciousness was that it acted as a boomerang: instead of aiding the cause of the underpriviliged whites, it enormously strengthened the position of the slaveholders in Southern society. In general, it has been difficult to arouse class-consciousness in America because of its agrarian tradition and its open society, which have made it possible for poor men of energy to rise to the top. The studies of Professor Owsley and his students at Vanderbilt show that a very large proportion of the slaveless white farmers owned the land that they tilled. They therefore occupied quite a different position from the industrial proletariat and the peasants of Europe, who formed the basis of Karl Marx's revolutionary class. The position of the latter in bourgeois society was fixed and could not be escaped. The non-slaveholders of the Old South, on the other hand, did not think of themselves as trapped in a stratified society; they had the opportunity to become slaveholders, and as a matter of fact many of them did acquire slaves.

Even if the non-slaveholders had had the opportunity to read Helper's book, it is doubtful if they would have accepted his revolutionary doctrine. They were afraid of the consequences of emancipating the Negro. Frederick Law Olmsted in 1857 talked to a poor farmer emigrating from Alabama to Texas who accurately expressed these fears. Slavery, he said to the Northern traveler, was a bad institution, but he was opposed to freeing the slaves and allowing them to remain in the country. "It wouldn't do no good," he observed, "to free 'em, and let 'em hang round, because they is so monstrous lazy; if they hadn't nobody to take keer of 'em, you see, they wouldn't do nothin' but juss natrally laze round, and steal, and pilfer, and no man couldn't live, you see, whar they was—if they was free no man couldn't live." And he had another objection to emancipating the Negroes: they would think themselves as good as the poor white man. "Now just suppose you had a family of children, how would you like to hev a nigger feeling just as good as a white man? how'd you like to hev a niggar steppin' up to your darter?"

Such race prejudice operated strongly in the border state of Kentucky in 1849 during the campaign to elect delegates to a constitutional convention. Despite a vigorous canvass of reformers to secure the election of emancipationists to the convention, the Kentuckians failed to elect a single avowed antislavery delegate. Robert Jefferson Breckinridge gave an interesting psychological explanation for the profound conservatism of his fellow citizens. He attributed the defeat of the liberal forces primarily to the unwavering support of slavery by the common man.

The common people, he observed, felt a sense of superiority by having the Negroes kept in slavery as a class below themselves. Moreover, they dreaded the liberation of the slaves, who could then move freely about to become their economic competitors. The workingmen of the North, he conjectured, had a similar psychology: they would vote to free the distant slaves but almost certainly would oppose receiving Negroes in large numbers as their neighbors and competitors.

The antipathy of the poor white and yeoman to the Negro was a deeply rooted folk prejudice, extending back to colonial times and to seventeenth-century England. It was illustrated by the discriminations against the free Negro in the North and by the aversion among the common soldiers of the Union Army to serving with Negro soldiers. Even in India, which so passionately has resented color prejudice in the world, the caste system, as Prime Minister Nehru has observed, "in its origin was based on color." Here the lighter-skinned Aryan invaders preserved a prejudice against the dark-skinned Dravidians, whom they had conquered in prehistoric times. In the Southern states Alexis de Tocqueville was surprised to find that the mulattoes held themselves aloof from the "darkies" and combined with the whites against the slaves.

Helper shared this deep racial antipathy of the class from which he came. When the New England abolitionist Mrs. Maria Child was seeking in 1860 to obtain the addresses of prominent Southerners to whom she could mail her antislavery tract, she solicited the aid of Helper. On his reply, she commented in a letter to John C. Underwood, October 26: "I sent to Mr. Helper for a list of names of persons to whom I could send it, but he declined on the ground that 'the negro was too prominent' for the tract to be acceptable in his native State." Furthermore, in an annotated copy of *The Impending Crisis*, dated Asheville, 1870, Helper cites numerous references in his famous book to show that it was not written in behalf of the Negroes but in sympathy for the non-slaveholding whites of the South. The poor whites, warped by race prejudice, wished to keep the Negroes in slavery, but Helper sought to emancipate the slaves and deport them in order to free the poor whites.

Helper's solution to the problem of the poor whites in the

South was not to destroy the capitalistic system. Indeed, he favored William Gregg's plan of gathering the unproductive poor whites into cotton mill villages, enforcing a moral and sober course of life upon them, and enabling them to earn money. He protested strongly, however, against paying white laborers less than the wage of hired Negro slaves, as was often the custom in the Southern states. His remedies for the ills of the South were: (1) to abolish slavery, (2) to educate the poor whites, (3) to establish the freedom of the press and of speech, and (4) to bring the poor whites into politics. All of these were sound and enlightened measures and should have brought him honor rather than hate in his section.

To Cassius Clay, Frank Blair, Jr., of Missouri, and Benjamin Sherwood Hedrick of North Carolina, Helper had dedicated the 1859 edition of his compendium of *The Impending Crisis of the South*. All of these antislavery leaders came from the border slave states. In comparison with the radicals of the North—such men as Garrison, Philips, Parker, and Weld—they appear to be moderate reformers. Observing slavery at first hand, they realized that the drastic plans of the Northern abolitionists were utterly impracticable. The Northern radicals approached slavery from the point of view of sympathy for the Negro; the Southern antislavery men, from the point of view of sympathy for the white non-slaveholding class or from a realization of the economic evils of the institution. Many of the Northern abolitionists became interested in radical causes other than the emancipation of the slaves, but the Southern antislavery men generally confined their efforts to the one great reform.

Both Cassius Clay and Hinton Rowan Helper found it more politic and effective to emphasize the economic argument against slavery than the moral one. Long before the North Carolina radical began his agitation against slavery, Clay attacked it as an institution that prevented the industrialization of Kentucky and the South and injured the mass of non-slaveholders. Both he and Helper saw also the injurious social and moral effects of the institution upon Southern society. They spoke out passionately and often rashly against a social institution whose evils they magnified. Neither reformer, however, proposed the immediate abolition of slavery; neither advocated the higher law doctrine or disunion as did the Garrisonians; and neither appealed to the slaves.

In seeking to organize the non-slaveholders for political action against the slaveholding oligarchy with their "hectoring spirit," as Clay put it, the two Southern reformers ran against almost insuperable odds. They had to overcome the voters' unthinking attachments and loyalties to the political parties; above all, on the question of liberating the slaves, they encountered race prejudice and vague fears of danger to the order of society. Daniel R. Hundley, who had a sound knowledge of Southern society, which he revealed in his *Social Relations in Our Southern States,* declared (p. 219): "although not as a class pecuniarily interested in slave property, the Southern Yeomanry are almost unanimously pro-slavery in sentiment." Both Clay and Helper, agitating for their society to take immediate steps to do something about the removal of slavery, made incautious statements that could be interpreted as incitements to revolutionary violence. Their position as reformers was always vulnerable because in the popular mind they were associated with the radical abolitionists of the North.

Helper and Clay, in their zeal to abolish slavery, seem to have been little affected by the moral and religious spirit which constituted the great strength of the antislavery movement in the Northern states. But another Southerner who should be compared with them, James G. Birney, was profoundly moved by the idealistic strain in the antislavery movement. The turning point in Birney's career that made him give his life to the antislavery cause was a religious conversion. A worldly young aristocrat like Clay, Birney was born in 1792 in Danville, Kentucky, and like Clay he received a Northern education—at Princeton College. Moreover, he had a similar experience to Clay's in being frustrated in his political ambitions. In northern Alabama to which he had emigrated as a young man and had established a plantation, he was defeated for public office on several occasions because he was an adherent of Henry Clay in an area that was ardently pro-Jackson. In the summer of 1832 on a visit to Huntsville Theodore D. Weld convinced him that slavery was a sin, a violation of the Golden Rule of the New Testament. He decided to become an agent of the American Colonization Society, but after a year of

proselyting he became so discouraged by his failure to arouse the
people of the lower South from their apathy toward colonization
that he returned to Kentucky. Here his antislavery views developed more strongly, particularly after a visit in 1834 to Lane
Theological Seminary in Cincinnati, a center of abolitionism,
which induced him to change from a gradualist to a moderate
abolitionist.

An incident in Danville in 1836 reveals the great difference between Birney and Cassius Marcellus Clay: a mob blocked Birney's
attempt to establish an antislavery newspaper, *The Philanthropist*. Although he had demonstrated great moral courage on numerous occasions, he moved to Cincinnati and published his paper
there. But he found no more tolerant spirit in the Northern city,
for a mob attacked his printing office and dumped his press into
the Ohio River. Thereafter, Birney's crusade against slavery
turned into a fight to preserve freedom of speech and of the
press in the North as well as to advance the antislavery cause.
Both Kentucky reformers had a keen sense of the use of politics
as a tool to advance their cause, and accordingly they parted
company with the Garrisonians. Though Birney became a candidate for President in 1840 and 1844, he refused to make any
compromises with his principles and, unlike Clay, did not seek
self-aggrandizement: in the Abolition movement he represented
the pure spirit of humanitarianism and Christianity. The contrast
between Helper and Birney was even more striking: the older
man came from a more aristocratic culture and was better
balanced than the angry young agitator. Birney sought to make
the voice of conscience prevail in the United States; Helper, on
the other hand, was a racist who spoke for the cause of the under-
privileged Southern whites.

Chapter IX

THE MIND
OF THE SOUTHERN NEGRO:
THE REMARKABLE INDIVIDUALS

EVER since Pavlov performed his epoch-making experiments on conditioning, men have had a deeper understanding of the importance of circumstance and habit upon the development of human nature. Slavery was a powerful conditioner of the mind of the Southern Negro, and this chapter is partly the story of that long-continued process. But it is also an account of how a considerable number of slave and free Negroes in the South, despite the tremendous handicaps that all Negroes in America suffered, were able to rise above the general level of the culture of their race and confute the prevailing Sambo image. They were the remarkable individuals.

White Southerners maintained that, having lived intimately with Negroes for generations, they knew the Negro mind. Yet their views of the Negro were distorted by powerful stereotypes, especially concerning a belief in the inherent inferiority of the Negro. The slave studied closely the white man, and seems to have been far more astute in reading the mind of the master than was the latter in penetrating the psychology of the black man. Beverly Nash, a prominent colored leader of the Reconstruction, observed that the Negro "will know more of your character in three days than you [the white man] will of his in three months. It has been his business all his life to find out the ways of the white man—to watch him—what he means." Even highly intelligent masters and mistresses whose interest it was to understand the subject race found the inner thoughts of the slaves veiled and inscrutable, for they were noncommittal and evasive in conversation with the white man.

The history of the Negro in the antebellum South has been based almost exclusively on white sources. There does exist, however, a large body of evidence by ex-slaves who lived on into the twentieth century. In 1936 the W.P.A. began a federal writers' project to interview these old people whose youth and young manhood and womanhood had been passed in the slave regime. Hundreds of ex-slaves living in the Southern states were interviewed, and the typewritten testimony of these witnesses of Southern slavery has been gathered into thirty-four bound volumes, arranged according to states and deposited in the Rare Book Room of the Library of Congress. A selection of this source material has been published by Benjamin Botkin in a slender volume entitled *Lay My Burden Down: A Folk History of Slavery*. I have read many of the original narratives and from them have derived a different impression of the conditions of slavery than Mr. Botkin's selection presents. In drawing conclusions from these narratives, one must take account of the fact that the narrators were very old persons whose memories were in some cases clear and reliable, but in others vague and capricious. Also, I found such a large proportion of these ex-slaves praising the kindness and humanity of their own masters, but giving a dark picture of cruelty of masters on neighboring plantations, that I began to wonder if these old ex-slaves were giving answers that they thought might please their Southern interviewers.

The ex-slave narratives, nevertheless, reveal much about the mind of the slaves and of the masters. In general they depict a semi-frontier environment on the plantation, where nearly everything was home-produced; one ex-slave in Georgia recalled the howling at night of painters (panthers) close to the slave cabins. Frontier conditions on the plantation coexisted with a strong sense of social distinctions. Minnie Davis, who lived on a plantation near Athens, Georgia, and was owned by John Crawford, a son of the statesman William H. Crawford, described the family of her master as "uppity people" and the slaves of Crawford were uppish also. Frank Adamson, a former slave on a South Carolina plantation, said of his master: "Them poor folks looked up to him lak God Almighty." Julia Cole said that though the overseers on the plantation in Georgia where she grew up were decent and "spectable," they were "not in a class with marse Billy's family." Her testimony as to overseers was an exception, for most slaves described them as a rough and cruel group of men. The Negro's awareness of social stratification was expressed in referring with contempt to the "poor whites" as "white trash."

The Southern Negro's strong sense of social distinctions (which he may have absorbed from the white master class) extended into social relations among the slaves and free Negroes. Horace Fitchett in a Ph.D. dissertation entitled "The Free Negro in Charleston, S. C.," has observed that the mulatto segment of the free Negro population of Charleston emphasized the difference between themselves and darker slaves or free Negroes. They formed an exclusive social and fraternal organization called the Brown Fellowship Society; qualifications for membership were that one be free, light-skinned, economically independent, and "devoted to the basic tenets of the social system." The excluded Negroes of dark color formed a rival society named the "Society of Free Dark Men," headed by Thomas Small, a carpenter who owned eleven slaves. William Tiler Johnson, a mulatto barber of Natchez, Mississippi, seems also to have been strongly influenced by the colored caste system, for he never attended "darkey parties, dances," or other social occasions, and apparently did not mingle socially with the slaves. An elderly planter and doctor of Greenville, South Carolina, told John William De Forest, the Freedmen's Bureau agent stationed there, that he had only once flogged a slave, but the cause for this unique occasion throws a sombre light on "the peculiar institution" and on the Negro caste system. After his slave girl, Julia, had borne a mulatto baby, she defied his command to take a Negro husband, declaring, "Doctor, I've had one white man's child. I'm never going to have no black man's child." Moreover, in referring to each other, the slaves often used the term "Nigger," a designation employed by the lower class whites but not generally by planters of good breeding.

The ex-slave narratives vividly portray the lights and shadows of plantation life. Over the remembrance of some of them lingered the pathos of being separated by the slave trade from their mothers and fathers and wives, never again to see them on this earth. They describe trained dogs tracking fugitives; cruel floggings by overseers, the indignities of pulling up the petticoats of slave women and whipping them on the bare buttocks; the evils of miscegenation; masters forcing Negro girls to take husbands that they did not love and compelling Negroes to aid in catching fugitives and punishing their fellow slaves. Stark as are these stories of the sinister side of slavery, they are counter-balanced by recollections of kind masters and mistresses. Minnie Davis of the Crawford plantation, for example, told how the master read the Bible to the slaves and asked the smart ones to repeat passages from memory; the Crawford children taught Minnie's mother to read newspapers and write letters; the slaves that were punished, she said, needed it; the slaves loved "Marse John" and when the Civil War ended the slave regime, "Mother was glad and sorry too that she was free." Minnie was one of the remarkable Negroes who developed on the antebellum plantation; after the war she attended Atlanta University and later taught school.

Some of the ex-slaves expressed a nostalgia for slavery times. They remembered with relish the ash cakes they ate—"de best thing you ever et," said Shorty Clemons of Alabama—the pleasures of hunting the opossum, trapping rabbits, and fishing for catfish, the slaves singing in the cotton fields, hog-killing time, little black boys swimming in the pond with the master's son, Negroes dancing on Saturday night to music played on homemade instruments, the uninhibited religious meetings, etc. Esther Casey in Alabama remembered her master as a fine man who treated his slaves like members of the family; the mistress taught them to read and write. Rufus Dirt spoke of his pride in once being a driver on an Alabama plantation; "the Niggers looked up to me," he said, and he liked to strut before them. Charlie Aarons said, "I loved master John and he loved me"; Charlie accompanied his master to war as his body servant. Mose Davis, son of the coachman on the plantation, was a warm friend of Colonel Davis' son Manning, with whom he hunted and fished and rode to town; occasionally he and Manning slept in the same bed. The colonel, Mose said, was against any form of whipping and punished delinquent slaves by depriving them of privileges and assigning extra work. Georgia Baker, who lived on Alexander Stephens' plantation, recalled that both Stephens and the overseer, his cousin, Lordnorth Stephens, were kind to the slaves—there was no whipping, no runaways, and no teaching of reading and writing on the plantation near Crawfordville. The slaves were allowed to hunt and were given plenty of food and milk. In fact they enjoyed so many privileges that they were called "Stephens' Free Negroes."

Besides the recollections of aged ex-slaves concerning the Negro's life in slavery, there is the testimony of escaped slaves who published their autobiographies. In general, these narratives were heavily edited by white abolitionists and are little more than anti-slavery propaganda. Typical of this literature is the *Narrative of the Life and Adventures of Henry Bibb, an American Slave, Written by Himself* (New York, 1849). According to his account, Bibb's father was a white man. As he grew up, or "was flogged up," on a Kentucky plantation he did not have half enough to eat and no shoes until December. Ill treatment led him to escape when he was twenty-two years old to Cincinnati. Perhaps the most valuable part of his book is the description of superstitions and "conjuring" among the slaves. The most significant of the published narratives of escaped slaves was written by the mulatto Frederick Douglass, certainly the most remarkable Negro reared in the antebellum South. In his *Narrative of the Life of Frederick Douglass, an American Slave* (Boston, 1845), later expanded into *My Bondage and My Freedom,* Douglass gives a deeply sensitive and vivid picture of life on a great slave plantation in Maryland. As a small boy he was the frequent companion of the master's youngest son. This circumstance accounted for the fact that, as the great orator he became, his speech showed very little of the slave accent. He noted several favorable characteristics of the Negroes, especially their native politeness and their respect for the Old "Uncles" and "Aunties" of their race. He observed, too, that those Negroes who resisted whipping were, after the first encounters with overseers or masters, punished less often than docile slaves. The career of this gifted Negro indicates the danger of teaching slaves to read, for his reading of the speeches on liberty in the *Columbia Orator,* he tells us, gave him the impulse to freedom that led him to form an escape plot among his fellow slaves.

The letters that slaves and free Negroes wrote to antislavery newspapers, to the American Colonization Society, and especially to each other—some of which Carter Woodson has published in his *The Mind of the Negro as Reflected in Letters Written during the Crisis, 1800–1860*—show that uppermost in the thoughts of the superior Negroes was the great longing to be free. Next to this major goal was the desire to educate their children and to be respected as men and, accordingly, to be called "Mr." Furthermore, they wished to receive fair wages as workers, to enjoy a family life free from the fear of separation by the slave trade, to safeguard their daughters and wives from the licentiousness of the white man, and finally to live a religious life that would entitle them after death to enter heaven. This Negro correspondence reveals a division of opinion among them on the desirability of emigrating to Liberia, the overwhelming majority being opposed to leaving their homes in America.

Especially poignant in expressing the desire to be free not only from slavery but from race prejudice in America are some of the letters of Negroes who had been emancipated and sent to Liberia. Such a liberated slave, Robert Johnson, wrote to Thomas Dolan of Lexington, Kentucky, August 20, 1846, in praise of Liberia, "that country where I am known as a man and the only country in which the colored man enjoys undisturbed liberty." Nelson Sanders wrote to his old mistress in Kentucky, January 5, 1848, "Liberia is unquestionably the happiest territory for the black man on the globe —we enjoy liberty here . . ." (Manuscripts in the University of Kentucky Library). And Peter Skipwith, one of General John Hartwell Cocke's former slaves, wrote to his old master in Virginia, August 20, 1859, that after a hard struggle for freedom and independence the Negro colonists were enjoying "the Golden sun of liberty" and that Liberia is "doing her part in the Great Work of improving human affairs—" (Bremo Slave Letters in John Hartwell Cocke Papers, University of Virginia Library). The desire for freedom from bondage was so great that whenever a chance for escape, such as the approach of the Union army, presented itself, they eagerly seized the opportunity. Among the first to flee were those Negroes who had been closely associated with the whites— the trusted house servant and the skilled mechanic. Eliza Andrews recorded in the *War-Time Jounral of a Georgia Girl* that the servant her father trusted most of all absconded when the Yankee army arrived.

Below the Mason-Dixon Line the Negroes, whether slave or free, were afraid to reveal their inmost thoughts or aspirations or to show the slightest sign of insubordination. Consequently it has been extremely difficult to find a Southern Negro spokesman who left records of his thought. I have selected for this purpose (in accordance with the plan of the other chapters of the volume) two Negroes: a remarkable Negro who represented the philosophy of accomodation to the white man and counseled the resigned acceptance of slavery; and at the opposite end of the spectrum of Negro thought, one who emigrated from the South to Boston, from whence he sought to send revolutionary literature to arouse the slaves from their apathy.

The Reverend John Chavis, a free Negro who taught a famous school for white children in the 1830's in Raleigh, North Carolina, was a striking representative of the attitude of Negro accomodation. Chavis had received an education in the classics and rhetoric in Washington Academy (now Washington and Lee University) and according to tradition had also studied at Princeton as a private pupil of President Witherspoon. Tradition maintains that he was sent to Princeton because of a wager between two white men about whether a Negro could learn Greek and Latin. In 1800 he was licensed as a preacher by the Lexington, Virginia, Presbytery, and five years later he emigrated to the Piedmont region of North Carolina, where he preached for many years. His main occupation, however, was teaching. In 1808 the Raleigh *Register* carried a prospectus of his school in that city—for white children in the day and for free colored children in the evening. In 1830 the editor of the Raleigh *Register*, Joseph Gales, praised Chavis' conduct of the Negro school, describing the intellectual attainments of his colored pupils as "almost incredible." He also commended the teacher for his "sensible" address at the public examination of his students. Chavis impressed on them that "though they occupied an inferior and subordinate status in society and were possessed of but limited privileges, even they might become useful in their particular sphere by making a proper improvement of the advantages offered them."

The career of Chavis is a fascinating demonstration of how a relatively liberal atmosphere in the upper South in the 1820's and early 1830's was changed. During this period the Negro, in his white school, taught some of the most prominent political leaders of the state as well as James H. Horner, founder of a famous classical academy. Chavis' remarkable correspondence with Senator Willie P. Mangum of North Carolina indicates that the senator and his brother Priestley were both his pupils; he refers to each of them as "My Son." In his correspondence with Mangum between 1825 and 1838 Chavis freely advised the senator on political as well as personal affairs. On August 8, 1832, for example, he sternly rebuked him for his temporizing course in politics: "How often have you changed your Federal Coat for a Democratic or Republic one?—and have I not often browbeaten you for your shifting conduct?" In addition to his correspondence with Mangum, Chavis wrote letters to General Daniel Barringer and to "My Son, Abraham Rencher," congressman and later minister to Portugal. When they neglected to reply, he asked Mangum to "tell them if I am Black I am free born American & a revolutionary soldier & therefore ought not to be thrown entirely out of the scale of notice." He applied to the white senator in the 1830's to let him teach his daughter Juliana. He was anxious to teach her "the Theory of the English Language which she never will be taught unless I teach her." He boasted, "I learnt my theory from Lindley Murrey's spelling book, which no other teacher in this part of the Country Teaches but myself & I think it preferable to the English Grammar."

Chavis' philosophy of life was eminently pragmatic and conservative. He criticized Priestley Mangum for being a poor political campaigner because he was too stubborn and unyielding. To be useful in this world, he observed, a man must be "condesending." Priestley should realize "that the ignorance and prejudice of mankind must be met and overcome by genuine Phylosophy." He lamented, therefore, that "proud dignity and independency of character, as he calls it, appears to have swept all Idea of Philosophic experiments from his mind."

The conservative views of the Negro teacher and preacher were reflected especially in his political principles. He was an ardent and undeviating Federalist, believing in the principles of Hamilton,

Jay, and John Adams, "bottomed on G. Washington." He wrote to Mangum in 1832, "I do not believe that mankind are capable of living under, either a Democratic, or a Republican Government. The bonds of such Governments are not sufficient to retain the corruptions of human nature." The federal constitution he regarded as a supreme achievement of political science, and he accordingly opposed any amendment of it. He became a zealous Whig, voting for Mangum (free Negroes were not disfranchised in North Carolina until 1835), and supporting a protective tariff, internal improvements, the renewal of the charter of the Second National Bank. He supported Henry Clay's candidacy for president, and he severely condemned Andrew Jackson as despotic and unfit to hold high office. A strong nationalist and patriot, he violently opposed the nullification movement, basing his opposition on a very intelligent discussion of political theory.

The most extraordinary of Chavis' views was his strong opposition to abolitionism. In 1825 he had advised Mangum to oppose the recognition of the Negro republic of Haiti. When Nat Turner revolted against the oppression of slavery in August, 1831, Chavis condemned this futile attempt to liberate the slaves as "that abominable insurrection in Southampton." He regarded the abolitionists as attacking the foundation of property rights, in which he believed strongly, by petitioning Congress to abolish slavery in the District of Columbia. "That slavery is a National evil," he wrote, "no one doubts, but what is to be done? All that can be done is to make the best of a bad bargain. For I am clearly of the opinion that immediate emancipation would be to entail the greatest earthly curse upon my bretheren according to the flesh that could be conferred upon them especially in a Country like ours. I suppose if they knew I said this they would be ready to take my life, but as I wish them well I feel no disposition to see them any more miserable than they are."

Chavis' long and honorable career took place in a time when Southerners had a more liberal attitude toward Negroes than they later developed. During this period of kindly tolerance, Hiram R. Revels, the first Negro elected to the United States Senate, grew up as a free Negro in Fayetteville, North Carolina. In his brief manuscript autobiography Revels observed that despite the increased restrictions that followed the Nat Turner insurrection, "so much of the former generous feeling toward the free people of color remained that in many parts of the state, especially in the cities and larger towns, colored schools were tolerated through the sympathy of the better class of white people" (Carter Woodson Papers in the Library of Congress). He himself attended a school in Fayetteville taught by a Negro, and there was another colored school in the town taught by a white woman.

But in the 1830's, the liberal atmosphere changed. Motivated by fear of insurrection, North Carolina passed laws to prohibit the teaching of slaves to read or write; and free Negroes, as well as slaves, were prohibited from preaching in assemblies where slaves of different families were collected together. These laws struck a severe blow at Chavis, and he was hard put to support himself, though the Orange Presbytery voted him a small life pension. On February 1, 1837, he wrote a pathetic letter to Senator Mangum asking him to defend him, "respecting my being charged with my going to Raleigh to teach the children of the free people of colour." He suggested that the senator base his defense of him on the letters that he had written to Mangum on abolitionism. During the following year he died; his epitaph should record that he was a forerunner of Booker T. Washington, an advocate of education for the Negro and of accomodation with the white people.

Most Southern Negroes seemed, like Chavis, to be convinced that slavery was too powerful and strongly entrenched to be resisted and that the best policy was to submit. Nevertheless, there were some slaves who could not endure human bondage and either sought to escape or planned slave revolts, such as Gabriel and Nat Turner in Virginia and Denmark Vesey in South Carolina. Potentially more dangerous to the white community than these sporadic and futile acts of resistance was the agitation of David Walker, the free Negro author of a revolutionary pamphlet. Born on September 28, 1785, in Wilmington, North Carolina, Walker was the son of a slave father and a free mother. Virtually nothing is known of his life in North Carolina, but according to the reputable Negro historian George W. Williams (1883), Walker wrote that he could not endure living in "this bloody land" where he continually heard the clanking of the chains of slaves. Feeling that he would be goaded into open rebellion and lose his life if he remained in his native state, he emigrated to Boston sometime before 1827.

Here he opened a shop on Brattle Street near the wharves, where he sold old clothes. In 1827 he became an agent of the Negro antislavery newspaper, *Freedom's Journal,* one of whose editors, John B. Russworm, was the first Negro to receive a degree from an American college (Bowdoin). Walker lectured to small groups in Boston, and in 1829 published at his own expense a revolutionary pamphlet entitled *David Walker's Appeal—to the Colored Citizens of the World.* . . . During the following year two other editions appeared, in which he added new and more radical comments; the third edition has recently been edited by Charles M. Wiltse, the biographer of Calhoun, and published as a paperback. The brief career of this unhappy Negro revolutionist ended in 1830, when he was found dead in front of his shop.

Walker's flaming pamphlet has a new relevance today, for the author was a forerunner of the civil rights movement of the 1950's and 1960's. In many respects he was a prototype of those Negro agitators of the twentieth century, William E. B. Du Bois and the Reverend Martin Luther King. By his revolutionary pamphlet Walker aroused the Southern states to a vivid sense of danger and thus contributed greatly to a change in the slave code and the suppression of free speech in the South. His pamphlet is an important document in the intellectual history of the Negro, revealing the attitude of the sensitive and intelligent members of his race not only toward slavery but toward racial discrimination.

The *Appeal* is divided into four chapters, portraying the wretchedness of the Negroes in this country in consequence of slavery, ignorance, the propaganda of Christian ministers, and the colonization movement. Despite its repetitiveness and tone of hyperbole, the pamphlet is well written and shows that the Negro author had read widely in ancient and European history as well as in the political discussions of his time. It is dominated by a poignant sense of anguish and outrage that the Negro was treated in America not as a man but as a "talking ape." The author maintained that the Negroes were kept ignorant in order that the white man might dominate them. He has words of scorn for the Christian ministry who, in violation of the spirit of their religion, supported slavery, preaching to the slaves to be obedient to their masters. He condemns Henry Clay severely for his support of the colonization movement, which he regarded as designed to get rid of the free

Negro and thus fasten the chains of slavery more securely upon the Southern bondsmen.

Walker's analysis of the Negro mind and personality was perceptive and has largely been confirmed by the progress of the race within recent years. He quotes Thomas Jefferson's opinion (advanced as a suspicion only) that the Negro was inferior in mentality to the white man. This remark of the great statesman whom Walker admired deeply pained him, for he felt that Jefferson's unfavorable opinion of the Negro had "sunk deeply into the hearts of millions of the whites and never will be removed this side of eternity." But the Negroes, he declared, must prove that Jefferson was wrong. Recognizing that the Negroes in America had developed a servile attitude and a trembling fear and awe of the white man, and that they were pathetically ignorant, he believed that these ignoble characteristics were caused by their enslavement. He maintained that Negroes had a primitive valor and emotional fervor, so that if they were aroused, one good black man could put to death six white men. When properly excited, he maintained, they would show great courage and even glory in death. It was the duty of Negro leaders to go to work to enlighten their people and give them confidence and self-respect. He conceived of himself in the role of a colored "John the Baptist," preaching deliverance of his people. His objective was the emancipation of the Negroes throughout the world.

The *Appeal to the Colored Citizens of the World* undoubtedly would have been a dangerous document had it been widely circulated among the slaves and free Negroes. The first edition closed with the ominous warning: "The Americans may be as vigilant as they please but they cannot be vigilant enough for the Lord, neither can they hide themselves where he will not find them and bring them out." In the second edition, he predicted the rise of a sable general like Hannibal, "that mighty son of Africa," to lead the Negroes out of bondage and destroy their cruel and inhuman masters. One of the elements that made his message so dangerous was his appeal to religious sentiment; he also invoked the natural rights philosophy of the Declaration of Independence. In this latter edition he passionately exclaimed that no man of good sense would submit himself to be a slave to a cruel master: "No! No! he would cut his throat from ear to ear and well do the slave-holders know it." He predicted, "As true as the sun ever shone in its meridian splendor, my color will root some of them out of the very face of the earth." In the third and final edition he declared "that the man who would not fight for freedom deserved to be kept in chains"; nevertheless, he cautioned the slaves not to make an attempt to gain their freedom "until you see your way clear," but "when that hour arrives and you move," he exhorted them not to be afraid, for the God of justice would lead them.

The Walker pamphlet made a tremendous sensation in the Southern states. The governor of Georgia sent it to the legislature, stating that sixty copies brought by ship to a Negro preacher in Savannah for distribution had been seized by the police. Greatly alarmed, the legislature passed some severe restrictive laws, including an act prohibiting the teaching of slaves to read or write. Also, the mayor of Richmond, Virginia, finding a copy of the dreaded pamphlet in the home of a free Negro, turned it over to the governor who brought the matter to the attention of the General Assembly. This body debated whether to prohibit the teaching of slaves to read and write, but by one vote rejected such a measure. After the Nat Turner revolt in 1831 had frightened the state, the legislature passed the bill that it had refused to adopt the year before. In North Carolina the distribution of Walker's revolutionary pamphlet led the legislature to enact such a law in 1830. Earlier, South Carolina, following the wave of fear produced by the Stono insurrection of 1739, had forbade the teaching of slaves to read and write. By the time of the Civil War all of the Southern states except Maryland, Kentucky, Tennessee, and Arkansas prohibited the teaching of slaves to read and write, but these laws were often evaded. There was a striking case of enforcement in Virginia, nevertheless, when Mrs. Margaret Douglass who for almost a year had conducted a school for Negro children in Norfolk was tried in 1853 for violating the state law and sentenced to a month in jail.

Most literate Negroes acquired a knowledge of reading and writing without openly flouting the law; they were often taught by indulgent masters or by the masters' children or by other Negroes. Carter Woodson, the colored historian who made an extensive study of Negro education before 1860, concluded, probably with exaggeration, that approximately 10 per cent of the adult Negroes could read. Literacy was much higher among the city and free

Negroes than among the plantation slaves. According to some statistics cited by John Hope Franklin, among free Negroes who emigrated from North Carolina to Liberia in the 1850's, 33 out of 153, or approximately 21 per cent, were literate. Whitelaw Reid, during his trip to the South in 1865, made a point to visit the recently established freedmen's schools and to ask the teachers whether Negro children learned as rapidly and well as white children, and the answer was invariably an affirmative one.

Although slavery greatly retarded the normal development of Negroes in the South, many made progress in positions that did not require a knowledge of reading and writing. Thousands of slaves took pride in becoming superior blacksmiths, brickmasons, cabinet makers, coopers, and mechanics. Sir Charles Lyell, on his second visit to the United States in 1845, was surprised to note the rank of black mechanics on some of the large plantations of Georgia. "When these mechanics came to consult Mr. Couper [one of the large planters of Georgia] on business," the English scientist observed, "their manner of speaking to him is quite as independent as that of English artisans to their employers. Their aptitude for the practice of such mechanic arts may encourage every philanthropist who has had misgivings in regard to the progressive powers of the race. . . ." Furthermore, there were humble heroes of daily living, like "Little Mary" of Hyland Plantation in Mississippi who led the gang of cotton pickers, who during one week in 1852 picked three hundred and fifty pounds of cotton per day. Stephen, a slave of Abisha Slade of Caswell County, North Carolina, was another exceptional Negro of the antebellum period. In 1838 he discovered a method of curing a local variety of tobacco, Bright Tobacco, that after the Civil War became the basis of the cigarette industry. On numerous plantations, slaves were encouraged by various incentives besides the fear of the whip to put forth their best effort.

The outstanding leaders in the plantation hierarchy were the Negro preachers and the drivers, *i.e.*, the Negro assistants of the overseers. One of the most remarkable of these religious leaders was Sam Drayton, who preached to colored congregations in Georgia and South Carolina. An appealing portrait of this Negro minister is found in the diary of Gertrude Thomas, the wife of a large planter who lived near Augusta, Georgia (manuscript in the

Duke University Library). A graduate of Wesleyan College in Macon, Mrs. Thomas was a widely read and intelligent woman who made perceptive observations; she had grave doubts about the morality of holding slaves. On several occasions she notes in her diary that she and her husband attended services conducted by the eloquent Negro preacher. After hearing Drayton preach, she wrote on April 8, 1855, "He is one of the most intellectual Negroes I have ever met with and has a decidedly fine command of language." Again she described him as "a man of extraordinary talent, well cultivated and well repays me for listening to his sermons." Yet one may wonder at the appeal of his sermons, for she wrote that when Sam Drayton called for members to come to the mourning bench, one of the Negro women, after swaying to and fro, fell flat on the floor and a moan arose from the audience that grew in volume until it became a loud wail, the scene and Sam's preaching greatly affecting Gertrude Thomas. On May 2, 1855, she hurried dinner in order to go to the Negro church to hear Sam Drayton preach, but instead of him, the Baptist preacher Peter Johnson exhorted the congregation. He was a fine-looking mulatto man, she wrote, who ostentatiously displayed a gold watch and chain and fob and put on gold-rimmed spectacles. Disappointed in not being able to hear her favorite preacher, Mrs. Thomas wrote in her diary, "He is not as polished nor by no means so talented a man as Sam Drayton."

The abolition stereotype of the Negro driver, as well as the testimony of some ex-slaves, was an unfavorable one—a traitor to his race, cruel, carrying a whip in his hand, hated by the field hands. On the contrary, many of the drivers were the best products of the race, who had attained their positions by virtue of superior intelligence and character. They were frequently tall, strong men who commanded a certain respect because of their physical superiority. The driver supervised the field tasks of the slaves, set the pace of work, and exercised the duties of a policeman in the slave quarters. He did the whipping of delinquent slaves under the eye of the overseer, but on many well-managed plantations he was not allowed to carry his whip into the field with him.

The driver was a man of experience, both in handling his fellow slaves and in the agricultural operations of the plantation. Master and overseer often deferred to his judgment and knowledge.

"Where drivers are discreet, experienced and trusty," wrote Olmsted, "the overseer is frequently employed as a matter of form, to comply with the laws requiring the superintendence or presence of a white man among every body of slaves—." The master of a South Carolina plantation told the Northern traveler that he had sometimes left his plantation in the care of a driver for a considerable length of time after having discharged an overseer, and that "he thinks it has been quite as well conducted as ever. His overseer consults the drivers on all important points, and is governed by their advice."

Captain Basil Hall drew an attractive picture with his camera lucida of two slave drivers in the rice country of South Carolina. Of Solomon, who was in charge of the Heyward plantation, he wrote: "He was a man of information and really very well bred— though he could neither read nor write. I did not suppose it possible that a negro in the situation of a slave driver could be so much of a gentleman—but so it was." The other driver had been born near Timbuctoo and had been captured when he was twelve years old and shipped to America as a slave—there were marks of a lion's claw on his chest.

A considerable number of planters, disgusted with the type of overseers available, preferred to operate their plantations with the aid of a Negro foreman or driver. Such was the case of the agricultural reformer Edmund Ruffin of *Marlbourne* plantation in Virginia. Here the faithful Jem Sykes performed the functions of overseer, having "charge of the keys," the emblem of authority. Universally respected by the master and his family as well as by the slaves, he was faithful until the Union army approached and then he absconded. Likewise, Joseph and Jefferson Davis employed Ben Montgomery, an intelligent and literate slave, to oversee the farming on their large plantations near Vicksburg. Ben's sons, Isaiah and Montgomery, were taught to read and write and were so apt that Joseph Davis employed them as his amanuenses to copy his business and political correspondence. Ben was ambitious to become a rich man, and in 1867 he and his sons bought both of the Davis plantations for $300,000 on the security of their notes.

Widely scattered over the South, indeed, were Negroes that differed greatly from the denigratory stereotype of Sambo. An important body of evidence concerning these Negroes, far more

reliable than the slave narratives written under abolitionist influence, is gradually being uncovered in the plantation records and
papers of the planters. In the papers of the Tait family of Georgia
and Alabama, of the Pettigrew family of eastern North Carolina,
and of Archibald Arrington of Nash County, North Carolina, for
example, are records of remarkable slaves. They show slaves who
were so intelligent and experienced that the master constantly
consulted them on plantation policies. There were slaves like
Harford on the Tait plantation, who wrote to his master away on
a trip intelligently reporting on plantation affairs, slaves who made
excellent progress in acquiring skills, slaves who had a passionate
attachment to the plantation and a pride in the crops.

Among these extraordinary plantation Negroes were two slaves,
Moses and Henry, who served as overseers on William Pettigrew's
plantations of Belgrade and Magnolia on Scuppernong Lake and
Scuppernong River in eastern North Carolina. Pettigrew left these
two capable and faithful Negroes in complete charge of his plantations while he was spending the summers at the Virginia springs.
They wrote weekly accounts to him of plantation affairs, dictating
letters to a white man, Malachi White, who lived in the neighborhood and hired himself at harvest time to Pettigrew. Pettigrew
wrote to Moses on June 24, 1856, while he was at Healing Springs
in Virginia: "I have placed much reliance in your management,
industry, & honesty by thus leaving the plantation & all on it in
your charge, nor have I any fear that you will fall short of the
confidence I have placed in you. The people promised to be
industrious & obedient to you, you must remind them of this
promise should any of them be disposed to forget it." Moses was
given the authority to decide how much rest and free time the
slaves were to be allowed; he punished delinquents, placing them
in the plantation penitentiary and depriving them of their molasses
and tobacco allowance; he purchased plantation supplies, gave out
the clothing allotments, and even had charge of the whiskey supply,
which was the supreme mark of trust. Both he and Henry reported
constantly that the slaves were working well. Moses wrote affectionate letters to his master signed "your friend," observing (July
5, 1856), "the people has been faithful and dutiful to me an to
thare work and all have agreed together since master left home."
When he died (probably in 1860), Pettigrew wrote that he cher-

ished the highest respect for his memory. In his place he appointed a young slave, Glasgow, thirty-two years old, whom he described as honest, industrious, "not too talkative (a necessary qualification)" and a man of good sense, who had been faithful in the discharge of duty.

The least favorable conditions for the development of the mind and personality of the slave were to be found on the large absentee plantations, run solely for commerical profit. Such was Stephen A. Douglas' two-thousand-acre plantation in the delta country near Greenville, Mississippi. The plantation was very efficiently managed; Douglas required the overseer to send him each week a copy of the detailed record of the plantation activities that must be kept in Thomas Affleck's model Record and Occasional Book for planters. He also stipulated that "the slaves were to be well-fed, well clothed, and humanely treated and kindly and properly cared for according to the laws of the state and the customs and usages of the best regulated plantations under the most kind and humane masters." The plantation continued to produce large crops of cotton and corn until Federal troops invaded it in March, 1863. The soldiers carried off and partly burned 1,486 bales of cotton, 15,000 bushels of corn, 93 mules, 63 cattle, 292 hogs, and "3 fine horses," one of which was the horse Douglas rode when he visited the plantation. The large profits of the plantation afford valuable evidence in the controversy among scholars as to whether Southern slavery was a profitable form of labor. In 1861 the 120 slaves on the Douglas plantation produced nearly 900 bales of cotton (500 pounds to the bale) on a thousand acres, as well as huge quantities of corn and other crops. The partner of Douglas in operating the plantation testified in the United States Court of Claims that the Douglas estate in Mississippi, had not the war intervened to prevent the marketing of the cotton, would have amounted to "an enormous fortune." In the 1870's Douglas' sons sought damages from the United States government in the Court of Claims to the amount of $325,648.

The testimony of ex-slaves, overseers, and planters before the United States Court of Claims throws some light upon the lives of Negroes in the delta region. When Federal troops threatened to occupy the Douglas plantation, the overseer ordered the accumulated cotton to be hidden in the canebrake at the rear of the plantation. This operation was carried out by five slaves, with Evans the carpenter in charge; all of them, according to the testimony of the overseer, were "smart and likely men." The written testimony of the ex-slaves of the Douglas and adjoining plantations was signed by all of them with a mark—although one slave, Alfred Loan, declared, "I can read a little by hard Spelling in easy places." The testimony of these former slaves shows that they did a variety of work besides cultivating the cotton and corn crops. John Brown, a slave on the Douglas place and a preacher, testified that he had cut the first rails for the plantation and had burned the brick for the buildings; James Henry Williams had helped to construct the cistern and to make bricks; another slave held the responsible position of being the engineer for the steam engine and four gins on the Silver Lake plantation where the Douglas cotton was ginned; he escaped on the transports when the Federal troops arrived in the neighborhood. Alfred Loan, on the other hand, also a preacher, remained loyal to his old mistress to whom he had given a promise to stay and take care of the plantation. Apparently some of the slaves were allowed to hunt, for Loan said in his testimony that "there is no telling how many bears and deer I have killed in that neighborhood." When the Federal troops searched for cotton they were guided by Negroes to the hidden Douglas cotton.

In the urban communities conditions were the most favorable for the development of the Negro. One remarkable free Negro, Jehu Jones, was noted for his excellent hotel in Charleston patronized by whites. Solomon Humphreys of Macon, Georgia, was an enterprising merchant. After he had emancipated himself by saving small sums he opened a store in Macon, and as a result of extraordinary energy, shrewdness, and a reputation for honesty became rich. Though he was unable to read or write, he employed white clerks to keep his accounts. With his wealth he practised Southern hospitality, entertaining his white friends at dinner, but observing the taboo of Southern society by refraining from sitting at the table with them. There were enterprising business men like Lunsford Lane of Raleigh who emancipated himself (by hiring his time from his master) and established a thriving business of manufacturing pipe tobacco until he was driven from Raleigh in 1842 because he was reported to have given some antislavery lectures during a trip in the Northern states.

Some of the most intelligent and spirited Negroes who grew up in the slave regime attained distinction by escaping to the North and there pursuing antislavery activities. Harriet Tubman, a Maryland slave, and Josiah Henson, regarded as the original of "Uncle Tom," became important conductors of the underground railroad. Especially notable was William Wells Brown, born a slave in Lexington, Kentucky, who escaped to the North and became an agent of the American Anti-Slavery Society and a prominent Negro author and historian. The autobiographies and lectures of such escaped slaves, detailing the cruelties of Southern slavery, were an important force in arousing the Northern people to support the abolitionist cause.

The Creole mulattoes, griffes, quadroons, and octoroons of Louisiana represented the highest development of Negro culture in the South during the antebellum period. In Victor Séjour and Camille Thierry, this class produced the two most accomplished literary Negroes of the period in America, but it is significant that they emigrated to France to escape racial prejudice. On the other hand, Norbert Rillieux, a Creole Negro who studied in France returned to Louisiana. In 1843 he invented an improved process of boiling cane juice in vacuum pans which was adopted by the progressive planters. Some of the Negro Creole planters like Alexander Durnford, whose *Sainte Rosalie* sugar plantation was cultivated by fifty slaves, and the colored planters in the Natchitoches region were wealthy. They spoke both French and English, had reserved manners for fear of being insulted by crude whites, and sent their children to France to be educated.

The free Negro community in Charleston, South Carolina, also contained some remarkable individuals. The Weston family, for example, started their progress upward in the Charleston world when the white slave master Plowdon Weston gave his mulatto slave Toney one half of his time to work for himself. After Toney was emancipated he became a highly successful millwright and inventor. In the 1860 list of taxpayers in Charleston his wife Maria was the largest taxpayer among the free Negroes. The Westons, who included the tailors, Jacob and Samuel, jointly paid taxes on $75,975 valuation of real estate as well as on thirty slaves. The Charleston free Negroes supported a school for their children taught by a white man.

Certainly an extraordinary town Negro of the Old South was the quadroon, William Tiler Johnson. He kept a diary from 1835 to 1851 which is one of the most valuable documents extant for studying the mind of the antebellum Southern Negro. In pursuing his trade of barber Johnson constantly came into contact with white patrons with whom he talked and joked freely. He improved his opportunities to make money by lending numerous small sums of money to whites at high interest; at the time when he was murdered in 1851, he had accumulated an estate of $25,000, including fifteen slaves. He bought a farm on which he employed some of his slaves; they were supervised by a white overseer he hired. He seems to have developed precisely the same attitudes toward his slaves as did white masters—flogging them severely on occasions, hiring them out for wages, buying and selling human chattels. He exercised most of the rights of free whites—suing debtors in court, owning a gun with which he hunted, attending the threatre, but always sitting in the gallery reserved for Negroes. He took a keen interest in local politics, owned gamecocks, gambled, and subscribed to five or six newspapers, including the New York *Mirror*, the sporting periodical, *The Spirit of the Times*, and the *Saturday Evening Post*.

Evidence for the existence of remarkable Negroes in the society of the old South is often found in the source material of the Reconstruction period. For example, Margaret Thorpe, one of the New England schoolmistresses who came to teach the freedmen in the village of Warrenton, North Carolina, recorded in her diary the residence of several outstanding Negro citizens who had been reared during slavery days. One of these was "Uncle" Albert Burgess, who rented the house in which General Braxton Bragg was born, and with whom Miss Thorpe boarded. "Uncle" Albert had been the slave of General Hawkins, who had taught him the courtly manners characteristic of many of the old slaves. He was well informed in local history and was a leader among the Negroes, but he refused a nomination for Congress because he did not think that Negroes were fit for political office. Another notable colored resident of Warrenton was a "Mr. Alston" in whose home Miss Thorpe dined, despite the strong condemnation of the villagers. Before the war he had, by saving extra earnings, bought his freedom from his master. Subsequently he had acquired a store, a small farm, and sixteen slaves whom he permitted to work out their freedom. Miss Thorpe described him as a handsome man with silvery hair, delicate features, and elegant manners. It is only by chance that a knowledge of such Negroes (remarkable in relation to their limited opportunities) in one small village of the South has survived, a circumstance that leads one to suspect the presence of many others like them throughout the slave states.

Many of the superior Negroes who grew up in the slavery regime were not able to display their ability until the Reconstruction period gave them an opportunity. The Freedman's Convention that assembled in Raleigh in 1865 contemporaneously with the white constitutional convention, for example, brought forward some hitherto obscure Negroes. Its deliberations so favorably impressed Sidney Andrews, correspondent for the Boston *Advertiser* and author of *The South Since the War* (1866) that he wrote: "In sober truth the Freedman's Convention was a body of which the Negroes of this or any other Southern State might well be proud—." The leader of the convention was John H. Harris of Raleigh, dark in color, a former slave field hand who had educated himself after the day's work, like Lincoln, "with a pine knot in one hand and a book in the other." After emancipation he became an upholsterer and a teacher—"a plain, patient, unassuming man, whose wise judgment, catholic views, genuine culture and honest manhood fit him to adorn any station in society." It was he who drafted the address presented by the freedman's convention to the white constitutional convention. Other leaders in the convention were Isham Sweet, a barber of Fayetteville, "of rare dramatic talent, mature years, ready speech, and moderate views"; George Rue, a "pure African" who had preached in Massachusetts and served as chaplain in a regiment of colored troops; and John Randolph, Jr., of Greensboro, a carpenter by trade and a teacher, "radical in desire, but conservative in action, longing for much, but content to make haste slowly." The convention rejected the proposals of the more radical members such as A. W. Galloway, who had associated much with Northern people and was dominated by an "exceedingly radical and Jacobinical spirit." The address of the colored convention revealed that the Negro leaders who had matured in the slave regime were capable of making wise political decisions and expressing their views and hopes in moving language.

The Negro newspaper, the New Orleans *Tribune*, on July 4, 1865, reported a meeting of colored citizens of Petersburg, Virginia, on the preceding March 31st. They passed resolutions that poignantly expressed some of the dominant thoughts in the Negro mind. "We can compare favorably" the meeting resolved, "with a large number of our white fellow-citizens, both native and foreigners, in point of intelligence—many of them can neither read nor write and know nothing of the country." Proudly they pointed to the record of bravery of Negro soldiers in the battles of Olustee, Milliken's Bend, Port Hudson, Fort Wagner, and Petersburg. They demanded the right of American citizens of no taxation without representation, and they scorned the allegation against Negroes, "that we understand freedom to be idleness and indolence."

The most notable of the Negroes who matured during the slave regime were the politicians of the Reconstruction period. Between 1870 (when Jefferson Long of Macon, Georgia, was the first Negro elected to the House of Representatives) and 1900 twenty-two Negroes served in Congress. Several held the office of lieutenant governor, one became a justice of a state supreme court, and numerous Negroes were legislators and state officers. Although a few were black carpetbaggers, the overwhelming majority were born in the South and reared during the days of slavery. They, therefore, represented an extension of the mind of the antebellum Negro into the Reconstruction period. A large portion of these Negro leaders had considerable white blood in their veins. Robert Smalls, for example, who seized the Confederate transport *Planter* and brought it within the Union lines, was the son of a Jewish father and Negro mother. After the capture of the *Planter*, of which he was made captain, he became the great hero of the South Carolina Negroes and was elected to four terms in Congress. The black politicians seem to have been as able as the lighter-skinned individuals. Good examples of the "smart" full-blood Negroes in politics were Prince Rivers and Beverly Nash in the South Carolina legislature and Jere Haralson, Congressman from Alabama, "black as the ace of spades and with the brogue of the cornfield." Rivers was a slave coachman in Beaufort before the war. He had learned to read and write, and he became a sergeant in a colored regiment commanded by Reverend Thomas Wentworth Higginson, who said of him, "If there should ever be a black monarchy in South Carolina, he will be its king."

Quite a number of the Negro politicians had managed to obtain a fair education before the war, and some were polished and cultivated gentlemen. Francis Louis Cardozo, the son of a Jewish editor in Charleston and a slave woman, studied before the war in the University of Glasgow and became secretary of state in South Carolina. Private tutors provided by their white fathers had taught Senator Blanche K. Bruce of Mississippi and Representative James Napier of Alabama on the plantation. The Negro politicians who held the higher offices were usually well dressed and decorous in conduct, and some were accomplished parliamentarians and eloquent speakers. Their principal weakness was a susceptibility to bribes. To balance this fault, however, most of them displayed a forgiving spirit toward the whites who had kept them in slavery, and generally they voted in Congress to remove the political disabilities of the former Confederates.

What is the explanation of the rise of these remarkable Negroes of the Old South and of the early days of Reconstruction? Most of them had enjoyed unusual opportunities and incentives for self-development. They advanced to a higher level of culture as a result of the encouragement and privileges granted to them by considerate and enlightened masters. Most of them had learned to read and write despite restrictive laws. By taking advantage of opportunities in the hiring system, by acquiring mechanical skills through apprenticeships, and by being placed in positions of responsibility on the plantation, they had developed self-respect and pride. The colonization movement gave to some of them a wider horizon and an incentive to struggle to buy their freedom. Lott Cary, a Virginia slave who had purchased his freedom and had learned to read and write, was the first American missionary to the Dark Continent (1820). He was an example of the power of the religious motive in elevating some slaves above the level of a mere animal existence. The first president of the republic of Liberia, Joseph J. Roberts, was a free Negro from Petersburg, Virginia, in blood seven-eighths white, who emigrated to that country in 1829. The struggle of some intelligent and spirited slaves to free themselves from bondage and to help other slaves to escape were potent stimulants of self-improvement. Of the thirty-six Negroes belonging to the period 1836–65 who are included in the *Dictionary of American Biography* and classified as "distinguished" in Professor Richard Bardolph's study, twenty-eight (most of them living North of the Mason-Dixon Line) were antislavery and Negro rights leaders.

One of the decisive influences in the growth of some of the remarkable Negroes was their close association with superior masters. Beverly Nash, for example, was the slave of W. C. Preston, president of South Carolina College and United States Senator; and William Finch, the first Negro elected to the Atlanta City Council (in 1870), was brought up in the households of the noted Unionist Judge Garnett Andrews and of Judge Joseph H. Lumpkin. Finch attributed much of his success in life to Judge Lumpkin's wise advice and to the interest that Lumpkin, a staunch upholder of slavery, had taken in him.

In the Slave Papers of the Library of Congress is a manuscript autobiography of the slave "Fields," dated at Richmond in 1847; the manuscript gives an example of the stimulus of white contacts upon the Negro. Fields relates that he never knew what "the yoke of oppression" was until he was nearly grown, for "the black and white children all faired alike." He became very attached to the master's son; but when the latter had become a teenager, he asserted his superiority over his dark-skinned playmate and friend, "like a peacock among chickens," and soon the master's son was sent away to school and the slave boy was put in the fields to work. But before this separation the master's son had taught Fields to read and had also stimulated his religious feelings. When a revival occurred in the neighborhood, he proposed that they both pray and see who got religion first.

This symbiosis of Negroes and whites living together, especially on the small plantations, was indeed an important influence in the advancement of the Negro, frequently leading to mutual respect and affection. The letter that the brilliant Virginia statesman Littleton W. Tazewell wrote to John Randolph of Roanoke on February 16, 1826, is only one of numerous testimonials of planters to the virtues of individual slaves and their affection for them. Tazewell wrote, "My faithful friend & servant John departed this life a few hours before I reached home—For seventy years had he filled his place in society with a fidelity which nothing could corrupt, and with an affection for his master which knew no bounds—I have never seen a better man and never can have a truer friend—we shall meet again hereafter, if I shall live like him, blameless, steady, and true to my trusts—" (Tazewell Papers, MSS in University of Virginia Library).

Progress of Southern Negroes was most evident where they had been exposed to the stimulus of town and city life. Northern travelers like Whitelaw Reid, John R. Dennett, and Robert Somers who observed the Negroes shortly after emancipation reported that on the isolated sea islands and interior plantations the slaves were most ignorant and degraded, but in the towns and city they were the most intelligent of the race. Sidney Andrews wrote from the Orangeburg court house, South Carolina, on September 9, 1865, "the city negro and the country negro are as much unlike as two races." Among those Negroes most closely associated with upper-class whites besides the house servants and drivers were the barbers, and this fact explains to some degree the important role Negro barbers played in politics and the leadership of the race immediately after the Civil War.

The remarkable individuals that arose in the slave society present only one facet of the Negro mind. The average slave could not overcome the handicaps of human bondage, which warped his mind and personality into what Ulrich B. Phillips, the eminent student of American Negro slavery, has described as "a standard plantation type." The slave was constantly accommodating himself to the pressures of an authoritarian society. Although the Negro was noted for his loud guffaw, which seemed to indicate an uninhibited sense of humor and a relaxed personality, there was another kind of laugh characteristic of the slave—a nervous laugh of ingratiation when he felt embarassed in the presence of the white man. After the Civil War the northern journalist Edward King visited a cotton plantation in Louisiana when a delegation of humble field hands came to see the master. "If I looked at them steadily," he wrote, "they burst into uneasy laughter and moved away." So common was this physical manifestation that he called it "the regulation laugh." He found the country Negroes diffident in expressing opinions before the white man. The sense of inferiority and insecurity, induced in part at least by the overlordship of the white man, seems to have been mainly responsible also for the shuffling gait, the slouching posture, and the downcast look in speaking to white men. Moreover the stuttering that advertise-ments for runaway slaves often mentioned probably resulted from this same sense of inferiority and insecurity.

Southern slavery, a modern student has observed, had much the same effect on the Negro's personality as confinement for a consider-able period in a German concentration camp of World War II had on white prisoners. It tended to produce a Sambo type of person-ality, reducing its subjects to a child-like behavior—submissive, irresponsible, living from day to day. The ardent abolitionist, Thomas Wentworth Higginson, colonel of the first colored regiment mustered into the United States army, studied closely the charac-teristics of his Negro soldiers, men who had just escaped from slavery. They displayed, he wrote, great docility, a child-like nature that alternated between extreme gravity and exhilaration, and an enduring patience. Other characteristics that he noted were a dramatic talent, a deep religious feeling which they expressed in their fervent singing of spirituals, and a freedom from vindictive-ness. Moreover, they proved in battle to be fully as brave as white soldiers. Since these jet black Negroes had grown up on isolated plantations they were comparatively free from the vices of towns and cities, such as drunkenness, profanity, and crimes of violence. Petty stealing and immorality were faults that had been stimulated by the conditions of the slave plantation. Higginson was impressed, though, by seeing how quickly the mores of the Negro changed after he had escaped from bondage. The freedman especially developed self-respect. Every day the Northern colonel observed with a feeling of half-regret that his affectionate, child-like soldiers were becoming more and more like the ordinary white soldier.

The Southern Negro, though he wished to be free, loved the region in which he was born—he was a Southerner. He was un-happy when he moved to the North, where the climate, food, urban customs, and stricter supervision by his employers were repugnant to him. In the North he encountered violent race prejudice and discrimination at every turn. Frederick Law Olm-sted, though a Northern antislavery man, was very observant and candid when he wrote: "I do not believe that there are any other people in the world with whom the Negro would be as con-tented, and, if contentment is happiness, so happy, as with those who are now his masters" (New York *Daily Times*, January 12,

1854). Northerners, Westerners, Europeans would not tolerate the constant indolence, shiftlessness, carelessness, and forgetfulness displayed by the Southern slaves that he witnessed. The influence of a warm climate and of the slave system on the mind and personality of the white Southerners for generations had made them less efficient directors of labor, more tolerant of human deficiencies, more shiftless themselves, and more relaxed taskmasters than the enterprising Northern men or Europeans who settled in the South.

Although the condition of the free Negro on the whole deteriorated during the latter part of the antebellum period, the condition of the slave seems to have improved. This reading of the evidence does not agree with the conclusion of one of the most recent scholarly studies of slavery *The Peculiar Institution* by Kenneth Stampp, who maintains: "In 1860 the peculiar institution was almost precisely what it had been thirty years before" (p. 28)—a strikingly vicious system. Sir Charles Lyell, the English geologist, who in 1845 observed the practical working of the institution, believed, on the other hand, that even in those districts where the slaves worked in large gangs, "the Negroes are very far from stationary" in acquiring a higher civilization. Moreover, where the slave associated closely with the white family on farms and small plantations (in 1860 nearly half, 47.6 per cent, of the slaves were owned by men who had fewer than 20 slaves) his progress was much greater. This acceleration of improvement from daily contacts with whites resulted from the exercise of what Lyell called "the imitative faculty," which the Negro possessed to a large degree.

Frederick Law Olmsted, who is generally regarded as a star witness against the Southern slave system, corroborated Lyell's observation, finding that "in general the relation of master and slave on small farms, and the relations of the family and its household servants everywhere, may be considered a happy one, developing, at the expense of decision, energy, self reliance and self-control, some of the most beautiful traits of human nature."

In the latter part of the antebellum period the progressive development of the practice of hiring slaves was modifying the slave system, giving some slaves new opportunities to develop. Although it applied to less than 10 per cent of the agricultural slaves, hiring was widely practiced in the towns and cities and in industrial occupations, such as the tobacco factories (where over half of the slaves were hired hands), in the building of railroads and the digging of canals, in mining, on steamboats, in hotels, in the turpentine industry, and especially in domestic service. In the hiring-out process the masters often permitted the slave to select his employer, and they used this opportunity to make terms with the hirer for special privileges. In the factories they were paid for extra work above a required task, thus furnishing them with money to spend on their pleasures or to save to buy their emancipation. In some cases the hired slaves were given an allowance to provide for their maintenance, which enabled them to select their food and quarters. Although some hired slaves were abused by their employers (who had little personal interest in protecting them), the system of hiring on a whole upgraded the lives of the slaves thus employed and was a step toward freedom. In the cities and towns where the majority of the hired slaves worked they became more sophisticated than their fellow slaves on the plantations, and they escaped the close surveillance of the master. Olmsted noted the effect of the hiring practice in the lumbering industry. The hired slaves cut a quota of shingles and were paid for extra shingles cut; they were, he observed, "more sprightly and straight-forward in their manner and conversation than any field-hand plantation negroes that I saw in the South." Some masters complained that hiring their slaves out in the towns ruined them, for they became "impudent," asserted their individuality more positively, became adept and sophisticated in evading the restrictions of the slave system—but these charges indicated that under the hiring system the slaves were developing some of the characteristics of free men. Indeed, the peculiar institution on the eve of the Civil War, partly as a result of the hiring system, was showing some signs in the cities and towns of breaking down.

Instead of being a Siberian prison camp for the Negro, as the abolitionists and neo-abolitionists have portrayed, Southern society of the antebellum period displayed a certain latitude in the treatment of the lowly race that permitted the rise of a considerable number of remarkable Negroes. In directing attention to this group, I have taken a path that has been traveled by few students of the Negro and of American history. The existence of these notable Negroes of the antebellum period (notable especially when one considers the tremendous handicaps placed on slaves in seeking a higher culture) has to be ferreted out from the obscurity of the past. They are among the examples that show the irrepressibility of the human spirit, whether in a black man or a white man, as well as the plastic nature of the human mind. The remarkable Negroes of the Old South should have proved to the Southerners the falsity of their stereotypes of the Negro. But so tenacious are stereotypes when supported by tradition, economic interest, and fear that they often defy both reason and observation. The stereotype of the Negro is a striking instance, for it has continued to affect public opinion, both in the South and the North, far into the twentieth century.

Chapter X

THE RELIGIOUS EXPERIENCE

THE antebellum period was probably the most religious age in the entire history of the South. Its spirit was exhibited in various ways—the camp meeting, "protracted meetings," the family altar at which the members daily knelt to offer prayer, the frequent readings of the Bible, the dramatic conversions and baptisms, and the letters of the time filled with a simple faith. Arthur M. Schlesinger, Sr., has noted that the American mind has displayed the remarkable phenomenon of an alternating freezing and thawing of thought resulting in periods of orthodoxy and of liberalism. The antebellum period in the South was one of the settling of religious thought and feeling into a rigid pattern of orthodoxy.

With the rise of the cotton kingdom, Southern religion took on more and more the character of anti-intellectualism. Rational, relatively nonemotional religions such as the Unitarian church, which had made so promising a beginning below the Mason-Dixon Line during the first quarter of the nineteenth century, declined to a shadow after 1830. Only foreign radicals such as the German Free Societies in Baltimore and Louisville during the

1850's dared to offend the mores of their communities by exercising free thought on religious matters. The German Turners of Louisville called down the condemnation of the community upon themselves when they paraded through the streets of the city in January, 1855, to pay honor to the memory of Thomas Paine, the author of *The Age of Reason*. The editor of the *Louisville Courier*, in criticizing these foreigners for their infidel beliefs, declared that American civilization was based on the acceptance of Christianity. He pronounced deluded those who subscribed to the teachings of *The Age of Reason*, Hume's *Essay on Miracles*, the skepticism of Voltaire and Gibbon, or Volney's *Ruins of Empire*.

By 1830 the deism and skepticism of the eighteenth-century Enlightenment had virtually disappeared in the South. The Great Revival and subsequent waves of evangelism had converted most of the doubters who had grown up in an age when skepticism was fashionable among the gentry. In 1835 John Hartwell Cocke was overjoyed at the conversion of one of the skeptics, Professor J. A. G. Davis of the University of Virginia (the same professor who some years later was elected chairman of the faculty). To his wife Louisa he wrote that the learned professor was until lately "the most outbreaking [*sic*] of all our Infidels," but that now he expected to meet him at the communion table in the Episcopal church in Charlottesville.

The elimination of deism and skepticism from the South was effected by many converging forces. Deism, the religion of a number of the statesmen of the early republic, was already dying a natural death when the evangelists of the Great Revival attacked it, for it was too cold and intellectual for the ordinary man. The spirit of the nineteenth century, moreover, was deeply affected by the enveloping movement of Romanticism, which was the antithesis of eighteenth-century rationalism. And the need to defend slavery against the attacks of the abolitionists fostered a fundamentalist form of religion.

The religion of the Southern masses in the nineteenth century was strongly evangelical. The manuscript diary of Richard Hugg King (which is preserved in the North Carolina Department of Archives at Raleigh) gives a remarkable insight into the evangelical mind of the Old South. Although King had been educated at Princeton, he was close to the common man in his religion and in his techniques of preaching. He was a backwoods farmer and collector of the odious excise tax on whiskey in North Carolina before he was converted in a violent religious paroxysm at a camp meeting during the period of the Great Revival. Since the Presbyterian church would not license him as a preacher because he had not studied theology, he joined the Methodist church and became a circuit rider in western North Carolina for twelve years. At this time the Methodist circuit riders were paid eighty dollars a year, plus traveling expenses, a fact that made it necessary for him to combine farming with riding the circuit.

The Reverend Eli Washington Caruthers, who wrote a manuscript biography entitled "Richard Hugg King and his Times" (also in the North Carolina Department of Archives) has sketched a striking portrait of him. He described this ardent evangelist, whom he had heard preach when he was a young student, as a tall portly man, well over six feet in height, inclining a little to corpulence. He had black hair and black eyes, a dark complexion, and an intellectual and impressive countenance. When he preached, he spoke slowly and calmly at first, in a loud but musical voice. Then he gradually warmed up to his subject until his eyes became fixed apparently on every person in the house, and soon he and his susceptible audience would weep together. The recurrent themes of his sermons were the redemption of sinners from the fate of Hell and the providence of God.

During his latter years in east Tennessee, he was much handicapped in his crusade to save souls by his great weight, for he weighed more than four hundred pounds and was affected by a swollen leg that forced him to preach sitting in a chair. Nevertheless, he was a man of such ardent temperament, who could "in tones of thunder deal out the terrors of the law," that he would at times involuntarily arise to his feet, to the alarm of his hearers, and appeal to sinners until he sank exhausted into his chair. He would on occasion preach in the groves, sitting in his chair, his audience "solemnly attentive." Periodically he went to Knoxville to attend religious services or he would set out in a sulky to administer the sacraments in lonely little places like Baker's Creek and Grassy Valley. Around him sickness raged, especially typhus or epidemic fever, the virulent ague, and after 1833, cholera epi-

demics, which took people from this earth with dramatic sudden-
ness. These recurring diseases that baffled the puny efforts of the
country doctors must have frightened the people and made them
susceptible to the kind of religion which the Methodist circuit
riders and the uneducated Baptist ministers preached.

The dramatic moment in American religion, in the North as
well as in the South, was the experience of "conversion." When
the scientist Joseph Le Conte was a student at Franklin College
(the University of Georgia) he was converted at a revival. His
description of his emotions at this time was typical of most conversions in the antebellum period: "I passed through all the stages
. . . a period of great distress, of earnest prayer, of exercise of
faith, followed by a sudden sense of acceptance, and intense
ecstatic joy for deliverance. . . ." The greatest effect of his conversion, he believed, was not in the change of his moral life, for he
was an exemplary young man, but in his emancipation from "the
bondage of the fear of death and the hereafter."

During the period of the Great Revival there was a remarkable
cooperation among the various sects, their doctrinal differences
being largely ignored in the common cause of saving souls. But
after the ebb of the Revival movement, men began to fight over
these differences and their attitudes hardened into an unyielding
denominationalism. Sectarianism, indeed, often influenced such
important decisions as to whether a Methodist should marry a
Baptist, or whether to vote for a staunch Baptist or an Episcopalian. The symbol around which the battle lines were drawn was
most often the rite of baptism, but there were other matters of
violent disagreement, such as closed or open communion, temperance, and missionary activity. A revealing example of the weight
attached to denominations in the Old South is found in the letters
of a Louisiana private in the Confederate Army to his wife. She
had wounded his feelings, he wrote, by becoming a Baptist, and
he begged her not to make Baptists of his children. "The ware
[war] and the Baptist and the sickness," he declared, "is a nuff
to make a man go crazy that dont have fare [far] to go no
how. . . ." Later he wrote in a glow of triumph concerning a debate in his company: "It was on the subject of Baptist and clost
communion. The scriptures was perused fore proof of the doc-

trine. The Baptist was as completly wound up as i ever saw in my life. This debate lasted 3 or 4 hours. It wound up by the Baptist saying that wee dident look at the scripures right."

When the Reverend Neal Gordon of Nicholasville, Kentucky, sought in 1850 to persuade his church, the Associated Reform Presbyterian, to engage in a missionary enterprise to Africa, he ran into difficulties over denominational prejudices. He proposed that the church buy four Negro boys and educate them to go to Liberia as missionaries and to establish a school in Africa. Some of the members were strongly opposed to merging their resources and efforts with other denominations in such a project. Gordon received letters saying that any merger would result in the loss of the distinctive characteristics of their branch of the Presbyterian church and that many of the wealthy members of the church, who were of "the straightest sect" and "sticklers for order and form," would not contribute.

The census statistics in the last decade of the antebellum period show that the more emotional sects had flourished in the South like the proverbial green bay tree. While population had increased during the decade at the rate, for example, of 24.06 per cent in Alabama, 21 per cent in Georgia, and 12.29 per cent in Virginia, the number of Methodist and Baptist churches increased 50, 34, and 30 per cent respectively. On the eve of the Civil War these churches, which appealed especially to the yeoman families and the Negroes, included well over three-fourths of the churches in the South, ranging in ratio from 70 per cent in Virginia to 90 per cent in Georgia.

The secession convention of Mississippi in 1861, which probably represented the leadership class of the state, presents an interesting picture of church membership. It contained twenty-three Methodists and sixteen Baptists—55.7 per cent of those of the convention who belonged to churches; the other denominations were represented by sixteen Presbyterians, twelve Episcopalians, two Roman Catholics, and one member of the Christian church; thirty of the hundred members of the convention apparently did not belong to a church, though some of these listed themselves as "friendly to all" churches.

The Presbyterians, from all indications, were far stronger among the leadership class than their numerical church membership would rank them. They sought more than any other sect to obtain control over the education of the youth and to mold it along Calvinistic lines. A good example of their strong-minded preachers who united the mystical with the intellectual in religion was James Henley Thornwell, outstanding leader of the Southern Presbyterian church at the end of the antebellum period. The son of a South Carolina overseer, he became the intellectual interpreter of the religion of the upper middle class. He had received his education as the result of the philanthropy of some gentlemen of Cheraw, and he repaid their confidence by becoming an intense student. At South Carolina College this small, sickly-looking youth was graduated at the head of his class. His erudition was such that he astonished people by his ability to recite from memory whole dramas of Shakespeare, numerous verses of Milton, and long extracts from the classic authors. He was a remarkable example of the effect of the classics upon the Southern mind—resulting in an appreciation of classical literature primarily for its value as a mental discipline rather than for its artistic and humanistic content.

In 1834 Thornwell enrolled as a student at Andover Divinity School in Cambridge, Massachusetts, and also studied briefly at Harvard College. Here he was shocked by the rationalistic attitude of professors and students toward the sacred mysteries of orthodox religion. He declared that the Unitarian doctrines of New England were "little better than downright infidelity" and quickly left those ungodly places where they flourished. Underlying his brilliant but dogmatic mind was a deeply passionate nature; religion was an emotional outlet for him and a passport to Heaven. Full of invective and sarcasm, he displayed a Hebraic intolerance toward unbelievers. He also exhibited the same type of puritanical asceticism that characterized the life of Alexander H. Stephens, especially when both men were young schoolteachers. He condemned dancing as "an insult to God," but he himself indulged in the pleasure of chewing tobacco from eleven years of age to his death.

From the time when his polemic career began during the great controversy in the Presbyterian church over the "New School" and the "Old School" until his death in 1862 Thornwell exercised great power in South Carolina and throughout the Southern Presbyterian church. Not only was he an influential preacher, but he served as president of South Carolina College from 1851 until 1855, when he resigned to become a professor in Presbyterian Theological Seminary located in Columbia. A large part of Thornwell's influence on his section emanated from his uncompromising convictions and his eloquence as a public speaker. Joseph Le Conte has observed in his autobiography that Thornwell by his personal eloquence and magnetism created a very high sense of honor among the students. Indeed, in referring to his joining the faculty of South Carolina College in the 1850's Le Conte wrote, "I had never previously seen (nor have I since) so high a sense of honor among students in their relations to one another and to the faculty."

A great polemicist, Thornwell fought mightily against modernism in religion as exhibited by the "New School" faction of the Northern Presbyterian church. He fought side by side with another potent leader of the "Old School" theologians—Robert Jefferson Breckinridge, professor in the Theological Seminary at Danville, Kentucky. These churchmen stoutly upheld the Calvinistic doctrines of the Westminster Confession of Faith, especially the depravity of human nature and Christ's atonement for the ancient sin of man by his sacrifice on the cross. In Thornwell's religious philosophy, sin and God's grace to repentant sinners played a central role; he had no doubt about the existence of positive evil in the world, both in the carnal nature of man and in the Devil being abroad. In these beliefs he reflected the universal faith of the South, as well as of the great majority of the devout rural folk of the North. There was no room in his religion for the toleration of heresy or free thought, such as atheism, unitarianism, or "the abomination of Popery."

A pillar of conservatism in religious matters, Thornwell was also a staunch conservative in the defense of slavery. He had a plantation named Dryburgh Abbey near Lancaster, South Carolina, which he would visit periodically for relaxation and refreshment of his soul. He was a kind and indulgent master who was careful to provide religious instruction for his slaves. Although he made virtually no profit from the slaves, his ownership of a plantation obtained for him the prestige and advantage of a planter in South Carolina society. In the General Assembly of the Presbyterian church in 1845 this doughty debater fought against any condemnation of Southern slavery. He maintained that slavery was not sinful: it was justified by the Holy Scriptures and was a civil relation with which the church had no right to interfere.

An ardent and ruthless expansionist, Thornwell desired to annex Texas and to take California and Mexico. To his wife he wrote from Wheeling, Virginia, on June 14, 1845: "The more I reflect upon the subject, the more I am satisfied that the mission of our Republic will not be accomplished, until we embrace in our Union the whole of this North American continent. If the New England people are disposed to kick up a dust about the annexation of Texas, I am prepared to take the ground that it would be better for this country, and for the interests of the human race, to give up New England, than to abandon any new territory which we may be able to acquire."

Though he had opposed the Nullification movement in 1832 and secession in 1850, he became intensely sectional in his outlook during the decade of the 1850's. He advocated, for example, that Southern youth should be educated in the South and not sent to Northern schools and colleges. In a famous Fast Day sermon on November 21, 1860, he preached a strongly political sermon setting forth the Southern point of view. God was scourging the nation, he declared, for its "national sins"—abolitionism and subversion of the Constitution by selfish Northern interests. He excoriated the free states for refusing to return fugitive slaves and for seeking to exclude slaveholders from federal territories. He seems also to have adopted George Fitzhugh's views, expressed in the latter's books *Sociology for the South* (1854) and *Cannibals All* (1857), that Southern slavery was not based on race but on a natural and beneficial relation between capital and labor. He scorned the recently propounded doctrine of the diversity of the races as opposed to God's word and maintained that the Negroes were of the same origin as white men, having the same heavenly Father and the same everlasting destiny. When the Southern Confederacy was established, he was the leading figure in the organization of the Southern Presbyterian church and until his death at the height of Confederate success in battle was confident that God was on the side of the Southern people.

A comparison of Thornwell with another extremist, Theodore

Parker of New England, illustrates the wide difference between the Southern point of view on religion and that of the Northern reformers. Reform was in the New England air during the antebellum period, as it was not in the South, and a number of its leading ministers were deeply influenced by the reform impulse. Probably the main difference between Southern and Northern forms of Christianity lay in this fact, for the great masses throughout the United States held to an orthodox and traditional religion. While the Southern preachers, in general, centered religion on the "saving of souls," the reform-minded ministers of New England regarded religion as an agent of social reform.

Parker was a product of this reform movement just as Thornwell was deeply influenced by the changing social environment of the Southern states around 1830. Both men came from humble families. Parker was born in Lexington, Massachusetts, into a deeply religious and austere family of farmers and mechanics. By hard physical work on the farm and by teaching school he was able to earn enough money to put himself through Harvard Divinity School. He became a Unitarian minister at West Roxbury, Massachusetts, and when he came under the influence of Emerson and the transcendentalists, he broke completely with orthodox religion. While J.H. Thornwell and most Southerners relied on the authority of the literal word of the Bible as the basis of their religion, Parker shocked the orthodox by maintaining that true religion existed independently of the revelation of the Bible. Thornwell, on the other hand, was a man of conventional and orthodox views. Though he was a scholar, his scholarship was narrow and unaffected by the fresh breezes of the critical study of the Bible that moved European scholars. Parker, in contrast, was a student of tremendous energy who read widely not only works in the English language but also German philosophy and literature. He read so voraciously that Professor Henry Steele Commager has called him an "intellectual gourmand." In Parker's sermons there was little, if any, of the gentlemanly tradition of religion that the Episcopal clergy preached; they were blunt, forthright, uncompromising, appealing to the intellect and the New England conscience. This Boston preacher, deeply influenced by the reform impulse, was a universal reformer, concerned with prison reform and the abolition of capital punishment, the rights of women, free school education, Sabbath reform, temperance, and the improvement of the lot of industrial workers, but the reform in which he became an extremist was the Abolition movement and the higher law doctrine.

Quite different from the reformist preaching of New England and the stern Presbyterian faith of Thornwell was the decorous Episcopal church in the South. This church represented the way to Heaven for the Southern gentry. Highly dignified, it was not noted for its evangelical zeal or its missionary activities. The sermons of its well-educated, restrained rectors could not compete with the emotional, hell-fire preaching of the Baptists and Methodists; the practice of charging rent for pews was repugnant to the common man; the latitudinarian ideas of its members in regard to dancing, card-playing and wine-drinking seemed "worldly" to many Southerners, and its ritual smacked of Roman Catholic practices. Though it grew vigorously after 1825, as did the evangelical churches, the Episcopal church never appealed to more than a very small fraction of the Southern people. In 1860 it had only 33 of the 572 churches in Louisiana, only 25 of the 1,441 churches in Mississippi, and only 188 of the 3,105 churches in Virginia where its strength was greatest.

No more admirable leader of this church, according to Southern standards, existed at the close of the antebellum period than the bishop of Louisiana, Leonidas Polk. Born in Raleigh, North Carolina, in 1806, he came from a family that had acquired large landed estates. After attending the University of North Carolina for a year he received an appointment to West Point, where he roomed with Albert Sidney Johnston. At West Point, Polk was an exemplary young man, enamoured with military life, enjoying the pleasures of the fashionable world—such as attending a dancing school—yet at the same time a good student, ranking eighth in his graduating class in 1827.

Until he was twenty years old, the aristocratic Carolinian paid little attention to religion. Indeed, zealous devotion to religion was derided by most of the cadets. But in the spring of his junior year he was deeply troubled by a mistake that he had made which lowered his standing in his class and darkened his future. Coincidentally he had a dream of the Day of Judgment which disturbed him. He went to the chaplain, the Reverend Charles

McIlvaine, for consolation and instruction as to how he might save his soul. The chaplain gave him a textbook on the evidences of Christianity, which aided him in becoming a deeply religious convert. It was a courageous step for him as a cadet to practice his faith openly, but he wrote to his father that he had fortified himself against the opinions of the world and that instead of finding the religious life one of gloom and austerity, he was happy in carrying out the duties of his faith.

Shortly before he was graduated from the academy, he startled his father, Colonel William Polk of Revolutionary fame, by asking permission to resign from the army and accept a position as a teacher at Amherst Academy (the precursor of Amherst College). He gave as his reason his desire to educate himself further, especially in the liberal arts, the classics, and history, in which he felt that his knowledge was only superficial. His father vetoed this request, attributing it to an impulse, a wild and silly scheme which blinded him from following an honorable military career worthy of his family and his station in life. Leonidas accepted this verdict but shortly afterwards announced that he intended to study theology and become an Episcopal rector. His father was unable to dissuade him; he resigned his commission in the army and in November, 1828, enrolled in the Episcopal Theological Seminary at Alexandria, Virginia. After completing his training there, he was ordained in the spring of 1830. He then received the appointment of assistant to Bishop Moore at the fashionable Monumental Church in Richmond.

Ill-health forced him temporarily to abandon the ministry and to seek a cure for a year by travel in Europe. Upon his return he settled as a planter in Maury County, Tennessee, on land which his father gave him. Here, surrounded by his brothers who were prominent planters, he was very happy supervising his plantation, and operating a small hemp bagging factory on his plantation. He also preached regularly to a parish in the nearby village of Columbia and founded a girl's school. Several years passed in this way when in 1838 at the age of thirty-two, he was unexpectedly appointed Missionary Bishop of the Southwest. His territory was vast, including Alabama, Mississippi, Louisiana, Arkansas, the Indian Territory, and the Republic of Texas.

The westward movement of population had uprooted many

families from their churches, and in the crude conditions of a newly settled country they often did not have the advantages of regular worship. When Bishop Polk made his first visitation in 1839, he did not find a single Episcopal church in Louisiana west of the Mississippi River, and so absorbed were the inhabitants in worldly affairs and amusements on Sunday that it was difficult to assemble an audience to hear him preach. His appointment as Missionary Bishop was a great break in the established usages of the church, marking an adaptation to western conditions.

Polk was admirably suited to the arduous task before him. A handsome man of imposing appearance, great energy, and decisive character, he accommodated himself to the crude conditions that he met, and fortunately he was not a stickler for ritual and form. He carried into his work the spirit of a soldier, and he was dominated by the evangelical zeal to save souls. He wrote to his mother in 1839 that the urgent calls of Bishop Kemper and himself for coworkers in their respective fields of missionary endeavor had met with little response, so that he must make a tour eastward to recruit; it was useless for him to travel and preach unless there were laborers "to nourish the Seed Sown" and aid in founding and fostering congregations in the Southwest. On his first visitation, he traveled five thousand miles—on horseback, in steamboats, and on stages—preached forty-four sermons, baptized fourteen, confirmed forty-one, and established two churches.

In 1841 he was elected bishop of Louisiana. Accordingly, he decided to leave Tennessee and establish his family on a plantation in the state where his diocese was located. Mrs. Polk, in the meanwhile, had received a large inheritance, with the choice of taking either money or four hundred slaves. The Bishop made the unfortunate decision to take the slaves and operate a large sugar plantation in Louisiana with them. His motives were twofold, as his son explains in his biography—a belief that he could exercise a greater influence with the planters of Louisiana by joining their ranks and a desire to persuade them to a kinder treatment of their slaves by setting the example of paternalism and of ministering to their spiritual needs.

His plantation Leighton on Bayou La Fourche, sixty miles from New Orleans, became a showplace among Louisiana plantations, the scene of an idyllic family life, and a model of the patriarchal slave plantation. Polk would not follow the custom of the sugar plantations of the region by working the slaves on Sundays during the critical grinding season between the harvest and the coming of frost. Thus, because of his scruples, he sacrificed his own financial interest at times. Zealous in holding religious services among his black dependents, he required them to belong to the Episcopal church, although most religious slaves preferred the more emotional sects of the Baptists and Methodists. He appealed to them to do their duties on the plantation out of motives of self-respect, but whenever they persistently erred, he punished them as children were punished in that age. Sometimes instead of whipping, he ordered humiliating penalties such as requiring a chicken thief to stand for several hours on Sunday with the stolen property tied around his neck, to the great amusement of the other slaves.

The good bishop divided his energies between the administration of his diocese and the superintendence of his large plantation. Such a dual role led to the neglect of his plantation and his worldly affairs. Moreover, he suffered extraordinarily bad luck: in 1849 an epidemic of cholera carried away 106 of his slaves; during the next year a tornado destroyed a large part of his property, including the sugarhouse valued at $75,000; and in the fall of that year an early frost reduced his sugar crop by one-third. These misfortunes and the heavy debts which he had accumulated forced him to turn over Leighton to his creditors and move his family to New Orleans.

The great but unfulfilled work of Leonidas Polk was the establishment of the University of the South. Though the Presbyterians, Methodists, and Baptists had founded denominational colleges in the Southern states, the Episcopal church in the 1850's had none. Bishop Polk resolved to establish an educational institution that would go far beyond being a church college and become a truly regional university. He made the first public announcement of his plan in the summer of 1856 in a printed letter addressed to the Southern bishops of the Episcopal church. He dreamed of founding a university in the South that in five years would rival Harvard, Yale, and the University of Virginia.

Polk urged the foundation of a regional Southern university because he believed that an emergency existed, "a stern necessity." Southern youth were being forced to abandon Northern schools and colleges because of their aversion to the antislavery doctrines taught in these institutions. Southern parents, he observed, "would rather their children go half-educated than send them to the North." The good bishop looked with apprehension upon the growth of radicalism, especially of abolition fanaticism, in the Northern states. Writing to Bishop Elliott of Georgia, August 20, 1856, he expressed a fear (in a passage omitted from the letter as published in the biography by his son) that the Northern Episcopal church, which had hitherto resisted fanaticism, would surrender to the antislavery movement and that secession would inevitably follow. The South then, he believed, would be in a bad way for education.

The founder planned to establish the University of the South on the solid rock of conservatism. There would be no Yankee professors on its faculty. In a passage also omitted from the published letter of August 20, he wrote, "We are afraid of Northern domination in our schools and pulpits of the South, 'these Northern men with southern principles.'" He also warned of danger from the influence of Northern seminaries and colleges; his university would protect Southern students from subversive doctrines.

The University of the South, he decided, should be different from the bourgeois schools and colleges of the Northern states; it should incorporate an aristocratic element by training the sons of planters to be Southern gentlemen. Only the Episcopal church was suited, he thought, to found this type of university. "The Baptists and Methodists," he observed in a letter of January 21, 1856, "have not the bearing or the social position or prestige, required to command the public confidence." In the projected university he proposed that there should be thirty-two schools—a far too ambitious undertaking—including architecture, civil engineering, agriculture, commerce, mining, and fine arts. One unique feature of his plan for the university was that its long vacation should be in the winter months and that it should operate throughout the summer when the students could closely associate with their parents who would be spending their vacations in nearby cottages.

His vision began to take practical shape when delegates from all over the South met on top of Lookout Mountain near Chattanooga on July 4, 1857, for the purpose of establishing the University of the South. The following year the legislature granted a charter. A great rivalry then ensued over the location of the projected university. Bishop Polk favored a site on Sewanee Mountain in eastern Tennessee because of its easy rail communication through Chattanooga with the lower South and because of its salubrious climate and charming landscape, which he thought would attract cotton and sugar planters to make their summer homes there. One of the promoters of the Sewanee site was John Armfield of the famous slave-trading firm of Franklin and Armfield; he owned the fashionable summer resort Beersheba Springs, which was located near the Sewanee site. Armfield entertained the Episcopal bishops at the Springs, contributed money to print promotional literature for the site, and built cabins on his land for Bishops Polk and Otey. The Sewanee Mining Company gave 9,500 acres of land for a campus and endowment. When the Sewanee property was finally selected in preference to the town of Chattanooga, its citizens became so vituperative over the loss of a moneymaking project that the good bishop commented: "They are a repulsive set of vulgarians." He devoted his energies until the coming of the Civil War to fund-raising campaigns; he traveled in the North to observe its universities and corresponded with leading men in Europe in regard to plans for the grand design.

In his efforts to found a religious proslavery university, Polk revealed that he had changed his views on slavery since he was a student at Episcopal Theological Seminary. At that time he had regarded colonization as a means of gradually eliminating slavery from the South. In a letter to his father, dated January 21, 1829, he had written: "Now I believe in the course of not many years one State after another will be willing to abolish slavery. This is proved by the state of things in Maryland and Virginia, the slave states farthest north. . . ." Three years later when he was traveling in England he observed in a letter to his mother: "I confess I am quite charmed with the neatness of the country houses, and the manner in which the fields are arranged, hedged, and tilled; and when I think of our own vast plantations, with our dirty careless thriftless Negro population, I could, and do, wish that we were thoroughly quit of them. The more I see of those without slaves, the more I am prepared to say that we are seriously wronging ourselves by retaining them. . . ."

By 1856, however, his views on the "peculiar institution" seem to have changed decidedly along with the changing attitude of his section. In August of that year he wrote to Bishop Elliott that "those madcaps at the North" did not understand slavery at all. Polk believed that Southern slavery was a patriarchal institution and that his projected university would train the sons of planters to be humane masters and to bring up their slaves in Christianity. The premature emancipation of the slaves, he held, would be a great wrong both to the slaves and to the masters.

For the remainder of his career until he became a general in the Confederate Army, Bishop Polk devoted his main efforts to founding the university. He wrote numerous letters to prominent Episcopalians, studied the organization and government of the best European universities, especially Oxford, and sought for a liberal endowment for the new institution. On October 9, 1860, the cornerstone of the first building was laid. Both the Honorable John S. Preston of South Carolina and Matthew Fontaine Maury spoke at the exercises on Sewanee Mountain. A few months earlier Maury had written to Bishop James Otey that his heart was in the great enterprise of building a Southern university. "You will not have it up a whit too soon," he warned, for the Union was in danger, and in the event of its dissolution the South would have the means of educating its leaders.

When the Secession movement interrupted the great work of his life, the Bishop took a loyal sectional stand on the issue of preserving the Union. Bishop Otey of Tennessee, one of the most important promoters of the university project, rebuked him for following the drift of public opinion instead of opposing the Secession movement. "It is God alone," Otey declared, "that can still the madness of the people. To what quarter shall we look, when such men as you and Elliott deliberately favor secession?"

Polk did endeavor, nevertheless, to prevent the Secession movement from resulting in a civil war. On December 26, 1860, before Louisiana had seceded, he wrote to President Buchanan, urging him to take no step toward coercing the Southern states and thus precipitating a civil war. He declared that in his opinion there was not "the remotest prospect for the reunion of the two sections as long as slave labor shall prove advantageously applicable to the agricultural wants of the Southern Confederacy."

Though the Bishop had no military experience after he left West Point, President Davis offered him a commission as major general in the Confederate Army to take charge of the defense of the Mississippi Valley. Polk conferred with Bishop Elliott and with the venerable Bishop Meade of Virginia on the advisability of accepting the commission. Upon their approval, he decided that it was his duty to accept the call to arms. On June 25, 1861, he became a major general in the Confederate Army. From then until June 14, 1864, when he was killed at Pine Mountain near Marietta, Georgia, opposing Sherman's advance, he served creditably in high command and was promoted before his death to the rank of lieutenant general. Rejecting the ruthless principles of total war, he believed that fighting men should behave as Christian gentlemen.

The career of Leonidas Polk as a churchman and that of the leader of the Northern branch of the church, Bishop Philander Chase, bear many striking resemblances. Chase was much older than Leonidas (he was born in 1775 in Cornish, New Hampshire), but they had virtually the same attitude toward religion, and their careers as missionaries in the West were similar. After graduating from Dartmouth College, Chase served as a pioneering clergyman in western New York and in 1817 went to the crude, recently settled area of Ohio. Here in 1819 he became the first bishop of Ohio. He found great difficulty, as did Polk, in securing ministers from the East who were willing to serve in the rough settlements of the West, and accordingly he determined to found a theological seminary and college in the West to train native sons for the ministry. In 1824 he was able to raise funds in England for the founding of Kenyon College, which he named after one of his English patrons. The location of the college was called Gambier after another patron, Lord Gambier, to whom Henry Clay had given Chase a letter of recommendation. He decided to locate his college in the woods rather than in a town, a plan which led to bitter opposition.

Bishop Chase had a more Puritan attitude toward life than

LEONIDAS POLK, Episcopal Bishop of Louisiana.

did his Southern counterpart. He fought strenuously in the temperance cause and would allow no drinking of whiskey among the students or even among the workmen who erected the college buildings. Both men seem to have been equally zealous in overcoming obstacles and enduring wilderness hardships to establish the Episcopal church in the West, and both had masterful and dominating personalities. It was this last quality that caused the faculty of Kenyon College to rise in rebellion against the rule of the autocratic Chase and led to his resignation as president in 1831. Both churchmen were warriors fighting under the banner of the Episcopal church against sin in the world. Chase had spent six years as a minister and teacher in New Orleans, and he always entertained a warm friendship for Southern people. In New Orleans he had bought a slave (who ran away from him), and the reminiscences which he composed in 1847 give no indication that he shared the abolitionist zeal of his nephew, Salmon P. Chase. Indeed, the religion of the Northern and the Southern champions of Episcopalianism in the West appear to be almost identical: both were Low Churchmen, who emphasized in their sermons prayer, the confession of sins, the weaning of the soul away from "the world," the preparation of the soul for death, and faith in the literal word of the Bible.

In Leonidas Polk there was a commingling of several religious traditions, as was often the case in both the South and the North. Polk was at the same time a missionary, the founder of a university, an exemplar of plantation paternalism, and an Episcopal clergyman. Not a profound thinker, he was a doer. Nor was he a pulpit orator like Thornwell or the eloquent Presbyterian minister of New Orleans Benjamin M. Palmer, the open advocate of secession. In manner and tastes he seemed far removed from the evangelical leaders, the fervent exhorters of the camp meetings; nevertheless, he did not differ basically in his religious ideas from these simple men—his thoughts, like theirs, were centered on "salvation," the winning of immortality in Heaven.

The Episcopal leader held the belief, common both to the evangelical and the gentlemanly traditions that the Christian life would be rewarded by practical benefits on this earth. To his brother Lucius who had recently joined the church, he wrote in

1843 that God would bless him in mind and estate: "For truly Godliness is profitable for all things, the life that now is as well as that which is to come." But the worldly success of the righteous was not to be compared to the salvation in the life beyond the grave. He warned against the folly of men who delayed the repentance of sins and preparation for death. "The time to prepare to meet death," he wrote to Lucius "is when we are in full health and have all our faculties at liberty to give to the wish."

Both the evangelical and the genteel traditions were obsessed with the idea of man's prepartion for death. Throughout Polk's writings, for example, there is a strong sense of the tragic element of life—the lurking of death. Life was short in the Old South, and the presence of death was emphasized by the mourning costume of women. Death would not have been so fearful, had not the sense of sin and guilt been emphasized by the preachers. The concept of sin varied to some degree among different groups but the deadliest sin was the sin of the mind—unbelief in Christian orthodoxy.

In the Petrie Papers at Auburn University is a letter which reveals what Freud might call the guilt complex of Americans of the prewar generation. To George H. Petrie, a student at the Presbyterian Theological Seminary in Columbia, South Carolina, John P. Porcher wrote on December 31, 1831, a description of a protracted meeting in the Presbyterian Church of Charleston, lasting four days, in which a minister from Savannah created a great sensation. As a result of his forceful preaching, wrote Porcher, "many have been convinced of the enormity of Sin and its awful consequence.—He preaches the terrors of the Law, and every one who hears him must feel and tremble."

Wilbur Cash in his *Mind of the South* has argued that the Southern people had a guilt complex because of the immoral relations of Southern men with slave women, and Mrs. Chesnut has lent support to this idea in her *Diary of Dixie*. Some modern liberals have attributed the emotional fundamentalism of the Old South to a guilt complex over the wrongs of slavery, but many Northern people had a similar feeling of sin. The more probable explanation for the great consciousness of sin in antebellum America was the resurgence of Calvinism with its great emphasis on the depravity of human nature.

The evangelical tradition in Southern religion had generally been opposed to slavery until the decade of the 1820's. Thereafter, with the rise of the cotton kingdom and the renewed profitability of slavery, both the evangelical and the gentlemanly traditions were able to accommodate the existence of slavery in the South with high Christian ideals. This feat was accomplished by a literal interpretation of the Bible, which immeasurably strengthened conservative trends in Southern society. There were so many contradictions in the Scriptures that both North and South could claim its authority for opposing views of the rightfulness of slavery. Probably the vast majority of Southerners after the 1830's came to accept without question the views of preachers, editors, and politicians who sanctioned slavery through the Holy Scriptures, for it seemed a profitable institution and the natural order of life.

Nevertheless, some brilliant and sensitive Southern men were troubled by doubts, such as the cultured former Senator William C. Preston, who had been president of South Carolina College. In 1857 while he was visiting in Virginia, Preston wrote to Waddy Thompson concerning his meeting with Phillip St. George, son of John Hartwell Cocke: "He put into my hands an essay on the *Scriptural* and statistical views of slavery, vastly the best work I have ever read on the subject, especially the *Scriptural*. It has wrought a change in my views which have been worrying me all my life. The work is by a Mr. Stringfellow, a Baptist preacher. Do get it and read it."

The great change in Southern religion in 1860 from that of 1800 arose from the intervening Romantic movement. The romantic aspects of Southern religion of the antebellum period are indeed striking. Thousands of planter families were fascinated by the allegory of John Bunyan's *Pilgrim's Progress* with its dream of Beulah Land and the Celestial City. In the Fackler Papers at the University of Kentucky there is a letter from young Calvin Fackler, who wrote to his mother in Huntsville, Alabama, April 21, 1850, that he had presented a copy of *Pilgrim's Progress* to his sweetheart. "I have always from childhood admired it more than any work I have ever read, though then I regarded it only in the light of a strange, mysterious piece of romance. I sincerely believe that there is more in it of satisfaction to the young convert than of any work ever published, not of inspiration." In January, 1855, John Hartwell Cocke of Bremo sent word to Lucy Skipwith, the slave teacher on his Alabama plantation, to read *Pilgrim's Progress* to the Negro children in her school. The puritan cavalier was in the habit of opening his Bible at random to seek guidance and encouragement. He almost certainly would have approved of the faith of Maria Fleet, mistress of Green Mount in Virginia, who consulted the prophecies in the Book of Revelation to obtain light upon the troubled times of Virginia during the Civil War.

The religion of William L. Yancey, the great orator of secession, is another illustration of the influence of the Romantic movement on Southern religion. To Yancey religion was a matter of the heart rather than of the mind. To one of his closest friends, the Presbyterian minister William H. Mitchell, he revealed his feelings of guilt and his doubts that he was a Christian. In the Yancey Papers in the Alabama State Department of Archives is a remarkable letter from Congressman Yancey, who wrote to Mitchell in 1846 from Washington, D. C. He confessed that he was sorely beset with temptations. Though his mind was brilliantly illuminated with a sense of duty, his heart seemed to be cold and torpid. Morning and evening, and sometimes at noonday, he prayed. He also attended a weekly Congressional prayer meeting with "some few praying spirits." Nevertheless, he lamented: "But lo! how little of life—of living and lively faith now dominates me! How feeble is the practice of a Christian duty & oh! how often—too often is that duty neglected, and sometimes shamefully violated!" It was Yancey who moved that the secession convention of Alabama should open its meetings with prayer.

The most apparent difference between the faith of the Old South and modern religion is the changed views of sin. The evangelical preachers, with their eyes turned heavenward, were a powerful force in imposing on the Old South a form of puritanism such as the region had never seen. The novelist William Gilmore Simms, who belonged to the Episcopalian or gentlemanly tradition, believed that this asceticism injured the cause of true religion in the South. In a review of Mrs. Trollope's *Domestic Manners of the Americans* he observed that this denial of wholesome amusements by the evangelical clergy

was an important cause of the fanaticism of the revival movements. He also pointed out that the loneliness of the rural
population and the rivalry of religious sects to outdo each other
in their appeal to the masses contributed to the emotional
excesses of the camp meetings.

Among upper class families there was often a conflict between
puritan asceticism and cavalier attitudes, as was illustrated by the
Fleet family of Green Mount in King and Queen County,
Virginia. Originally the family had been Episcopalians, but the
generation of 1860 were Baptists. Dr. Fleet could not control
himself from periodically going on drinking bouts, and finally,
to prevent from being excommunicated, he resigned from
the church. While the strict Baptists in the neighborhood were
excommunicating some girls for dancing, the Fleets accommodated their religion to the aristocratic tradition. "Pa" Fleet
and his teen-age son Benny went to dances; on one occasion they
stayed up dancing until morning and Pa was tired out. Mrs. Fleet
made currant wine; and Benny read novels, an indulgence which
was frowned upon by the devout—such novels as Caruthers'
The Knights of the Horse-Shoe, the Waverly novels of Scott,
and Dickens' *Great Expectations.* He patronized the circus, and
when he visited Richmond to sell the plantation produce, he
often went to the theater.

At the same time, Benny Fleet's diary is filled with the religious
activities of the family. They went to "protracted meetings,"
where contrite sinners were welcomed at the "Mourner's Bench";
they watched baptisms in the mill pond; and they attended
regular services on Sundays, when Benny invariably noted the
Bible text upon which the sermon was based. The Fleet diary
and letters give an intimate glimpse into the religion of the Old
South, especially the strong faith in Providence, the belief that
"good works" will not get you to Heaven, the great reliance on
prayer, the belief that in order to enter Heaven a man must be
"prepared" for death, that is, have his sins forgiven beforehand.
The Fleets derived great strength and consolation from their
religion, enabling them to meet the disappointments and crises of
life with fortitude.

In 1860 there was little disagreement between the fundamental
beliefs of the lower and the upper classes of the South, in con-

trast with the dichotomy that had existed in the early American republic and in many creative periods of history; all classes in the South adhered to a conservative faith, a common orthodoxy. The variations between the different forms of Protestantism—the evangelical, the Calvinistic, and the genteel—were principally in matters of ritual such as baptism and communion, the practice of a decorous religion, the toleration of worldly pleasures, or the policy of sending missionaries to foreign countries. In the beliefs that mattered—the role of the supernatural in life, the efficacy of prayer, ideas of sin, salvation, and an over-ruling Providence—there was virtually no disagreement. This unity of religious belief, as well as the restrictive influence of slavery, may explain why the South, though a strongly religious section, produced no theologian with new ideas (with the possible exception of Alexander Campbell)—no William Ellery Channing, no Emerson, no Joseph Smith—only pulpit orators. Instead of being a reasoned orthodoxy, the religion of the Southern people on the eve of the Civil War was truly a faith, deeply imbued with the spirit of the Romantic movement of the time.

Chapter XI

THE SCIENTIFIC MIND:
THE EMPIRIC AGE

PURE science may seem to be far removed from the struggles of crusading social reformers such as Hinton Rowan Helper and Cassius Marcellus Clay. But scientists are complex human beings who inevitably are influenced by the controlling assumptions of the society in which they live. They are affected by its attitude toward free thinking, by its religious taboos, and by its economic organization. Indeed, they do not formulate their scientific ideas or make their discoveries in a vacuum.

In the 1820's and early 1830's the South was a favorable place for the pursuit of pure science—that is, before the religious and proslavery orthodoxies had hardened. It was during this period that Transylvania University in Lexington, Kentucky, became one of the most advanced centers of science and humanistic learning in America. Here from 1819 to 1826 was a curious professor of natural science, Constantine Rafinesque, whose body is today buried in a vault under Transylvania's Morrison Hall. Rafinesque found the South of the 1820's and 1830's a veritable paradise for the discovery of new species in the fields of botany and zoology. This eccentric scientist, who was born near Constantinople of French and German parents, had a colorful and unhappy life. He traveled extensively in Europe and was for a time a merchant in Sicily until a faithless wife and his own restless temperament drove him to emigrate to America. In Lexington his activities were richly varied; while he was professor of natural philosophy at Transylvania University he taught modern languages; in Lexington he established a Botanical Garden; he made frequent expeditions into the western wilderness to seek new species; and he found time to write poetry and draw sensitive portraits of beautiful Kentucky women.

He published many books and made large claims for discoveries of unknown plants, fishes, shells, fossils, and even quadrupeds. The unspecialized nature of science in his day (as well as his fantastic conceit) was indicated in his letter to Jefferson applying for a job at the University of Virginia: "I do not know a single individual either in the U. St., or in Europe who is *at the same time* equally acquainted with Geology, Mineralogy, Meteorology, Zoology and Botany as I am." Despite the fact that there seems to have been something of the charlatan in him, he made valuable contributions as a pioneer scientist in the West, and he was ahead of his time in forecasting in 1832 the theory of organic evolution by mutations.

Rafinesque was not typical of the men who taught science in the South, however, except that he was a non-Southerner. Usually the science teacher in the Old South was a Northerner or a foreigner, a man such as the Dutchman Gerard Troost, who for many years taught science at the University of Nashville in the midst of stuffed birds, turtles, fossils, minerals, chemical apparatus, and books; or Michael Tuomey and John W. Mallet, born in Ireland, at the University of Alabama; or Denison Olmstead and Elisha Mitchell, Connecticut Yankees at the University of North Carolina. Most of the trained scientists in the South as well as in the North supported themselves by teaching in colleges and universities where they were so overburdened with academic duties and were required to teach such a variety of sciences that it was difficult for them to specialize. Moreover, the libraries in the South were poorly supplied with scientific works, and the colleges and universities lacked equipment and adequate laboratories for the professors to carry on experiments.

Although the South depended heavily upon the Northern states and European countries for its supply of science teachers, several of the most eminent were natives—notably Joseph Le Conte and Matthew Fontaine Maury. An aristocratic Virginian of Huguenot extraction, Maury was born near Fredericksburg in 1806 but was reared in Tennessee. He spent virtually his whole career in the navy. At first he was on active duty, but in 1842 after he was lamed by a stagecoach accident, he was placed in charge of the Depot of Charts and Instruments in Washington, the forerunner of the Naval Observatory and Hydrographical Office. He is also regarded as the founder of the United States Weather Bureau. Maury's study of winds and currents enabled him to determine the course of the Gulf Stream and to provide ships with information that saved many hours of sailing time between ports. A devoted Southerner, he wrote a number of popular scientific articles for the *Southern Literary Messenger* and *De Bow's Review*. Before the Civil War he won international recognition for his scientific work and played a leading role in the Maritime Conference at Brussels in 1853. Though his great work, *The Physical Geography of the Sea* (1855), did not represent the best scientific knowledge of his time, it had an immense popularity. Its inflated style, arguments from divine design, and many biblical quotations strengthened its appeal to his generation. As a result of his deep-sea soundings, Maury advised Cyrus W. Field of the existence of the Atlantic plateau, upon which Field afterwards laid his cable to Europe.

Since Maury had great popularity and, moreover, left a large collection of personal papers (now in the Library of Congress), he would seem to be an excellent representative of the scientific mind in the South. But he spent most of his career outside the South, and his papers relate very little to the region of his birth and rearing. A more representative Southern scientist was the geologist William Barton Rogers, professor for many years at the University of Virginia. Next to Maury, Rogers was the most distinguished scientist of the Old South. His father Patrick had emigrated from Ireland to Philadelphia, where William was born in 1804. Fifteen years later Patrick was elected professor of natural philosophy and chemistry at William and Mary College. Here he trained his four sons in scientific studies, and they all became brilliant scientists whose names are included in the *Dictionary of American Biography.*

In the summer of 1828 Patrick died, and William Barton, then twenty-four, succeeded his father as professor of natural philosophy at William and Mary. William lectured twice a day on such subjects as electricity, light, meteorology, and dew, and edited a monthly magazine of the college entitled *The Messenger of Useful Knowledge.* His classes, he wrote to his brother Henry (November 8, 1829), were the largest in the college and had not been equaled in size during the past ten years. A general teacher of science, he began to concentrate on geology. In 1833 he published articles on marl and greensand in Edmund Ruffin's *Farmers' Register* and in 1834, an article on the Voltaic battery in the *American Journal of Science.* His ability now began to be recognized, and in 1835 he was elected professor of natural philosophy in the University of Virginia shortly after he had been appointed state geologist.

The great work of William Barton Rogers in the South was a study of the Appalachian mountain chain, in cooperation with his brother Henry. This project began when he persuaded the Virginia legislature to authorize and support a geological survey of the state. In behalf of his idea he spoke before a legislative committee and prepared its report in favor of the project, and, perhaps most effective of all, made an extemporaneous speech before the House of Delegates. The act establishing the geological survey passed the legislature on March 6, 1835, virtually without opposition, and William was appointed to conduct it. He had great difficulty in securing trained assistants but was able to employ his youngest brother Robert to explore the northern part of the state, especially to locate marl beds and fossils. Later he added the oldest brother, James Blythe, to his staff. In 1836 Henry Rogers, now a professor of geology at the University of Pennsylvania, was appointed director of the geological surveys of Pennsylvania and New Jersey, with the result that William and Henry assisted each other in their investigations.

The decade of the 1830's was an era of state geological surveys, a subject which Charles S. Sydnor has explored in his essay "State Geological Surveys in the Old South." All the Southern states except Florida and Louisiana undertook such surveys, and they employed able Southern scientists to conduct them, notably Oscar M. Lieber, Gerard Troost, Michael Tuomey, Robert Dale Owen, James M. Safford, and Professor Elisha Mitchell, who lost his life in 1857 while exploring the mountain in North Carolina that today bears his name. Legislatures were willing to appropriate money for this type of scientific investigation because they anticipated practical benefits from it. When William Barton Rogers wrote the report of the committee recommending a geological survey of Virginia, he made it an alluring statement of practical advantages: the farmers would benefit from the location of marl and greensand beds; the owners of mineral springs, from the analysis of their waters; and the speculators and manufacturing interests, from the discovery of vast strata of coal, gold mines, iron, copper, and lead ores, porcelain earth, salt deposits, and Epsom salts—the great purgative of the era.

After the panic of 1837, legislatures were reluctant to grant funds to continue the surveys or print the reports. Rogers found it necessary to go to Richmond in 1839 to defend the continuation of the Virginia survey at state expense. This project was attacked in the legislature with ignorant and outlandish speeches. But William was an eloquent speaker and finally prevailed in securing appropriations to continue the survey until April, 1842.

All during these years the Virginia scientist was growing in national and international reputation. In the summer vacations he made frequent excursions into the Northern states, where he became acquainted with the leading scientists of America. When the National Institution for the Promotion of Science in Washington was founded, he was elected to membership and was invited to deliver one of its lectures. In 1842 at the meeting of the Association of American Geologists and Naturalists in Boston, William and Henry Rogers read a notable paper entitled "On the Physical Structure of the Appalachian Chain as Exemplifying the Laws which Have Regulated the Elevation of Great Mountain Chains Generally." The revolutionary ideas of this paper were also presented to a meeting of British scientists at Manchester, and the Rogers brothers were elected members of the Geological Society of London.

William was so respected by his colleagues at the University of Virginia that he was chosen chairman of the faculty (equivalent to president). While he was serving in this position, a movement arose in the legislature to cut off the annual university appropriation of $15,000, but he met this menace by writing a strong memorial justifying the appropriation, whereupon the legislature abandoned the attempt to deprive the university of its vital revenues. Antebellum colleges were subject to chronic irruptions of student violence and disorder; in 1845 there was such a serious riot at the University of Virginia that the civil authorities were called in to restore order. After this event William wrote to Henry that he intended to look for another place, "a more tranquil home" than he had found in Charlottesville. At the same time he had another cause to be dissatisfied with Virginia: the legislature refused his request for an appropriation to publish his final digested report of the geological survey of the state.

Disillusioned, he resigned from the university in 1848 but then changed his mind and decided to remain a few years longer. His plaint to Henry, "I long for an atmosphere of more stimulating power," reminds one of Francis Lieber's similar disenchantment with South Carolina College. In 1849 William married a cultivated New England woman, and four years later he resigned his professorship and moved to Boston, where his brother had preceded him. While in Virginia he had cherished the dream of establishing a great polytechnic school, but not until 1862 was he able to realize his vision with the founding of Massachusetts Institute of Technology, of which he became the first president.

Most of the outstanding scientists of the Old South received their principal stimulus toward scientific study from the North, particularly from the great teachers—Louis Agassiz and Asa Gray at Harvard; Benjamin Silliman at Yale, and Amos Eaton, the New York geologist and botanist. Joseph Le Conte was one of these students who went North for instruction. Of Huguenot family background, Le Conte was born in 1823 at Woodmanston, a spacious plantation in Liberty County, Georgia. His father Louis was a Northerner, whose hobbies aroused the scientific curiosity of Joseph and his older brother John: he experimented with chemistry in the attic laboratory of the mansion and cultivated a botanical garden on the grounds of the estate.

Joseph's schooling in academic subjects was very haphazard;

in nine years he had nine teachers, one of whom was Alexander H. Stephens. When he was fourteen years old, he entered the University of Georgia at Athens (then called Franklin College). After graduation he enrolled in the College of Physicians and Surgeons in New York City and in 1845 received the degree of doctor of medicine. For several years he practiced medicine in Macon, Georgia, but the life of a doctor bored him. In 1850 he abandoned his profession and went to Harvard College to study under Louis Agassiz, the greatest scientist in America. Agassiz was attracted to the enthusiastic young student from Georgia and took him as his assistant to study the coral reefs and keys of Florida. Le Conte's interest in both zoology and geology was deeply aroused by daily contact with the enthusiastic Swiss-born scientist.

In 1851 Le Conte accepted a position as teacher of all the sciences except astronomy at Oglethorpe University in Midway, Georgia, at a salary of $1,000. Here he had no laboratory for teaching zoology, and there was not even a textbook available, but in botany he did have an excellent text prepared by Elisha Gray, whose course he had taken at Harvard. After a year at the provincial little college, he sought a position teaching geology and botany at the University of Georgia, where his able brother John was a professor of chemistry and physics. Agassiz wrote a recommendation saying that he had never known a better student than Le Conte, who had fitted himself to become an original investigator of the natural sciences. An ardent worker and an independent observer, he had the penetration of mind to see the essential characteristic of natural objects.

The young scientist obtained the appointment, but he was not happy at the University of Georgia. Both of the Le Contes regarded the faculty duty of policing the turbulent students as highly repugnant and refused to do so. After an academic revolution against the tyranny of President Alonzo Church, a Northerner, Joseph followed his brother in resigning his professorship and in 1857 obtained a position as professor of chemistry and geology at South Carolina College. Later in the year John, who had taught briefly in the College of Physicians and Surgeons in New York, joined him on the faculty as professor of physics. Though Joseph Le Conte had a delightful social life in Columbia, he was burdened with classwork—three lectures a week in both geology and chemistry, and four recitations in algebra and geometry—so that he had little time to do any original work.

Le Conte's first important scientific paper was based on his observations while working with Agassiz in Florida. It was entitled "On the Agency of the Gulf Stream in the Formation of the Peninsula and Keys of Florida" and was read before the American Association for the Advancement of Science in 1855. He advanced the theory that the peninsula of Florida had been gradually prolonged by the deposit of sediment carried by the Gulf Stream from the Mississippi Valley. Upon this substratum of sediment, coral reefs had formed, and then the waves completed the work of land-building by their deposits. He thought that this process had narrowed the channel at the tip of Florida, thus forcing the Gulf Stream farther into the Atlantic and thereby ameliorating the climate of England.

At the 1860 meeting of the association Le Conte was elected general secretary at the same time that Frederick A. P. Barnard of the University of Mississippi was elected president. This meeting was the last one held until after the war. On December 20 South Carolina seceded, and although Le Conte opposed secession, he was loyal to his section and served during the war as a chemist for the Confederate government—first in the government factory for medicines in Columbia and then with his brother John in the Niter and Mining Bureau. He fled from Sherman's army before it marched into Columbia but returned to continue teaching at the University of South Carolina until 1869 when John and he joined the newly organized faculty of the University of California. Here he taught until his death in 1902 and won a national reputation by his books and articles, which supported the theory of evolution and demonstrated that it was compatible with the Christian religion.

The Le Conte brothers were important contributors to the *American Journal of Science*, founded by Benjamin Silliman. In 1858 the *Journal* carried an article by John entitled "On the Influence of Musical Sound on the Flames of a Jet of Coal-gas" (LXXV, 62–67). He reported that at a performance of Beethoven's music by a piano, violin, and violincello, he had observed that the gas burners lighting the room flared at certain sounds: there were pulsations in the height of the flames that synchronized with audible beats of the music. In the next year Joseph published an article in the *Journal* (LXXVIII, 305-19) which he had read before the American Association for the Advancement of Science at Springfield, Massachusetts, entitled "The Correlation of Physical, Chemical and Vital Force and the Conservation of Force in Vital Phenomenon." In this paper he maintained that the question of the origin of the species was "utterly beyond the limits of human experience and will thus remain." He expressed the view that although mankind could never hope "by the light of science to know how organisms originated, still all that we do know of the laws of the organic and inorganic world seem to negative the idea that physical or chemical forces acting upon inorganic matter can produce them."

The *American Journal of Science* might be regarded as an index of the research that was going on in the United States from its founding in 1818 to the Civil War. A perusal of the volumes from 1850 to 1860 indicates that the South had its proper proportion of scientists engaged in research. William Barton Rogers, Oscar M. Lieber, and James M. Safford published articles on geology. Frederick A. P. Barnard contributed an article "On the Pendulum . . . with a Description of an Electric Clock" (LXXVII, 184-97), constructed for the University of Mississippi by E. S. Ritchie of Boston under Barnard's supervision; an article on the zodiacal light; and an article examining the theory of a nebulous ring around the earth. John Lawrence Smith, professor of chemistry at the University of Louisville, published two articles in 1855 (LXIX, 153-63, 322-43) on meteorites; from observation of their iron composition he speculated on their origin, holding that they were fragments from the moon. Frederick Barnard and C. S. Venable of South Carolina College were selected to sail with the United States expedition to Labrador in 1860 to observe a total eclipse of the sun. John W. Mallet wrote several articles on the atomic weight of lithium, on brewsterite, and on zirconium. The *Journal* reviewed the study of Southern flora by A. W. Chapman of Florida and the work on fossils in South Carolina by Michael Tuomey and Francis S.

Holmes—fossils that contained the bones of the ancient horse, the mastodon, the giant sloth, the tapir, and the broad-footed bison.

The scientific men in the Old South demonstrate that objectivity in scholarship does not insure a similar detachment of mind in social and political matters. So strong were the social pressures in the Old South for conformity of opinion, expecially with regard to slavery and religion, that it took an exceptionally independent personality to resist them. A large proportion of the science professors in Southern colleges came from Northern states, and these men had to be especially prudent in their remarks on sensitive subjects. James Woodrow, who was teaching natural history at Oglethorpe University in 1855 was circumspect in regard to discussing slavery and was orthodox in his religious views. Nevertheless, the fact that he had spent his youth in the North and had received his education there made him an object of suspicion at the close of the antebellum period. When a new chair of chemistry was established in the college, he was not appointed to it; the reason, he felt, was that the damning cry of "Northerner" had been raised against him.

Frederick A. P. Barnard, a native of Sheffield, Massachusetts, while professor of science at the University of Alabama and later president of the University of Mississippi, accommodated himself to Southern mores, and even owned slaves. Notwithstanding, he got into trouble at the University of Mississippi: he accepted Negro evidence against a student who had assaulted his slave girl and on the basis of it, dismissed the boy from the university. Southern laws did not permit courts to accept Negro testimony against white persons, and accordingly he was accused of "unsoundness" in regard to the peculiar institution. At his own request, he was tried by the board of trustees on February 29, 1860. He vigorously defended himself in a written statement to the board, in which he declared, "If I entertain now, or if your investigation shall discover that I have ever entertained, sentiments which shall justify any man, however captious, in pronouncing me 'unsound on the slavery question,' then, gentlemen, do your duty and remove me from a position for which I am morally disqualified."

The board unanimously acquitted him and stated furthermore

that their confidence in his ability and integrity had been increased rather than diminished by his conduct. But he was a strong Union man, and when Mississippi seceded, he returned to the North. It was a great loss to the South that this fine scholar and university administrator should give up his position because of unorthodox political views. He became president of Columbia University where he had a long and distinguished career.

William Barton Rogers, though an antislavery man at heart, pursued a prudent course while he was teaching at the University of Virginia. In his correspondence there is no hint of his opposition to slavery until the Hungarian patriot Louis Kossuth came to America and excited his admiration. On January 6, 1852, he wrote that the opposition to Kossuth in the South arose from the circumstance that he was so enthusiastically received by the abolitionists of the North. The rejection of Kossuth by Southerners, he observed, was "the natural result of that conservatism which of late has become the strong feeling of the politicians of the South, a feeling which could not fail to spring up in antagonism to the aggressive philanthropy of other parts of the Union. The result shows how deeply these feelings operate, since from the excitable character of the South, and its great admiration for eloquence and chivalrous daring, Kossuth is a person for whom, under other circumstances, an unbounded enthusiasm would be aroused."

After Rogers left the South and was surrounded by his antislavery friends in New England, he became decidedly more vocal in his opposition to slavery. He strongly opposed the expansion of slavery into the federal territories and in 1856 supported Frémont, the Republican candidate for President. He condemned Buchanan's proslavery Kansas policy and wrote bitterly of the agitation of Southern demagogues and of the evil nature of "the slave power." Though he thought that John Brown's raid was "a crazy effort," he admired the heroism of the man. He wrote to Henry that the nation should adhere to "the principles and doctrines of Washington, Jefferson, and Madison —the principles and doctrines which when we were youths in Virginia, were almost universally received among educated and patriotic men." So ardent in the antislavery cause had he become by February 18, 1861, that he declared, "Better secession than grant one iota of Southern demands for slavery extension."

Two of the most eminent of the native-born scientists of the Old South, Matthew F. Maury and Joseph Le Conte, concurred with the public opinion of their section that slavery was the best condition for the Negroes. Until the end of the Civil War Le Conte continued to hold slaves on the family plantation in Georgia and to treat them paternally. Maury, like many Virginians, was opposed to the Secession movement, but when Virginia joined the Confederacy, he resigned his commission in Washington and was appointed an officer in the Confederate Navy.

At the University of North Carolina a paradoxical situation existed among the scientists: Professor Elisha Mitchell, a Yankee who had received his scientific training at Yale, wrote a curious pamphlet in defense of slavery, entitled *The Other Leaf of the Book of Nature and the Word of God*. On the other hand, Professor Benjamin Sherwood Hedrick, a native of the North Carolina Piedmont, bravely opposed the extension of slavery into the federal territories.

Hedrick was graduated from the University of North Carolina in 1851 with highest honors and then secured a position in the office of the American Nautical Almanac in Cambridge, Massachusetts. Ambitious, and eager for knowledge, he attended the Harvard lectures of Agassiz, Gray, Pierce, and Horsford. In 1853 the trustees of the University of North Carolina established a school of science and elected Hedrick to the chair of agricultural chemistry. The young professor drew up an idealistic blueprint for developing the courses in the scientific school. His plan required that the students should analyze and perform all the experiments themselves in laboratories—an innovation in his era—and that professors should lecture only two or three times a week in each course. But the carrying out of this enlightened program was rudely interrupted when he dared to express unorthodox opinions on slavery.

In talking with some students in Chapel Hill in the autumn of 1856 Hedrick said he would vote for Frémont, the Republican candidate for President, because he believed in the principle of free soil. The editor of the leading Democratic newspaper of the state, William W. Holden, heard of this casual remark and thereupon began a campaign in the Raleigh *North Carolina Standard* to drive the liberal professor from his chair. During the violent controversy that followed, the *Carolina Watchman* of Salisbury on October 28, 1856, declared: "The professorships should be sifted and weeded of those who may covertly circulate opinions not in sympathy with our social institutions." The president and the faculty tried to get Hedrick quietly to resign. When he refused, a committee of the faculty, headed by Professor Elisha Mitchell, reported that the course of the independent professor "was not warranted by our usages and that the political opinions expressed [by him] are not those entertained by any member of this body." Only one member of the faculty voted against these resolutions—Henry Harrise, the professor of French. Hedrick was then summarily dismissed from his position, and he left his native state for the North.

In the realm of religion Southern scientists, with one notable exception, seem to have accepted orthodox views without question. The exception was Dr. Thomas Cooper, professor of chemistry and president of South Carolina College from 1819 until 1834. Cooper was an English émigré who was continually shocking people by his radical ideas. In his course in geology he felt compelled by the lack of other adequate texts to use Bakewell's *Introduction to Geology*, an American edition of which had been published by Professor Benjamin Silliman, combined with a syllabus of Silliman's lectures at Yale College. Cooper thought that Silliman's effort to harmonize the findings of geology with the biblical account of the Creation and of Noah's flood represented "an absolute surrender of his common sense to clerical orthodoxy." Accordingly, he attacked the views of the Yale professor in a resounding pamphlet, entitled "On the Connection between Geology and the Pentateuch" (1833). He declared that the Pentateuch was not written by Moses or a divinely inspired writer and that the Book of Genesis was a collection of "absurd and frivolous tales." Though Cooper had survived several attempts by the legislature to remove him from his position, he was finally forced to resign in 1834 by a campaign of intolerant religious groups.

The scientific theories about the age of the earth, particularly the views of the English geologist Sir Charles Lyell and the implications of the fossils in the strata of the earth, seemed to many of the orthodox to contradict the word of the Bible. Accordingly in 1857 a presbytery in Mississippi raised the alarm against this menace to religion in adopting the following resolution: "*Whereas,* we live in an age in which the most insidious attacks are made upon revealed religion through the natural sciences, and as it behooves the church, at all times to have men capable of defending the faith once delivered to the Saints, therefore, *Resolved* that the Presbytery recommend the endowment of a professorship of the natural sciences, as connected with revealed religion in one or more of our theological seminaries. . . ." In 1861 such a professorship was established in the Presbyterian Theological Seminary in Columbia, South Carolina, and James Woodrow of Oglethorpe University was appointed to the new chair.

Actually the Southern scientists as a group were not guilty of "insidious attacks" upon revealed religion. Joseph Le Conte, for example, in his inaugural address as professor at South Carolina College—once the citadel of freethinking—tried to alleviate any fears of the orthodox over the teaching of geology by observing that there was no collision between the new science and the Scriptures. "There was a time," he declared, "when the battleground of Faith and Infidelity was situated in the domain of the metaphysical science—the attacks of Voltaire and Hume," but that time, he asserted, had well-nigh passed away; "the atheist is nearly extinct—is a fossil not an enemy." Geology, he predicted, would strengthen Christian faith and would be universally acknowledged as "the chief handmaid of religion among the sciences."

Matthew Fontaine Maury, though bold and independent in his criticism of the educational practices of the day and in his scientific investigations, was quite orthodox in his religious views. In a letter to his brother Richard, November 16, 1834, protesting against his adopting the doctrines of Alexander Campbell as an easy way to Heaven, he advised, "Learn your duties, Dick, from the Bible." The findings of modern geology did not shake his belief that the Mosaic account of the creation of the earth and of man was literally correct. "If the two cannot be reconciled," he argued, "the fault is ours, and is because in our blindness and weakness we have not been able to interpret aright either the one or the other." Shortly before the Civil War began, he was invited to speak at the laying of the cornerstone of the first building of the University of the South. On this occasion he reaffirmed his belief that the views of the Bible should take precedence over the theories of modern science. "I have been blamed," he said, "by men of science both in this country and in England for quoting the Bible in confirmation of the doctrines of Physical Geography. The Bible, they say, was not written for scientific purposes and is therefore no authority in matters of science. I beg pardon: the Bible is authority for everything it touches."

Maury's attitude was characteristic of the age rather than peculiar to the South; even the great English geologist Sir Charles Lyell, Louis Agassiz at Harvard, and Benjamin Silliman at Yale made concessions to religious orthodoxy. A writer in the *Southern Quarterly Review* (April, 1851) reviewing recent books on science declared: "Fallible man may err in his interpretations of some portion of the sacred text, and thus, for a time, discordance [with science] may exist; but if we have full faith that the works of God, as seen through nature, must be consistent with His revealed word, as they are both emanations from the same supreme intelligence, we need have no fear that the faith which the Christian holds more precious to him than life itself can be exposed to any jeopardy."

With a similar view Professor R. T. Brumby of South Carolina College gave an address on December 8, 1849, in the South Carolina House of Representatives assuring the legislators that the study of geology was not anti-Christian. He followed up this address by an article in the *Southern Quarterly Review* entitled "The Pre-Adamite Earth—Relations of Theology to Geology" (January, 1852); he wrote that geology was profoundly Christian in tendency, for its spirit was that of awe and reverence for the great design of God in nature. All established principles of physical science, he maintained, were in harmony with the Sacred Scriptures.

Although Darwin's *Origin of Species* was not published until 1859, some of the Southern scientists were acquainted with the earlier evolutionary theories, particularly Lamarck's theory.

Dr. John Wesley Monette of Washington, Mississippi, a graduate of Transylvania University, anticipated some of Darwin's ideas on evolution as early as 1824 in an essay on "the causes of the Variety of Complexion and Form of the Human Species"; and still earlier William Charles Wells, a native of Charleston, had suggested the theory of evolution by natural selection. Joseph Le Conte states in his autobiography that he was introduced to the theory of evolution in the spring of 1845 by reading Robert Chambers' *Vestiges of the Natural History of Creation*. In 1857, two years before Darwin's famous book was published, he talked with the South Carolina planter and statesman Langdon Cheves, who advanced the theory of the evolution of species by transmutation. Le Conte opposed this theory, adhering to the view of his old teacher Louis Agassiz, who taught the doctrine of a preordained plan of creation. William Barton Rogers read the *Origin of Species* shortly after it was published and wrote a favorable review of Darwin's revolutionary theory in a Boston newspaper. Henry W. Ravenel, an amateur botanist of South Carolina, recorded in his diary as early as September, 1860, that he had read reviews of Darwin's book, but he was opposed to evolution because he thought it conflicted with the Bible. So did most Americans in 1860, educated as well as uneducated, including the great professor of natural science at Harvard Louis Agassiz. It was not until approximately twenty years later that the theory began generally to be accepted by scientists in this country.

In the thirties and forties the natural and physical sciences were relative newcomers in the curriculum of Southern colleges and universities; the premier place was held by the Greek and Roman classics. In 1842 Sir Charles Lyell reported in his travel account of the United States that at Harvard College only Latin, Greek, and mathematics were required for graduation. Matthew Maury protested against the excessive emphasis placed in the college curriculum upon the dead languages. In a letter to his daughter Anne, August 28, 1836, he declared: "When our young men leave college most of them (some exceptions) are prepared as little for entering upon the world as they were when they entered college, the reason of this is that every young man is taught to believe Latin and Greek of the first importance;

consequently everything that is solid & practical, such as mathematics, chemistry, & the like, is made to occupy a subordinate place & only a smattering of them is obtained. West Point I consider to be the only tolerable institution in the United States; & why it is so is owing to the circumstance that the humbuggery of the Learned Languages is not tolerated there."

On the other hand, Frederick A. P. Barnard, while he was teaching science at the University of Alabama, took an opposite view of the comparative value of the classics and the sciences in the college curriculum. In 1856 he published a pamphlet entitled *Improvements Practicable in Southern Colleges,* in which he observed that the science courses in the college and universities of the United States were usually mere outlines that gave the student only a smattering of knowledge: "the present teaching of them is little better than a farce." He proposed, therefore, to eliminate from the college curriculum many of the branches of natural history; he declared that they were valuable mainly for information, whereas the great object of college teaching was mental discipline. The absolutely indispensable disciplinary subjects, he maintained, were Latin, Greek, rhetoric, logic, and metaphysics. Instead of students scattering their energies and frittering away their time on diluted scientific courses, he thought that they should concentrate on the disciplinary subjects.

In this stern prescription of undergraduate studies Barnard would seem to have been a complete reactionary, but actually he tried to advance the cause of the natural sciences in the South. When he became president of the University of Mississippi in 1856, he proposed that a postgraduate course leading to a master's degree be offered, in which the sciences should be studied. He appealed to the local patriotism of the people by urging the state to establish advanced studies so that "the flower of Southern youth" would not have to go to the North to be educated. He devoted great efforts to establishing an astronomical observatory at Oxford, to be paid for by an appropriation of the legislature. His project was adopted, and in 1859 the observatory building was erected. A telescope with a nineteen-inch lens— larger than that of Harvard's telescope—was ordered from Cambridge, but it was not completed until the summer of 1861, too late to be delivered before Mississippi seceded.

Despite the popularity of the Greek and Latin classics, the sciences were not seriously neglected, as Professor T. Cary Johnson's study *Scientific Interests in the Old South* demonstrates. He has found that in 1832–33, of the 140 students enrolled at the University of Virginia where the elective system was in effect, seventy were taking chemistry and eighty-two natural philosophy; twenty-three years later when the university had 558 students (a larger number than at Harvard), 191 were taking chemistry; and 143, courses in natural philosophy. A comparison can be made of the relative popularity of the courses in the classics and those in the sciences from statistics presented in a *Documentary History of Education in the South before 1860*, edited by Edgar W. Knight, which show that at the University of Virginia in 1857, 249 students were attending courses in Latin; 248, courses in chemistry; 168, courses in Greek; and 171, courses in natural philosophy.

At the University of Georgia a curious episode occurred at this time: the trustees ruled that students who failed to pass only their science courses could still be promoted with their class. This lowering of standards led Joseph Le Conte and some of his colleagues to introduce a resolution before the faculty protesting the ruling on the ground that one-third of the courses were in the sciences.

Outside of college halls there was a considerable interest in natural science. Even "sweet Southern girls," Professor Johnson notes, studied natural science in their seminaries and academies. A surprisingly large number of cultivated planters and professional men were amateur scientists, who collected specimens of plants which they dried and pressed and exchanged with each other, very much as boys collect and exchange foreign postage stamps; they also dabbled in chemical experiments and established cabinets for mineral rocks, fossils, and stuffed animals. A step above these amateurs were some nonprofessional scientists scattered over the South who made serious and intelligent studies of natural phenomena, such as Dr. Lewis David de Schweinitz who, while living in the Moravian village of Salem, North Carolina, published a volume on the fungi of the state; or Nicholas M. Hentz, born in Versailles, France, who became an outstanding authority on spiders during his many years teaching in Southern schools and colleges; and Benjamin L. C. Wailes of Washington, Mississippi, who published a report on the geology of Mississippi.

South Carolina was pre-eminent in the cultivation of scientific studies, probably because of the presence of the cultural center of Charleston and because the aristocratic organization of its society provided leisure. Charleston had the most important museum of natural history in the South. Here lived the Lutheran minister John Bachman, a native of New York and a graduate of Williams College, who collaborated with John James Audubon on *The Viviparous Quadrupeds of North America*. He also attacked the theory of diverse origins of the races, advanced by Josiah C. Nott of Mobile and George R. Gliddon in their book *Types of Mankind* (1854). Earlier, in 1821, the planter Stephen Elliott of Beaufort published a volume on the botany of South Carolina; John Edward Holbrook wrote a multi-volume work on reptiles entitled *North American Herpetology* (1842); and Henry W. Ravenel, a low-country planter, published a five-volume study of Carolina fungi.

Perhaps the most important contributions to science in the South were made by Southerners who were not strictly scientists, notably John James Audubon, Edmund Ruffin, and Dr. Crawford W. Long. Audubon combined the functions of artist and scientist in his study of ornithology and in his book on *Birds of America* (1838). Doctor Long, experimenting in an obscure Georgia village where he practiced medicine, in 1842 stumbled upon one of the greatest discoveries of the nineteenth century, the use of ether as an anesthetic. Edmund Ruffin, a Virginia planter, influenced by reading Humphrey Davy's *Agricultural Chemistry*, conceived of the idea of using marl to correct the excessive acidity of the exhausted soils of tidewater Virginia and thus revolutionized the agriculture of the upper South.

The society of the Old South appreciated most fully those individuals such as Ruffin who applied science to solving practical problems. Many planters in the South closely observed nature, read agricultural publications, and experimented with new crops. They were what Solon Robinson, the Northern agricultural editor, called "improving planters," and there was a surprising number of them below the Mason-Dixon Line.

Though they were empiricists, they contributed to the accumulation of valuable scientific data in their region. A good example of these amateur scientists was Benjamin L. C. Wailes, who combined the occupation of cotton planter with the avocations of geologist and student of the fauna and flora of his region.

The Southern mind of the antebellum period was, on the whole, essentially unscientific. There were not the incentives for scientific study that exist in our modern society—less so in the South than in the North. The typical college student in the Old South planned to become a lawyer, a politican, a doctor, or a planter. How could science as it was then taught be of much use to him? When the British geologist George Featherstonhaugh was touring America in 1844, he talked to Gerard Troost, the professor of sciences at the University of Nashville; Troost told the visitor that though he had had some competent students during his long service at the university he had never found one with an enthusiasm for science.

In the Old South the free pursuit of science was limited by the Romantic movement and the inhibiting influence of slavery. It was a time when romanticism strongly affected Southern society, and Southern scientists revealed both in their public lectures and their letters that they viewed science in a somewhat romantic light. Romanticism affected scientific thought in the North and the South in varying degrees; but in the Southern states there existed a special influence that militated against the development of the scientific attitude, namely, the subtle and pervasive effect of slavery. It is impossible, however, to separate the effects of slavery on the Southern mind from the influence of the rural Southern environment. Frederick Law Olmsted in an article in the New York *Times*, January 12, 1856, attempted to make this analysis on the basis of his observations during three trips to the South. He believed that the close association of Southerners with shiftless Negro slaves tended to develop the habit of ignoring small things because the masters' patience was constantly tried by infinite vexations on the part of the careless slaves—irritations that would have infuriated a Northerner. The lax, slipshod methods of the Southern plantation tended to develop habits of mind unsuited to progress in science. The typical Southerner, in contrast to the Northerner, Olmsted observed, was given to vague generalizations and inexact speech: his mind was oratorical and romantic; he lacked an aptitude for "close observation," a quality which is pre-eminent in Olmsted's own writing; and he disliked applying himself to details. Especially, wrote Olmsted, were Southerners "disinclined to exact and careful reasoning." The Northern traveler, who had a strong antislavery bias, may have attributed too much to the influence of slavery in developing these characteristics, but it unquestionably had an important part in forming the Southern mind.

All of the characteristics cited by Olmsted were the antithesis of the scientific mind. The study of science requires concentration, perseverance, and great curiosity—qualities in which Southerners as a whole seem to have been deficient in comparison with Northerners. But even more destructive of the detachment and bold imagination essential to scientific discovery was the effect of slavery in closing the Southern mind after 1830 to new and liberal ideas. Thus a climate distinctively unfavorable to the pursuit of science and scholarship developed in the Old South, which caused some of its more eminent scientists and scholars, notably William Barton Rogers, Frederick A. P. Barnard, and Francis Lieber, to leave for the freer and more stimulating atmosphere of the North. Furthermore, the progress of science was restricted to a greater degree in the South than in the North by religious taboos and a remarkably strong fundamentalist religion.

Chapter XII

THE ROMANTIC MIND

O N APRIL 30, 1848, William Gilmore Simms in a letter to a
Northern friend described a *tableau vivant* staged in his
plantation home, Woodlands. His daughters and their guests
were costumed as queens, princesses, sultanas, and sylphs. "I
too," he wrote, "made a figure—a very fearful one—as a
Cumanché Indian in three scenes which I planned myself, and
had for an opponent a fair & vigorous damsel who personated a
Texas Hunter—and I let her—throw me!" It was a gala occasion
not only for the white family but for the slaves. "You should have
seen our Negroes, the whole plantation gathered to the Spectacle.
Our piazza was crowded with them leaping over each others
heads & much more delighted than you & I have even been at
Niblo's." Here was a display of Southern paternalism toward
the black members of the family as well as a manifestation of the
romantic vogue in the Old South.

Much deeper than literature, affecting men who scorned
novels and poetry, was the romantic spirit that subtly permeated
the society of the Old South. It made men touchy of their honor
and impelled them to do things that were the negation of

economic realism. It lay behind the demand of the South that its citizens should have the right to carry their slaves into western territory, a land economically unsuited to this form of labor. It nourished the illusion at the time of the Civil War that the Southern spirit could prevail against tremendous economic odds. It infused Southern religion with a mystic quality that enabled weak human beings to triumph over the Devil, the flesh, and the world.

The romantic spirit expressed itself most patently in the arts and in social manners: men and women wrote sentimental novels, poetry, and acrostics; artists painted "the sublime" in wild nature; young girls fashioned garlands of artificial flowers and treasured locks of hair; young men engaged in ridiculous ring tournaments; politicians practiced a florid oratory; would-be aristocrats developed the "Cavalier Myth"; and all classes of society but the poor whites placed woman upon a pedestal. Mary Boykin Chesnut described one aspect of the romantic vogue when she wrote in her diary of the popularity of the song "Lorena": "Maggie Howell [the sister of Jefferson Davis's wife] says there is a girl in large hoops and a calico frock—at every piano between Richmond and the Mississippi, banging on the out-of-tune thing and looking up into a man's face, singing that song."

Romanticism has been exhibited by individuals in all ages, but as a broad social movement it developed in Europe and America between the years 1800 and 1860. Vernon Parrington has rightly described this period in the United States as constituting a "Romantic Revolution." Romanticism in the South was in part a reaction from the eighteenth-century Enlightenment—a de-emphasis of reason in favor of feeling and intuition. The difference in the two modes of viewing life was illustrated by the attitude of the aged Jefferson: he tried to read Scott's *Ivanhoe,* which had an immense vogue in his region, but was bored by its artificialities and sentimentality and could not get through it. His generation loved order, uniformity, reason; the succeeding generation emphasized feeling over reason, delighted in the mysterious and supernatural. Writers such as Poe and Chivers chose exotic subjects that were remote both in time and place from the society in which they were living. Moreover, one of the aspects of the Romantic movement in Europe—diversity— which exalted the peculiar qualities of each nation or region—its folk culture—appealed increasingly to Southerners as a result of the slavery controversy. Professor Rollin Osterweis in his study *Romanticism and Nationalism in the Old South* has pointed out the force of romanticism during this period in developing the concept of two separate societies—the North and the South— and consequently in the stimulation of romantic Southern nationalism.

The Romantic movement would probably have developed in the South of the nineteenth century independently of foreign literary influences, such as the novels of Sir Walter Scott or the poetry of Byron and Moore. A new type of economics resulting from the westward movement laid the foundations for its growth. The rapid exploitation of the virgin lands of the Southwest produced a class of self-made men—"cotton capitalists" (in some cases, "cotton snobs," as Daniel R. Hundley called them in his *Social Relations in Our Southern States*); they very much needed, as did the capitalists of the later Gilded Age, to embellish their lives with showy colonnaded houses, aristocratic trappings, fine race horses, and libraries of books they did not read. The rise of Jacksonian democracy, moreover, greatly enlarged the electorate to include many poorly educated, emotional people, who responded to the florid oratory of politicians and new dramatic techniques of the political art that were in contrast to the old aristocratic spirit of restraint and dignity. Perhaps the brooding loneliness of the plantation houses and the idleness of the younger members of the family encouraged the development of romantic tastes. The existence of slavery in the South in defiance of world opinion almost certainly contributed to the growth of a school of Southern novelists who idealized the plantation and the relationship of master and slave.

The Romantic movement that flourished in Europe and America from 1800 to 1860 took many forms, as Professor Arthur Lovejoy has pointed out in "The Meaning of Romanticism for the Historian of Ideas" (*Journal of the History of Ideas*, 1941). In the Northern states it underlay transcendentalism and the agitation for the *immediate* abolition of slavery; it was directed toward reform, toward establishing utopias. In the South the movement took a different turn; it was backward-looking and strengthened conservative trends. Expecially did it nourish "chivalry" and an archaic conception of honor. Instead of the endless striving for perfection and the renovation of society, which were characteristic of the North, romanticism in the South glorified the status quo of the slave-based plantation society. The historical novels of Sir Walter Scott fitted in perfectly with this trend of thought and feeling. Accordingly, though the Scottish writer was popular in the North, he was the rage in the South.

A prominent characteristic of the Romantic movement was the development of a luxuriant individualism, which in the Old South was reinforced by the survival of frontier traits. Indeed, the Romantic movement produced some extreme characters who could hardly have been found in Northern society. Colonel Alexander McClung of Mississippi, a famous duellist, was one of these romantic individualists. A nephew of Chief Justice John Marshall, he was born in Fauquier County, Virginia, in 1812 but grew up in Kentucky. After serving for a while as a midshipman and wasting his patrimony, he emigrated in 1832 to Jackson, Mississippi. Here he became a Whig leader and editor of *The Crisis* and later, the *True Issue*. But he injured his influence by heavy drinking and reckless gambling.

The Mexican War came along and gave to the dissipated colonel the opportunity to become a hero. At the battle of Monterey he was the first man to scale the fort in the face of whistling bullets. For a moment he stood poised on the rampart waving his sword in glee. Then a Mexican bullet cut him down. When his regiment returned to Natchez, the ladies prepared a great celebration. The hero was called upon for a speech. The Natchez papers reported his flowery address, in which he spoke of the laurel wreath of glory which each of the soldiers and officers had won. To Colonel McClung, glory was enough.

This brandishing of his sword on the ramparts of Monterey was the apogee in the life of the romantic colonel. During the year following his return from Mexico he ran for Congress but was defeated. President Taylor, however, appointed him chargé d'affaires to Bolivia, where he served until 1851. He returned to Mississippi in time to work strenuously against secessionism in the state campaign that year. When Henry Clay died, the

Mississippi legislature requested that Colonel McClung deliver a eulogy on the departed Whig leader. His oration, which became famous throughout the South, was a masterpiece of eloquence in the ornate style of the period.

Reuben Davis in his *Recollections of Mississippi and Mississippians* writes of him: "His personal appearance was singularly noble and impressive. McClung was an athlete, tall and symmetrical, perfectly and powerfully formed. His fine head was covered with a profusion of curly auburn hair." A portrait of him in the Capitol at Jackson shows a handsome, voluptuous face with aristocratic features; only a tantalizing smile on his lips might indicate that he could be a dangerous man.

He never married but was a great favorite with the ladies of Jackson, who would invite him to ride in their carriages as they were driven in the cool of the evening. When he was sober, he was a very polite gentleman. Mrs. Clement C. Clay declared that as a girl she loved him madly while she was in his presence but feared him during his absence. "He was the gallantest lover that ever knelt at a lady's feet," she wrote in reminiscence. He was subject to fits of melancholy, when he would mount his spirited horse Rob Roy, ride to the cemetery, and throw himself upon a grave, where he would stare into the sky for hours.

Colonel McClung manifested two aspects of the Romantic movement as it developed in the Old South—a devotion to the military tradition and a quixotic sense of honor that made him swift to resent an insult. He was the challenger or second in many duels, and his encounters usually resulted in the death of his opponent, for he was regarded as the second-best shot in Mississippi. Belonging to an aristocratic political party, he was defeated in his frequent efforts to win election to office. "Poor McClung!" wrote Reuben Davis. "His nature was too highly strung. The disappointments and difficulties of life maddened him and he died by his own hand [in 1855]."

A fusion of classical and romantic elements in many individuals of the Old South produced a cavalier type of personality. Such a person was Colonel John S. Mosby, the semi-legendary leader of the Confederate Rangers on the Virginia front. This mobile fighter wrote to his wife in December, 1862, to send him the following books: Plutarch's *Lives*, Macaulay's *History*, Sir Walter Scott's novels and poems, Shakespeare, Byron, and Hazlitt's *Life of Napoleon.* In the first twenty-one pages of Mosby's *Reminiscences,* as Edmund Wilson has pointed out, there were quotations from or references to Homer, Virgil, Gibbon, Sterne, Byron, Moore, Macaulay, and Longfellow. In his taste for both the classic and the romantic writers and in his opposition to secession (though he became one of the most redoubtable fighters of the Confederacy), Mosby illustrated some of the cross-currents that affected the Southern mind.

The seminal literary influence in the rise of Southern romanticism came from Scotland and England—from the novels of Scott and the English romantic poets—but it was a delayed development. It was not until the 1830's that Southerners began to write novels after the Scott fashion, twenty years after Sir Walter had published his first historical novel, *Waverly.* Southerners had, of course, read these captivating novels about feudal times and probably had found some justification for their own slave-based society in the chivalrous society described by the Scottish writer. Nevertheless, they themselves were not stirred to write novels about their own sections until they became more self-conscious of their regionalism, partly as a result of the attack upon their society by the abolitionists and the resentment arising from the Nullification controversy. Moreover, the old Atlantic seaboard culture was being challenged at this time by the rapid growth of a strident cotton kingdom in the Gulf region and by the democratic upheaval of the Jacksonian period. The Southerners now had something new to write about—the plantation and the frontier—and Sir Walter had set them an example of dealing with native literary material.

In 1832 John Pendleton Kennedy, a Maryland lawyer, published *Swallow Barn,* a nostalgic novel that set the pattern of glamorizing the Southern plantation and the country gentry. In it he even had a hawking scene reminiscent of Scott. Shortly afterwards, William Alexander Caruthers began to publish his historical novels of Virginia—*The Kentuckian in New-York* (1834) and *The Cavaliers of Virginia* (1835). These novels evoked the stately image of an aristocratic society in Virginia that contributed much to distorting actual history and creating the plantation legend. In the preface to his last novel, *The Knights of the*

Horse-Shoe, a Traditionary Tale of the Cocked Hat Gentry in the Old Dominion (1845), he frankly acknowledged his obligation to Sir Walter Scott. At approximately the time that Caruthers and Kennedy were publishing their filial novels about the South, Beverley Tucker, the half brother of John Randolph of Roanoke, was publishing novels with an even more partisan Southern accent. In 1834 the *Southern Literary Messenger* was founded in Richmond, whose editor for a brief while was Edgar Allan Poe. Through his trenchant criticism Poe tried to deflate the artificial and excessively romantic style of the period, but the *Messenger* remained throughout the antebellum period the vehicle of amateur literary romanticism.

The most significant representative of the romantic spirit in the South, in literature as well as in politics, was William Gilmore Simms. Born in Charleston in 1806, Simms grew up in an unfavorable literary environment, though his youthful surroundings led him to a life of the imagination. He was only two years old when his mother died and his father, an Irish immigrant and unsuccessful merchant, wandered off to Mississippi to become a planter, leaving his son to be reared by his grandmother. Unhappy and lonely in his childhood the boy compensated for his sense of alienation by reading passionately and omnivorously. His grandmother also contributed to his literary development by telling him stirring tales of the Revolution in South Carolina. He was at first apprenticed to a druggist but later studied law and was admitted to the bar. Failure in this profession and subsequently in editing a newspaper propelled him toward a literary career. Selling his newspaper in Charleston at a great loss, he went to New York carrying various literary manuscripts with him, and in this city in 1832 he published his long romantic poem *Atalantis*. He continued to compose romantic poetry during the rest of his life, but he won his reputation with historical romances.

In his historical novels Simms contributed much to the formation of the legend of the Old South. Like his model, Sir Walter Scott, he tended to portray the extremes of society, thus giving the impression that Southern society was composed principally of the gentry, the poor whites, and the slaves. Simms's first novel, *Martin Faber* (1833), however, was a psychological study of crime in the Gothic tradition. It attracted little attention, but in the following year he gained national recognition with the publication of *Guy Rivers*, a novel about the rough mining region of Georgia in the 1820's. He quickly followed up his success by publishing *The Yemassee*, a story of Indian warfare in colonial South Carolina, and *The Partisan*, his first romance of the American Revolution. The novel which he considered his best, *Beauchampe* (1842)—a melodramatic story based on the murder of Colonel Solomon Sharp of Kentucky in 1826 by Beauchampe to avenge the seduction of his wife—was his last full-length novel until 1851 when he began to publish a notable series of Revolutionary romances. The panic of 1837 and the competition from cheap reprints of British novels had temporarily ruined the market.

The popular taste of the period, both North and South, forced him to compose in the romantic style, but his natural bent was toward realism. He exhibited this predilection in his portraits of frontier characters—poor whites and Negroes and especially in the creation of the earthy guerrilla leader Captain Porgy, a Falstaffian character, who was nevertheless—as William R. Taylor has observed—a Southern gentleman. He rebelled at times against some of the romantic conventions and the excessive prudery of Victorian society in America. His story "Caloya; or the Loves of the Driver," which described the immoral acts of a Negro driver, aroused a storm of protest from the readers of the Charleston magazine *The Magnolia;* but Simms defended it as moral because it was truthful and did not make vice attractive —the Bible, he pointed out, told stories of crime, yet it was not immoral. Scornfully he wrote of that type of censorship exerted by public opinion which prevented refined people from calling things by their proper names. "We are reluctant in very nice society," he wrote to the editor of *The Magnolia* on August 12, 1841, "to call things by their proper names. We dare not speak of legs or thighs in the presence of many very nice ladies; and the young woman who would be shocked beyond recovery if you craved permission to embrace her, has no sort of objection if you will only substitute the word 'waltz' for that of 'embrace.' The act is very much the same. . . ."

Although he enjoyed the pleasures of life, Simms was sincerely religious. The numerous deaths in his family chastened his spirit and made him more devout. He advised his Northern friend James Lawson to have daily prayers in his family. In his writings he inculcated Christian ideals; indeed, he regarded the function of literature to be the elevation and refinement of human life. His novels exemplified, he believed, "the moral imaginative" and his romances took the place of the heroic epic that had disappeared. The Romantic revolution in America had by this time elevated novels to a position of respectability, in sharp contrast to their low estate when Jefferson wrote to Nathaniel Burwell on March 14, 1818: when the poison of inordinate novel reading infects the mind, "it destroys its tone and revolts it against wholesome reading. . . . The result is a bloated imagination, sickly judgment, and disgust toward all the real businesses of life."

In his novels Simms exhibited both the virtues and faults of the Southern literary man. His best work was his Revolutionary romances written in the 1850's—*Katherine Walton, Woodcraft,* and *Eutaw.* Here he excelled in portraying the Southern landscape and in catching something of the spirit of the civil conflict between the Tory and the patriot. His women in most cases are too fragile, romantic, and stilted in language, but occasionally he drew a vivid and credible female character, such as the widow Eveleigh in *Woodcraft.* Though his strong common sense and his out-of-doors life moderated the extravagances of the Romantic school in making its heroes too perfect, its villains too black, and its ladies too angelic, he too created highly romantic figures such as "the noble red man" in *The Yemassee.*

Simms believed that a genuine literature could be produced only by American authors writing about the regions in which they lived and which they knew intimately. His formula for a novel was high romance enacted in a setting of reality. His novels, therefore, deal with Southern landscape, native characters, and heroic episodes in Southern history or with melodramatic border incidents. He had a passion for the Southern frontier and a strong interest in the history of the Revolution in the South, which led him to visit and study the battlefields. Two of his border romances, *Richard Hurdis, a Tale of Alabama,* and *Border Beagles, a Tale of Mississippi,* were based on the life of John A. Murrel, colorful leader of a gang of outlaws and slave-stealers in the Southwest. He had conversed with Virgil Stewart, the captor of Murrel, and from him had learned many details that went into his novels. Though he was successful in creating true settings, he continued to use the artificial and worn-out molds of Sir Walter Scott and failed to appreciate the emergence of a new type of American novel represented by the work of Hawthorne and Melville.

In 1842 he joined the "Young America" group of writers who were intense nationalists, Loco Foco Democrats, exponents of the cause of westward expansion, and advocates of an international copyright law. Like them, Simms was much opposed to the practice of American authors and critics toadying to British literary men. His advocacy of an international copyright law was motivated not only by the desire to protect the profits of American writers but also "to emancipate us from the dictation of the British mind." In 1846–47 he published two volumes of criticism entitled *Views and Reviews* (dated 1845) that were the Southern manifesto of the "Young America" movement. In these volumes he urged American writers to use their unique history and their frontier as the subjects of a distinctive national literature and to write with manly and independent spirit.

His chief faults as a writer arose from his romantic conception of literary inspiration and from his prolific production: he published eighty-two volumes of novels, verse, history, criticism, and biography. He wrote entirely too rapidly and carelessly, seldom revising in order to produce a finished work of art. He composed *Beauchampe*, "as fast as pen could fly over paper," a mode suited to his impetuous temperament, he said. His life illustrated the myriad distractions of the country gentleman who tried to write: he wasted time in being hospitable, spent long hours in nursing his sick wife and numerous children, cared for his slaves, managed a plantation, edited magazines, lectured, and finally sought to enter politics. He composed for the popular taste—hence his bloodcurdling, melodramatic novels. He did not take time to contemplate, and consequently his works do not penetrate deeply into the universal problems of human existence, as do those of his New England contemporaries—Melville in

Moby Dick, Hawthorne in the *Scarlet Letter*, Emerson in his essays, and Thoreau in *Walden*.

Simms considered himself not only a poet and novelist but also a historian. In 1840 he published *The History of South Carolina from its First European Discovery to its Erection into a Republic*. It is a surprisingly dull and conventional chronicle, based principally on secondary works and intended for school children and the general reader. In 1847 he planned to revise it, "to do justice to the up country," but he did not publish a revised edition until 1860. In a letter to Benjamin F. Perry in 1847 he observed, "our people do not seem to care a straw whether they have ancestors or not. The work [of revision] will not pay for any labor bestowed upon it and [my *History of South Carolina*] has not paid me as much money as I have realized in one weeks labor, writing stories!"

To Simms the making of history was the work of great men, a conception which led him to write admiring biographies of Francis Marion, Captain John Smith, and Nathanael Greene. At the same time he held a mystic faith in the influence of race on history, which he applied to explaining the superiority of the "Southrons" to the New Englanders; for the latter came from the plebeian class of Roundheads, whereas the former were descended from the Cavaliers of Norman ancestry. When Commodore Paulding arrested William Walker in 1857, Simms wrote in condemnation: "Filibustiering [*sic*] is the moral necessity of all of Anglo-Norman breed. It is the necessity of all progressive races."

The publication of Lorenzo Sabine's *The American Loyalists* (Boston, 1847), which criticized the conduct of South Carolina in the Revolutionary War, provoked Simms to a vigorous defense of the patriotism of his state. He wrote caustic and ironic reviews in the *Southern Quarterly Review*, which he later published in a small volume entitled *South Carolina in the Revolutionary War, being a Reply to Certain Misrepresentations and Mistakes of Recent Writers in Relation to the Cause and Conduct of the State* (Charleston, 1853). He admitted that public opinion in South Carolina was equally divided between the Loyalists and the Whigs, but he maintained that most of the Tories were of foreign

birth or lower class or had come into the state as refugees from
Florida. At the same time he criticized New England as being
dominated by mercenary motives in its support of the Revolutionary movement—in contrast to South Carolina. In the fall of
1856 he began a lecture tour in New York State, speaking on
the subject of South Carolina in the Revolution. It was an unfortunate time for a Southerner to address a Northern audience
since they had been aroused by the attack of Brooks on Sumner
and by the recent presidential election. His tour was a flat
failure, and he returned home much humiliated. He deserved a
better fate, for he was well informed on the history of the
Revolution in his state, especially as to partisan warfare; and
he had a sound view of the nature of the conflict, as degenerating
into a civil war between the aristocrats and the poor.

Although Simms was a romantic historian, he had a good
critical sense. He had learned to be skeptical of the accuracy of
the historical recollections of old people. In 1852 in a letter to
the novelist John Pendleton Kennedy discussing their different
views on politics and slavery he observed that there was one
area of agreement: ". . . we believe that Yankee Histories of the
United States are generally fraudulent from Peter Parley to
George Bancroft." He advised Henry S. Randall, who was
writing a biography of Jefferson, to examine public resolutions
and remonstrances in the colonies from 1764 to 1776 to show
that Jefferson's phraseology in the Declaration of Independence
was quite common at the time and thus confute the claims of the
proponents of the Mecklenburg Resolves. In his novels he sought
scrupulously to preserve historical accuracy, but he thought that
only fragments of the evidence of past events had survived and
that the role of the historical novelist lay in that no-man's-land:
"the free use which the imaginative mind may make of that
which is unknown, fragmentary & in ruins—the *debris* of history"
(letter to Evert A. Duyckinck, February 2, 1847). Unquestionably his novels illustrate and preserve much of the social
history of the times that has escaped the notice of the professional historian.

In his young manhood Simms was a pronounced unionist. He
was a staunch supporter of Andrew Jackson, partly because of his
attachment to his wandering father who had fought under

Jackson in his Indian campaigns. From 1830 to 1832 he edited the Charleston *City Gazette*, in which he took such a strong stand against the nullifiers that a mob menaced him and he lost many subscribers. By middle age, however, he had become an ardent sectionalist, a bitter critic of New England, and an advocate of secession. Moreoever, he had changed from being a mild apologist for slavery to a strong advocate of the "peculiar institution" as a positive good.

It is difficult to date the turning point in his attitude toward the nation and the slavery issue, for the change was subtle and gradual. Some writers have attributed his reversal of views primarily to his marriage in 1836 to Chevillette Roach, daughter of a large planter, an event that brought the young writer into the possession of Woodlands and allied him with the plantation aristocracy. Though his marriage probably did have an unconscious effect on his attitude, there were more decisive forces altering his outlook. Simms wrote to Hammond in 1847 that "I should have arrived at my [present] conclusions without your aid, if I had not, after my repudiation 20 years ago as a Union man, dismissed as much as possible from my mind the consideration of subjects over which it appeared to me I was destined to have no control." In the thirties and forties the social and political environment around him was changing profoundly, affecting such powerful minds as that of John C. Calhoun, who abandoned his nationalistic point of view to become a sectionalist. From his mother's estate Simms had inherited twenty-five slaves (whom he lost because of debts), and it is unlikely that his attitude toward slavery was altered by his marriage to the heiress of a plantation. Much more important in causing the change were the attacks of the abolitionists on the South and the condescending attitude of Northern critics to Southern writers, for Simms had a passionate devotion to the South.

The aristocratic social tradition in the South encouraged ambitious men to desire political office, and Simms heeded this siren call. He had the old-fashioned idea that the call to serve in office should come, not from the voice *within*, but from *without*. Nevertheless, in December, 1841, he changed his attitude, for he felt insulted when the legislature rejected a resolution to appropriate $2,000 to purchase copies of his *History of South*

WILLIAM GILMORE SIMMS, romantic novelist of South Carolina.

Carolina for distribution in the free schools of the state, while at the same time voting to adopt a "paltry geography" of the state by Thomas Lockwood. Accordingly he decided to enter the race for election as representative to the legislature. A man of moods, he decided in the following spring to withdraw his candidacy. But his neighbors and friends persuaded him to become a candidate again in 1844, though he declared that he would not electioneer—would neither "treat nor speechify—will not in short cross the road for their suffrages." He was elected and took his seat in November, 1844.

Simms's participation in the Young America movement led him to join hands with its Northern exponents and to dilute his sectional feelings. In politics, he became for awhile a foe of conservatism. In the latter 1840's he sought to initiate a "Young Carolina" movement to overthrow the dominance of Calhoun and the conservative Charleston group of politicians. This clique was connected with the potent Bank of South Carolina, which Simms believed exerted a baleful influence on South Carolina politics. He tried unsuccessfully to persuade Hammond to lead the Young Carolina movement against the combined forces of the bank, the old "Hunkers," and the all-powerful Calhoun.

In no other state did the political dictatorship of one man suppress dissent so effectively as in South Carolina. For twenty years Calhoun ruled the state almost as an uncrowned monarch. From 1828 to his death in 1850 he sought and succeeded in keeping the state unified, not only to advance his unquenchable ambition but also to make the little state the leader of the whole South. Simms wrote to Hammond in 1847 that ambitious men in South Carolina were afraid to differ with Calhoun. He hoped, therefore, that the great Carolinian might attain his goal of being elected President so that there might be "a resurgence of that independence among our people which can never be as long as his ambition remains ungratified. His shadow falls heavily upon our young men and darkens all their pathways." Calhoun opposed all changes in the state government for fear that agitation for reform would upset the political harmony of the state.

Simms was naturally a democratic person who had a democratic conception of literature. In an autobiographical letter of 1839 he described himself as a Democrat of the Jackson school and a state rights man, opposed to tariffs, banks, internal improvements, American Systems, Fancy Rail Roads, Floats, Land Companies, and humbugs. "I believe in the people," he wrote, "and prefer trusting their impulses, than the craft, the cupidity & the selfishness of trades & Whiggery." In 1844 he was elected to the South Carolina legislature, and here he advocated the adoption of a plan for popular education and made a speech favoring the abolition of capital punishment. He also was in favor of letting the people vote for presidential electors. In 1849 in a letter to Beverley Tucker, Professor of Law at William and Mary College, he gave a noble definition of democracy as a principle that lifts men into responsibility and trust, but he declared at the same time that he was a conservative democrat.

Simms's faith in democracy diminished when he saw it put in practice against himself. In 1846 he was defeated for re-election to the legislature partly because of his frequent visits to the North: the cry against him was that he was a "Northern man." Moreover, he refused to electioneer or treat the voters with liquor. To his New York friend James Lawson he commented: "Among a people so ignorant as many of our poor farmers are, it is not difficult for cunning men who are also unprincipled, to effect a great deal, and a great many slanders and misrepresentations have been used against me." In December of that year he was defeated in the legislature for election to the office of lieutenant governor—but only by one vote. Hammond explained the defeat of his friend on the ground that Simms was a novelist, and the people of the state did not think a man of letters could be a statesman.

The rise of the Abolition movement and of the proslavery argument also made Simms less domocratic in feeling and thought. When he was thirty-one years old he wrote a review of Harriet Martineau's *Society in America* for the *Southern Literary Messenger*, in which he defended Southern slavery as a beneficial institution for the Negro, acting as a school for his development. He then wrote: "The time will come, I doubt not, when the negro slave of Carolina will be raised to a condition which will enable him to go forth out of bondage. When that time comes it may be, that we, like Pharaoh, will be loth to give them up." But he thought that the day of deliverance was "very far remote"

(III [October, 1837] 656). In 1852 he revised this article and published it as an essay—"The Morals of Slavery"—in *The Pro-Slavery Argument*. In this apology for the "peculiar institution" he modified his liberal sentiment of 1837: "I do not believe he [the Southern slave] will ever be other than a slave." He also dismissed the statement in the Declaration of Independence about the equality of men as merely a "finely sounding" phrase, made only as an assertion of the equality of the Americans against the British.

Simms made a further contribution to the Southern apology for slavery in his novel *The Sword and the Distaff* (later renamed *Woodcraft*), which was published in the same year. To Hammond he complained on December 15, 1852, "My last Book, 'The Sword & Distaff' has not been named by a single Carolina Press, though it is probably as good an answer to Mrs. Stowe as has been published." In this romance (perhaps his best novel) he described Tom the slave cook who attended Captain Porgy during the Revolutionary War as wholly devoted to his master and as being treated by the captain with the greatest of kindness and affection. Simms himself was such an indulgent master that he got very little work from his field hands, and his plantation was not profitable.

By 1847 Simms had become an ardent expansionist, principally to bolster the strength of the South by the acquisition of slave territory. He wanted not only California and the Southwest but a large part of Mexico itself. Within fifteen or twenty years, he predicted, Maryland, Virginia, and North Carolina would lose their attachment to slavery, but the acquisition of Texas and Mexico would assure the future safety of the "peculiar institution." Almost solely because Zachary Taylor was a slaveholder and presumably favorable to the cause of the slaveholders, Simms departed from his Democratic affiliation to work for the election of Taylor as President in 1848.

After his disillusionment with Taylor, who refused to support the Southern demand to open the territories to slavery, he wholeheartedly adopted the Calhoun doctrine that the South must ignore national parties and unite as a bloc for protection against an aggressive antislavery North. During the Southern movement of 1849–50 he opposed compromise and hoped for secession, but like Hammond he regarded the seccession of South Carolina alone as inexpedient. When Hammond was elected to the Senate in 1857 Simms lectured him on his duties as the potential leader of a united South. Above all, he urged, the South Carolina Senator should emphasize the honor of the South, which required him to stand firm for the admission of Kansas to the Union under the Lecompton Constitution.

In the secession crisis and during the Civil War Simms was an ardent sectional patriot who let his emotions dominate his mind. He advocated that if Lincoln were elected President, South Carolina should secede without awaiting any overt act of oppression and without waiting for other Southern states to secede. He anticipated a glorious future for the Confederacy founded at Montgomery, and when war threatened, he wrote that he felt like a bear chained at the stake. His active mind was constantly making suggestions as to how the war should be fought. One of his proposals was to use psychological warfare against the enemy, whom he regarded as very cowardly. To General Beauregard he proposed on June 8, 1861, that to each company a band of ten men should be attached—painted and disguised as Indians, with yellow hunting shirts, turbans, and faces dyed red with the bloodroot. "If there be anything which will inspire terror in the souls of the citizen soldiery of the North," he wrote, "it will be the idea that scalps are to be taken by the redmen. Encourage this idea."

The buoyant enthusiasm of Simms at the beginning of the war ended in stark tragedy: his wife and two of his children died during the war years (indeed, of his fifteen children only six survived at his death in 1870); and the mansion at Woodlands with his library of 10,700 volumes was burned by Sherman's troops. Among the last sad records of the aging romancer was his letter to Governor Andrew Magrath: he appealed for exemption from the state draft (he was then fifty-nine years old) on the ground that he could hardly walk any distance because of hemorrhoids and an enlarged testicle. He also wrote a moving indictment of Sherman's army in a pamphlet entitled *The Sack of Columbia, South Carolina.* By this time Simms had passed the meridian of his writing days, and the remainder of his life was a brave and forlorn struggle to earn a living by hack writing and to aid his impoverished literary friends.

In his prime, Simms had stood in the front rank of the Southern novelists who created a romantic image of plantation life and of the gentility of the Southern people. The prewar generation of novelists, unlike the later school of local color, chose the colonial, Revolutionary, or early nineteenth-century periods in which to locate their novels. They placed great emphasis on inheritance—the Cavalier blood—interacting with the mystique of the Southern climate and land.

Perhaps because he himself had no illustrious family background of which to boast Simms could mildly satirize some of the decayed aristocracy of his state. In *The Golden Christmas*, for example, he described Mrs. Girardin, proud of her French Huguenot ancestry—"blue blood"—as she went shopping on King Street in Charleston. Her face, he wrote, was a barometer of the caste of the people whom she met. Nevertheless, his novels contain nostalgia for baronial estates in South Carolina, respectful Negro servants in livery, coaches of four with outriders, heirlooms, coats of arms, and Madeira of rare vintage. He also lamented the manners of the old school—including the courtly bow—which were passing away with the exit of the generation educated in England. The old families needed fresh blood, he said, for their insularity had increased their self-esteem and prejudices, and they were losing their vigor. His prescription was for them to marry vigorous commoners.

Though Simms's novels are scarcely read today, he was certainly one of the most representative figures in the intellectual history of the Old South. He was a greater man than his literary work. Paul Hamilton Hayne described him in a letter to Richard H. Stoddard (December 15, 1856) as "having great nobility at the bottom of his nature but the surface is not prepossessing"; and his lack of tact, discretion, and judgment were attributed to his humble rearing. A tall, leonine figure, somewhat blustering in personality, he was very fond of talking and was inclined to be dogmatic. It was this propensity that caused John Pendleton Kennedy, who differed with him in politics, to call Simms "Sir Oracle." But such faults were far overshadowed by great virtues

—his courage in adversity, his capacity for unselfish friendship, his frankness and cordiality, and his patriotism in the cause of the South.

With the destruction of the Confederacy, the Romantic movement in the South did not come to an abrupt end; rather, a new form of romanticism arose with the glorification of the lost cause, as for example, in the novels of John Esten Cooke. Augusta Jane Evans of Mobile, Alabama, the author of the highly romantic novel *Macaria* (dedicated "To the Brave Soldiers of the Confederate Army") continued to write in the romantic vein after the war, achieving her greatest success in *St. Elmo,* a novel that was almost as popular in the United States following the war as *Uncle Tom's Cabin* had been in the 1850's. Thomas Nelson Page and Grace King—the school of local color—perpetuated the glamorous legend of the Old South. These writers portrayed the Southern plantation a more sentimental and less realistic spirit than the older Southern novelists. The prewar generation of Southern writers—Kennedy, George Tucker, Caruthers, and Simms (though not Beverley Tucker)—could see some faults in the society that they romanticized.

If the Romantic movement permeated Southern life, why did the Old South give so little support and honor to the creators of romances and to their good poets such as Timrod and Hayne? Simms's novels sold readily in the North but very slightly below the Mason-Dixon Line. In one of his moods of deep discouragement, he wrote to Hammond on December 14, 1847: "The South don't care a d——n for literature or art. Your best neighbour & kindred never think to buy books. They will borrow from you and beg, but the same man who will always have his wine, has no idea of a library. You will write for and defend their institutions in vain. . . . At the North the usual gift to a young lady is a book—in the South, a ring, a chain, or a bottle of Eau de Cologne."

Simms's sense of frustration was especially felt in the failure of his efforts to develop Southern literary magazines. He spent much of his energy and time attempting to keep Southern literary magazines alive, and through this medium he tried to encourage young writers. In 1842–43 he was editor of *The Magnolia* at Charleston; in 1845, of *The Southern and Western Mag-*

azine; in 1849–55, of the *Southern Quarterly Review;* and from 1857 to 1860 he actively supported *Russell's Magazine,* which was edited by Paul Hamilton Hayne. These magazines had to compete with the superior Northern and English periodicals, and quite naturally the Southern people preferred the latter. As a rule Southern magazines could not pay authors, and even Simms, despite his devotion to the South, sent his best stories and articles to Northern magazines such as *Godey's Lady's Book,* which paid him.

Southerners were much more interested in politics than in belles lettres. Hammond bluntly told Simms that the Southern people were not a reading people and that it was unrealistic for him to expect them to honor the literary man. The low repute in which the literary man was held in the Old South is illustrated by the struggling Virginia lawyer John Esten Cooke, who had published his *Leather Stocking and Silk* anonymously. In a letter to Evert Duyckinck in 1854 asking not to include his name in the *Cyclopaedia of American Literature,* he wrote: "Literature has seriously injured me already and putting my name *on file* as an author would well nigh overthrow my professional prospects." Though Simms exaggerated the neglect of himself and his work by his native section, he was essentially correct in believing that the South had little interest in the development of a Southern literature; even today the writer or artist is appreciated by only a very small fraction of Southern society.

Simms's life was full of harassment and frustration—"a drawing of water in a sieve," he said—but he could retreat into his study and enter the romantic world of literature. He read widely; Shakespeare was his favorite, and the character of Hamlet intrigued him perhaps more than any other figure in literature. He was also drawn to the novels of Scott, whom he made his standard of writing, to Froissart's chronicles of chivalric days, to Grote's history of ancient Greece, and to romantic passages in the Spanish conquest of the New World. His review of Prescott's *Conquest of Mexico* is a glowing piece of romanticism and he wrote a life of the Chevalier Bayard, the knight *sans peur et sans reproche.* A neighbor and close friend, the planter David Flavel Jamison, also followed the romantic vogue by publishing a life of the knightly hero Bertrand du Guesclin.

In Simms the romantic literary mind of the Old South had a blighted flowering. It could not express itself freely within the limitations of the slavery controversy and a conservative religion. The native writers were too concerned with creating a peculiarly Southern literature rather than a literature that transcended sectional boundaries. It was unfortunate that Simms and other writers of the Old South felt that regional patriotism required them to make their literary works a vehicle in defense of slavery and "Southern rights." What Simms needed, and his section too, was to travel abroad and see themselves in the context of Western civilization. On several occasions he tried to obtain a government post in one of the European capitals but was not successful. He needed a better education, as did the mass of Southerners, and greater discipline of mind; especially did he suffer from the lack of intellectual detachment or the critical spirit (which the classic spirit might have remedied); but such were the faults of the "Southrons." Although they were a people of honor, frank, manly, brave, and courteous, they were also provincial in outlook, violent, highly susceptible to oratory, and easily aroused to emotional decisions by spellbinders such as William L. Yancey.

Chapter XIII

THE VOICE OF EMOTION

THE stereotype of the Southerner on the eve of the Civil
War contrasted him—a warm-hearted, hospitable emotional
person—with the cold, calculating Yankee. Wrote William Gilmore Simms to his New York friend James Lawson on July 16,
1830, "But we Southrons, you know, are creatures of impulse and
prejudice." The Southerners, indeed, appeared to be more
emotional than the inhabitants of the more urbanized North.
Having a much higher ratio of illiteracy than the New Englanders, they were more susceptible to florid oratory, more unre-
strained in expressing emotion at religious revivals, and quicker
to resent insults and to appeal to the code of honor or the bowie
knife. When De Tocqueville asked the eminent Baltimore lawyer
John L. B. Latrobe what was the distinguishing characteristic
between the Northerner and the Southerner, he replied that the
Northerner was animated by the spirit of enterprise, the
Southerner by the spirit of chivalry. Senator Jeremiah Clemens
of Alabama, declared in the Senate in 1850 that Southerners were
"a race constitutionally brave, even to rashness, and as prone to
resentment as 'the sparks to fly upward.'" The Southerner of

1860 who represented most powerfully this emotional quality of his section in politics was the orator and fire-eater William Lowndes Yancey of Alabama.

Yancey was truly a man of deep and uncontrollable feelings, possessed of an antique and quixotic pride. It was unfortunate for the nation that in the crisis of 1860–61 such a man came to the front and like Hitler in modern Germany swayed great political audiences in the South, almost hypnotically, by his appeal to their resentment, pride, and fear of the future. Concerning his easily aroused and passionate nature, Benjamin F. Perry, the South Carolina unionist, wrote: "He had strong feelings and impulses, which generally controlled his action and judgment. He was a man of high spirit and dauntless courage. His impulses and his passions involved him in a great many difficulties of a serious nature." On one occasion while Yancey was reading law in Perry's office in Greenville, he and a fellow student had a heated political discussion which ended by both of them drawing their pistols. Perry had to rush between the impetuous young men to prevent them from shooting each other. Later Yancey killed his wife's uncle (apparently in self-defense) as the result of a quarrel arising from a verbal insult. Perry felt that Yancey was responsible for the breakup of the Democratic party at Charleston with its train of evils, and his estimate of the fire-eater was therefore unfavorable: "With all his talents, attractions, and brilliancy, he was not a man of wisdom, or judgment, or stability of character."

In the Alexander Beaufort Meek Papers there is a letter written by Yancey in response to a wedding invitation that shows a very appealing side to his warm-hearted, emotional nature. He complimented his friend, W. O. Baldwin, for the unconscious influence the latter had exerted over him by setting an example of purity and refinement. "You have insensibly influenced my own heart, Baldwin," he wrote. "You just made me feel that I had become tarnished in too rude an intercourse with the world and excited me to an examination of myself." Yet he warned the prospective bridegroom that "in a married life you must find more crosses and vexations than you ever dreamed of."

It is frequently the recourse of a highly emotional man, subject to fits of depression as Yancey was, to find solace or support in excessive drinking. Although Edmund Ruffin asserted that Yancey was inspired by alcohol when he made his famous speech on the African slave trade at the Montgomery Commercial Convention in 1859, other testimony indicates that he was temperate in drink. In the Benjamin F. Perry Papers at Montgomery is a letter from Yancey to Perry dated February 10, 1861, thanking Perry for procuring a barrel of South Carolina whiskey. Yancey commented that he took a dram a day but could not endure drinking the common stuff of commerce; for that reason he desired the pure "mountain dew" which Perry had sent him—to the amount of forty-three gallons. Yancey apparently at this time drank whiskey as a medicine, for he was suffering from what he called his "terrible disease"—arthritis of the spine.

Yancey had a very unusual background for one who became an agitator for Southern rights. Born in 1814 on his grandfather's Georgia plantation, he was educated largely in the North. After the death of his father (a prominent lawyer of Abbeville, South Carolina) when Yancey was three years old, his mother married a Yankee schoolteacher, the Reverend Nathan Beman, who conducted an academy in Georgia. Later the family moved to Troy, New York, where his stepfather became pastor of a Presbyterian church. Tensions developed between the abolitionist stepfather and the Southern mother that finally led to divorce. No one can tell the effect of family clashes upon the emotional youth. Possibly his intransigent course as a fire-eater had its roots in these family tensions. He attended Williams College but left before graduation to take up the study of law, first in the office of a lawyer at Sparta, Georgia, and later in Perry's office at Greenville, South Carolina.

While he was reading law in Perry's office his mentor observed that Yancey was too much interested in politics and literature to be an assiduous law student. Though he was fond of feminine society and very susceptible to the charms of a vivacious woman, "nothing," according to Perry, "could make him forego the pleasures of political excitement." He threw himself passionately into the party struggles over nullification. For a short time in 1834–35 he edited a unionist newspaper, the Greenville *Moun-*

taineer. He was only nineteen years old then, but he did not hesitate to denounce the nullifiers boldly, especially for the passage of the Test Act, which imposed upon all civil and military officers a test oath of superior allegiance to the state. Thus he early demonstrated his flair for dramatic and extreme language. On December 6, 1834, for example, he declared that the test oath would make nearly half of the people of the state serfs, and a week later he appealed to the heroic men of South Carolina not to submit to shackles but to be animated by "the spirit of 76." At this early age also, in speaking to mass meetings in South Carolina, he discovered his great oratorical gift.

Everything that Yancey did, he did with ardor. In 1836, after marrying a woman who had inherited thirty-five slaves, he moved to Alabama and set up as a planter. He practiced agriculture with great enthusiasm, but also edited newspapers, first at Cahaba and then at Wetumpka. In 1839 an event occurred which his biographer John Witherspoon Du Bose has described as "the turning point in his career." As a result of a feud between his overseer and the overseer of a neighbor, his slaves were poisoned. After this great financial loss he abandoned the occupation of planter, again took up the study of law which he had neglected for six years, and sought to support his family by a return to his old profession.

Nevertheless, Yancey was more interested in politics and in honor than in making money at his law practice. In this respect he was like thousands of other ambitious young Southerners, especially those who had the gift of oratory. During the presidential campaign of 1840 he made ardent speeches at barbecues and public gatherings for the Democratic candidate Martin Van Buren. In the following year he was elected to the lower house of the legislature and in 1843 to the state senate. The great issue in Alabama politics at this time was the basis of the reapportionment of the legislature. The planter class favored the federal basis, by which slaves were to be counted in determining representation at three-fifths of their number. Yancey, on the other hand, campaigned in behalf of the more democratic principle of counting only the white population.

Indeed, until he became warped by an obsession with Southern rights, his political career was characterized by strong liberalism. He strove vigorously for the adoption of an adequate free school system. He was also active in trying to secure fairer legal rights for women. In 1839 Mississippi had been the first state in the Union to grant women the right to own and control their property after marriage, without the liability that it might be sold to pay the husband's debts. Yancey proposed the adoption of a similar law for the state of Alabama. In his papers preserved at Montgomery is the manuscript copy of a fifty-six-page speech entitled "The Rights and Wrongs of Women," which advocated revising Alabama laws to permit women not only to control their property but also to act as the legal guardian of their children. Toward achieving these reforms he urged the women of the state to use all their powers of persuasion. ". . . your smiles and your graces," he reminded them, "are irresistible." The present laws of the state "shock a gallant heart." Although he championed the cause of women in many respects, he was not an advocate of the extreme Northern brand of feminism; he would not "disturb man's supremacy in the management of the political world."

Yancey's role in national politics was brief and undistinguished; his great influence was exerted in political conventions and in moving popular assemblages by his oratory. In 1844 he was elected to Congress to fill the unexpired term of Dixon H. Lewis, Calhoun's lieutenant in Alabama, and he was later re-elected to a full term. In his campaigns of stump speaking he traveled much through his district, but so hospitable were the Southern people that he never had to pay a hotel bill. "I was elected twice to Congress," he said, "and my canvasses did not cost me $5."

In Congress he began to display a sectional bent that contrasted with his earlier unionism. When the Whig Congressman Thomas L. Clingman of North Carolina attacked Southern Democratic Congressmen in a speech opposing the annexation of Texas, they selected Yancey to reply. His scathing attack of Clingman led to a bloodless duel. Alabama law declared that the participant in a duel was disqualified to hold office, but the legislature passed a special act relieving him of this penalty and when the governor vetoed it, repassed the bill over the veto. Yancey did not enjoy his life as a Congressman and resigned in June, 1846, explaining that he needed to return to his law practice to support his family. In his letter of resignation he expressed his disgust with the Northern members of the Democratic party, whom he accused of sacrificing principle and Southern interests for personal advantage.

In February, 1848, Yancey took a bold and decisive step that determined his future career in politics. At the state convention to select delegates to attend the Democratic National Convention at Baltimore he introduced a set of resolutions that came to be known as the "Alabama platform." They stated the extreme position of the fire-eaters, namely, that the territory about to be ceded by Mexico should be opened for settlement to "all citizens of the United States together with their property of every description and that the same should remain protected by the United States while the territories are under its authority." This statement not only repudiated the Wilmot Proviso but also the popular sovereignty doctrine advocated by Lewis Cass, one of the principal candidates for nomination for President. The resolutions furthermore declared that no one who held views contrary to the Alabama position should be nominated by the party for President or vice-president. When the Baltimore convention overwhelmingly rejected the Alabama platform, Yancey and one other delegate withdrew.

On his way home he stopped at Charleston, South Carolina, where he made a violent speech denouncing the action of the Baltimore convention, observing ironically that "virtuous" politicians from the South, including his Alabama colleagues, had sacrificed their principles to win an election and to secure the nominaion for vice-president of Senator William R. King of Alabama. In Alabama Yancey was widely criticized for his intractable course. So wounded in spirit was he by this repudiation that he wrote to Senator Dixon Lewis proposing the formation of a new party.

Lewis's reply, June 29, 1848, extended to seventeen manuscript pages (preserved in the Alabama State Department of History and Archives) and was highly pragmatic. His obesity (he weighed 430 pounds and had a special chair in the Senate) may explain the unusual exordium of his letter: "Two doses of Calomel & the hottest weather I ever felt, must be my excuse for

WILLIAM LOWNDES YANCEY, fire-eating orator of Alabama.

not answering your letter as fully as its importance demands." He approved completely of the principles in the Alabama platform and of Yancey's course in the convention but flatly rejected the idea of a separate party, doubting that such a party would carry a single county in the state. It was foolish, he wrote, to break up the Democratic party and deny support to Cass, who had opposed the Wilmot Proviso and was sound on slavery. He criticized Yancey's impetuous speech at Charleston because it was too full of denunciation and lacked a calm and quiet statement of the facts. He tried to soothe the proud politician by subtle flattery: '"It is natural that you should feel deeply the assaults that have been made on you, & that you should consider the unanimity with which our Party friends have gone to the support of Gen. Cass as a rebuke to the fidelity—and as all will admit—the ability—with which in obedience to your pledges as a Delegate—you resisted the nomination, but does your personal honour or your party position require you to indicate your sense of personal injury by your present purpose of forming a new political organization?'"

After his great rejection, Yancey virtually isolated himself from party politics for the next eight years. In 1851 the people of Alabama were presented with the question of whether they would accept the Compromise of 1850, an issue that dominated the election of Congressional and state officers. Yancey made many vehement speeches against the adoption of this sectional truce, maintaining that the Compromise violated the Constitution and sacrificed Southern rights. At this time Southern rights organizations were formed in the various communities of the state, and these extremist groups invited Yancey to become a candidate for governor. In a letter of May 10, 1851, he declined the invitation but announced that he approved of the principles adopted by the state convention of Southern rights associations. He attacked the submissionists—the moderates—but at the same time he disapproved of a proposal for the Southern states to levy prohibitive taxes on the purchase of goods manufactured in the North. He urged the secession party to perfect its organization, regardless of all former party distinctions, to create a nucleus for action when the next great emergency produced by fresh Northern aggressions should arise. This group, he wrote, could then take advantage of "the warmth and indignation of the hour . . . to place the State triumphantly in a position of independence and honor—such will be our glorious destiny."

In 1852 he refused to vote for the Democratic candidate, Franklin Pierce, but instead cast his ballot for the candidates of the fire-eaters, George M. Troup of Georgia for President and John A. Quitman of Mississippi for vice-president. When the American or Know-Nothing party arose, he vigorously denounced it as being anti-American in seeking to deny Catholics the full privileges of American citizenship. He returned to the fold of the Democratic party in 1856 and campaigned to secure the election of the pro-Southern James Buchanan. The refusal of the North to accept the Dred Scott decision and the Lecompton Constitution aroused in him a mood of deep resentment and defiance.

In such a mood, he began a renewed agitation for the secession of the South unless the North would grant justice and equality to his section within the Union. In a famous letter of June 15, 1858, to James S. Slaughter of Georgia he expressed his disillusionment as to the efficacy of a political party to protect Southern rights and advocated the organization of "Committees of Safety" throughout the cotton states, "to fire the Southern heart—instruct the Southern mind—give courage to each other, and at the proper moment, by one organized concerted action, we can precipitate the cotton States into a revolution." Accordingly, he supported Edmund Ruffin's proposal to form "Leagues of United Southerners" to protect Southern rights, and he himself drafted the constitution of the Montgomery organization. Despite these secession sentiments he sought but failed to secure an election by the legislature to a seat in the United States Senate.

The passionate addiction of Southern people to florid and emotional oratory was one of the social conditions that gave Yancey the opportunity to become something more than an ordinary politician. It was not that he said original or striking things in his speeches, but he lived at a time when his manner of delivery, as well as his appeal to emotions of resentment and of honor, enthralled the rural audiences of the Old South. An examination of Yancey's style of oratory and its effect upon Southern audiences, therefore, affords a clue to a significant facet of the Southern mind on the eve of the Civil War. To a great extent Yancey employed the technique of the camp meeting in moving the masses. A deeply religious man himself, he allied the cause of obtaining justice within the Union or the alternative of secession with great moral forces and with the ineluctable dictates of honor. Much of his success as an orator also depended on the fact that both he and his audiences were strongly affected by the Romantic movement.

This romantic influence is indicated by the Eufaula, Alabama, *Spirit of the South* (July 15, 1851), reporting a speech by Yancey over the acceptance of the Compromise of 1850. The orator was escorted from the home of a prominent citizen of Eufaula, John G. Shorter, to the place of the meeting by a splendid procession of "State Rights citizens"—riding in fifty carriages and buggies accompanied by more than one hundred horsemen and by numerous citizens on foot. Cannons were booming, drums were rolling, and "loud wild cheers" reverberated from the van to the rear of the long procession. In front of Young's Store, Colonel Shorter arose from his buggy and in a loud voice challenged and defied the champion of the submissionists, Henry W. Hilliard, "to come forth and measure arms" with the secession leader. In the audience were a 150 ladies; at the Blue Springs barbecue held the week before when the secessionist and submissionist orators spoke, "The occasion was graced," observed the *Spirit of the South,* "by the presence of a large number of ladies, who now, as in the days of the revolution, are found espousing the cause of their country." On this exciting occasion, before the tournament of oratory began, there was a soul-stirring song modeled on the Marseillaise and composed for the occasion. Though Hilliard was a mighty warrior of speech, he was vanquished in the opinion of the *Spirit of the South* by the "burning eloquence, the massive reasoning, and the just denunciations" of William L. Yancey.

At Uniontown, Alabama, in September, 1856, a three-day political meeting took place; relays of orators spoke, Yancey being the last. His speech, according to a manuscript in the Du Bose Papers, alternated between a conversational tone and "the grandest flights of oratory." In his peroration Yancey used the dramatic incident of the advance of Napoleon's troops against the Austrians at Wagram, and in the words of the manuscript version, which is different from the printed version: "As the orator began to describe the movement of the advancing troops, he moved with measured tread toward the brink of the stage facing the great audience, every man and woman before him in deepest tension; the black coachmen on the margin ardently interested. Reaching the end of the platform, his countenance aglow, the wonderful voice cried out the soldier's command to rushing, crowding ranks, 'Keep time, My Men! Keep Time.'" So deeply moved was the crowd that they sprang to their feet as one man; yells and shouts filled the air; and hats were thrown up in abandon. The ladies presented the orator with a gorgeous bouquet, and when he had retired, men mounted the platform and confessed that they had been converted by his speech from being Fillmore men to Buchanan supporters.

Yancey's remarkable qualities as a public speaker were contrasted vividly with the style of Henry W. Hilliard, who was rated by contemporaries in Alabama as Yancey's only match as a speaker. William R. Smith, one of the unionist leaders in 1860–61, pointed up the striking contrast between the two men in this way: "In all that was soft and smooth, easy and graceful Mr. Hilliard was unquestionably the better [Hilliard had been an English professor at the University of Alabama and an occasional Methodist minister before he became a politician]; in all that was fierce, stormy, vituperative, denunciatory, impetuous and scornful Mr. Yancey excelled." Yancey spoke with great rapidity and he had a fondness for high-sounding phrases, nor did he scruple at using "plausible claptrap." He was fond, too, of taking illustrations from mythology and from the history of classical Greece and Rome. Hilliard himself paid tribute to his opponent's ability to manipulate the emotions of a crowd; "he exhibited a vehemence unsurpassed in our country since the time of Patrick Henry."

What was the secret of his magical power over a Southern rural audience? Thomas H. Watts, who opposed Yancey's extremism in politics but who later became the attorney general in Davis's cabinet, answered the question as follows (in a manuscript reminiscence in the Du Bose Papers): "He was a man of remarkably fine presence before a jury or an audience, and then the peculiar charm about his speaking was the sweet voice and the annumciation [sic] of every syllable of every word that he spoke so that even in conversational tone he was distinctly heard in any room and at a great distance when speaking in the open air. His was a peculiarly mellow and sweet voice which was attractive. He was always deeply in earnest, and I may say that he carried out—whether he knew it or not—the rule which Garrick adopted when he was in the very height of his fame as an actor—he spoke truth as though it was truth, and that he felt from the innermost recesses of his heart the full measure of its truth. In that way he manifested in my judgment, the magnetic power which he had over audiences and juries."

Yancey's great moment of destiny came in the Democratic National Convention at Charleston in April, 1860. Murat Halsted, editor of the Cincinnati *Commerical* and a Republican in politics, has described Yancey as he observed him on this occasion—a man of medium height, compactly built, though with "a decided stoop in his shoulders" (owing to his spinal affliction), with light brown hair and gray eyes (a portrait in the Alabama State Department of History and Archives, however, has brown eyes), dressed in the style of a tidy businessman, and with the frank and unassuming manners of a boy. The Alabama leader, he noted, was unlike the professional politicians at the convention, who were smoking, drinking, and hobnobbing confidentially with other trading politicians. Yancey rather avoided talking politics and mingling with the crowd. "He is mild and bland in manner as [the pro-Southern New York mayor] Fernando Wood, and has an air of perfect sincerity, which Wood has not." Indeed, Halsted portrays Yancey as the very opposite of the stereotyped image of the fire-eater: "There is not the slightest symptom of a fanatic about him. . . ."

Yancey did not speak in the convention until the fifth day, April 27, when he arose to make his famous speech urging that the party adopt the extreme Southern position—actually the Alabama platform of twelve years before. It was an able speech, in which he enumerated the various grievances of the South caused by a violation of the Constitution. He argued emphatically against the right of a territorial legislature, which represented only the firstcomers, to exclude slavery from the territories. On this occasion as in other recent statements he declared that he was not a disunionist per se; he would prefer that the South remain in the Union as long as the Constitution was strictly observed.

When the convention adopted the platform of Stephen A. Douglas, or popular sovereignty, the Alabama delegation led by its chairman, Leroy P. Walker, walked out. This bolt was the beginning of the breakup of the Democratic party into two factions, the National Democratic party, which met in Baltimore and nominated Douglas, and the Constitutional Democratic party, which chose John C. Breckinridge as its candidate. Another group, largely from the border states and consisting of many old Whigs, formed the Constitutional Union party and nominated John Bell of Tennessee. In his account of the Charleston convention Murat Halsted indicates that the bolting Southern delegations were not trying to precipitate a secession movement by splitting the party and thus insuring the election of the Republican candidate. Rather they sought by this desperate maneuver to throw the presidential election into the House of Representatives, where they hoped to elect a President favorable to Southern views.

In support of Breckinridge, Yancey made a campaign tour in the Northern states during the fall. Dressed in a gray suit of Southern-manufactured cloth, he dramatically appealed to a large audience in New York City to vote for Breckinridge in order to do justice to the South and save the Union. In Boston he defended slavery as a kindly institution, condemned the doctrine of popular sovereignty, maintained that cotton was the source of New England prosperity, and affirmed his devotion to the Union provided that the Constitution was faithfully observed.

The Alabama unionist Jeremiah Clemens thought that Yancey's tour of the North would injure rather than help the cause of the South and the Union. To John Bell he wrote on October 14, 1860, (letter in the John Bell Papers, Library of Congress): "You have no doubt seen the report of Yancey's speech in New York. I see by the Telegraph to-night that he has been repeating it in Boston. There is a wonderful backing down from the extreme position he took at home in the early part of the canvass, but mischief always dogs his steps & his presence there will strengthen the hands of the Black Republicans. With all his speaking talent he has not one particle of common sense & if he went North for any other purpose than that of helping the Republicans, it must have been under the influence of a weak and childish vanity of which a lunatic ought to be ashamed."

The election of Lincoln on November 6 was the spark that touched off the Secession movement. Alabama was among the first states to act, for its legislature eight months before had made it obligatory for the governor to call a convention should the Republican candidate be elected. The hundred delegates who assembled in Montgomery on January 7 were divided in opinion into fifty-four secessionists and forty-six unionists and cooperationists. There was a clear sectional alignment among the delegates; almost all of the unionists and cooperationists came from the northern hilly part of the state where slavery and the plantation system were relatively weak. Northern Alabama was closely connected with Tennessee, where its markets lay, and it is understandable that the people of this section were reluctant to secede, for Tennessee at this time showed no signs of leaving the Union. Moreover, bad feeling existed between the people of the Southern Appalachians, to which the northern section of the state belonged, and the people of the lowlands and black belts. This old feeling flared up when Yancey declared that those who would not submit to an ordinance of secession passed by the convention would be traitors branded as Tories. Nicholas Davis of the Tennessee Valley replied that the people of north Alabama would meet Yancey and his cohorts at the foot of the mountains and settle with arms the question of the sovereignty of the people.

The two dominating figures in the convention were Yancey and Jeremiah Clemens, leader of the cooperationists. The leader of the cooperationists was a complex and contradictory character who ended his career as an exile from his native state in Philadelphia, where he advocated the re-election of Lincoln in 1864. Born in Huntsville in the Tennessee Valley of northern Alabama, he was a very brilliant and handsome young man, well educated at La Grange College and Transylvania University. The Romantic movement had affected him deeply, leading him to write several romantic novels, notably *Bernard Lile*, and to follow the martial tradition of the aristocratic class of the South. In 1842 he volunteered in the Texas army to protect the republic from the threat of a Mexican invasion, and he rose to the rank of colonel during the Mexican War. Mrs. Clement C. Clay, Jr., who danced with him at a ball when she was a teen-aged girl, wrote: "He was the personification of manly beauty. His head was as shapely as Tasso's . . . and in his eyes there burned a romantic fire that enslaved me from the moment their gaze rested upon me." But Clemens was much more than a gallant ladies' man; he was an able lawyer and a very ambitious politican.

There is a sadness in contemplating the ruin of a career that promised so much but ended so dismally. In the 1840's Clemens was a member of the Young America group that tried to wrest control of the Democratic party from the old fogies. In 1849 after the death of Dixon Lewis, he was elected to the United States Senate as the youngest member of that body. But his election in the legislature had apparently been won by a deal with the Whigs, and ever afterwards he was distrusted. In the Senate he at first took a pro-Southern stand that exceeded even Yancey's ultraism. In opposing the Vermont resolutions on slavery, he declared in a speech in the Senate on January 10, 1850: "The Union is valuable only for the privileges that it confers and the rights it secures. When the [federal] government is so administered to oppress and grind down one portion of the Confederacy it ceases to be an object of veneration to me, and I am ready to rend asunder its firmest bonds." He violently op-posed the adoption of the Compromise of 1850, declaring that the admission of California as a free state was worse than the enactment of the Wilmot Proviso. But after the Compromise was adopted by Congress, he suddenly changed his position and upon his return to Alabama campaigned against Yancey and the secessionists in favor of accepting the Compromise. He was not re-elected to the Senate; in 1856 he joined the American party and in 1860 supported John Bell as candidate of the Constitu-tional Union party.

In the crisis following the election of Lincoln, Clemens' corre-spondence with Senator John J. Crittenden (in the Crittenden Papers, Library of Congress) reveals an agonizing conflict of opinion in his mind. On November 24 he wrote that the personal liberty acts of the Northern states and their refusal to return fugitive slaves were greater grievances than the election of a Republican candidate in the constitutional way. "I am unwilling to remain in the Union with these grievances unredressed. The difference between Mr. Yancey & myself is that I believe that redress may be obtained in the Union while Separate State action will only aggravate the evil." A month later he wrote to Crittenden that though he did not believe in the right of secession, he did believe in the right of revolution and that if the Northern states persisted in retaining their unconstitutional laws and refused to give the South guarantees for the future protection of slavery, "I am for taking the sword in hand and trusting to God for the consequences." At this time and throughout the debates he maintained that secession would inevitably lead to civil war, while Yancey and the ardent secessionists promised the people that the course which they advocated would not lead to war.

In the convention Clemens and the cooperationists pursued the tactics of delay. Thus, he hoped that the North would be given time to make concessions which would assure the South of the safety of their institutions within the Union. He presented the minority report of the "Committee of Thirteen," appointed to recommend a course of action for the convention. The report contained a list of proposed guarantees for the protection of slavery and Southern rights to be used as a basis of settlement between the North and the South. It recommended the calling of a convention of slave states at Nashville on February 22 and demanded the submission of any ordinance of secession to the vote of the people for ratification.

The disunionists probably could have passed an ordinance of secession on the first day, but they gave the cooperationists abundant opportunity to speak against precipitate secession. On January 11 the convention passed the fateful ordinance by a majority of sixty-one affirmative to thirty-nine negative votes. Clemens voted for the ordinance because he realized that it would pass and he believed it desirable for the state to present a united front to the North. Thirty-three delegates of the convention, however, stood by their principles and drew up a protest against the passage of the secession ordinance.

The debates in the Alabama convention were not an isolated case of the divided mind of the South on the question of seceding from the Union. In Georgia a momentous debate took place over the same issue; Alexander H. Stephens made a plea for the state to wait before taking the drastic step of secession in order to see what the action of the Lincoln administration would be. His was the voice of reason: "Let us not anticipate a threatened evil," he advised. In the upper South too there were many men, former supporters of John Bell, who held back the hotheads from carrying their states into secession until Lincoln's call for troops after the firing on Fort Sumter forced them to make a decision between fighting with the South or the North.

The great decision which the Southern people made to secede from the Union seems to have been based on emotion rather than on a realistic assessment of their best interests. They did not coolly weigh the chances of war that were involved in their decision, nor consider actually whether slavery was safer out of the Union than in it. They acted largely on a wave of resentment, on an artificial sense of honor, with entirely too much haste. No single fire-eater such as Yancey can reasonably be held responsible for the secession of the Southern states. Indeed, there is some evidence, presented by Professor Austin Venable in the *Journal of Southern History*, that at the last moment Yancey tried to persuade the Alabama delegation to break their instructions and stay in the convention at Charleston. Nor does there seem to have been any important segment of Southern opinion that desired separation from the Union and the formation of a new nation as an end in itself. Rather, the decision for secession was the boiling over of a sense of accumulated grievances.

By 1860 the Southern mind had become very sensitive to the harsh criticism of the North and to the assumption of Northern reformers that they were morally superior to the people of the South. A resident of Burke County in western North Carolina where the slaves composed only 26 per cent of the population had noted earlier that there existed "a great sensitiveness of the community to everything connected with slavery." Were

Southerners reticent in discussing the "peculiar institution" because they had feelings of guilt over holding slaves? I have found little evidence of a guilt complex among the Southern people after 1835. Nevertheless, I believe, Southerners could no more isolate themselves from world opinion then than can the supporters of *apartheid* in South Africa today ignore for long the censure of world opinion.

Moreover, between the 1830's and 1860 the sentiment of nationalism had declined sharply in the South. The Italian Count Francesco Arese during his travels in the South in 1837–38 had observed a moving demonstration of devotion to the Union and pride in it during the celebration of the Fourth of July in Lexington, Virginia. After the usual fireworks, the marching of the militia, and the playing of "Yankee Doodle" and "Hail, Columbia!" the townspeople sat down to an elaborate dinner, where many patriotic toasts were given. Among the banqueters was an old Negro, who had served Washington during the Revolution, and "for that reason," the Count relates, "a half-century later, he was allowed the honor once every year of sitting down to table with white men!" Had the Count returned a generation later he would have found Southerners far less enthusiastic about belonging to a great undivided nation, whose mission was to set an example of democracy to the rest of the world. Had he visited Montgomery or Charleston or Jackson or Tallahassee or New Orleans after the passage of the secession ordinances, he would have seen the people thronging the streets, congratulating each other that they had come out of the house of bondage; and he would have heard church bells ringing, cannons firing, the sounds of revelry as young girls in crinoline skirts danced and sang, and the applauding of crowds as fervid orators such as Yancey predicted a glorious future for a Southern republic.

What had happened to the concept of "the glorious Union" that had prevailed when Count Arese visited the South? Ever since 1844 when the Methodist church had broken asunder over the slavery question, the mystic bonds of sentiment holding the Union together had begun to snap. Especially destructive was the struggle over the expansion of slavery into the territories acquired from Mexico. Today this seems largely a fight over an

abstraction, for slavery was unsuited to expansion in this territory
—with slight exceptions. To the North, however, it involved a
moral principle. To the South it was primarily a question of
honor. Again and again Southern speech echoed the refrain that
the obligations of honor would not permit the South to accept
inequality in the Union, which the territorial policies of the
Republicans threatened to impose upon the section. The climax
of sectional feeling came when Southern people realized the
depth of feeling in the North against slavery, as demonstrated
by the reaction to the John Brown raid and by the election of a
Republican President. The election of Lincoln, Yancey said,
was the last straw.

The Southern people became emotional not only over an
accumulation of sectional grievances but also over their fears for
the future. Certainly a powerful element in the secession crisis
was this vague fear of the future—the anticipation that Lincoln's
election was only a first step toward the eventual destruction of
slavery. With prophetic insight, Calhoun had voiced this fear a
decade before and had sketched the course of development.
First, he predicted, the Northern states would "monopolize"
the federal territories; then they would gain a three-fourths
majority of the states to pass a constitutional amendment setting
free the slaves. After the bondsmen were emancipated, they
would be given a vote, and subsequently their votes would be
controlled by the Northern party to whom they owed their
freedom. Former slaves and profligate native whites (the future
scalawags) alone would receive the federal offices in the
Southern states. The South at last would become an appanage
of the North. Bitterness between the two races would become
unbearable. Nor would the condition of the Negroes be greatly
improved, for though they would be freed from the protective
care of their old masters, they would become the slaves of
society. Moreover, Southerners feared that amalgamation of the
races would be the final result. Much of what Calhoun predicted
came to pass in the Reconstruction period. In 1860 subcon-
sciously, if not consciously, the Southern people were afraid of
the darkening future.

The change of opinion of many conservatives in the lower
South during the crisis is illustrated by the case of Thomas H.

Watts of Montgomery, a prominent Whig leader and a strong opponent of the fire-eaters. After the election of Lincoln, on November 10, 1860, he published a letter in the Montgomery *Weekly Post* reversing his former position and advocating the secession of Alabama. He explained his change of opinion as follows: "Fanaticism rules the North." The hostile state of feeling in that section toward the South, he said, was indicated by the personal liberty acts, the recent overwhelming election of John A. Andrew as governor of Massachusetts (a zealous supporter of the fanatic John Brown), the rejection of John Bell for president, and the election of Lincoln. Moreover, the failure of the Crittenden Compromise in the Senate discouraged many conservative men.

In the emotional crisis following Lincoln's election the secession of the lower South was rushed through. The radicals held the initiative, and they realized the need to strike while the iron was hot. The moderates of 1860–61, like the moderates in the integration crisis a hundred years later, were reduced to quiet acquiescence. The fate of the Southern moderates who failed to speak out boldly in opposition to the passion of the hour, bears some resemblance to the fate of Greek moderates during the Peloponnesian War, when extremists ruled. Thucydides wrote: "The meaning of words had no longer the same relation to things, but was changed as they thought proper. Reckless daring was held to be loyal courage; prudent delay was the excuse of the coward; moderation was the disguise of unmanly weakness. . . ." In the states of the lower South, likewise, the cry of "submissionist," "Tory," "Lincolnite" was raised against those who advocated a course of delay and of calm consideration whether the election of Lincoln actually endangered the rights of the South.

The Mobile *Daily Register* of December 23, 1860, maintained that nine-tenths of the people of the South on the eve of the presidential election were devoted to the Union but that the election of Lincoln had converted them to secession. Nevertheless, many former Whigs and Bell supporters still hoped to preserve the Union and continued to hold to the concept of a glorious undivided country. Among these was Robert Jemison, Jr., of Tuscaloosa, the unionist candidate for President of the

Alabama convention of 1861. In the hall of the convention on January 10 he penned an eloquent statement of his devotion to the Union in a letter to his daughter (manuscript in the University of Alabama Library): "The grave will be the only asylum to which we may flee from the destruction precipitated upon this happy & prosperous people. A set of ruthless rash reckless politicians had laid ruthless hands on the pillars of the fairest noblest temple of political liberty ever enacted by human wisdom & crushing friends & foes in its ruins." But these die-hard unionists were largely old men—most of them were like Sam Houston or Richard K. Call, the great nationalist figure in Florida politics, men who retained memories of Jacksonian nationalism. They were ignored in the rush; the voice of emotion had prevailed in the South.

Chapter XIV

THE DYNAMICS
OF THE SOUTHERN MIND

THE mores of a people have been considered so tenacious, at least from the days of William Graham Sumner, that they supposedly change at a glacial pace. But David Riesman has shown in *The Lonely Crowd* that this is not always true. The impact of the recent accelerated growth of population on the United States has changed the American character, particularly in the large cities. This generation has also witnessed within a few climactic years a remarkable overturning of the folkways of large parts of the South in respect to the Negro. Sumner's thesis therefore applies more authentically to an isolated, rural community such as existed in the Old South than it does to modern America. Yet even in the Old South some of the mores changed appreciably in the time between Thomas Jefferson and Jefferson Davis. This chapter is an attempt to probe the social dynamics of the region and to discover those aspects of the Southern mind that changed between the 1820's and 1860 and those that remained back in the eighteenth and early nineteenth centuries.

It is to the aristocracy—the country gentlemen—of the South

that one must look for the most marked differences between the North and the South. They cherished a set of values that were different from those of the North and which have virtually disappeared from our modern society. William Faulkner in "An Odor of Verbena" has described some of these archaic virtues, notably a deep sense of obligation to the family and a willingness to put one's life in jeopardy for the sake of honor. A striking example of this latter characteristic is found in the record of a court of honor held in 1836 at the University of Virginia (manuscript in the Huntington Library). At a dance given by Professor Bonnycastle a student from South Carolina, Louis Wigfall, felt insulted by the refusal of a Southern belle, a Miss Leiper, to dance with him. Believing that he was "elevated by wine," to use her expression, she took the arm of another student and hastened precipitately away. Wigfall was a youth of high mettle and fiery spirit and accordingly sent a challenge to Miss Leiper's escort for uttering language during the altercation "that I could suffer from no one."

When the civil authorities prevented the duel, a court of honor was appointed by the students to adjudicate the question whether Wigfall had been insulted. The court acted scrupulously according to legal forms. Miss Leiper's testimony, presented in a letter, informed the court of honor that she was mistaken in thinking that Wigfall was under the influence of wine when he insisted upon dancing with her. The court of honor reported that the affair between the two students had arisen out of "a delicate sensibility" which each party displayed, and because of a misconception. It ruled that there was no point of honor involved and that Wigfall's conduct in the presence of a lady was not rude or due to alcohol but was owing to "a natural impetuosity" which Miss Leiper had wrongly attributed to intoxication. Thus the matter ended without bloodshed and with the honor of both students preserved. Louis Wigfall lived to become a secession leader in Texas and a senator in the Confederate Congress.

Southern pride was displayed in various other ways than in quick resentment to insult. Many Southerners had a high sense of pride in regard to money matters; they did not wish to appear petty or mean in financial transactions. When James Atherton was touring Kentucky in 1832 he noted how different the

Kentuckians were from New Englanders in money matters. "To offer a Kentuckian cents in change," he wrote to his father, "would be deemed almost an insult" (manuscript in the University of Kentucky Library). Indeed, the values of Southerners were not those of sharp-trading Yankees. Horace Holley, who came from Boston to be president of Transylvania University, observed in 1832 that the people of Kentucky and Tennessee were influenced in their manners and character by slavery and the subtle forces of an agricultural interior. "Commerce," he remarked, "makes a different sort of population from agriculture."

A keen sense of personal pride and honor was, of course, not peculiar to the Southern people of the antebellum period. The Japanese, for example, have had until recently a code of conduct which exalts honor to fantastic extremes and seems to be the vestigial remains of a feudal society. The Southern sense of honor, too, had a feudal background, but it was powerfully nourished by the institution of slavery. Although Southerners as a whole did not display much vanity about personal appearance, they were overwhelmingly proud of standing up for the rights of their section. Southern pride, indeed, had an important role in bringing on the Civil War.

Honor and personal pride were part of the code of a gentleman in the Old South. Another obligation of the code, affecting even the humblest farmer, was the practice of hospitality. One visitor in the 1850's, the Northern journalist Frederick Law Olmsted, was not impressed by Southern hospitality. He was refused lodging for the night by planters both in Virginia and Mississippi; and often when he was accommodated, he paid f r his meals and lodging. When Edmund Ruffin was making his agricultural survey of South Carolina in 1843, the great planters who knew of his reputation entertained him hospitably, but he found that when his route lay through the region of small farms, the inhabitants accommodated travelers for the money. Even a state senator who lived near the Salkehatchie River was not too proud to charge him for lodging and meals, whereas Ruffin assumed that he was receiving hospitality and that it would be an insult to his host to offer payment.

Quite different, however, were the experiences of most travelers in the Old South. Henry Barnard, a Northern schoolteacher who traveled in this region in 1833, was touched by the many evidences of Southern hospitality, especially among the Virginians. "These Virginians," he noted, "won't take anything for their hospitality." For example, on his way to the scenic Peaks of Otter, he spent the night in the home of an intelligent farmer who refused to accept any compensation for lodging and food. "This is the way they do things in Virginia," Barnard commented. A Scottish textile worker, William Thomson, who traveled through the Southern states in 1840–42 and wrote *A Tradesman's Travels in the United States and Canada*, commented on Southern hospitality and sense of honor: "The character of the southern states, for hospitality, stands high, and it is not overrated. They are quite a distinct race from the 'Yankees.' They have a high sense of honour; treating every white man as a gentleman, but rigidly exacting the same respect in return; and although many young men carry bowie-knives, sword-canes, or pistols, after I knew them I felt myself as safe from injury or outrage as in my own house. In short, the society in this part of the country was the most agreeable I ever associated with.— Ladies are treated on all occasions with great deference and respect."

The plantation society of the Old South exhibited a strong patriarchal character owing to its isolation and to slavery. These same influences, young Charles Darwin discovered, produced a similar characteristic in Brazilian plantation society. He visited a Brazilian plantation in 1832 while the *Beagle* was in port. His description of it, except for the great pile of coffee beans drying before the residence, bears a striking similarity to accounts of some Southern plantations of the same period: "The house was simple, and, though like a barn in form, was well suited to the climate. In the sitting room gilded chairs and sofas were oddly contrasted with the white-washed walls, thatched roofs and windows without glass. . . . This profusion of food showed itself at dinner, where, if the table did not groan, the guests surely did: for each person is expected to eat of every dish. One day, having, as I thought, nicely calculated so that nothing should go away untasted, to my utter dismay a roast turkey and a pig appeared in all their substantial reality. During the meals, it was the employment of a man to drive out of the room sundry old hounds, and dozens of little black children, which crawled in together, at every opportunity. As long as the idea of slavery could be abolished, there was something exceedingly fascinating in this simple and patriarchal style of living: it was such a perfect retirement and independence from the rest of the world. . . . On such fazendas as these I have no doubt the slaves pass happy and contented lives."

The plantation society of the Old South emphasized the family to a much greater degree than was done in the North. Family graveyards were a familiar sight in the landscape of the Old South; the family altar was a part of its religious mores; and the devotion to kin was expressed in the phrase "kissing cousins." Southerners tended to evaluate people not so much as individuals but as belonging to a family, a clan. This characteristic has survived into the twentieth century in many villages of the Deep South, as Harper Lee's recent novel *To Kill a Mockingbird* has demonstrated. Here, far from the industrial world, the villagers judged people within the family context, as displaying hereditary characteristics. They were accustomed to lump all the Ewells together as being no-account for generations; the Cunninghams could always be trusted to pay their debts; "all the Burfords walked like that"; the Penfields had a "flighty streak"; the Crawfords, a "mean streak"; and the Goforths, a "stingy streak."

John William De Forest, who observed society in the up-country of South Carolina at the close of the Civil War, compared Southerners with his fellow New Englanders. "They are more simple than us," he wrote, "more provincial, more antique, more picturesque; they have fewer of the virtues of modern society, and more of the primitive, the natural virtues; they care less for wealth, art, learning, and the other delicacies; they care more for individual character and reputation of honor."

The traits of the Southern people were brightly illuminated during the Civil War. Von Clausewitz, the great German student of war, has argued that a nation fights the kind of war that the nature of its society determines. By 1860 the upper class of Southern society had developed the habit of command and a remarkable sense of pride. They were not accustomed to subordinate their wills to a central authority. Mrs. Chesnut's description of her father-in-law, in 1865—old Colonel Chesnut of South Carolina—points up this characteristic. "Partly patriarch, partly grand seigneur, this old man is of a species that we shall see no more—the last of a race of lordly planters who ruled this Southern world, but now a splendid wreck. His manners are unequaled still, but underneath this smooth exterior lies the grip of a tyrant whose will has never been crossed." Not all Southern planters were like Colonel Chesnut, but many of them were highly individualistic. Most of them, even the well-educated, were provincial in their outlook and in their loyalties.

The higher officers of the Confederate Army (who were not elected) came mainly from the plantation aristocracy, from the professional soldiers, the lawyers, and, suprisingly, from the business class. Ezra Warren establishes in *Generals in Gray* that of the 425 Confederate officers of general rank, 129 were lawyers before the war; 125, professional soldiers; 55, businessmen (including bankers, manufacturers, and merchants); 42, farmers and planters; 24, politicians; and 15, educators. The elected officers below the rank of colonel, however, were often drawn from humble citizens. They nevertheless commanded the sons of aristocratic planters; for example, Kate Stone's brother of Brokenburn in Louisiana served as a private in a company whose officers included a livery stable keeper, an overseer, and a butcher. The Confederate armies were, as David Donald has observed, "a product of the paradoxical world that was the antebellum South, devoted to the principles of democracy and the practice of aristocracy."

The old South was also different from our own age in its greater devotion to the classics, which meant a greater devotion to tradition. The whole educational system of the South from grammar school through college was based on the classic tradition, as was also the case in the North, though perhaps to a lesser degree. Hugh Swinton Legaré, editor of the Charleston *Southern Review* and John Tyler's attorney general and secretary of state, advocated that Southern youth should be thoroughly taught in the ancient languages from their eighth to their sixteenth year. The study of the classics, he observed, would form in them a pure taste, kindle their imaginations "with the most beautiful and glowing passages of Greek and Roman poetry and eloquence," store their minds with "the sayings of the sages," and indelibly impress upon their hearts the achievements of the Greek and Roman heroes.

Accordingly, the "gentleman" of the Old South was expected to have a classical education. The lack of such a training gave the novelist William Gilmore Simms an inferiority complex when conversing with the polished gentlemen of Charleston. In a letter to Hammond (1845) requesting that he be called neither doctor nor colonel, he commented: "I have as little claim to be a Dr. of Laws as any literary man in the country. Never was education so worthless as mine—i.e. in a classical point of view. . . . Through painful necessities I have come to the acquisition of an Independent Mind. . . . I must submit to be called Dr. & Col. by that silly class of persons who attach much importance to these things." In advising a young girl on her education Simms wrote (July 13, 1854): "I would have you make yourself familiar with Plutarch, Anacharsis [one of the Seven Sages of antiquity], Froissart, & C." Plutarch's *Lives* was regarded in the Old South, next to the Bible, as the great character-builder and was perhaps the most important single source of the classic tradition.

Legaré was the outstanding champion of the Greek and Roman classics in the Old South. This Charleston intellectual reminds one somewhat of Lord Byron in his temperament and in the circumstances of his life; the lock of hair that he wore over his forehead, his long sideburns, his fastidiousness, and his melancholic temperament were Byronic. Like the English poet, too, his personality suffered a permanent trauma from the fact that he was lame from childhood. In all probability Legaré would have been a literary man had he lived in a different environment. But ambitious of honor, he turned to politics and made literature an avocation. He never married, though apparently he was in love with a South Carolina girl, whom he described as "the most thorough-bred young lady in the country"; she had the same tastes as Legaré but nevertheless married another man, leaving him "alone in society" in Charleston. His affections thenceforth centered on his mother and sister.

The frank letters that Legaré wrote to former Senator William C. Rives of Virginia in 1839 reveal to some degree the paradox of the Southern intellectual of the period—a conflict between classicism and romanticism. He buried himself in the study of the ancient world, especially of Roman law, and wrote to Rives: "I have lately read Greek and German enough to choke ten professors." From 1832 to 1836 Legaré had served as chargé d'affaires at Brussels, where he had cultivated his mind by contact both with books and a continental society, which may explain his discontent with "this humdrum American world." To Rives he described himself as desolate and wretched, like Prometheus on the rock, with a "chained spirit." His letters are full of romantic longing instead of the serene acceptance of life as it is, typical of classical Greek art and literature. To Rives he also lamented that his mind was preternaturally calm, like the Dead Sea: "I want a tempest, anything that can stir it up to some passionate effort." He found this outlet in politics—at first, in a strong opposition to the Nullification movement; then toward the end of his life, in fighting the "putrid democracy" of Van Buren.

In this last struggle before his early death in 1843 he displayed the spirit of a strong conservative, reflecting some of the characteristics of the South Carolina mind. Lacking the economic basis for the aristocratic life, he nevertheless despised the pursuit of money. "What is there to awaken me," he exclaimed to Rives, "but the sordid love of pelf—which unfortunately does not come to me?" He was disgusted with the vote-getting appeals that the Van Buren democracy made to the common people, which aroused hostility between the rich and the poor, between the North and the South, and between agriculture and commerce. What had these self-styled friends of the poor actually done for them? "Did they encourage them to work as [John Jacob] Astor had done?" Despite such conservative individualism, Legaré rendered an official opinion as attorney general in 1841 that was decidedly liberal for his time, holding that free Negroes were entitled to the same civil rights as white men.

The cross currents in Southern thought that Legaré exhibited were also apparent in the pages of the Southern literary magazines. These reflected a much greater trend toward romanticism than toward a strong and vital interest in the Greek and Roman classics. Their articles on classicism were usually related to practical Southern interests and were often dictated by the desire to justify Southern institutions. The *Southern Quarterly Review* of Charleston, for example, published articles in the 1840's and 1850's on such subjects as "Classical Literature" (July, 1842), "Socrates" (January, 1843), "Rome and the Romans" (October, 1844), "Cicero's Letters" (October, 1844), "The Roman Law" (July, 1845), "Athens and the Athenians" (April, 1847), "Slavery among the Romans," which justified Southern as better than Roman slavery because of the influence of Christianity (October, 1848), "The Condition of Women in Ancient Greece" (January, 1850), "An Inquiry into Roman Jurisprudence" (April, 1851), "The Athenian Orators" (October, 1851), "Marcus Aurelius" (October, 1853), "Necessity of the Classics" (July, 1854), "Plato's Phaedon" (August, 1856), and "Cicero's *De Officiis*" (November, 1856). Professor Frank Ryan, who has written a doctor's dissertation on the *Southern Quarterly Review,* has found that approximately 5 per cent of the articles in this magazine dealt with the ancient world.

The *Southern Literary Messenger* of Richmond, the most enduring of Southern magazines, showed even less interest in the classics. A considerable number of the issues from August, 1834, the date of its founding, until the beginning of the Civil War contain very little material on the ancient world. In the March, 1836, issue is an article on "The Classics," in which the writer noted a growing neglect of the classics as well as continued attempts of many prominent men "to cast contempt on those studies which were once considered essential to the scholar and the gentleman." The writer defended the study of the classics as providing the best mental discipline for students and the best models of literature. Mathew Carey, the Philadelphia economist and publisher, replied in articles in the *Southern Literary Messenger* (August, 1836 and January, 1837), in which he maintained that too much time was spent in grammar school and college on the dead languages, to the detriment of the study of science and modern languages, which were more useful, especially for youths intended for business.

The issues in the 1850 volume were unusual in the number (six) of articles and translations relating to classic Greece and Rome, including an article entitled "Aristotle on Slavery." In other years the *Southern Literary Messenger* published such articles as "Zenobia, Queen of Palmyra" (May, 1849); "Modern Oratory" (June, 1852), which discussed the differences in style of Demosthenes and Cicero with the conclusion, "Demosthenes is, perhaps, the noblest model of oratory" (p. 371); and an alluring article entitled "Good Eating among the Greeks and Romans" (December, 1855). The general tone of the Southern literary magazines indicated a waning influence of the classics in Southern life after 1830 and the overwhelming dominance of the Romantic movement.

Especially significant, however, was the influence of the classics on the development of Southern oratory. Demosthenes and Cicero were held up by schoolmasters as the supreme models. Hugh Swinton Legaré, while a student at South Carolina College, displayed a passion for the classics that reminds one of a Renaissance scholar; he fashioned his style of oratory upon classic examples and like many other Southern boys practiced the art of declaiming in secluded places with appropriate gestures. Calhoun used the example of the Roman consulate to bolster his proposal of a dual Presidency for the nation, and he modeled one of his major speeches on Demosthenes' "Oration on the Crown." Thomas Hamilton, the supercilious British traveler, observed in *Men and Manners in America* (1833) that one heard more Latin quoted in Congress than in the British Parliament but that it consisted of hackneyed phrases and revealed no deep acquaintance with classical literature. Northern speakers as well as Southern orators engaged in this lip service to the classics, but in the rural South, oratory derived from Periclean Athens and imperial Rome could not compete successfully with romantically styled speeches.

The interest in ancient history and the classics might very well have been a liberating force on the Southern mind. Instead of emulating the liberal side of the classical tradition, however, Southerners of the antebellum period were attracted to the conservative elements. From the examples of Greek and Roman society, Southerners drew some of their strongest arguments for justifying slavery. They regarded their own society as an extension of a Greek type of democracy, which had been based on slavery. Yet writers in *De Bow's Review* and the literary magazines, taking note of the fact that the Southern states gave little support to literature, considered the Southern character to be closer to the Roman than to the Greek, for Southerners prided themselves on their genius for government, their military exploits, and their practical ability.

Although Legaré, was probably the outstanding classical scholar in public life in the South, the classically trained individual who may have most deeply influenced the Southern mind was Professor Thomas Roderick Dew of William and Mary College. Born in 1802 on a stately plantation at Dewsville, Virginia, he received a splendid classical education, including two years of study in Europe. When he returned to America he was appointed professor of history, political economy, and metaphysics at William and Mary College. Very early he became the subject of jealousy on the part of his less gifted colleagues. They harassed him by influencing the board of visitors to mutilate his course in ancient and modern history. In this course, as he himself observed, he did not go much into the dry details but concentrated on the philosophy of history. Though it was not required for a degree, his history course was exceedingly popular with the students. Moreover, Dew was receiving state-wide acclaim for his pamphlet opposing a protective tariff, which he used as a text in his course in political economy.

Dew's greatest fame came in 1832 when he published his *Review of the Debate in the Virginia Legislature of 1831 and 1832*, later to be included in *The Pro-Slavery Argument* (Charleston, 1852). In this work Dew emphasized the practical objections to the emancipation of the slaves and using his knowledge of Greek and Roman history and of Aristotle, he justified the institution as the natural order of life. His essay was the first important polemic in the development of the proslavery argument in the South, and its seeds fell on fertile ground, for the Southerners were ready to be convinced that they were doing nothing wrong in holding slaves. Few in the South controverted his ideas publicly, but one brilliant contemporary, Jesse Burton Harrison of Lynchburg, Virginia, who was also a student of the classics, published a noble refutation of the proslavery argument —*Review of the Slave Question by a Virginian* (Richmond,

1833). Dew was rewarded in 1836 by being chosen
of William and Mary College.

In the struggle between the classic tradition and the romantic
spirit for supremacy over the Southern mind, the victory went
decidedly to romanticism; even classic culture was viewed in a
romantic and unhistorical light. The antebellum South was filled
with neo-classic architecture. Greek Revival colonnades deco-
rated courthouses, churches, banks, theaters, and mansions. Yet
behind the imposing facades there was little to suggest the classic
tradition except perhaps for libraries representing an accumulation of several generations; occasionally the mantels were of
marble and the wallpaper derived from classical motifs, as in
Andrew Jackson's Hermitage. The spirit of the architecture of
the Old South, both the Greek Revival and the Gothic Revival,
was indeed romantic. As Oliver Larkin has phrased it, "under
the colonnades and pediments they had created something which
the Greeks never knew."

In no aspect of Southern life during the antebellum period
was the romantic vogue carried to greater excess than in the
treatment of women. "Years ago," said one of Faulkner's characters in *Absalom, Absalom!*, "We in the South made our women
into ladies. Then the War came and made the ladies into ghosts."
The ladies of that old time did not walk on their legs beneath
their crinoline dresses, Faulkner observed—they floated. It was
not always so in the South, for the mores had changed greatly in
respect to woman's role from the days of William Byrd II of
Westover. The Romantic movement had intervened, so that
Southern society of the nineteenth century frowned upon the
realism with which Byrd regarded his wife, and women in
general. Travelers from Europe between 1830 and 1860 were
impressed with the politeness of American men, particularly in
the South, who gave up their seats in stagecoaches and railroad
cars to women. And in the South men were far more gallant in
making compliments to ladies—and still are—than was the
custom in the North.

The attitude toward women in the Old South was highly
romantic, but actually not many Southern women lived according to romantic standards. Maria Louisa Fleet, the mistress of
Green Mount in Tidewater Virginia, seems to have well repre-

sented the superior type of Southern "lady" on the plantation. Her letters in 1860–65 and the diary of her son Benny reveal that she was so busy being the mistress of a plantation of fifty slaves and rearing a family of seven children that she had little time to be a romantic lady. Nevertheless, she was strongly influenced by the romantic vogue of her society; she displayed a taste for sentimental songs and novels that were flavored with a moral or religious ingredient. On June 16, 1863, she wrote to her son in the Confederate Army: "I wish you would do a favor for me the next time you go to Richmond, if you can—I have still a hankering after Northern newspapers, illustrated ones particularly. Books and papers are the only things that I want from Yankee land and England."

Maria Louisa Fleet held the Victorian idea that woman's place in society was definitely subordinate to the male. Yet she also believed that most men were easy to manage, "*if you go about it in the right way*," and she seems to have had great influence in making family decisions. She shared the spirit of *noblesse oblige* that elevated the Southern gentry and scorned those men who, lacking courage and the martial spirit, failed to volunteer to fight for "their country" (the South). At various times she reveals in her letters her aristocratic prejudices; she belonged to an ardent Whig family, who made a distinction between "gentlemen" and other people. When she heard that an effort was being made during the early part of the war to array the poor against the rich, she wrote to her soldier son, "Ah! my child too much democracy will ruin this country." Yet the mistress of Green Mount was a kind and generous woman; she treated the slaves maternally, taught her children high ideals of character, worked unceasingly for the Confederate soldiers (sewing and knitting and sending them food), and practiced a cordial hospitality.

Very different from Mrs. Fleet in personality was Louisa McCord of Lang Syne plantation and Charleston, South Carolina; nevertheless, the two women were both ardent Southerners. Louisa was the brilliant daughter of Langdon Cheves, a prominent Southern nationalist. He sent her North to Miss Grimshaw's School in Philadelphia, but Louisa also learned much from the politicians and planters who came to her father's home. She studied the Greek and Latin classics, and they made such a great impression on her that she tried to mold her life on that of the Roman matron Cornelia; in middle life she wrote a five-act drama entitled *Caius Gracchus*. Like the lady of Green Mount, she worked hard at being a good mistress of the slaves. In articles in the *Southern Quarterly Review* she passionately defended slavery, and Simms therefore selected her to write the review of *Uncle Tom's Cabin*. She advocated the philosophy of conservatism, condemning the "isms" of the North, such as feminism, which she believed took women out of the sphere assigned to them by divine law.

When war came, Louisa McCord became the embodiment of feminine heroism and Southern patriotism. At her own expense she raised a company for her son, and after he died in battle, she worked day and night in the hospitals caring for wounded soldiers and served as president of the Ladies Clothing Association of South Carolina for the benefit of Confederate troops. In her famous diary Mrs. Chesnut recorded: "She has the brains and energy of a man." But Louisa also had the passionate spirit of defiance that animated the women of New Orleans before the surrender of the city in the spring of 1862. The *Southern Literary Messenger* of July, 1863, celebrated their patriotism in a poem by Tenella entitled a "Lament for New Orleans." These heroic women were compared to the cowardly men who had bartered their honor to save their gold; the anonymous poet declared:

"In wrath and defiance they boldly arose
And scorned to concede one inch to their foes."

In Louisa McCord's view there were no blemishes on the "Christian slavery" of the South. Her friend Mrs. Chesnut, though she supported Southern institutions loyally, had her doubts and wrote in her diary (with great exaggeration) on March 14, 1861: "I wonder if it be a sin to think slavery a curse to any land. Men and women are punished when their masters and mistresses are brutes, not when they do wrong. Under slavery we live surrounded by prostitutes, yet an abandoned woman is sent out of any decent house. . . . Like the patriarchs of old, our men live all in one house with their wives and their concubines;

and the mulattoes one sees in every family partly resemble the white children."

Mrs. Mary Minor Blackford of Fredericksburg, Virginia, also recognized the evils of slavery and in 1832 began to keep a journal entitled "Notes Illustrative of the Wrongs of Slavery." Mrs. Blackford became an ardent colonizationist and taught her children to hate slavery and worship God devoutly. She and her family were strongly unionist in sentiment, but after Virginia seceded, her sons became devoted Confederate soldiers. Mrs. Blackford, Mrs. Chesnut, Mrs. McCord, and Mrs. Fleet all belonged to the aristocratic strata of Southern life, and though differing in many respects, they displayed certain common characteristics—intense regional patriotism, romantic tastes, strong religious feeling, and a conservative philosophy of life.

Another powerful agent of change in the South that paralleled the Romantic movement was the rise of Jacksonian democracy. This great uprising of the common people altered the political mores of the South very decidedly. Fletcher Green in an article entitled "Democracy in the Old South" (*Journal Of Southern History,* February, 1946) and Charles S. Sydnor in *The Development of Southern Sectionalism* (1948) have shown the existence of a large measure of political democracy in the Old South. The Jacksonian movement gave poor men the opportunity to become politicians, but the yeomen, though voting in large numbers, never really developed a leadership responsive to their needs. In most instances the members of this class who rose to party leadership forgot their early background, went over to the side of the aristocrats, and became vociferous advocates of planter interests.

Such was a familiar pattern in the history of the Old South from the time of Davy Crockett of Tennessee to the era of Joseph E. Brown of Georgia and Albert Gallatin Brown of Mississippi. J. D. B. De Bow in a pamphlet on *The Interest in Slavery of the Southern Non-Slaveholder* pointed out the ever recurring absorption of the ambitious sons of yeomen into the ranks of the planters: "The sons of the non-slaveholders are and always have been the leading and ruling spirits of the South in industry as well as in politics—[he himself was one of the examples]. In this class are the McDuffies, Langdon Cheves,

Andrew Jacksons, Henry Clays, and Rusks of the past; the Hammonds, Yanceys, Orrs, Memmingers, Benjamins, Stephens, Soulés, Browns of Mississippi, Simms, Porters, Magraths, Aikens, Maunsel Whites, and an innumerable host of the present; and what is to be noted, these men have not been made demagogues, but are among the most conservative among us."

The extent and depth of democracy below the Mason-Dixon Line may be gauged by examining the power structure on two levels—the county courthouse rings and the legislatures. The apportionment of representation in the legislatures was the most significant indicator of democratic or aristocratic control. The most democratic method of determining representation was the white basis, defined variously as "free white males," as in Arkansas; or "qualified voters," as in Tennessee; or "free white inhabitants," as in Mississippi. The most aristocratic arrangement was the counting of total population, slave and free, which was done only in Louisiana and Maryland (after 1852). Between these extremes were the federal basis, where slaves were counted at three-fifths of their number, and the mixed basis, which was a combination of taxes and population. The states of the Mississippi Valley, with the exception of Louisiana, belonged in the first category, that of white democracy; North Carolina, Georgia, Florida, and Maryland (until 1852) used the federal basis; and South Carolina and Virginia adopted the mixed basis. South Carolina unquestionably was the most aristocratic, and Mississippi—according to the judgment of Professor Charles S. Sydnor—the most democratic of Southern states. In the latter state the people elected even the judges, high and low.

But the existence of democratic political machinery is, of course, no guarantee that democracy will prevail in the functioning of government. No one can tell, for example, if rich and powerful men in the local communities intimidated poor men as a result of the viva voce system of voting that prevailed in the South (Louisiana, one of the aristocratic states, however, elected its officers by ballot). Nor is it possible to determine the weight of courthouse rings or of family influence in politics, which in colonial days had been so powerful. A former source of aristocratic control, the appointment of the justice of the peace, was undermined greatly by the middle of the century, for only a few of the Southern states, notably Virginia and Kentucky, kept the old system; eight of thirteen Southern states elected all of their county officials. Moreover, the cause of democracy was advanced during most of the period from 1828 to 1856 by the existence of a genuine two-party system. It is ironic, nevertheless, that during this time of ever expanding democratic practice, the political theory of the South became more antidemocratic—a repudiation of Jeffersonian liberalism by such leading proslavery writers as Calhoun, Hammond, and George Fitzhugh.

The Jacksonian movement changed the common man's psychology toward government. Government became no longer a province to be administered by men of the upper class but was a possession of the "sovereign people." After the 1820's most of the leading politicians of the South were not of aristocratic lineage but sons of yeomen. Stump speaking, florid oratory, violent partisanship, the instruction of the senators by the legislatures, and demagoguery were characteristic of the new politics. The Jacksonian movement also brought with it a wave of anti-intellectualism and increased the intolerant atmosphere in the South that the Abolition movement had stirred up. The wide use of the vigilance committee and of mobs, representing the direct action of the people, became the order of the day, seriously threatening freedom of speech and of the press.

Coinciding with the Jacksonian movement and connected also with rising sectionalism, there appeared disturbing evidence of anti-intellectualism in Southern society. Sadly, Jefferson, the great liberal of an earlier epoch, modified some of his liberal views as a result of the Missouri Compromise struggle and supported some aspects of the emerging anti-intellectual trend. In 1821 he was distressed to learn that a large number of Southern youths were attending Northern colleges (more than half of the students at Princeton, he heard, came from Virginia). He feared that Southern youths attending Northern schools and colleges would learn "the lessons of Anti-Missourianism" and would return to their native states "deeply impressed with the sacred principles of our Holy Alliance of restrictionists." It is disconcerting also to observe him deviating from his principles of intellectual freedom in seeking to impose a censorship on the textbooks to be used by the professors of law in the University of Virginia and on the reading matter of

American students. He had too great a faith in the power of books to change the minds of college students. He feared, for example, the pernicious influence of their reading David Hume's history, which he believed was the more insidious because the British historian wrote in such an elegant and appealing style. Accordingly, he tried to persuade the Philadelphia publisher, William Duane, to bring out an American edition of Hume based on the revision of the Englishman John Baxter: "Wherever he has found him endeavoring to mislead by either the suppression of a truth or by giving it a false coloring," he commented, "he has changed the text to what it should be, so that we may properly call it Hume's history republicanised."

In the 1840's and 1850's the growth of anti-intellectualism was particularly manifested in efforts to purge textbooks from any criticism of slavery or of Southern life. At the same time editors, preachers, and politicians launched a vigorous propaganda campaign against Southern youth attending Northern schools and colleges; the University of the South was founded at Sewanee, Tennessee, partly to provide safe instruction for the sons of the slaveholders. Simultaneously, anti-intellectualism was exhibited in a decline in the movement for public education that had developed in the 1840's and early 1850's in some of the states, notably Virginia. In the minds of conservative Southerners public education now became associated with the "isms" of the North—abolitionism, feminism, pacifism, Fourierism, Grahamism. Thus Southerners tended to regard the great majority of Northern people as sympathetic to the wild visions and schemes of reform advocated by the Northern extremists.

For many years Yankee professors and teachers had staffed Southern colleges and schools to a large extent, but in the last two decades of the antebellum period a pronounced hostility arose against the employment of educators from the North. In 1858 the Fayetteville *Observer*, for example, protested against the appointment of a Northern man to the faculty of the University of North Carolina. When President David L. Swain defended his appointment by citing the earlier examples of the University of Virginia and South Carolina College in employing foreign professors, the highly influential editor, E. J. Hale, replied: "In both of those institutions, filled with foreigners and Northern men, there have been most deplorable outbreaks & riots & rows. Both have been noted for the prevalence and propagation of infidel notions in religion" (E. J. Hale and son to David L. Swain, February 5, 1858, MS in Swain Papers, Southern Collection, University of North Carolina).

In various forms and from time to time anti-intellectualism crops up in American democratic society. In the 1950's, when the country was disturbed by "the cold war," it permeated the Republican party, producing the McCarthy era. Then intellectuals, "the egg heads," were often looked upon as subversives or "pinks," and powerful Senators were afraid to voice dissent. In the Old South, which was likewise suffering from a cold war atmosphere, anti-intellectualism throve, denigrating the intellectuals of the region— the literary men, the critics, the independent thinkers, the profession of teaching—and severely repressing dissent.

This mood of the Southern people, however, represented only one aspect of the complex mind of the Old South. Some historians have sought to reduce the complexity of Southern life to a simple concept, a "central theme," but such a quest for a unifying principle is as illusive as the search for the Holy Grail. An early example of "the central theme" syndrome was the answer that the eminent Baltimore lawyer, John H. B. Latrobe, gave to Alexis de Tocqueville, when the Frenchman asked him what was the distinguishing characteristic between the North and the South. The Marylander replied that the North was the land of enterprise, the South, the land of chivalry. This sweeping generalization may have had some validity if only the upper class is considered, but it hardly applied to the great mass of yeoman farmers. Furthermore, the South was a sprawling land divided into many subregions in which different conditions left their imprint upon the inhabitants.

The Southwestern mind, for illustration, was somewhat different from the Virginia or the South Carolina mind. The pen pictures of planters in the Yazoo Valley of Mississippi drawn in 1859 by Dupuy Van Buren, a young Northern teacher, show vividly the imprint of Western conditions upon the Southerners of the lower Mississippi Valley. Most of these planters had been born in other Southern states, as was the case of Jefferson Davis, and by their own efforts had created cotton plantations in a region from which the Indians had been expelled less than a generation before. They lived, accordingly, in primitive surroundings, in roughly hewn log cabins, with the wild forest a short distance away. Some of them, however, brought with them the culture of Tidewater South Carolina, Georgia, and Virginia, and in the semi-wilderness they exhibited also some old English traits. Van Buren noted that some of them slept in heavy high poster beds of Elizabethan design; like the English squires, they loved hunting, horses, and dogs; they practised a courtly politeness, using the term "Sir" in addressing their peers. They enjoyed a leisurely and informal life; they did not bolt their food as was frequently done in the Northern states; they reverently said the blessing at the table; and they were exceedingly hospitable. Virtually little kings on their plantations, they displayed a cavalier attitude toward the law, often settling personal difficulties that the New Englander would have taken to court with the pistol, the bowie knife, or their fists. Sam Houston was a representative in hyperbole of the Southwesterner. An Indian fighter and diplomat, duelist, land speculator, Jacksonian politician, and ardent expansionist, he expressed most of the facets of the Southwestern mind.

In the shaping of the Southern mind, what was the role of leaders or of human personality? The perceptive Northerner, John William De Forrest, agent of the Freedman's Bureau in Greenville, South Carolina, thought that the influence of prominent men in Southern communities was peculiarly powerful. "Every community" [of the state], he wrote, "had its great man, or its little great men, around whom his fellow citizens gather when they want information, and to whose monologues they listen with a respect akin to humility." This reliance upon the leader was to be expected in a region where a large part of the people were illiterate, where the circulation of newspapers was small, where slavery elevated the master's ego, and where semi-frontier conditions influenced men to admire excessively the martial qualities of personality. More subtle in the development of a cult of personal leadership in the Old South, were the traditions of *noblesse oblige* and of honor, stretching back to the colonial gentry, and the conservative aspects of the Romantic movement of the nineteenth century.

In trying to glimpse the Southern mind as it was in 1860, I have studied twenty men whom I think represented the major points of view of Southern society. Only five of them—Simms,

Thornwell, Polk, Yancey and Barnwell—favored secession in 1860, and on that single issue this study of the Southern mind may be a minority report. Also, only four—Hammond, Clay, Wise, and Yancey—practiced the code duello. Simms contemplated sending a challenge to an insulting Northern critic and went so far as to submit the question of whether or not his honor was involved to Hammond, who dissuaded him from making a fool of himself. On the other hand, in regard to deeper issues, religion for example, only one—Cassius Marcellus Clay—could be classified as unorthodox, and he was reticent about his religious opinions. In respect to another fundamental issue, the preservation of slavery, only three differed from majority opinion; and, with the possible exception of Hinton Rowan Helper, they seem to have been affected in varying degrees by the Romantic movement. All but five owned plantations, thus setting them apart from most Northerners, and upon the Southern mind of the antebellum period, the way of agriculture left deeper traces than did the more limited issue of slavery.

Virtually all of them, moreover, were powerfully influenced by their varied economic environments. John Hartwell Cocke, born in 1780, grew up in Virginia during the sunset of the Enlightenment when the decline of the tobacco industry and the consequent unprofitability of slavery predisposed Virginians toward liberal ideas. Hammond was *nouveau riche,* as were many cotton planters in a society that found slavery profitable and planter control of the government necessary to protect their property interests. He was a Hamlet type who changed his ideas and wavered often over the means of "saving" the South but was consistent in his devotion to slavery. Maunsel White illustrates the evolution of the successful businessman into the planter, the economic goal of Southern society. Wise represents the divided mind of Virginia that revealed itself so clearly in the secession crisis. The western half of the state was dominated by the interests of the yeoman farmer; the eastern half, by the old aristocracy. Wise tried to pour new wine into old bottles in seeking progressive reforms in his state. He had one foot in the East and one in the West, a personality half Jeffersonian and half demagogue.

On the surface, Cassius Marcellus Clay and Hinton Rowan

Helper seem clearly eccentrics. Yet on closer view Clay appears to have represented a crosscurrent in Kentucky life. From the days of David Rice, the father of Presbyterianism in the West, who published his pamphlet *Slavery Inconsistent with Justice and Good Policy* (1792) to the Pindell letter of Henry Clay in 1849, Kentucky had nourished a sizable group of emancipationists. In 1860 less than one-fifth of the people of the state belonged to slave-owning families, and these were concentrated largely in the Bluegrass region. Hinton Rowan Helper also represented a diverse element in Southern society. The German settlers in the South from whom he sprang had a background of opposing slavery. In the Piedmont section where he lived, slaveholding was a minor interest, and the section had produced other critics of slavery, notably Dr. Henry Ruffner, also of German extraction.

The three men whom I chose to represent the religious mind came from different economic and cultural levels of society. Yet they were in remarkable agreement on the essentials of their theology; they illustrated indeed the typical orthodoxy of the South. A crosscurrent of skepticism, started by the iconoclastic Dr. Thomas Cooper of South Carolina and the discoveries of the new geology of Sir Thomas Lyell, was overwhelmed by the powerful force of orthodoxy. The scientists Maury, Rogers, and Le Conte were all devout religionists who did not permit the critical spirit of science to invade the religious realm.

The career of William Gilmore Simms especially revealed the great changes that came over the Southern mind—changes that converted a realist into a romanticist, a natural democrat into an apostate, and a liberal young man—enthusiastic for nationalism and Southern leader of the Young America movement—into a very conservative older man and an ardent sectionalist. His career was paralleled in some respects by that of William L. Yancey, who as a young man also fought against nullification and for the idea of the Union but in later life used his matchless power of oratory to destroy the Union. On the other hand, Jeremiah Clemens changed from an ardent sectionalist in 1850 to a strong unionist in 1860, apparently influenced strongly by the sentiment of the southern Appalachian area that he represented.

The lives of these twenty men were encompassed by the powerful mores of Southern society. Extraordinarily potent, because entrenched in an isolated and beleaguered society, Southern folkways and attitudes were based on tradition and deep folk feelings as well as on economic interests. Consequently, the method of studying only the economic interests of leading men —the technique adopted by Charles A. Beard in interpreting the origin of the Constitution—is inadequate to explain the nature of the Southern mind in 1860. Indeed, beneath the play of changing economic conditions and political opinions, the ways of the Old South altered very slowly—not fundamentally until the coming of the Industrial Revolution to the South in the twentieth century.

In comparison with these ineluctable forces, the role of individual leaders in molding the Southern mind, despite the most favorable influences for the exercise of personal leadership, seems very slight. The great man, or little "great men," of the region, instead of creating masterful ideas and dominating the movements of history in their region were themselves bent and warped by the powerful economic and social forces of their times. Even Calhoun, who most nearly played the role of "the great man," despite his brilliant mind and strong personality, could not withstand such pressures. The Carolina leader himself realized the futility of opposing the strongly flowing tide of popular emotion in the nullification crisis which was carrying him away from his goal of being elected president. To his friend Virgil Maxcy in Maryland, who advised him against joining the nullification movement, he replied, "My friends out of the state think I should step forward in order to arrest the current of events. They appear to take it for granted, that it is in my power." This notion, he wrote, was based on a great misconception of his influence (Galloway, Maxcy, Markoe Papers, Vol. 35, September 11, 1830, Library of Congress). Likewise, William Gilmore Simms surrendered to the powerful currents of politics and to the dominant sense of values of his society, changing from a liberal to a conservative attitude. Yet both of these men were, like their contemporaries, only partly conscious of the extent to which they were influenced by their social environment and by circumstances; they both sincerely believed that in their public life they were guided by great ideas and noble principles—certainly not by opportunism.

The great dynamic of Southern thought in the period from 1820 to 1860 was a revolutionary change in thinking concerning slavery, which influenced virtually every facet of the Southern mind. After 1832 when the Virginia legislature examined the very foundations of the social structure of the state and resolutely turned its back on any change, the South followed an accelerating course of conservatism. Calhoun and George Fitzhugh proclaimed that the Southern states formed the balance wheel of the nation, conserving the federal principle of government against the centralizing tendency of the North, and that their stable labor system served as a mighty bulwark against the advance of communism. During the years when the cotton kingdom was expanding, the Southern people seem to have grown more materialistic, for the opportunities of wealth were greater and society had become more fluid; their talk, travelers reported, was incessantly of "cotton, niggers, and land." The relative prosperity of the region in the 1850's subtly influenced their minds to complacency concerning the rightness of their way of life. The British correspondent William H. ("Bull Run") Russell observed at Charleston in 1861, "These tall, thin, fine-faced Carolinians are great materialists"—as much concerned with profits as the Yankees whom they denounced.

As the Southerners became increasingly materialistic, they retreated within the fortress of religious orthodoxy. Their fundamentalist religion tended to remove any sense of guilt over slavery that their fathers and grandfathers may have had and to strengthen them in confronting outside critics. Southern women, however, seem to have been less convinced of the rightness of slavery than the men. Gertrude Thomas in Georgia echoed the sentiment about the immorality of slavery in Mrs. Chesnut's famous diary when she recorded in her own diary, January 2, 1858, her revulsion at seeing the child of a slave woman who was nearly white in color. The immoral relations between white men and Negroes, she commented, were "a great point for the abolitionists to argue . . . oh, is it not enough to make us shudder for the standard of morality in our Southern homes . . . Southern women are I believe all at heart abolitionists, but there I expect I have made a very broad assertion, but I *will stand* to the opinion that the institution of slavery degrades the white man more than the Negro and oh exerts a most deleterious effect upon our children." In a similar vein Laura Beecher Comer commented on this dark side of slavery. "It is a terrible life," she confided to her diary, January 5, 1862—"married to a Bachelor who has lived with his negroes as equals, at bed and board! What a life many poor wives have to live in uncomplaining silence" (Southern Collection, University of North Carolina). Mrs. Comer, though she had been a New England schoolteacher before she married her slave-holding husband, did not condemn the institution of slavery and ardently supported the Confederate cause.

In 1860 the Southern mind, having reconciled the existence of slavery within a Christian society, cherished a romantic delusion that Southern civilization was superior to that of the North—in all that constitutes the gentleman and a gallant people. Nevertheless, there remained a deep sense of insecurity in the mind of the Southerner as he looked into the future and realized that the South was becoming more and more a minority section in the nation. In these years, in a changing world, Southerners sought desperately to preserve the landmarks of the past. It was during the antebellum period that the Southern mind acquired the habit of conservatism, a staunch, ingrown feeling, that was to extend far into the future.

A NOTE ON SOURCES

Chapter I

The principal sources for this chapter are the Jesse Burton Harrison Papers in the Library of Congress and the Harrison Papers, including his manuscript diary while a student in Europe, in the Alderman Library of the University of Virginia, both of which are rich in historical materials. Harrison's speech before the Lynchburg Colonization Society in July, 1827, was published in the *African Repository and Colonial Journal*, September, 1827; his *A Disquisition on the Prospects of Letters and Taste in Virginia* was published as a pamphlet at Cambridge, Massachusetts in 1828; his essay on "English Civilization" appeared in the *Southern Review*, February, 1832; and his article, "The Slavery Question in Virginia" was first published in the *American Quarterly Review*, December, 1833, and then as a pamphlet under the title *Review of the Slave Question by a Virginian* (Richmond, 1833); a large number of clippings of editorials by Harrison in the *Louisiana Advertiser* for 1836 are among the Harrison Papers in the Alderman Library. There is no biography of Harrison in the *Dictionary of American Biography*, but there is a valuable account of him by Fairfax Harrison in *Aris Sonis Facisque, Being a Memoir of an American Family, the Harrisons of Skimino* (privately printed, 1910). Harrison's career as a student in Germany is briefly presented in John T. Krumpelmann, *Southern Scholars in Goethe's Germany* (Chapel Hill, 1965). Richard B. Davis has written two valuable studies of the intellectual life of Virginia during

Harrison's residence there, *Francis Walker Gilmer; Life and Learning
in Jefferson's Virginia* (Richmond, 1939), and *Intellectual Life in Jefferson's Virginia, 1790–1830* (Chapel Hill, 1964); William R. Taylor's
volume *Cavalier and Yankee; The Old South and American National
Character* (New York, 1961) is also very illuminating on the intellectual
life of Harrison's time.

The main sources for the study of the young reformers in the Virginia
legislature of 1832 are their speeches which were printed in the Richmond *Enquirer* and the Richmond *Constitutional Whig* in the early part
of 1832. The most prominent of these speeches were also reprinted as
pamphlets in 1832. There are small collections of the papers of James
McDowell, Jr., and of Charles James Faulkner in the Duke University
Library and the Alderman Library. McDowell's speeches on J. Q. Adams
and opposing the Wilmot Proviso are in the *Congressional Globe*, 30th
Cong., 1st. Sess., 386, and *Congressional Globe*, 31st Cong., 1st Sess.,
1678. A valuable source on public opinion of the time is to be found in
Charles H. Ambler, *The Life and Diary of John Floyd* (Richmond,
1918), and J. H. Johnston (ed.), "Antislavery Petitions Presented to
the Virginia Legislature by Citizens of Various Counties," *Journal of
Negro History*, XII (October, 1927), 670–91. Brief biographies of the
principal participants in the debate of 1832 are included in the *Dictionary of American Biography*. There are two scholarly studies of the
Virginia debate of 1832: Theodore M. Whitfield, *Slavery Agitation in
Virginia, 1829–1832* (Baltimore, 1930), and Joseph C. Robert, *The
Road from Monticello: A Study of the Virginia Slavery Debate of 1832*
(Durham, 1941). I am indebted to Professor William G. Bean for
valuable information from two articles: "The Ruffner Pamphlet of 1847:
An Antislavery Aspect of Virginia Sectionalism," *Virginia Magazine of
History and Biography*, LXI, (July, 1953), 260–82, and "John Letcher
and the Slavery Issue in Virginia's Gubernatorial Contest of 1858–
1859," *Journal of Southern History*, XX (February, 1954), 22–49. My
article, "The Freedom of the Press in the Upper South," *Mississippi
Valley Historical Review*, XVIII (March, 1932), 479–99, and book,
The Freedom-of-Thought Struggle in the Old South (New York, 1964),
deal with the transient period of free discussion in 1832 in the Virginia
newspapers. The quotation from Judge Porter of Louisiana concerning
the effect of the Virginia debate of 1832 is derived from Joseph Tregle,
Jr., "Through Friends and Foes with Alexander Porter," *Louisiana
History*, III (Summer, 1962), 173–91.

Chapter 11

The Cocke Papers in the Alderman Library at the University of
Virginia are both voluminous and revealing. At Bremo in Virginia is
a large collection of Cocke papers, including diaries of John Hartwell

Cocke and the papers of his son Dr. Charles Cary Cocke, which are owned by Mrs. Forney Johnston of Bremo and Birmingham, Alabama; microfilms of these papers are in the Southern Collection at the University of North Carolina. The Ellis-Allan Papers, factors of Cocke, in the Library of Congress, contain a few letters from Cocke. The William C. Rives Papers in the Library of Congress also contain some Cocke material.

Philip Alexander Bruce, *History of the University of Virginia* (5 vols., New York, 1920), includes some valuable letters of Cocke relating to the University of Virginia. Armistead C. Gordon planned to write a biography of the Virginia reformer and left some notes which are in the Alderman Library, and he has a slight account of Cocke in his *William Fitzhugh Gordon* (New York, 1909). Though there is no published biography of Cocke, there is an account in the *Dictionary of American Biography* and a Ph.D. dissertation, at the University of Virginia, entitled "John Hartwell Cocke of Bremo: Agriculture and Slavery in the Ante-Bellum South," by M. Boyd Coyner, Jr. I have not seen Mr. Coyner's study, but I have derived valuable information from him through correspondence.

For studies of the shift of Southern thought from liberal to conservative, see William E. Dodd, *The Cotton Kingdom* (New Haven, 1919); Clement Eaton, *Freedom of Thought in the Old South* (Durham, 1940); and Joseph C. Robert, *The Road from Monticello: A Study of the Virginia Slavery Debate of 1832* (Durham, 1941).

Chapter III

The Hammond Papers in the Library of Congress constitute one of the most valuable and extensive collections of the political and social history of the Old South. This collection is supplemented by another large deposit of letters and papers in the South Caroliniana Library of the University of South Carolina, which is indispensable in the study of the Carolina statesman. There are some executive papers and a secret diary in the South Carolina Archives building at Columbia; the Southern Collection of the University of North Carolina contains some forty letters from Hammond to Edmund Ruffin, 1842–1857; and the Duke University Library has a small collection of Hammond papers, especially the correspondence with W. B. Hodgson of Georgia. Extremely valuable for an understanding of the complex personality of Hammond is his considerable correspondence with William Gilmore Simms published in Mary C. Simms Oliphant *et al.* (eds.), *The Letters of William Gilmore Simms* (5 vols., Columbia, 1954–56). Edmund Ruffin in his manuscript diary (Library of Congress) and Solon Robinson in his travel accounts of the South have left interesting descriptions of Hammond's personality and his agricultural operations. A number of significant letters from Hammond to Calhoun are found in J. F. Jameson (ed.), "Correspondence of John C. Calhoun," *Annual Report of the American Historical Association for the Year 1899* (Washington, 1900), Vol. II. I have found useful the Charleston *Courier* (of which the University of Kentucky Library has a microfilm copy of the files 1803–22, 1852–72) in following Hammond's political career and in its reporting of some of Hammond's speeches. Many of his speeches are also to be found in the *Congressional Globe* and in *Selections from the Letters and Speeches of Hon. James H. Hammond of South Carolina* (New York, 1866), including particularly his "Oration on the Death of Calhoun." Hammond's arguments in defense of slavery are to be found in *The Proslavery Argument* (Charleston, 1852), and in E. N. Elliott (ed.), *Cotton is King and Pro-Slavery Arguments* (Augusta, Ga., 1860). The only published biography is a very inadequate study by Elizabeth Merritt, "James Henry Hammond, 1807–1864" in *John Hopkins University Studies in Historical and Political Science*, XLI (1923), No. 4. Robert G. Tucker has written a Ph.D. dissertation titled "James Henry Hammond, South Carolinian" (University of North Carolina, 1958), which I have seen. Charles Wiltse, *John Calhoun, Sectionalist, 1840–1850* (Indianapolis, 1951), and Broadus Mitchell, *William Gregg, Factory Master of the Old South* (Chapel Hill, 1928), contain some interesting Hammond material.

Chapter iv

The extensive Maunsel White papers, journals, and letterbooks in the Southern Collection of the University of North Carolina (of which there are microfilms in the University of Kentucky Library) form the basis of this study. In the Louisiana State University Archives there are a few Maunsel White papers, a valuable letter in the George Lanaux Papers, April 15, 1859, and some letters in the Nathaniel Evans Family Papers; in Tulane University library is a manuscript account of White by J. J. Wieskinson in his "Pioneer Planters of Plaquemines Parish," and letters and references in the J. D. B. De Bow Papers in Duke University Library. Letters and references to White are also contained in John Spencer Bassett (ed.), *Correspondence of Andrew Jackson* (6 vols., Washington, 1926–35); Ralph W. Haskins, "Planter and Cotton Factor in the Old South: Some Areas of Friction," *Agricultural History*, XXIX (January, 1953), 1–14; *De Bow's Review*, XIV (January, 1853), 85 (frontispiece has a picture of White); XXV (October, 1958), 480–82; and other volumes have brief biographies of prominent Southern business leaders. Otis C. Skipper, *J. D. B. De Bow, Magazinist of the Old South* (Athens, 1958), and Lyle Saxon, *Fabulous New Orleans* (New York, 1928) contain brief references to White. See also Freeman Hunt, *Lives of American Merchants* (New York, 1858), Vol. II.

Background studies of White's interests in sugar production and plantation slavery are to be found in P. A. Champomier, *Statement of the Sugar Crop Made in Louisiana* (New Orleans, 1844–62); J. Carlyle Sitterson, *Sugar Country, the Cane Sugar Industry in the South, 1753–1950* (Lexington, 1953); Alton V. Moody, "Slavery on the Louisiana Sugar Plantations," *Louisiana Historical Review* (April, 1924); J. G. Taylor, *Slavery in Louisiana* (Baton Rouge, 1963). Clement Eaton, *The Growth of Southern Civilization, 1790–1860* (New York, 1961); and Harold D. Woodman, "The Profitability of Slavery: A Historical Perennial," *Journal of Southern History*, XXIX (August, 1963), 303–25.

Three studies that give information about the political attitudes of Southern businessmen are Ollinger Crenshaw, "Urban and Rural Voting in the Election of 1860," in E. F. Goldman (ed.) *Historiography and Urbanization* (Baltimore, 1941); A. F. Sanford (ed.), *Reminiscences of Richard Lathers* (New York, 1909); and Ralph A. Wooster, *The Secession Conventions of the South* (Princeton, 1962).

Chapter v

The most important collection of Wise manuscripts is the correspondence between the Virginia politician and his cousin Naval lieutenant Henry Augustus Wise in the Library of Congress. The Southern Collection of the University of North Carolina has microfilm of valuable letters and pamphlets owned by Miss Ellen Wise of Richmond, Virginia. Wise letters are also included in the Richard K. Crallé Papers and the George W. Gordon Papers in the Library of Congress, the Kemper Papers in the Alderman Library of the University of Virginia, and the James Buchanan Papers in the archives of the Pennsylvania Historical Society. There are a few Wise manuscripts, as well as references to him, in the Hugh Blair Grigsby Papers in the archives of the Virginia Historical Society at Richmond. Vivid descriptions of the Virginia political leader are to be found in the Rosina Mix Papers in the Southern Collection of the University of North Carolina, a sketch by a Northern school teacher at Puntoteaque, Virginia in the Duke University Library, and Thomas Hicks Wynne's diary of life in Richmond at the Huntington Library.

Among the most valuable sources for the study of Wise's political career are the Executive Papers (over forty boxes in the Virginia State Library at Richmond) and his speeches in the *Virginia Constitutional Convention Debates and Proceedings,* issued as supplements to the Richmond newspapers, Nos. 13–19 (in the Virginia State Library). The diary of Benny Fleet and of his brother Fred, who was in Wise's command, give interesting details of Wise as a general, in Betsy Fleet, John D. P. Fuller (eds.), and Clement Eaton, historical consultant, *Green Mount, a Virginia Plantation Family during the Civil War* (Lexington, Ky., 1962).

John Quincy Adams's diary presents a distorted picture of Wise in Congress; Wise's son, John S. Wise, on the other hand, in his reminiscences, *The End of an Era* (Boston, 1902) draws a warm, sympathetic portrait of his father. Numerous letters from Wise are included in Lyon G. Tyler (ed.), *The Letters and Times of the Tylers* (2 vols., Richmond, 1884). J. P. Hambleton published *A Biographical Sketch of Henry A. Wise with a History of the Political Campaign in Virginia in 1855* (Richmond, 1856). In his old age Wise composed a political reminiscence, entitled *Seven Decades of the Union* (Philadelphia, 1876). Barton H. Wise, a grandson, wrote a biography entitled *The Life of Henry A. Wise of Virginia, 1806–1876* (New York, 1889), and there is a sketch in the *Dictionary of American Biography*.

I have published three articles on Wise: "Henry A. Wise and the Virginia Fire Eaters of 1856," *Mississippi Valley Historical Review*, XXI (March, 1935), 495–512; "Henry A. Wise, A Liberal of the Old South," *Journal of Southern History*, VII (November, 1941), 482–94; and "Henry A. Wise, a Study in Virginia Leadership, 1850–1861," *West Virginia History* (April, 1942).

Chapter VI

There are small collections of Clay letters in the University of Kentucky Library, the Berea College Library, and the Filson Club Library at Louisville, and in the Salmon P. Chase Papers in the archives of the Pennsylvania Historical Society at Philadelphia. The Brutus J. Clay Papers at Auvergne, the home of Mrs. Cassius M. Clay near Paris, Kentucky, contain important Clay documents, including letters from Clay to his brother Brutus and the unpublished second volume of Clay's memoirs, largely a collection of newspaper clippings, speeches, and writings. Some of this material has been published by a later Cassius M. Clay under the title *Letters from the Correspondence of Brutus J. Clay* (Paris, 1958), which is a reprint of edited documents appearing in the *Filson Club History Quarterly*, XXXI (January and April, 1957) 3–21; 122–46; XXXII (April, 1958), 136–50. In 1886 Clay published at Cincinnati the first volume of *The Life of Cassius Marcellus Clay, Memoirs, Writings, and Speeches*, which is a rambling, prejudiced, egotistical account of his career. Two most valuable sources are the Clay letters in the Salmon P. Chase Papers in the Library of Congress and in the William H. Seward and Thurlow Weed Collections at Rochester University. I have been able to use these indispensable sources through microfilms lent to me by Professor David L. Smiley of Wake Forest College.

A complete file of the *True American* is in the Lexington Public Library and a partial file, after the paper was moved to Cincinnati, in the University of Kentucky Library. A file of the Louisville *Examiner*, October 16, 1847–December 8, 1849, is in the Filson Club

Library in Louisville. Horace Greeley edited *The Writings of Cassius Marcellus Clay, including Speeches and Addresses* (New York, 1848). Some of Clay's speeches were printed as pamphlets, notably: C. M. Clay, *A Review of the Late Canvass and R. Wickliffe's Speech on the "Negro Law"* (Lexington, 1840); *Speech of C. M. Clay at Lexington, Ky. Delivered August 1, 1851,* (n.p., n.d.), all in the University of Kentucky Library. Perhaps the most important of these addresses is the *Appeal of Cassius M. Clay to Kentucky and the World* (Boston, 1845) in refutation of the *History and Record of the Proceedings of the People of Lexington and its Vicinity in the Suppression of the True American from the Commencement of the Movement of the 14th August 1845 to its Final Termination on Monday, the 18th of the Same Month* (Lexington, 1845). Thomas Marshall's speech urging the suppression of *The True American* is published in W. L. Barré (ed.), *Writings and Speeches of Thomas F. Marshall* (Cincinnati, 1858).

There are valuable sidelights on Clay's personality in Frederick Law Olmsted, *A Journey Through Texas* (New York, 1860); S. A. Wallace and F. E. Gillispie (eds.), *The Journal of Benjamin Moran, 1857–1861* (Chicago, 1948), I, 810; *Autobiography of John G. Fee* (Chicago, 1891), and A. W. Campbell, *Cassius Marcellus Clay, A Visit to his Home in Kentucky* (Richmond, Ky., 1888). There is a brief article on Clay in the *Dictionary of American Biography;* William H. Townsend's *Lincoln and the Bluegrass* (Lexington, 1955) contains some colorful pages on the Kentucky crusader; I discuss Clay's fight for the freedom of the press in my volume *Freedom of Thought in the Old South;* and David L. Smiley has written an article, "Cassius M. Clay and John G. Fee: A Study in Southern Anti-Slavery Thought," *Journal of Negro History,* XLII (July, 1957), 201–13, and an interesting biography, *Lion of White Hall, the Life of Cassius M. Clay* (Madison, 1962).

Chapter VII

The manuscript citations from Francis Orray Ticknor are taken from the Ticknor Papers in the Duke University Library. Contemporary collections of Southern humor include Thomas A. Burke (ed.), *Polly Peablossom's Wedding: and other Tales* (Philadelphia, 1851); William T. Porter (ed.), *A Quarter Race in Kentucky and Other Sketches* (Philadelphia, 1858); Joseph M. Field, *The Drama in Pokerville* (Philadelphia, 1846); William T. Porter (ed.), *The Big Bear of Arkansas* (Philadelphia, 1845); and Thomas Bangs Thorpe, *The Hive of the Bee-Hunter* (New York, 1854).

The classics of Southern humor in the antebellum period are Augustus Baldwin Longstreet, *Georgia Scenes, Characters, Incidents, etc. in the First Half Century of the Republic* (Augusta, Ga., 1835);

William Tappan Thompson, *Major Jones' Courtship* (Madison, Ga.,
1843), and *Major Jones' Chronicles of Pineville* (Philadelphia, 1845);
David Crockett, *A Narrative of the Life of David Crockett . . .
Written by Himself* (Baltimore, 1834); Johnson Jones Hooper, *Some
Adventures of Simon Suggs, Late Captain of the Tallapoosa Volun-
teers* (Philadelphia, 1845); and *A Ride with Old Kit Kuncker*
(Tuscaloosa, 1849), reissued as *The Widow Rugby's Husband* (Phila-
delphia, 1851); Joseph G. Baldwin, *Flush Times of Alabama and
Mississippi* (New York, 1853); John Q. Anderson (ed.), *Louisiana
Swamp Doctor; the Life of Henry Clay Lewis; the Writings of Henry
Clay Lewis, Alias "Madison Tensas M.D."* (Baton Rouge, 1962);
Harden E. Taliaferro, *Fisher's River (North Carolina), Scenes and
Characters* (New York, 1859); John S. Robb, *Streaks of Squatter
Life* (Philadelphia, 1847); Sol Smith, *Theatrical Apprenticeship*
(Philadelphia, 1845); George W. Harris, *Sut Lovingood's Yarns*
(New York, 1857); Brom Weber (ed.), *Sut Lovingood, by George
Washington Harris* (New York, 1954); George William Bagby, "The
Letters of Mozis Addums to Billy Ivvins," *Southern Literary Messen-
ger* (February–December, 1858); Charles Henry Smith, *Bill Arp, So
Called* (New York, 1866); and F. D. Srygley, *Seventy Years in Dixie*
(Nashville, 1914). Excellent modern anthologies are Franklin G.
Meine (ed.), *Tall Tales of the Southwest* (New York, 1937);
Arthur P. Hudson, *Humor of the Old Deep South* (New York, 1936);
Kenneth Lynn, *The Comic Tradition in America* (Garden City, 1958);
and James R. Masterton, *Tall Tales of Arkansas* (Boston, 1942).

For critical evaluations of Southern humorists see Walter Blair,
Native American Humor, 1800–1900 (Durham, 1954); Kenneth S.
Lynn, *Mark Twain and Southwestern Humor* (Boston, 1959); and
Edmund Wilson, *Patriotic Gore* (New York, 1962). I have written an
article entitled "The Humor of the Southern Yeoman," *Sewanee
Review* (April, 1941). Useful works on Southern humor include
John D. Wade, *Augustus Baldwin Longstreet; A Study of the Devel-
opment of Culture in the South* (New York, 1924); W. S. Hoole,
Alias Simon Suggs, the Life and Times of Johnson Jones Hooper
(University, Alabama, 1952); Thomas D. Clark, *The Rampaging
Frontier* (Indianapolis, 1939); Shields McIwaine, *The Southern Poor-
White from Lubberland to Tobacco Road* (Chicago, 1939); N. Y.
Yates, *William T. Porter and the Spirit of the Times* (Baton Rouge,
1957); and Milton Rickels, *Thomas Bangs Thorpe, Humorist of the
Old Southwest* (Baton Rouge, 1962).

Chapter VIII

There is no collection, as far as I know, of Helper papers. A number
of letters written to Benjamin Sherwood Hedrick in the Duke University Library contains some information, mostly after 1860. In the
Thomas Nelson Page Papers, also in the Duke University Library, is

an interesting letter from Helper written in 1902. There are several Helper letters to John C. Underwood in the Underwood Papers in the Library of Congress and a significant letter (typed copy) to John Sherman written in 1896 in the Southern Collection of the University of North Carolina. I have a letter written to me from Professor John Spencer Bassett, dated Northampton, Mass., February 19, 1926, giving some impressions of the personality of Helper, whom Bassett knew in Helper's old age.

The principal sources for a study of Helper's career before the Civil War are his books, especially those in which he gives autobiographical details: *The Land of Gold, or Romance Unveiled* (Baltimore, 1855); *The Impending Crisis of the South, and How to Meet It* (New York, 1857); *Compendium of the Impending Crisis of the South* (New York, 1859); *Nojoque: A Question for a Continent* (New York, 1867); and *The Negroes in Negroland* (New York, 1871). The most important refutations of Helper's attacks on slavery are Samuel M. Wolfe, *Helper's Impending Crisis Dissected* (Philadelphia, 1860), and Gilbert J. Beebe, *A Review and Refutation of Helper's Impending Crisis* (Middleton, N. Y.). Thomas D. Clark of the University of Kentucky has an autograph copy of *The Impending Crisis*, dated Asheville, 1870, which Helper annotated in pencil. John Sherman, *Recollections of Forty Years in the House, Senate, and Cabinet* (Chicago, 1896) contains a valuable account of the controversy over the *Compendium* in the House of Representatives. E. W. Newman ("Savoyard"), *In the "Pennyrile" of Old Kentucky, and Men, Things, and Events* (Washington, 1911), gives a vivid description of Helper in his old age.

Hugh Bailey has published a biography (1965), and Bassett has an account of him in his "Anti-Slavery Leaders of North Carolina," in *Johns Hopkins University Studies in Historical and Political Science,* XVI (1898); Hugh T. Lefler has published a brochure, entitled *Hinton Rowan Helper, Advocate of a "White America"* (Charlottesville, 1935); see also a bitterly anti-Helper article by David R. Barbee, "Hinton Rowan Helper," *Tyler's Historical Quarterly and Genealogical Magazine,* XV (1934); article in *Dictionary of American Biography* by J. G. deR. Hamilton; Hugh C. Bailey, "Hinton Rowan Helper and *The Impending Crisis,*" *Louisiana Historical Quarterly,* XI (April, 1957), 133–45; Theodore V. Theobald, "Hinton Rowan Helper and *The Impending Crisis*" (M.A. thesis, Columbia University, 1949); and Harvey Wish (ed.), *Ante-Bellum Writings of George Fitzhugh and Hinton Rowan Helper on Slavery* (New York, 1960).

Chapter ix

Since the slaves and free Negroes in the South wrote few manuscripts, the primary sources reflecting Negro thought are relatively few. In the Rare Books Division of the Library of Congress are the records of W.P.A. writers who interviewed old slaves still living in 1936, 34 vols.; a selection of this material was made by Benjamin A. Botkin in *Lay My Burden Down: A Folk History of Slavery* (Chicago, 1945). Other interviews with ex-slaves have been published by: Hampton Institute, *The Negro in Virginia* (Richmond, 1939); and John B. Cade, "Out of the Mouths of Ex-Slaves," *Journal of Negro History*, XX (July, 1935), 294–337. The John Hartwell Cocke Papers contain letters from slaves who emigrated to Liberia and the Bremo Slave Letters; and in the University of Kentucky Library there is a collection of letters from Kentucky slaves in Liberia to their former masters. Some interesting letters written in the 1840's by a Negro Creole planter Alexander Durnford to John McDonogh are in the John McDonogh Papers, Tulane University Library. A rather extensive group of letters from the Negro preacher and teacher, John Chavis, is published in Henry T. Shanks (ed.), *The Papers of Willie Person Mangum* (Raleigh, 1950–52), Vols. I and II. In the Carter Woodson Papers in the Library of Congress is the manuscript autobiography of Hiram R. Revels, and there is a brief but fascinating autobiography of a slave, "Fields," dated Richmond, 1847, in the Slave Papers of the Library of Congress. Carter Woodson has collected letters that Negroes in the South wrote to the American Colonization Society (files in the Library of Congress) to the *Liberator,* the *Anti-Slavery Standard,* and the *African Repository;* he has published these in *The Mind of the Negro as Reflected in Letters Written During the Crisis, 1800–1860* (Washington, 1926). The *Journal of Negro History* also has published letters and papers of Southern Negroes, such as John Hope Franklin (ed.), "James Boon, Free Negro Artisan," XXX (April, 1945), 150–80.

The mind of the revolutionary Negro is disclosed in C. M. Wiltse (ed.), *David Walker's Appeal in Four Articles; Together With A Preamble to the Coloured Citizens of the World, But in Particular, and Very expressly, To those of the United States of America* (New York, 1965). Henry Highland Garnet, a New York Negro preacher and abolitionist, published an edition in 1848 entitled *David Walker's Appeal With a Brief Sketch of His Life* (New York, 1848). The mind of a free Negro is vividly revealed in W. R. Hogan and E. A. Davis (eds.), *William Johnson's Natchez: The Ante-Bellum Diary of a Free Negro* (Baton Rouge, 1951). Some insights into the mind of the slave on large plantations are afforded by the testimony of former slaves on the plantation of Stephen Douglas, in the suit of his sons to recover damages suffered during the Civil War: Records of the United States Court of Claims, General Jurisdiction Cases, Nos. 9192 and 9740, MSS, National Archives. Also the Negro newspaper, New Orleans *Tribune,* reported meetings of Negroes held in various Southern states during the Reconstruction period revealing the philosophy of Negroes trained in the slave regime (Microfilm in the Howard University Library). Much information about the Negro in the Old South can be gleaned from H. T. Catterall (ed.), *Judicial Cases Concerning American Slavery and the Negro* (Washington, 1926–36).

Contemporary testimony of the Negro concerning his life in slavery found in the narratives of escaped slaves is often edited by abolitionists and highly prejudiced. Many of these are recorded in Daniel Drew, *The Refuge: Or the Narratives of Fugitive Slaves in Canada, Related by Themselves* (Boston, 1856), and William Still, *The Underground Rail Road: A Record of Facts, Authentic Narratives, Letters, etc.* (Philadelphia, 1872). Some of the better narratives of escaped slaves are Frederick Douglass, *Narrative of the Life of an American Slave* (Boston, 1845); William Wells Brown, *Narrative of William Wells Brown, a Fugitive Slave, Written by Himself* (Boston, 1847); Josiah Henson, *Father Henson's Story of His Own Life, with an Introduction by Harriet Beecher Stowe* (Boston, 1858); Irving Lowery, *Life on the Old Plantation in Ante-Bellum Days* (Columbia, S. C., 1911); James W. C. Pennington, *The Fugitive Blacksmith: Or Events in the Life of James W. C. Pennington* (London, 1848); Henry Bibb, *Narrative of the Life and Adventures of Henry Bibb, written by Himself* (New York, 1849); Solomon Northrup, *Twelve Years a Slave: Narrative of Solomon Northrup* (Auburn, N. Y., 1853); and Harvey Wish (ed.), *Slavery in the South: First-Hand Accounts* (New York, 1964).

The sources cited above are primary Negro sources. Sources written by white people are to be found scattered in the papers, diaries, and records of the planters. I have done research in the following: Littleton W. Tazewell Papers, in the Alderman Library of the University of Virginia; Benjamin F. Perry Diary, John Houston Bills Diary, Daniel R. Hundley Diary, Magnolia Plantation Papers, Ebenezer Pettigrew Papers, Private Diary of Ed Ruffin, Maunsel White Papers, the Laura Beecher Comer Diary, and a collection of letters culled from the Pettigrew Papers by Professor J. G. D. Hamilton, entitled "Some Plantation Letters," in the Library of the University of North Carolina; James H. Hammond Papers, Edmund Ruffin Diary, Richard Eppes Plantation Journal, and Moses Waddel Diary, in the Library of Congress; the Buckner Family Papers, William Moody Pratt Diary, Lulbegrud Baptist Church Minutes, Providence Baptist Church Minutes, Shelby Family Papers, Augustus Woodward Diary, Henry Clay Papers, William Reynold's Journal, in the University of Kentucky Library; Ball Family Papers, Micajah Clark Travel Journal, James H. Hammond Papers, in South Caroliniana Library, University of South Carolina; Thomas B. Chaplin Plantation Journal and Jacob S. Schirmer Diary, in South Carolina Historical Society Archives at Charleston; Thomas Watson Papers and the valuable Gertrude Thomas diary in Duke University Library; John Witherspoon DuBose Papers, in Alabama State Library; John J. Cabell Papers, Lewis and Robert Hill (slave-hiring agents) Papers, Francis Lieber Papers, James and W. H. Lyons Papers, in Huntington Library, San Marino, California; W. S. Hyland Plantation Journal, near Warrenton, Mississippi, owned by Professor Thomas D. Clark, University of Kentucky, and the Brutus J. Clay Papers, owned by Rudolph Berle Clay of Paris, Kentucky.

Published diaries and journals affording some insight into the mind of the Southern Negro of the antebellum period include Edwin A.

Davis (ed.), *Plantation Life in the Florida Parishes of Louisiana, 1836–1846, As Reflected in the Diary of Bennet H. Barrow* (New York, 1943); J. S. Bassett, *The Southern Plantation Overseer, as Revealed in His Letters* (Northampton, Mass., 1925); U. B. Phillips and J. D. Glunt (eds.), *Florida Plantation Records* (St. Louis, 1927); Susan D. Smedes, *Memorials of a Southern Planter, a [reminiscence]*, ed. Fletcher M. Green (New York, 1964); Fletcher M. Green (ed.), *Ferry Hill Plantation Journal* (Chapel Hill, 1961); Betsy Fleet and Clement Eaton (eds.), *Green Mount: A Virginia Plantation Family During the Civil War* (Lexington, 1962); J. Q. Anderson (ed.), *Brokenburn: The Journal of Kate Stone, 1861–1868* (Baton Rouge, 1955); John William De Forest, *A Union Officer in the Reconstruction*, ed. J. H. Croushire and D. M. Potter (New Haven, 1948); Mary Boykin Chesnut, *A Diary from Dixie*, ed. B. A. Williams (New York, 1949); Eliza F. Andrews, *The War-Time Journal of a Georgia Girl*, ed. Spencer King (Macon, 1960); Frances Anne Kemble, *Journal of a Residence on a Georgia Plantation*, ed. J. A. Scott (New York, 1961). There are also some diaries and journals of the Civil War and early reconstruction periods that throw light on the mind of the Negroes who were molded by the institution of slavery, notably: Margaret N. Thorpe, "A 'Yankee Teacher' in North Carolina [extracts from her diary, 1869–71,]" ed. R. L. Morton, in *North Carolina Historical Review*, XXX, (October, 1953); 564–82; Frances Butler Leigh, *Ten Years on a Georgia Plantation Since the War* (London, 1883); R. S. Holland (ed.), *Letters and Diary of Laura M. Towne* (Cambridge, 1912); Elizabeth W. Pearson, *Letters from Port Royal* (Boston, 1906); Ray A. Billington (ed.), *The Journal of Charlotte Forten* (New York, 1953); Mary Ames, *From a New England Woman's Diary in Dixie in 1865* (Springfield, Mass., 1906); Elizabeth H. Botume, *First Days Amongst the Contrabands* (Boston, 1893); and Cornelia Hancock, *The South After Gettysburg: The Letters of Cornelia Hancock, 1863–1868* (New York, 1956). Especially valuable is Thomas Wentworth Higginson, *Army Life in a Black Regiment* (Boston, 1870).

The accounts of white travelers in the antebellum South usually give superficial views of the characteristics of the slave. The most valuable works are: Frederick Law Olmsted, *A Journey in the Seaboard Slave States* (New York, 1856); *A Journey in the Back Country in the Winter of 1853–54* (New York, 1860); and *A Journey Through Texas* (New York, 1960); Sir Charles Lyell, *A Second Visit to the United States of North America* (2 vols.; London, 1849); James Silk Buckingham, *The Slave States of America* (2 vols.; London, 1842); Captain Basil Hall, *Forty Etchings from Sketches Made with the Camera Lucida in North America in 1827–1828* (Edinburgh, 1829); and *Travels in North America in the Years 1827–1828* (Edinburgh, 1830); Henry B. Whipple, *Bishop Whipple's Southern Diary, 1843–1844*, ed. L. B. Shippee (Minneapolis, 1937); Fredrika Bremer, *The Homes of the New World: Impressions of America* (2 vols.; New York, 1853); Harriet

Martineau, *Retrospect of Western Travel* (3 vols.; London, 1838); William H. Russell, *My Diary, North and South* (Boston, 1863); Herbert A. Kellar (ed.), *Solon Robinson, Pioneer and Agriculturist* (2 vols.; Indianapolis, 1936); and A. DePuy Van Buren, *Jottings of a Year's Sojourn in the South* (Battle Creek, Michigan, 1859). In the early Reconstruction period Northern travelers observed the characteristics of the recently freed slaves, among whom were: Sidney Andrews, *The South Since the War* (Boston, 1866); Whitelaw Reid, *After the War: A Tour of the Southern States, 1865–1866*, ed. C. Vann Woodward (New York, 1965); John Richard Dennett, *The South As It Is, 1865–1866*, ed. H. M. Christman (New York, 1965); John T. Trowbridge, *A Picture of the Desolated States* (Hartford, 1868); Robert Somers, *The Southern States Since the War*, ed. Malcolm MacMillan (Tuscaloosa, 1965); and Edward King, *The Great South: A Record of Journeys* (Hartford, 1875).

Among the scholarly books, articles, and monographs on the Southern slave and free Negro that I have found most useful are: Kenneth M. Stampp, *The Peculiar Institution: Slavery in the Antebellum South* (New York, 1950); Frederic Bancroft, *Slave-Trading in the Old South* (Baltimore, 1931); Eugene Genovese, *The Political Economy of Slavery* (New York, 1965); Stanley M. Elkins, *Slavery: A Problem in American Institutional Life* (Chicago, 1959); Basil Davidson, *The African Slave Trade* (Boston, 1961) and *The Lost Cities of Africa* (Boston, 1959); Melville J. Herskovitz, *The Myth of the African Past* (New York, 1941); Lorenzo D. Turner, *Africanisms in the Gullah Dialect* (Chicago, 1947); M. Crum, *Gullah; Negro Life on the Carolina Sea Islands* (Durham, 1941); Bell I. Wiley, *Southern Negroes, 1861–1865* (New Haven, 1938), John Hope Franklin, *The Free Negro in North Carolina, 1790–1860* (Chapel Hill, 1943), and *From Slavery to Freedom, A History of American Negroes* (New York, 1947); E. F. Frazier, *The Negro in the United States* (New York, 1949); Carter Woodson, *The Education of the Negro Prior to 1861* (Washington, 1919); Richard C. Wade, *Slavery in the Cities: The South, 1820–1860* (New York, 1964); William W. Freehling, *Prelude to Civil War: The Nullification Controversy in South Carolina, 1816–1836* (New York, 1966); John M. Lofton, *Insurrection in South Carolina: The Turbulent World of Denmark Vesey* (Yellow Springs, Ohio, 1964); Clement Eaton, *The Growth of Southern Civilization, 1790–1860* (New York, 1962), and *A History of the Old South* (rev. ed.; New York, 1966); Vernon Loggins, *The Negro Author* (New York, 1931); Benjamin Brawley, *The Negro Genius* (New York, 1937); William J. Simmons, *Men of Mark . . . .* (Cleveland, 1887); Horace Fitchett, "The Free Negro in Charleston, South Carolina" (Ph.D. dissertation, University of Chicago, 1950; Microfilm in Howard University Library); John Spencer Bassett, *The Southern Plantation Overseer as Revealed in His Letters* (Northampton, Mass., 1925); William K. Scarborough, *The Overseer: Plantation Management in the Old South* (Baton Rouge, 1966); Hudson Strode, *Jefferson Davis* (New York,

1964), III; Otto Klineberg (ed.), *Characteristics of the American Negro* (New York, 1944); Richard Bardolph, *The Negro Vanguard* (New York, 1961); George W. Williams, *History of the Negro Race in America* (2 vols., New York, 1882); Avery Craven, *Edmund Ruffin, Southerner: A Study in Secession* (New York, 1932); P. J. Staudenraus, *The African Colonization Movement, 1815–1865* (New York, 1961); Edgar W. Knight, "Notes on John Chavis," *North Carolina Historical Review*, VII (July, 1960), 326–45; Clement Eaton, "A Dangerous Pamphlet in the Old South," *Journal of Southern History*, II (August, 1936), 1–12, and "Slave-Hiring in the Upper South: A Step Toward Freedom," *Mississippi Valley Historical Review*, XXVI (1960), 663–78. In addition to the above works there are studies of slavery in the individual states by Charles S. Sydnor, Chase C. Mooney, James B. Sellers, J. Winston Coleman, Jr., Orville Taylor, John S. Bassett, Harrison S. Trexler, Rosser H. Taylor, Richard Taylor, and others. Studies of the Negroes in the Reconstruction period often give an insight into the Negro as he was influenced by slavery, such as Vernon Wharton, *The Negro in Mississippi, 1865–1890* (Chapel Hill, 1947); Joel Williamson, *After Slavery: The Negro in South Carolina During Reconstruction, 1861–1877* (Chapel Hill, 1965); Willie Lee Rose, *Rehearsal for Reconstruction: The Port Royal Experiment* (Indianapolis, 1964); Samuel D. Smith, *The Negro in Congress, 1870–1901* (Chapel Hill, 1940); James S. Pike, *The Prostrate State: South Carolina Under Negro Government*, introduction by Henry Steele Commager (New York, 1935); Robert F. Durden, *James Shepherd Pike: Republicanism and the American Negro, 1850–1882* (Durham, 1957); George B. Tindall, *South Carolina Negroes, 1877–1900* (Columbia, S. C., 1952).

Chapter x

The Leonidas Polk Papers in the archives of the library of the University of the South at Sewanee are quite extensive. I have used three reels of microfilm of these papers obtained on interlibrary loan. The George W. Polk Papers, containing a number of letters of Leonidas, are in the Southern Collection of the University of North Carolina. Other manuscript collections that I have found valuable in interpreting the religious mind of the Old South are the James Henly Thornwell Papers in the South Caroliniana Library, the Benny Fleet diary and letters, manuscripts owned by Miss Betsy Fleet of King and Queen County, Virginia, the John Hartwell Cocke Papers, the Richard Hugg King Diary and Letters in the North Carolina Department of Archives and History at Raleigh, the Matthew Fontaine Maury Papers in the Library of Congress, the Neal M. Gordon Papers in the University of Kentucky Library, the Joseph C. Stiles Papers in the Huntington Library, and the Petrie Papers, Auburn University.

Published works which I have found useful include: William M. Polk, *Leonidas Polk, Bishop and General* (2 vols. New York, 1915);

a scholarly biography of Polk which emphasizes his military career has recently been published by Joseph Parks, entitled *Leonidas Polk, Fighting Bishop* (Baton Rouge, 1962). Valuable studies of religion are to be found in Ernest T. Thompson, *Presbyterians in the South, 1607–1861,* I (Richmond, Va., 1963); William W. Sweet (ed.), *Religion on the American Frontier: The Baptists, 1783–1830* (New York, 1931); and *The Presbyterians, 1783–1840* (New York, 1936); and Benjamin M. Palmer, *The Life and Letters of James Henley Thornwell, D.D., LL.D.* (Richmond, 1875); the *Danville Quarterly Review,* I–IV (1860–64), especially the review article on David Friederich Strauss's *Das Leben Jesu* (Tübingen, 1840) by the editor, Robert J. Breckinridge, entitled "The New Gospel of Rationalism," I (September, 1861), 365–89; Thomas C. Johnson, *The Life and Letters of Benjamin Morgan Palmer* (Richmond, 1906); Walter B. Posey, "The Protestant Episcopal Church: An American Adaptation," *Journal of Southern History,* XXV (February, 1959), 3–30; *The Development of Methodism in the Old Southwest, 1783–1824* (Tuscaloosa, 1933); *The Baptist Church in the Lower Mississippi Valley* (Lexington, 1957). Thomas R. Ford (ed.), *The Southern Appalachian Region* (Lexington, 1962) shows how tenaciously old religious attitudes survive in the Appalachian region. Some aspects of the religion of the antebellum South are considered in my volume *A History of the Old South* (New York, 1949), Chap. XX, and in an article, "The Ebb of the Great Revival," *North Carolina Historical Review,* XXIII (January, 1946), 1–12. The quotation from the Confederate soldier is taken from John A. Cawthon (ed.), "Letters of a North Louisiana Private to his Wife, 1862–1865," *Mississippi Valley Historical Review,* XXX (March, 1944), 533–50.

Chapter xi

An extensive collection of manuscripts of William Barton Rogers as state geologist is in the Virginia State Library. His wife, Emma Savage Rogers, edited many of his papers in *Life and Letters of William Barton Rogers* (2 vols., Boston, 1896). Sir Charles Lyell has some important references to the Rogers brothers in his *Travels in North America in the Years 1841–42* (2 vols., New York, 1845). Jed Hotchkiss published *A Reprint of Annual Reports and Other Papers on the Geology of the Virginias by William Barton Rogers* (New York, 1884).

Joseph Le Conte's manuscript autobiography is in the Southern Collection of the University of North Carolina. A sizable number of letters of Le Conte are in the archives of the American Philosophical Society in Philadelphia, which I have used on microfilm. Several letters in the Elizabeth Furman Talley Papers and the journal of Le Conte's daughter Emma are in the Southern Collection of the University of North Carolina. A valuable document of Le Conte's career is his *Inaugural Address Delivered in the State House, Dec. 8, 1857* (Columbia, S. C., 1858), a copy of which is in the University of Kentucky Library. William D. Armes edited and published *The Autobiography of Joseph Le Conte* (New York, 1903), but he omitted some of the material of the original. After Le Conte left the South, he published *Evolution and Its Relation to Religious Thought* (New York, 1891).

The Matthew F. Maury Papers in the Library of Congress contain many volumes; the Lewis R. Gibbes Papers in the Library of Congress are also extensive. In the Southern Collection of the University of North Carolina are the William Le Roy Brown Papers, the Silas H. McDowell Papers, and the autobiography of Charles A. Hentz. In the the libraries of the University of Kentucky and Transylvania College there are extensive collections of papers of Dr. Robert Peter. At Transylvania College is a Ph.D. dissertation on Peter by Professor John Wright; and the college library also has a valuable collection of Rafinesque publications.

Valuable background studies are George P. Merrill, *The First One Hundred Years of American Geology* (New Haven, 1924); William M. Smallwood, *Natural History and the American Mind* (New York, 1941); David K. Jackson (ed.), *American Studies in Honor of William K. Boyd* (Durham, 1940), containing an essay by Charles S. Sydnor entitled "State Geological Surveys in the Old South"; Dumas Malone, *The Public Life of Thomas Cooper, 1783–1839* (New Haven, 1926); Thomas C. Johnson, *Scientific Interests in the Old South* (New York, 1936); A. R. Childs (ed.), *The Private Journal of Henry William Ravenel* (Columbia, S. C., 1947); E. M. Coulter, *College Life in the Old South* (New York, 1928); Matthew Fontaine Maury, *The Physical Geography of the Sea and its Meteorology*, ed. John Leighly (Cambridge, Mass., 1963); the recently published biography by Frances Leigh Williams, *Matthew Fontaine Maury, Scientist of the Sea* (2 vols., New Brunswick, 1962); Constantine S. Rafinesque, *A Life of Travels and Researches in North America and South Europe* (Philadelphia, 1836); Edwin M. Betts (ed.), "The Correspondence between Constantine Rafinesque and Thomas Jefferson," *Proceedings of the American Philosophical Society*, VIII, No. 5 (1944); Huntley Dupre, *Rafinesque in Lexington* (Lexington, 1945); Charles S. Sydnor, *A Gentleman of the Old Natchez Region: Benjamin L. C. Wailes* (Durham, 1938); Clement Eaton, "Professor James Woodrow and the Freedom of Teaching in the South," *Journal of Southern History*, XXVIII (February, 1962), 2–17. A number of articles by Southern scientists are published in the *American Journal of Science, De Bow's Review*, and the *Southern Quarterly Review*.

Chapter XII

The basic source for this study is the five volumes of Mary C. Simms Oliphant, *et al.* (eds.), *The Letters of William Gilmore Simms*

(Columbia, S. C., 1953–54). The James H. Hammond Papers (previously cited), the Paul Hamilton Hayne Papers in Duke University Library, and John Esten Cooke's letters in the Evert Duyckinck Papers in the New York City Public Library, the George Frederick Holmes Papers in Duke University Library, and the Hugh S. Legaré Papers in the South Caroliniana Library are invaluable sources for the study of the development of Southern literature during the period of Simms's literary activity. The only biography of Simms is the brilliant but prejudiced account by William P. Trent, *William Gilmore Simms* (New York, 1892). Excellent interpretations of Simms's significance are to be found in Vernon L. Parrington, *The Romantic Revolution in America, 1800–1860* in his *Main Currents in American Thought* (New York, 1927), II, 125–36; J. B. Hubbell, *The South in American Literature* (Durham, 1954), 572–602; C. Hugh Holman's introduction to William Gilmore Simms, *Views and Reviews* (Cambridge, 1962); and E. W. Parks, *William Gilmore Simms as Literary Critic* (Athens, Ga., 1961). Some interesting insights into Simms as an author are given in John W. Higham, "The Changing Loyalties of William Gilmore Simms," *Journal of Southern History*, IX (May, 1943), 210–23; C. Hugh Holman, "The Influence of Scott and Cooper on Simms," *American Literature*, XXIII (May, 1951), 203–18, and "William Gilmore Simms' Picture of the Revolution as a Civil Conflict," *Journal of Southern History*, XV (November, 1949) 441–62; Joseph V. Ridgely, "*Woodcraft*: Simms's First Answer to *Uncle Tom's Cabin*," *American Literature*, XXXI (January, 1960), 421–33; and John R. Welsh, "William Gilmore Simms, Critic of the South," *Journal of Southern History*, XXVI (May, 1960), 201–14. I have not listed Simms's numerous literary works, or articles in the *Southern Literary Messenger, The Southern Review, The Magnolia*, and the *Southern Quarterly Review*, which constitute a prime source for an understanding of the Romantic movement in the Old South.

The description of Alexander K. McClung is based on an article in the *Southern Literary Messenger*, XXI (January, 1855), 1–17, entitled "Sketches of Our Volunteer Officers: Alexander Keith McClung"; Henry S. Foote, *Casket of Reminiscences* (Washington, 1874); and Reuben Davis, *Recollections of Mississippi and Mississippians* (New York, 1889).

For a study of the Romantic movement in the Old South, the following works are recommended: Rollin S. Osterweis, *Romanticism and Nationalism in the Old South* (New Haven, 1949); William R. Taylor, *Cavalier and Yankee: The Old South and American National Character* (New York, 1961); Irving Babbitt, *Rousseau and Romanticism* (New York, 1919); Dallas C. Dickey, *Sergeant S. Prentiss, Whig Orator of the Old South* (Baton Rouge, 1954); Clement Eaton, *Henry Clay and the Art of American Politics* (Boston, 1959), and *Freedom of Thought in the Old South* (previously cited); Wilbur J. Cash, *The Mind of the South* (New York, 1941); John Hope Franklin, *The Militant South 1800–1861* (Cambridge, 1956); Charles H.

Watts, *Thomas Holley Chivers: His Literary Career and His Poetry* (Athens, Ga., 1956); Arthur H. Quinn, *Edgar Allan Poe, a Critical Biography* (New York, 1942); Francis Davenport, *Cultural Life in Nashville on the Eve of the Civil War* (Chapel Hill, 1941); T. Harry Williams, *Romance and Realism in Southern Politics* (Athens, Ga., 1961); Ben Ames Williams (ed.), *Mary Boykin Chesnut's Diary from Dixie* (Boston, 1949); John S. Mosby, *Memoirs,* ed. C. W. Russell (Bloomington, 1959); John Lyde Wilson, *The Code of Honor; or Rules for the Government of Principals and Seconds in Duelling* (Charleston, 1858); Jacques Barzun, *Romanticism and the Modern Ego* (Boston, 1943).

Chapter xiii

The papers of William L. Yancey are deposited in the library of the Alabama State Department of Archives and History at Montgomery; the Yancey Manuscripts in the Library of Congress are almost wholly concerned with his Confederate career when he was commissioner to Great Britain, but the Louis T. Wigfall Papers contain several Yancey letters prior to 1861, and the Yancey folder contains an interesting letter of February 27, 1861, to Governor Francis W. Pickens of South Carolina. In the Alabama Department of Archives and History are also the papers of John Witherspoon Du Bose, the biographer of Yancey. I found them very valuable, particularly the various reminiscences of Yancey's contemporaries who were still living when Du Bose was gathering the material for his biography. In the Southern Collection of the University of North Carolina are to be found the papers of Yancey's brother, Benjamin Cudworth Yancey, which threw light on Yancey's early life. The Benjamin F. Perry Papers in Montgomery are quite valuable for an appraisal of Yancey as a person. Other manuscript collections in the Alabama State Department of Archives and History which contribute to an understanding of Yancey's personality and career are the A. B. Moore Papers (governor of Alabama at the time of secession) and the Alexander Beaufort Meek Papers. Among the manuscripts at the University of Alabama that are pertinent to the secession of Alabama are the small collections of papers of Thomas H. Watts and Robert Jemison, Jr. (one of the leaders of the cooperationists).

In the Alabama Department of Archives and History there are files of the Greenville *Mountaineer,* 1834–35, and of the Wetumpka *Argus and Commercial Advertiser,* May 15, 1839–March 30, 1844, during Yancey's editorship. The Eufaula (Ala.) *Spirit of the South,* 1850–51, I found very useful. In the Library of Congress I consulted the files of the *Independent Monitor* of Tuscaloosa and the Mobile *Advertiser and Daily Register* for 1860–61. The Montgomery *Advertiser* and the *Daily Mail* are to be found in the Alabama Department of Archives and History at Montgomery.

Some of Yancey's speeches were published in pamplet form, notably *An Address on the Life and Character of John Caldwell Calhoun, Delivered before the Citizens of Montgomery, Alabama, On the Fourth of July, 1850* (Montgomery, 1850), and *Speech of the Hon. William L. Yancey of Alabama Delivered in the National Democratic Convention of Charleston April 28, 1860, With Protest of the Alabama Delegation* (Charleston, 1860). A pamphlet was issued concerning Yancey's duel with Clingman, entitled *Memoranda of the Late Affair of Honor between Hon. T. L. Clingman of North Carolina and William L. Yancey of Alabama* (printed for private circulation by W. L. Yancey, 1845). Yancey's manuscript speech "The Rights and Wrongs of Women" (55 pp.), is in the Alabama State Department of Archives and History. Yancey's speeches and remarks in Congress are to be found in *The Congressional Globe*, 1845–46.

The printed works that are most useful for the study of Yancey's career are: the only biography of Yancey, by John Witherspoon Du Bose, *The Life and Times of William Lowndes Yancey* (2 vols., Birmingham, 1892); Joseph Hodgson, *The Cradle of the Confederacy; or the Times of Troup, Quitman, and Yancey* (Mobile, 1876), which gives some valuable information on Yancey's political career; Willis Brewer, *Alabama: Her History from 1540 to 1872* (Montgomery, 1872), which contributes a sketch of Yancey's personality; and William G. Brown's valuable interpretation of Yancey's career in *The Lower South in American History* (New York, 1930); William Russell Smith, *Reminiscences of a Long Life* (Washington, 1889), Vol. I; Henry W. Hilliard, *Politics and Pen Pictures, at Home and Abroad* (New York, 1892); William Garrett, *Reminiscences of Public Men in Alabama for Thirty Years* (Atlanta, 1872); and Benjamin F. Perry, *Reminiscences of Public Men* (Philadelphia, 1883) were written by men who knew Yancey personally. The most recent studies of Yancey have been made by Austin L. Venable: *The Role of William L. Yancey in the Secession Movement* (Nashville, 1945), a summary of a Ph.D thesis at Vanderbilt University, 1937; "The Conflict between the Douglas and Yancey Forces in the Charleston Convention," *Journal of Southern History*, VIII (May, 1942), 226–41; and "The Public Career of William L. Yancey," *The Alabama Review* (July, 1963), 200–12.

For a study of Yancey's role in the Secession movement, see W. B. Hesseltine (ed.), *Three Against Lincoln: Murat Halsted Reports the Caucuses of 1860* (Baton Rouge, 1960). The story of secession in Alabama is presented in William Russell Smith, *The History and Debates of the Convention of the People of Alabama, Begun and Held in the City of Montgomery on the Seventh Day of January, 1861: in which is Preserved the Speeches of the Secret Sessions and Many Valuable Papers* (Montgomery, 1861); Walter L. Fleming, *Civil War and Reconstruction in Alabama* (New York, 1905); A. B. Moore, *History of Alabama* (University, Alabama, 1934); Lewy Dorman, *Party Politics in Alabama from 1850 through 1860* (Wetumpka,

1935); and Charles P. Denman, *The Secession Movement in Alabama* (Montgomery, 1933). The quotation about the sensitivity of Southerners on the question of slavery is taken from Edward W. Phifer "Slavery in Microcosm: Burke County, North Carolina," *Journal of Southern History*, XXVIII (May, 1962), 149.

There is no biography of Jeremiah Clemens, though there is a sketch in the *Dictionary of American Biography*. Only a few of his manuscript letters are preserved, notably in the John J. Crittenden Papers and the John Bell Papers in the Library of Congress. Virginia Clay-Clopton (Mrs. Clement C. Clay, Jr.) has given some vivid impressions of his personality in *A Belle of the Fifties* (New York, 1905); there is an account of his career in Garrett's *Reminiscences* and valuable material on his role in the Alabama secession convention in Smith's *History and Debates of the Convention*. Virgil L. Bedsole has written a good master's thesis on Clemens (1934), deposited at the University of Alabama, and there is a Clemens folder in the library of the Alabama State Department of Archives and History, which contains letters from his daughter (Mrs. W. W. Townsend) giving a small amount of information about her father. Clemens' novels, *Bernard Lile* (Philadelphia, 1856), *The Rivals*, and *Tobias Wilson, a Tale of the Great Rebellion* (Philadelphia, 1865), which, in Clemens' words, "omits all events that would shock a modest woman" have strong autobiographical overtones. R. A. Nueremberger, *The Clays of Alabama* (Lexington, 1958) present an unfavorable picture of Clemens. Besides the speeches of Clemens in the *Congressional Globe* there is in the Alabama Department of Archives and History the typewritten copy of a speech (20 pp.) delivered at Huntsville, August 6, 1860, and a broadside, *Letter from Hon. Jere Clemens, Defining his Position on the American Question* (Huntsville, July 12, 1855). Several of his speeches were published in pamphlet form: *Remarks of Messrs. Clemens, Butler, and Jefferson Davis on the Vermont Resolutions Relating to Slavery, Delivered in the Senate of the United States, January 10, 1850* (Washington, 1850); *Speech of Mr. Clemens of Alabama, in the Senate of the United States, Dec. 10, 1851, on the Resolution of Mr. Seward Relative to Louis Kossuth* (Washington, 1851); and *Speeches of Senator Rhett and Senator Clemens in Controversy, Delivered in the Senate of the United States on the 27th and 28th of February 1852* (Washington, 1852).

Chapter XIV

The manuscripts cited in this chapter are: the Fleet Papers, previously listed; the Brock Papers in the Huntington Library containing the record of the court of honor held at the University of Virginia in 1836; the travel journal of James Atherton in the University of Kentucky Library; the journal of Edmund Ruffin written while he was making his agricultural survey of South Carolina in 1843 in the Southern Collection of the University of North Carolina; the Whitney-Burnham Papers, Library of Congress; and the William C. Rives Papers, Library of Congress.

The following diaries, travel journals, and biographies I have found valuable in studying Southern characteristics: Ben Ames Williams (ed.), *A Diary from Dixie by Mary Boykin Chesnut* (Boston, 1961); John William De Forest, *A Union Officer in the Reconstruction*, eds. James H. Croushore and David Morris Potter (New Haven, 1948); L. Minor Blackford, *Mine Eyes Have Seen the Glory, the Story of a Virginia Lady, Mary Berkeley Minor Blackford* (Cambridge, 1954); Clement Eaton (ed., with Betsy Fleet), *Green Mount; A Virginia Plantation Family during the Civil War* (Lexington, 1962); Mrs. Clement C. Clay, Jr., *A Belle of the Fifties* (New York, 1905); Margaret Farrand Thorpe, *Female Persuasion, Six Strong Minded Women* [including Louisa McCord], (New Haven, 1949); Henry Barnard's travel journal, ed. Bernard C. Steiner under the title "The South Atlantic States in 1833, as Seen by a New Englander," *Maryland Historical Magazine*, XIII (September, 1918), 267–94 and (December, 1918), 295–386; John Q. Anderson (ed.), *Brokenburn; the Journal of Kate Stone 1861–1868* (Baton Rouge, 1955); J. C. Bonner (ed.), "Plantation Experiences of a New York Woman," *North Carolina Historical Review*, XXXIII (July, 1956), 384–417, and XXXIV (October, 1956), 529–64; Phoebe Y. Pember, *A Southern Woman's Story*, ed. Bell I. Wiley (Jackson, Tenn., 1959).

One of the most intelligent observers of the political mores of both Southerners and Northerners was Alexis de Tocqueville, who in 1835–40 published *Democracy in America*. The quotation from Latrobe on the differences between Southerners and Northerners is to be found in J. P. Mayer (ed.), *Alexis de Tocqueville, Journey to America* (London, 1959). The account of the court of honor at the University of Virginia is related by Clement Eaton, "Class Differences in the Old South," *Virginia Quarterly Review*, XXXIII (Summer, 1957), 357–70. Fletcher Green, "Democracy in the Old South," *Journal of Southern History*, XII (February, 1946), 3–24, and *Constitutional Development in the South Atlantic States, 1776–1860* (Chapel Hill, 1930); C. S. Sydnor, *The Development of Southern Sectionalism 1819–1848* (Baton Rouge, 1948); and Francis N. Thorpe (ed.), *The Federal and State Constitutions* . . . (6 vols., Washington, 1909), give valuable insights into the growth of democracy in the South.

The classic influence on the Southern mind is illustrated especially in the Hugh S. Legaré Papers in the South Caroliniana Library and his letters (forty-seven in number) to William C. Rives, September 19, 1832–June 12, 1843, in the Library of Congress; the Thomas Roderick Dew Papers in William and Mary College Library, and the diary of

Hugh Waddell (teacher of the classics in South Carolina) in the Library of Congress. For printed works see Linda Rhea, *Hugh S. Legaré, a Charleston Intellectual* (Chapel Hill, 1934); and the literary magazines—*The Southern Review*, 1828–32, the *Magnolia* (1841–43), the *Southern Quarterly Review*, 1843–56, and the *Southern Literary Messenger*, 1834–60. Frank Ryan illuminates the classic influence on Southern literature in his Ph.D. dissertation on the *Southern Quarterly Review* at the University of North Carolina Library.

In my volume the *Leaven of Democracy: The Growth of the Democratic Spirit in the Time of Jackson* (New York, 1963) are three chapters of sources on the South. Perceptive interpretations of Southernism are to be found in Frances Wright, *Views of Society and Manners in America*, ed. Paul R. Baker (Cambridge, 1963); C. Vann Woodward, *The Burden of Southern History* (Baton Rouge, 1960); T. Harry Williams, *Romance and Realism in Southern Politics* (Athens, 1961); John Hope Franklin, *The Militant South, 1800–1861* (Cambridge 1956); U. B. Phillips, "The Central Theme of Southern History," *American Historical Review*, XLIX (1928), 30–43; Wendell H. Stephenson, *The South Lives in History* (Baton Rouge, 1955); Charles G. Sellers (ed.), *The Southerner as American* (Chapel Hill, 1960), including especially a chapter by David Donald entitled "The Southerner as a Fighting Man"; and David Potter, "The Enigma of the South," *Yale Review*, LI (Autumn, 1961), 142–51.

INDEX